PRAISE FOR ROSEMARY SULLIVAN'S

SHADOW MAKER

"As any great biographer must be, Sullivan is also a
magician, for she has succeeded in making Gwendolyn
MacEwen rise from the pages of *Shadow Maker*, not to
be forgotten."

Anne Cimon,
The Gazette (Montreal)

"Her book is an excellent, painstakingly produced
chronicle of the artist as a young, haunted woman; it is a
supremely honorable, yet unhagiographic, tribute to
MacEwen, our greatest poet of the mind."

George Elliott Clarke,
The Halifax Chronicle-Herald

"This ability to be fully involved, emotionally and intel-
lectually, with her subject and yet to maintain balance
in her analysis sets [Rosemary Sullivan] apart from other
Canadian biographers. . . ."

Diana Brebner, *Books in Canada*

"A splendid book, rich in insight, ideas and the fruit of
dogged research. . . . Sullivan has taken on a fiercely
difficult and delicate task and acquitted herself with
thoroughness and intelligence."

Douglas Fetherling, *The Toronto Star*

"Rosemary Sullivan has two great virtues as a literary biographer. . . the ability to shape a compelling story and tell it with incomparable grace [and] an implicit sense of the moment in which her subject lives. Sullivan sets all her scenes as a dramatist would. . . Her other virtue is a deeply felt understanding of and respect for the creative process and for the intensity of the life that feeds it."

Joan Givner, *Quill & Quire*

"Sullivan does not idealize her subjects, but she is clearly in their camp, respectful and sympathetic, determined to see from the inside. . . And she is a poet herself, with a poet's understanding of just how much and how little about a writer's life can be inferred from her work. . . [She] crafts that intense bond between the reader and her subject."

Joan Thomas, *The Globe and Mail*

"It is hard to put down this book, both for the life being reconstructed . . . and for the probing intellect and engaging presence of the biographer."

Gary Geddes, *The Calgary Herald*

"*Shadow Maker* has an incisive, empathetic immediacy that raises it above the cumbersome, overly detailed work of so many biographers."

John Bemrose, *Maclean's*

". . . the reader's ultimate bonding to the central figure in this book is the crowning triumph of Rosemary Sullivan's skill and compassion. *Shadow Maker* is not a biography—it is a love affair between every one of its readers and Gwen MacEwen."

Timothy Findley

THE RED SHOES

MARGARET ATWOOD
STARTING OUT

ROSEMARY SULLIVAN

Harper*Flamingo*Canada

http://www.harpercollins.com/canada

HarperCollins books may be purchased for educational, business, or sales promotional use.
For information please write: Special Markets Department, HarperCollins Canada,
55 Avenue Road, Suite 2900, Toronto, Ontario M5R 3L2.

First edition

Canadian Cataloguing in Publication Data

Sullivan, Rosemary
The red shoes : Margaret Atwood starting out

Includes index.
ISBN 0-00-255423-2

1. Atwood, Margaret, 1939– – Biography.   2. Authors, Canadian (English) –
20th century – Biography.*   I. Title.

PS8501.T86Z885   1998   C813'.54   C98-931367-0
PR9199.3.A8Z885   1998

98 99 00 01 02 03 04 HC 10 9 8 7 6 5 4 3 2 1

Printed and bound in the United States

To Arlene, Jeni, and P.K., whose friendship
gives me ballast

CONTENTS

INTRODUCTION

THE RED SHOES

In my memory, it was a Thursday evening at Harbourfront, Toronto's arts centre at the edge of Lake Ontario. Greg Gatenby, artistic director of Harbourfront's literary events, had organized a reading in support of Abbey Bookstore, a bilingual Canadian bookstore in Paris. Many of the well-known Toronto writers had been invited to read.

The writers sat at the front of the Brigantine Room at small tables with checkered tablecloths and candles meant to conjure a Parisian cabaret. Margaret Atwood was on the programme.

For someone of such prominence, she has a way of slipping into a room quietly. She is tiny, with a taut, electric intensity. There is something bird-like about her. Magpieish, as she sometimes describes herself.

Rumours were in the air that night about her new book, *Alias Grace*. There had been a cool review in *The Globe and Mail*.

Her blue eyes are large, almost transparent, and as she greeted people I noted the anxiety in them. That may have been my projection. I was thinking about what it means to be a famous writer. Writing is the most personal and the most exposing of the arts. There is no buffer zone between the writer and her audience. If the writer fails, she fails alone.

Margaret Atwood is famous. That night she already knew that *Alias Grace* would be published in many countries. It would metamorphose into an alien text in numerous languages she couldn't read, and would enter into the minds of hundreds of thousands of people she would never meet. And yet, to me she seemed worried about what the literary world would do with her creation. But why should I be surprised by this?

Greg Gatenby had instructed us to read from a book we felt deserved more attention, one we would like to see translated into French and sold at Abbey Bookstore. Margaret Atwood read from *Green Grass, Running Water*, a novel by the Native writer Thomas King. She was hilarious, and almost seemed to become the Trickster figure in King's book. And I thought, yes, she is a Trickster. Mischievous, a shape-shifter, challenging assumptions and conventions. How could one ever get a fix on her?

For that is what I intended to do. I was writing a book about Margaret Atwood. Though I didn't quite know what to call it. A "not-biography" was the closest I'd come.

I wanted to write about her creative life. And yet I needed a phrase to describe my position. I had come up with "the middle distance." I would write from the middle distance, interfacing between the culture that had formed her and the mind of the writer. It wouldn't be a gossipy book. Who would tell me anything anyway? And besides, the little gossip that I already knew didn't interest me. Gossip is the surface story, usually meant to puncture and deflate another life.

A not-biography then. I knew that a real biography can only be crafted in retrospect. It is a nostalgic exercise, a synthesis of perspectives about the subject after the memoirs, letters, and anecdotes have been collected.

Instead, I wanted a book about the writing life. There is so much confusion about what makes a writing life possible. My book would be about what drives Margaret Atwood, about the doubts and confusions and triumphs on the way. It would put her in her time, the generation she was part of that helped to change the shape of Canadian writing. It would, I hoped, show that the mind and the imagination are central to the real pleasure of living, something almost lost on our literal-minded age in which stories about individuals seem to be told only at the level of lifestyles and bedroom gossip.

Still, I had a deeper motive. I wanted to write a third book to complete the narratives of two I had already written. Those had been real biographies. They were both about women writers. Though I hadn't expected it, they turned out to be stories about frustration, indeed agony, and, finally, about silence. The subject of my first biography, Elizabeth Smart, had written a masterpiece at the age of twenty-seven and then had fallen silent for thirty years. She claimed it was a problem of self-confidence. She always felt there was a shadowy hand on her shoulder, which she called the "maestro of the masculine." This phantom told her she could never be good enough. The second writer, Gwendolyn MacEwen, had died tragically, convinced, at least for long moments, that art was not worth the price of loneliness. My books had celebrated them as remarkable writers, but secretly I felt a kind of guilt. Had I not, inadvertently, perpetuated the stereotype of the tragic female artist? Surely, I felt, there are other narratives. I wanted a third version. I felt compelled to write about a woman who had managed to take control of her artistry and her life.

When I explained to Margaret Atwood what I wanted to do, she initially misunderstood my intention. "I'm not dead," she said. When I described my theory of not-biography, she was only a little mollified. What seemed to bother her most was the idea that I might turn her into a role model; being a role model was never what she intended. Or that I might create an artificial order out of the myriad details of her life simply by the act of turning it into a narrative. She had already had years of people inventing someone called Margaret Atwood that had little to do with the woman alone in her room writing a book. Would I not just be perpetuating that?

Why would I presume to write a book about Margaret Atwood? Because, privately, I am fascinated by the mystery of artistic confidence. Where does the strength come from to believe in yourself as a writer? Is it merely personal? Why do many talented people never take the gamble and set out on the costly journey to become artists? Why are others, like Elizabeth Smart, derailed? Does one need cultural support?

When I think of Margaret Atwood, I am haunted by an anecdote:

The year is 1948 or 1949. A little girl sits in a movie theatre. Seeing a film is a rare treat. This time, the occasion is someone's birthday. The film they are all watching is *The Red Shoes*, about a young woman called Victoria Page who becomes a world-famous ballerina. Victoria is beautiful, dressed like a princess in diamond tiara and gossamer tutu, dancing her way through elegant ballrooms and exotic European cities. The little girl is entranced and wants to be like that, but she begins to sink despondently into her seat. Victoria's life is turning into a tragedy. The maestro is angry with her, her young husband leaves her. In the end, she commits suicide by jumping in front of a train. The little girl understands the message and is devastated: if you are a girl, you cannot be an artist and a wife. If you try to be both, you will end up jumping in front of a train.

Margaret Atwood was the young girl in that movie theatre. She was born into an era when girls were still slapped down for creative ambition, and yet she went on to become a remarkable writer. How did that happen?

When Margaret Atwood tells the story of being devastated as a young girl watching *The Red Shoes*, the question that fascinates me is: although she was upset by it, why was she not derailed? If this was the vision she was offered, why and how did she escape? Many young girls born in 1939 still took that message into their bones. How did this young girl, in pre-feminist days, evolve the instinctive capacity to believe, unequivocally, in herself?

At one point in an interview, Margaret Atwood remarked: "We have a somewhat romantic notion on this side of the Atlantic about what an author is. We think of 'writing' not as something you do but as something you are."[1] This seems innocuous enough, until you stop to think about what she is saying.

In those cryptic sentences, she was sabotaging the history of romanticism that has attached to the artist. And this perception of the writer, more than anything else, had to go.

When she started out as a writer, it was not easy for a young woman to believe in herself. Twenty years ago she remarked: "Fewer women than men come through their early years strongly motivated to write seriously. . . . 'Being a writer' is more easily seen by them as a state of being, not of doing. When instant recognition is not forthcoming, it's easier to give up."[2] "Girls, particularly, are trained to please and conciliate, and when somebody doesn't like them they think that it's some failure of theirs."[3] The attempt to write well — "to investigate, to explore, to acknowledge an external discipline, to take risks, among them the risk of failure" — was discouraged in young women.[4]

How does one form an attitude of confidence and courage, "without which the project of being a writer becomes a joke"? "Your confidence as a writer," she explained, "has a lot to do with your total confidence as a person . . . and that comes from childhood."[5] Were the roots of her confidence to be found in her childhood?

The story of Margaret Atwood's journey from that movie theatre where she watched *The Red Shoes* to her international success as a writer is one of the narratives of this book. In many ways, I see the story as part of a collective narrative of women writers in the last thirty years. A list of the writers born in the same era as Margaret Atwood or coming to prominence when she did is impressive: A.S. Byatt, Nadine Gordimer, Joyce Carol Oates, Angela Carter, Maxine Hong Kingston, Margaret Drabble, Marie-Claire Blais, Marge Piercy, Marilynne Robinson, Toni Morrison, Alison Lurie, Ann Beattie, Elena Poniatowska, and many others. These women have irrevocably changed the iconography that attaches to both the male and the female artist.

If we go back to *The Red Shoes*, released in 1948, when war films had glutted the silver screen and the film industry was scrambling for new themes, we can easily see that film as a meditation on the role of women in art. The original script was by Emeric Pressburger, and its subject was the ballet career of Victoria Page, played by Moira Shearer. Victoria is an ambitious young dancer who is taken up by a famous impresario and choreographer, Boris Lermontov, a maestro of the old school who develops his dancers by using ruthless discipline and deliberate humiliation. Art is a religion for Lermontov, and Victoria is to be his creation.

Lermontov has written a ballet for her called *The Red Shoes*, based on a fairy tale by Hans Christian Anderson. He describes the story to her in the following way: "A girl is devoured by the ambition to dance in a pair of red shoes which she has bought from a gypsy. At first she is happy at the dance, but then she gets tired and wants to go home. But the shoes are not tired. They never get tired. They dance her out into the fields. Time rushes by, love rushes by, life rushes by. But the shoes dance on. In the end she dies."

Ingeniously, this is an allegory of the fate of the woman who presumed to be an artist. Jealously, possessively, Lermontov guards Victoria as his invention. She is the malleable material that will guarantee his immortality. But she makes the horrifying mistake of falling in love with and marrying the company's young composer. She becomes the pawn in a battle between the two men. Lermontov rages: "The dancer who relies on the doubtful comforts of human love will never be a great dancer. Never!" Her husband wants her to give up her art for his sake. He needs her beside him as his muse and inspiration. She tries to choose her art, but doing so destroys her. At the film's end, seemingly having chosen her career over her marriage, Victoria walks towards the stage entrance to perform the ballet *The Red Shoes*. But the red shoes suddenly have a will of their own.

They take her out to the balcony overlooking the train station where her husband is about to leave. They leap her over the balcony railing. As she lies dying, she begs her husband to remove the red shoes.

Clearly women were meant to be muses, not maestros. No wonder the young Margaret Atwood sank despondently into her seat in that movie theatre fifty years ago. What would be so dangerous about a woman having an artistic career of her own? The answer was simple. In what had become the traditional version of things, woman had to remain the passive inspiration for art since man could not create without her.

In 1948, after their emancipation in the workforce, women had to be returned to the nation's kitchens so that their jobs could be freed up for men coming back from the front. For those women who had enjoyed the public world, sustaining the pretence that they had never left the house must have felt like a brutal amnesia. *The Red Shoes* suggests that art, too, had to be aggressively re-established as a male prerogative.

What was the image of the male artist anyway, and where did it come from, that it had to be so desperately protected?

The iconography of the male artist was unrelievedly romantic. Of course, our notion of the artist has been a cliché, evolving as it did out of early nineteenth-century Romanticism. I think of Percy Bysshe Shelley, one of the first truly bohemian poets. As the industrial middle class pushed the artist to the periphery of society, the only solution was romantic rebellion. Art was more important than life. It was a religion. The artistic life was one of enormous sacrifice. (It was also, paradoxically, one of enormous indulgence.) The bohemian artist devoted to self-expression was born.

Women were necessary in that world, but as muses. And the male artist, notoriously promiscuous, needed a lot of them. Women were attracted to this role as handmaiden to genius because it meant selection (usually on the basis of beauty). Any woman who aspired to be an artist herself was a rival, not a handmaid. If indeed she had enough self-confidence for such an aspiration, she had to be bashed down. She was, after all, threatening to make her own art as important as a man's.

But was this really how it worked? Often, of course, only as a kind of overarching cliché mythology. Still, it is astonishing how deeply it stuck. As a consequence, art was a man's game. Women artists did not have a place in the world of art, nor would they. Not until there were enough women with the courage to kill off this shibboleth.

The women of Margaret Atwood's generation shattered the stereotype, and, perhaps more important, they destroyed a second one. In the history of female iconography, the image of mother and child categorically excluded the possibility of art, except as a subject. It was thought that a woman could not be both mother and artist. Many women of the generation prior to Margaret Atwood's had been convinced of the impossibility of mixing maternity and a career. Mavis Gallant, for instance, pursued a solitary life in Paris in order to be able to write. Jean Rhys, Marianne Moore, Flannery O'Connor, and others never had children. Of course, there were many women who did, but that fact never seemed to penetrate the collective imagination. Doris Lessing brought one of her children with her from South Africa when, determined to be a writer, she moved to England, but there she had to confront the dilemma of bringing up a child alone. It did not help that, in doing so, she was going against the prevailing mythology. One's life as an artist was meant to be monomaniacally single. It was said to require an almost ravenous egocentricity. If you had children, you were compromising your art. Today, it is still hard to bring up a child alone. But in the world of women like Margaret Atwood, at least the child can be, wonderfully, there. And the women can continue, undevastated, with their creative explorations, without its being a violation of the code of art.

I believe that what helped to perpetuate so many myths about the "artistic life" was that art had been separated from life. When I was at university in the 1960s, we were still being told that great literature was written by those, mostly men, who were different in kind from normal people. They were geniuses. On another plane. "Literature is not life," I was told. The writer's work had been cut off and floated in hyperspace without any connection to the person who wrote it. Those works were called "well-wrought urns," autonomous artefacts sealed in airtight rooms, and the space had a name: immortality. Art was never to be connected with the real world. But that was the mistake. We failed to understand that art is life; that it is made up of the hundreds of bits of household bric-a-brac, of the landscapes and mnemonic resonances that constitute our own existence.

Once I understood that, women's voices began to intrigue me: whether they had been heard; whether they had been distorted by the listener;

whether they surfaced whole from the speaker or had been undermined from within by self-doubt.

If you have heard Margaret Atwood speak, you will remember her voice. She speaks in a monotone with a deadpan delivery. It is a voice that has often been parodied as boring, or as condescending and dismissive, because, if you are not listening carefully, you will miss the wit. She is often wily, refusing to be cornered, since she is aware that that is what the world attempts to do. The voice makes it clear that this woman does not suffer fools gladly, and can be devastatingly ironic. And yet she can also be uncannily direct when offered a genuine response.

Over the years, Margaret Atwood has been the subject of many projections. In the beginning she was described as a pre-Raphaelite, with a nimbus of windswept hair. The characterization never really worked because she lacked the pliancy of the Victorian heroine, and, besides, she always wondered what *male* writer's hair was the subject of every commentary about him. Then, when she wrote *Power Politics*, she was called an astonishingly cruel talent, with an eye for the jugular. She was a "man hater," and "her stuff was bleak, dark, and negative." Later she was described as "really funny" and, finally, she became "maternal."[6] As times changed, the projections changed, though she remained essentially the same person.

Many people would have been set off stride by that barrage, but she bashed on, regardless. Certainly humour must have helped. But the real reason for her stamina was that, all along, she had the intrinsic self-confidence to believe in her art. She has, in fact, been remarkably consistent. Her voice is a Canadian voice, a woman's voice, and, most important, a voice evoking a unique vision that has struck deep, resonant chords in her readers.

In my mind's eye I see Margaret Atwood standing on a bridge: the woods are at her back, the city is before her, and she commands both worlds. There are bodies under the water, trolls under the bridge. This is, of course, an absurd image I have invented, but it conjures up a vision of a woman who, out of years of training and willed attention, has claimed deep mythological roots for her writing. She speaks with an incisiveness in which the pleasure of provocation is implicit. She takes herself very straightforwardly. She is a writer.

I think of this book as a meditation on what a particular woman means to her culture and to the readers whose lives she has entered by the sheer act of writing fictions about them. It is an effort to explore what makes a writer and a writing life possible, to watch, with pleasure, the unfolding of a remarkable writer's career.

But there is a second story that enfolds the first. This book is also a portrait of a generation starting out. Margaret Atwood began her career when Canadians were still in the deep-freeze of colonialism and only beginning to think of themselves as having a culture. Her generation changed all that.

It was in the sixties, that overdescribed and yet still elusive decade, that everything changed. While the sixties are characterized as the decade of war and psychedelics (and that was, of course, part of the story), there were other narratives. As countries fell to the sixties liberation ethic, which seemed to hit everywhere simultaneously, Canada had its own peculiar experience. It was a time of cultural nationalism in Canada, and Canada would never be quite the same again.

From 1966 until the end of the 1970s, Canada experienced a literary sea-change. In 1960, you could count on the fingers of one hand the number of novels published in this country. There were a few more books of poetry because they were cheaper to produce. By 1966, small publishing houses, literary magazines, and new theatres began to sprout up like the mushrooms people were eating to get high. By the end of the seventies, Canadian writers knew they were part of a culture that was their own. The colonialism that Northrop Frye had lamented, calling it a "frostbite at the roots of imagination," had thawed, and a confident culture emerged.

There were many young mavericks in those days, Margaret Atwood among them. A narrative of her writing life inevitably becomes a cultural and a generational narrative.

This book is a record of a woman writing in a particular time. It stops at the end of the 1970s. By that time Margaret Atwood had become the international writer we know today. And by that time the culture that nurtured her had also come into its own. It is the drama of beginning that is always the most compelling. Margaret Atwood once remarked about those years: "Everything was interesting, but the important thing was discovering the fact of our own existence as Canadians."[7]

1

KITCHEN STORIES

"I don't think in terms of 'usual' and 'unusual.' Of course it
was unusual for me to do a lot of the things I did in other
people's terms, but not in mine."

Margaret Atwood[1]

Margaret Atwood encapsulated her history for the potted version
required by blurb writers and interviewers in the following way:

> I was born in the Ottawa General Hospital right after the
> Grey Cup Football Game in 1939. Six months later I was
> backpacked into the Quebec bush. I grew up in and out of
> the bush, in and out of Ottawa, Sault Ste. Marie, and
> Toronto. I did not attend a full year of school until I was in
> grade eight. This was a definite advantage.[2]

We have to remember that, almost sixty years ago, there was nothing
mundanely diverting about backpacking into the woods (sometimes the
story varied and she was carried in a box), and certainly parents did not
carry a six-month-old child into the Canadian bush, which was not then,
nor is it now, a tourist romp. And it was 1939, the beginning of the Second
World War, which Canada was one of the first among the Allies to enter.

Though Margaret Atwood's laconic summary seems to suggest otherwise, it describes an eccentric beginning.

Who were these adults that they stepped so casually outside the norm of their times? To edge in on that world, we must start further back. We all believe our lives begin long before we do, with the people we call our ancestors, the ones who, literally and figuratively, make us up. Yet how much are we to be explained in terms of ancestry? Who are those lines of strangers we descend from to become ourselves? We use metaphors such as "roots" and "branches" to describe them, as if to locate ourselves like plants. But since genetic inheritance is so mysterious, perhaps our ancestors are most important as the stories, the mythologies, we use to explain ourselves to ourselves.

Margaret Atwood's favourite ancestor was tried as a witch a decade before the infamous Salem witch trials of 1692–93, during which almost two hundred people were accused of practising witchcraft and nineteen were executed.[3] If she had wanted to invent an ancestor for herself, Margaret could not have done better: this was a woman who stood up to authority and survived brutality with remarkable resilience.

Mary Reeve Webster, an ancestor of Margaret's grandmother Ora Louise Webster, on her mother's side, lived in Hadley, Massachusetts. It seems that her marriage to fifty-three-year-old William Webster in 1670[4] had initially been prosperous, but the public records report rather vaguely that the two became poor to the point of destitution and required public assistance. This was dangerous. Under New England's Puritan laws, the poor could petition the town for relief, and the townspeople were required to offer aid. Each inhabitant was expected to take turns providing the pauper with food, lodging, or other necessities. But so resistant were the colonists to such public charity that, to reduce the risk of public liability, towns passed ordinances forbidding both the entertainment of strangers and the sale of land to strangers without permission from the local selectmen. If one fell "on the town," as it was called, local citizens had the right, because poverty was considered a personal failing, to direct the pauper on how to live a more orderly existence.[5]

In her poverty, Mary Webster came under the care and scrutiny of one Philip Smith, who was to arrange for her poor relief. Smith was a member of the court, deacon of the church, lieutenant in the troop, and selectman of Hadley. Apparently, Mary, "being dissatisfied at some of his just cares about her, expressed herself unto him in such a manner that he declared himself apprehensive of receiving mischief at her hands."[6] It was not wise to insult the village benefactor.

Soon allegations began to collect that Mary was a witch and a termagant. The court records of the time report her crimes, which seem quaint until one realizes these were deadly accusations. Horses baulked as they approached her house, and would not drive past it. At such times, the drivers would enter the house to beat her, and only then were their horses able to move on. Rumours were rampant. On one occasion a load of hay overturned at her doorstep and, when the man in charge entered the house to whip her, the load was placed right side up by an invisible hand. She caused a neighbour's child to ascend in the air three times simply by looking at it. And once a hen flew down a chimney and was burned, and it was discovered that Mary Webster, at that very time, was suffering from a scald.[7]

Mary was brought before the Court at Northampton with Philip Smith, among others, officiating, and after many testimonials she was accused of being a witch. She was remanded to Boston Gaol in April 1683 and tried by the Court of Assistants on 22 May. When physically examined, she was found to have a devil's teat. Such a mark could be anything from a mole to a red welt caused by flea bites, but there could be no evidence more damning. The marks indicated the devil's familiars had come to suck her body at night.

The accusation read: "For that she not hauing the feare of God before hir eyes & being instigated by the divill hath entred into Couenant & familiarity wth him in the shape of a warraneage [an Indian name for black cat] & had hir Imps sucking hir & teats or marks found in hir secret parts as in & by seuerall testimonyes may Appeare Contrary to the peace of our Soueraigne Lord."[8]

Held in jail awaiting a further trial, she finally appeared again before the Court of Assistants on 4 September and was found not guilty. The records do not explain why, but a note accompanying the court records indicates that she was charged to pay twenty-three pounds, fifteen shillings, and two pence for the cost of her trial and travel to and from Boston.

This was not the end of it for Mary. Philip Smith died two years later, in 1685, and Mary was again accused, this time of his murder by witchcraft.

So famous was her case that it was reported by the Puritan preacher and writer Cotton Mather.

His report describes how, in the beginning of January, Smith "began to be very valetudinareous [unwell], laboring under Pains that seemed Ischiatic [sciatic]." In his eventual delirium, he cried out "in a Speech incessant and voluble and (as was judged) in various Languages," naming Mary as his tormentor.[9] Numerous ominous signs indicated that Smith's demise had been from supernatural causes. Pins were discovered under the bed, and the unmistakable scent of musk was in the air. Mysterious scratchings were heard. Fires appeared on the bed from no discernible source. Galley pots containing the victim's medicine were mysteriously emptied.

To relieve the suffering Smith, a number of the young men of Hadley went to Mary's house. They dragged her out and hanged her by the neck until she was almost dead. Then they cut her down and rolled her in the snow, finally burying her in it. By some trick of luck and extraordinary will, she survived.

This "snow trial" was a well-known, if little-used, counter-spell. Presumably by burying a witch in deep snow, her torturers were able to freeze her supernatural powers. It was claimed that Smith's sufferings abated during Mary's ordeal.[10]

When Smith finally died on the third day of his illness, eyewitnesses reported that his corpse turned blue and black, and blood flowed down his cheeks. The body was examined: there was a swelling of one breast, which "rendered" it like a woman's, and Smith's "privates were wounded or burned. On his back, besides bruises, there were several pricks, or holes, as if done with awls or pins."[11] It appears that the respectable Philip Smith was not only a reputed hypochondriac, but probably a self-flagellator as well.

After the failed hanging, Mary herself seems to have escaped further victimization by the locals. She died in Hadley in 1696. Little could Mary have known that she would make an impact on history. In 1990, she was still considered a blot on the Hadley public record, and a descendant requested that her name be removed from the family annals. Clearly he wanted the family history cleansed. But Mary had an unexpected defender. Another distant descendant would write her vindication.

When she came to write the poems collected in *Morning in the Burned House*, published in 1995, Margaret included a poem to Mary Webster titled "Half-hanged Mary." Once you know that Margaret is speaking about her own ancestor, the poem's impact is uncanny. She writes in the first person, and imagines the stages of Mary's ordeal through the night as she hung from that rope.

. . .

8 p.m.

The rope was an improvisation.
With time they'd have thought of axes.

Up I go like a windfall in reverse,
a blackened apple stuck back onto the tree.

Trussed hands, rag in my mouth,
a flag raised to salute the moon,

old bone-faced goddess, old original,
who once took blood in return for food.

The men of the town stalk homeward,
excited by their show of hate,

their own evil turned inside out like a glove,
and me wearing it. . . .

. . .

8 a.m.

When they came to harvest my corpse
(open your mouth, close your eyes)
cut my body from the rope,
surprise, surprise:
I was still alive.

Tough luck, folks,
I know the law:

you can't execute me twice
for the same thing. How nice.

I fell to the clover, breathed it in,
and bared my teeth at them
in a filthy grin.
You can imagine how that went over.

Now I only need to look
out at them through my sky-blue eyes.
They see their own ill will
staring them in the forehead
and turn tail.

Before, I was not a witch.
But now I am one . . .[12]

In a Radcliffe alumni address in 1980, Margaret spoke of her ancestor: "Mary Webster went free. I expect that if everyone thought she had occult powers before the hanging, they were even more convinced of it afterwards. She is my favorite ancestor, more dear to my heart even than the privateers and the massacred French Protestants, and if there's one thing I hope I've inherited from her, it's her neck."[13]

But, for Margaret, it is Nova Scotia, rather than New England, that is the landscape of origins and legends. The ancestral Atwoods sailed to Massachusetts in 1635, and in 1760 a branch of the family moved to Nova Scotia. Austin Killam, on her mother's side, arrived in Salem in 1637, and in 1766 one of his descendants, John Killam, also emigrated to Nova Scotia.

A peninsula attached by a thread of land to the eastern edge of the land mass that would become Canada, Nova Scotia was, as Margaret would fondly say, an "exotic place": from the sixteenth century on, the British and French fought like dogs to keep this gateway to a continent, until the final capture of the French fortress of Louisbourg in 1758 by General James Wolfe, he of the Plains of Abraham fame. In its heyday, Nova Scotia was a harbour, a garrison, and a wartime boomtown swarming with British sailors, privateers, and merchant seamen off ships from the West Indies.

It had been caught in the fray of two wars: the American Revolution and the War of 1812. In that colourful world Margaret could trace all the lines that ultimately led to her.

It was in 1766 that John Killam came from Massachusetts as one of the group later to be called the Pre-Loyalists. By proclamation, the British government offered New Englanders land vacated by the French Acadians (numbered conservatively at six thousand) who had been expelled in 1755. The New Englanders were among the "foreign Protestants" brought in by the British in an effort to populate Nova Scotia with non-Catholics. John Killam settled on a farm in Chegoggin Cove, a barren inlet in the county of Yarmouth (already, of course, home to Native people who called it "Isagogin," or "Place of Wares"). The relationship with the Native population was uneasy. Local legends focused on abductions. One of the most famous was of a young girl whose family had been carried off by Indians. It seems she, who never merits a name, had been away from home, picking berries, when this happened, and she returned to find her family gone. To the amazement of the people of Chegoggin, she fled to the Indians for safety. And stayed. Years later, the old woman who came to town with the Indians would be pointed out as a local phenomenon by John Killam's fellow villagers.[14]

John Killam's line of descendants (he had ten children) would branch out and make an impact on Nova Scotia. His son John Jr. became a Yarmouth merchant and shipowner, and helped to establish the Marine Insurance Company. When John's son Thomas (born in 1802) joined the family business, they prospered in the hazardous trade between North America and Great Britain. By mid-century, Thomas Killam owned some sixty vessels, although twenty-five were eventually lost at sea. Thomas's son Frank would be elected to the local legislature, and the Killam brothers would become leading shipowners (their office on Water Street is considered the most important historic building in modern Yarmouth). John Killam's great-great-grandson Albert became a judge and, after moving to Winnipeg, sat on Manitoba's Court of Queen's Bench to hear the appeal of Louis Riel. (The court, of course, upheld Riel's conviction, and he was hanged on 16 November 1885.) By the next generation, even the girls had caught up. Maud Killam Neave went to the Women's Medical College, New York Infirmary, obtaining her MD's licence in 1896, and became a medical missionary in Chengdu, China, sent there by the Women's Methodist Missionary Society of Canada.

In a family noted for enterprise, perhaps the most enterprising was Thomas's grandson Izaac, born in Yarmouth in 1885. From the poorer branch of the family, at the age of twelve or thirteen Izaac somehow realized there was money to be made in the newspaper business. Yarmouth had three or four local weeklies, but the dailies came by train from Halifax and Saint John. He got the franchise to supply them and, by the age of fifteen, had cornered the market. At sixteen he changed careers and became a junior clerk at a Yarmouth branch of the Union Bank of Halifax and never looked back. At twenty-nine, he replaced Max Aitken (later Lord Beaverbrook) as president of Royal Securities Corporation, one of Canada's most influential investment houses. He and his wife, Dorothy, moved to Montreal, where they lived with ten servants in a grey-stone mansion on Stanley Street. His gifts to her were legendary, including a *briolette* diamond that had once belonged to Henry II of France and the pearls that Mrs. John Astor had clutched as she jumped into a lifeboat to escape the sinking *Titanic*.

The Atwoods, Joshua and Mary, arrived from Truro, Massachusetts, shortly before the Killams, settling in Barrington on the South Shore around 1760.[15]

Margaret claims that one of her Atwood ancestors was Cornwallis Moreau, the son of a monk expelled from his order in France, and, as legend has it, the first white child born in the newly settled city of Halifax, in 1749.[16] The idea of his being the son of a monk probably appeals to Margaret.

Jean-Baptiste Moreau of Dijon, France, arrived in Halifax in 1749 to serve as an Anglican missionary. That he had once been a Benedictine seems clear. While prior of Saint-Mathieu's Abbey, near Brest, Abbé Moreau had become disenchanted with Catholic doctrines and practices, and was persecuted for his sympathy with the Huguenots. He fled to England, married, and from there sailed with Lord Cornwallis and his settlers on the *Canning* in June 1749. Cornwallis's mission in the new world was to establish a British town as a bulwark against French aggression. With Moreau came his pregnant wife, Elizabeth, and four servants. The settlement they arrived in was little more than wilderness, with only a sparse polyglot collection of French Protestants, Germans, and a few British. Assigned by the Society for the Propagation of the Gospel to the French Protestants, Moreau preached at the new St. Paul's, the first Protestant church built in Canada. He then travelled with about 1,600 French- and German-speaking immigrants, also "Foreign [European] Protestants," to the new settlement of Lunenburg. Though he took great pains, as he said, to "bring over the Savages to embrace our holy Religion," he didn't have much luck with the Mi'kmaq.

The abbé's son Cornwallis was born in December 1749, and thus was the first child born in the new settlement. A captain in the Lunenburg militia, he lived to be ninety-one. The impact his father, the monk, had in Nova Scotia outlived his son. When Halifax was devastated by the harbour munitions explosion in the First World War, the west gallery window of St. Paul's was shattered in such a way as to show the silhouette of a head — an astonishing likeness, it was claimed, of Abbé Moreau.[17]

By the time Margaret's parents came along, settlements had shifted. Her father's family had remained on the South Shore, and Atwood had become a common name there. There is even an Atwoods Brook near Shag Harbour on Nova Scotia's southernmost tip. The Killams were living on the North Shore, in the Annapolis Valley.

Born in November 1939, Margaret was a child of the Second World War. Unlike the fathers of some children, however, hers did not disappear for six years. His work as a scientist for the federal Department of Lands and Forests was declared essential, and he spent his war in Canada. But, for the Atwoods too, the war meant isolation from family. Margaret once described her mother and father as Depression refugees from Nova Scotia. At home, there had been no jobs. Now, because of wartime gas rationing, it was impossible to get back. One did not travel long distances except for official reasons. Nova Scotia, two thousand kilometres away, loomed in Margaret's childish imagination as HOME, peopled by mythic figures who wrote letters and evoked family sagas. When the letters were read out loud at the dining-room table, the family oral history was "dished up — along with the mashed potatoes." From the family photo albums, Margaret could give faces to these voices. They became like characters in stories — "as familiar to me," she later wrote, "as characters in books; and since we lived in isolated places and moved a lot, they were more familiar than most of the people I actually encountered. . . . I was kept up on the doings of my aunts, and also my great-aunts, my uncles, my cousins, my second cousins. . . . I grew up in a huge extended family of invisible people."[18]

The patriarch of the Killam family was Dr. Harold Edwin Killam. After getting his degree from Dalhousie Medical College in 1906, he practised for forty years in Kentville, and was also Medical Officer for the Kings County Militia Unit at Aldershot. He was well known as a fruit grower; his apple orchards were considered among the finest in the Annapolis Valley. From her mother, Margaret heard stories of how this "strict, awe-inspiring, but lovable grandfather . . . drove around the dirt roads in a horse and sleigh, through blizzards, delivering babies in the dead of night, or cutting off arms and legs, or stitching up gaping wounds made by objects unfamiliar to me — buzz saws, threshing machines."[19] Her mother often used the phrase "laid down the law" when referring to her own father, and Margaret would picture her grandfather, like Moses, setting down two great slabs of rock on the dining-room table. He and his wife, Ora Louise Webster, had five children: two sons, Fred and Harold, and three daughters, Margaret (Margaret's mother, born in 1909), Joyce, and Kathleen.

Margaret's mother was a wonderful storyteller, "a raconteur and deadly mimic," as her daughter described her. And so the stories built of the family that lived in a large white farmhouse, with a barn and a carriage house, and a kitchen that had a pantry. Her mother remembered the days when flour came in barrels and all the baking was done at home. She heard tales of the three sisters and their doings in the valley. "I did not have a sister myself, then, and the mystique of sisterhood was potent for me," Margaret explained.[20]

The ringleader and plot-planner of their escapades was Kathleen, "the brilliant one." She would complete her Master's degree in History at the University of Toronto in 1930 at the age of nineteen, and then, turning down her father's offer to finance her for an advanced degree at Oxford, she married and had six children. As a child hearing her aunt's story, Margaret wondered why Kathleen couldn't be brilliant, have six children, and also go to Oxford.

What is compelling to me is how Margaret would embellish these narratives. How we see our childhood is what counts, since that is the mythology out of which we invent ourselves.

In 1945, when she was six and the long-awaited car trip was made to Nova Scotia, these were the people whom Margaret finally met. It came as a shock to her that these figures from her mother's mythology were ordinary people. The family vacations in Nova Scotia left their traces in her memory. In one anecdotal account, she describes that world:

When my mother was a child, she and her family had crossed the North Mountain by horse-drawn wagon, on the way from the Annapolis Valley to the shore of the Bay of Fundy for their summer holidays, and we, too, made that trip, though by car. We stayed in my grandmother's cottage, which was on a cliff overlooking the Bay of Fundy and a wooden harborage that jutted out into it, defense for small fishing boats against battering storm waves and the sometimes 54-foot tides that, everyone knew, were the highest and most dangerous in the world.

During our stay the cottage bulged with cousins, in whose company I did many things I would not have the nerve, energy or foolhardiness to attempt now. At high tide we swam in the harbor, immersing ourselves in the subarctic waters of the Bay of Fundy until we turned bright purple. At low tide we explored the long, slippery stretches of rocky beach, with its tidal pools and the weirs set by fishermen, vertical nets in which fish, including such rarities as skate and jellyfish, would be stranded by the quickly receding tide. We scrambled into the caves in the cliffs, hunting for amethysts and barely heeding the dire stories we'd been told of children trapped in them, cut off from rescue by the inrushing tides and swept out to sea. When we were older we sailed out into the Bay of Fundy in a boat constructed by my cousins, once narrowly avoiding wreckage by hurricane. . . .

After the family network in the Annapolis Valley had been thoroughly negotiated, we would drive around the coast to my father's family, on the South Shore near Shelburne. The terrain there was different. On the coast were indented harbors instead of the smooth lines of the bay, and

inland the lush contours of the valley gave way to dark conif-
erous forests and cranberry bogs. Between some of the rocky
points were white sand beaches, on which you could stand
and look south and know that there was nothing between
you and South America.[21]

Her South Shore grandparents lived on a remote farm which hadn't
changed much since the nineteenth century. The house was lit only by
kerosene lamps, cooking was done on a wood-burning range, and the
water had to be hand-pumped. Everything was done by hand. Grandmother Atwood made her own butter in a wooden churn and served it in
moulded shapes. She also made her own patchwork quilts, following the
patterns and legends that had been passed down through the generations.

Writers have a special kind of memory. Memories are recorded as stories.
Anecdotes, textures, landscapes, sensory images are laid down in the mind
and can be called up decades later, when necessary. When Margaret came
to write her novel *Alias Grace*, details of her grandmother's house and the
texture of those handmade patchwork quilts would return to her as material to use in creating Grace Marks's mid-nineteenth-century world.

Margaret's father, too, had apocryphal stories of his South Shore world,
of "the neighbourhood witch he had known as a boy, who would never sit
in a chair in which you had hidden a pin; or the man with the circular
barn in which the cows' rears all faced inward, to save work on the muck-
ing; or the man who bought an entire barrel of mismatched buttons,
because they came out cheaper per button that way."[22]

For Margaret, Nova Scotia "abounded in eccentrics whose eccentricity took a practical form." And their social style to this day remains what
she calls "deadpan, ironic, skeptical, laconic," a style that overlays "a
generosity and helpfulness that will be brought out for you as a visitor
when it becomes clear that you are not malevolent or a total fool."[23]
There might be something after all to the argument that genetic inheritance is determinative. Many would come to describe Margaret herself
exactly this way. She would follow the basic Nova Scotia moral code,
which was against waste: against wasting things, of course, but also against
wasting your talent or time, or human life.

2

READING FAMILIES

For most of us, parents loom, almost iconic, in certain family photographs, particularly in those taken when we were young or before we were born. Who were those romantic figures, so fresh and expectant before life and age altered them irrevocably? We have a private romance with such photographs. They are more than pictures. They are myths of the individuals who exist beyond family, slipping, protean, from our needy grasp.

In 1996, Margaret wrote a fictionalized memoir titled *The Labrador Fiasco*. It reads as a thinly disguised and moving tribute to her father after his death. Two photographs are mentioned. They are of a young woodsman:

> Somewhere around the house there's a picture of my father himself — at the back of a photo album, perhaps, with the snapshots that haven't yet been stuck in. It shows him thirty years younger, on some canoe trip or other. . . . He's evidently crossing a portage. He hasn't shaved, he's got a bandanna tied around his head because of the blackflies and mosquitoes, and he's carrying a heavy pack, with the broad tumpline across his forehead. His hair is dark, his glistening face is deeply tanned and not what you'd call clean. He looks slightly villainous; like a pirate, or indeed, like a northwood's guide, the kind that might suddenly vanish in the middle of the night, along with your best rifle, just before the wolves arrive on the scene. But like someone who knows what he's doing. . . .

There's another photo of my father, perhaps from the same trip as the one with the portage; or he's wearing the same bandanna. This time he's grinning into the camera lens, pretending to shave himself with his axe. Two tall-tale points are being made: that his axe is as sharp as a razor, and that his bristles are so tough that only an axe could cut them. It's highjinks, a canoe-trip joke; although secretly of course he once believed both these things.[1]

What makes Margaret's story moving is that the membrane between fiction and life has thinned. Carl Atwood spent much of his life in the north woods. They were his passion and his profession. In anecdotal accounts, he is always surrounded by their paraphernalia, by the planes and spirit levels for building cabins for shelter, by the feathers for tying flies for fishing, by the stones for making arrows. In her story, the father is a man who could confront risk and transcend danger in those woods. "In extreme situations, you have to use your wits" was how her own father might have put it. But there was also his high-jinks humour, one of his most essential legacies to his daughter.

Carl Atwood was born in Clyde River, Nova Scotia, in 1906. Encouraged by his mother, he put himself through high school by correspondence course. Initially thinking of a teaching career, he went to Normal School in Truro, where he won a scholarship to Acadia University. This would have been remarkable enough for a young man from a backwoods farm in Nova Scotia, but he won a second scholarship that took him to McGill University, and then to the University of Toronto, where he got his Master's of Science in 1933. He put himself through university by working as a junior entomologist for the federal Department of Agriculture. Each summer from 1930 to 1935, his research into bees sent him back to the Annapolis–Cornwallis Valley to investigate the pollination of apples in the region. He probably spent research hours in Dr. Killam's apple orchard. He already knew the beautiful Margaret Killam. He had met her in the 1920s at Normal School, though one of the family stories was that, the first time he saw her, she was sliding down a banister.

From his 1933 article "Studies on the Apoidea of Western Nova Scotia. . ." one can imagine Carl Atwood, during those summers, scrambling among the grasses and low herbage, hunting the bees' tiny burrows as he studied their nesting habits and sought to understand their social organization. Or dissecting them in the Experimental Station in Kentville and mounting them in glycerine or balsam.[2] In 1937, he obtained his doctorate from the University of Toronto, studying longevity and reproduction in *Ephestia kuhniella* Zeller, a species of moth. His thesis was to prove how the current "sex-linked lethal theory" (i.e., continued inbreeding) was inadequate to explain decreasing fertility. Margaret would later say that her interest in metamorphosis might have begun with her father's passion for moths.

When his thesis was finally published, Carl Atwood acknowledged the invaluable help of Margaret Killam in the monotonous work of record taking. It wasn't surprising to find Margaret's mother out on those field trips, helping him to collect data.

In the family stories, Margaret Killam figured as "physically brave, a walker of fences and barn ridgepoles," but shy, so shy that she hid in the barn from strangers. It was her younger sister Kathleen, the ringleader, who thought up the plots and plans, all of which had to be kept from their father, the doctor, as "sins of horse-whipping proportions." Margaret may have been the beauty of the Killam family, with pre-Raphaelite eyes, wavy hair, and sculpted cheekbones, as well as the high-bridged Roman nose her daughter would inherit, but she had brains as well.

Dr. Killam was a conventional patriarch, and though he supported her sister Kathleen in her university education he thought Margaret was "a flighty, pleasure-bent flibbertigibbet."[3] But Margaret outwitted him. At seventeen, she took a degree at the Normal School in Truro and then taught in a one-room schoolhouse. Boarding in town, she rode to school on horseback each day. It took her two years to save enough to put herself through the first year of a degree in Home Economics at Mount Allison University, in New Brunswick, where she won a scholarship to complete her degree at the University of Toronto. Soon she found a job as a dietitian at the Toronto General Hospital.

Carl and Margaret married in 1935 (she was twenty-six) in a double wedding with her sister Kathleen, and then, as her daughter would embellish it, they "set off by canoe" down the Saint John River to begin their nomadic life. They had had to wait so long to get married because it was the depths of the Depression and they had no money. Margaret used to divide the meagre family paycheque into four envelopes: rent, food, other bills, and ten cents for entertainment. Their son, Harold, named after his grandfather, was born in February 1937. Margaret Eleanor, named after her mother and called Peggy in the family to avoid confusion, arrived two and a half years later. Their second daughter, Ruth, was born in 1951.

Shortly after Harold was born, Carl Atwood took a full-time job in Ottawa with the federal Department of Lands and Forests. Forests were seen as a resource vital to the war effort, since, among other things, healthy trees were needed in the shipbuilding industry, and so he spent the Second World War conducting research, primarily in northwestern Quebec.

The rhythm of Margaret's early childhood was dictated by her father's profession, researching tree-eating insects. The family lived in two worlds, the city world of her Ottawa childhood, which was mostly just a winter landscape of cold and snow, and the world of the remote bush, where they often spent stretches of the spring, summer, and fall while her father pursued his work.

Although it was Canada's capital, Ottawa, in the early forties, was still a small provincial city dedicated to the production of lumber. Margaret's earliest memories, as she sought to recover them, were of the smell of sawdust from freshly cut trees.

For the adults, the war meant deprivations as the economy was redirected to military necessities. Housing, which hadn't recovered from the Depression, was often substandard. Gas was rationed; by 1943, those who owned cars were allowed 120 gallons per year. Travel by bus was limited to round trips of fifty miles. There were government restrictions on movement: people were forbidden to relocate from, say, Vancouver to Toronto without proving that their reason for moving had to do with the war. Food items like sugar, butter, coffee, tea, and meat were also rationed.

But, for a young child, the only indication of war in Ottawa was the occasional blaring of the air-raid siren. And the anxiety of the adults as they listened to the news on the radio.

The Atwoods lived on Belmont Avenue and, then, when Margaret was two, at 1 Patterson Avenue, a lovely tree-lined street in the Glebe district of Ottawa. Their second-floor apartment was in a duplex just on the edge of the Rideau Canal. For Margaret, Ottawa would have been a city of snowdrifts so high children built tunnels through them. These were not exactly safe — they did collapse and sometimes a child was smothered — but, as every Canadian child knows, there was something uncanny about crawling into those white wombs, for inside they were very warm. And there was the canal — frozen, in her childhood memory — where she went to skate. Children in those days were muffled in snowsuits that looked like inflated tires. To skate, they strapped two-bladed runners onto their boots.

But the real centre of Margaret's childhood was those springs, summers, and autumns in the bush. In a compelling article titled "True North," written years later, Margaret returned to that landscape. "For me, the north used to be completely in force by the Trout Creek planing mill. Those stacks of fresh-cut lumber were the true gateway to the north, and north of that was North Bay, which used to be, to be blunt, a bit of an armpit. It was beef-sandwich-on-white-bread-with-gravy-and-canned-peas country."[4] Tourism in those days was perfunctory. One might see caged animals — a scraggly bear, raccoon, deer, or even a skunk — displayed as a curiosity at roadside gas stations. Kids would stick hot dogs or Popsicle sticks through the bars while their parents filled their tanks. Margaret remembered a fox gone mad, pacing the figure eight in manic frenzy, in one of those roadside cages. Past North Bay there was nothing but miles and miles of trees, until you hit the Quebec border at the Ottawa River.

"There, across the border in Québec, in Témiskaming, is an image straight from my childhood: a huge mountain of sawdust. I always wanted to slide down this sawdust mountain until I finally did, and discovered it was not like sand, dry and slippery, but damp and sticky and hard to get out of your clothes. This was my first lesson in the nature of illusion."[5] In this one-industry town, Margaret would have seen the Quebec *bûcherons*, heading into the bush with horse-drawn sledges to set up the lumber camp, and later sliding their logs across the ice for the spring run on the river.

"Sometimes we went the other way, across to Sudbury, the trees getting smaller and smaller and finally disappearing as you approached. Sudbury was another magic place of my childhood. It was like interplanetary travel, which we liked to imagine, which was still just imagination in those days. With its heaps of slag and its barren shoulders of stone, it looked like the moon."[6]

Dr. Carl Atwood set out most springs for his research station in northern Quebec, and the family would pack up their life in boxes and suitcases piled in the back of the car and go with him. A conventional mother might have stayed in the city, where there were hospitals, and friends, and perhaps even the tea parties that went with the government job. But Margaret's mother was not conventional. Margaret's parents were nomads who improvised their dwellings, and indeed their lives; both, according to Carl Atwood, liked being as far away from civilization as possible.[7]

There is never a suggestion that Mrs. Atwood wanted it otherwise. Margaret believed her mother had found the world she wanted. And why? Because she had slipped the noose of the staid world of starched propriety and antimacassars that her Nova Scotia childhood would have dictated for the doctor's daughter. In Margaret's mind, her mother had guts, a straightforward vision that was empowering. Looking back, she would call her mother a tomboy. "Mother loved the physical, unconstrained life in the bush. Cooking was hard work because it involved the endless chopping and getting of wood, fetching water and lighting the woodstove, all of which were time-consuming."[8] Forty years later, when Margaret wrote *Alias Grace*, she identified the most autobiographical moment in that murder mystery. It was when the character did the laundry. "When I lived in the north of Canada the laundry was done in washtubs, with water heated on a wood stove, and when I was Grace's age, much of it was done by me. Grace's pleasure when she has a line of clean white washing flapping in the breeze comes straight from the heart."[9]

Life in the bush, from Margaret's cumulative descriptions, was remarkably orderly. The family would live in tents while Carl Atwood built a small, just serviceable cabin; once he had them ensconced, he would start work on a bigger cabin. This process would be repeated casually when he moved to a new location. Margaret said, cryptically, "My father liked to chop wood."[10] Between 1936 and 1948, she explained, her parents moved twenty times: to the woods in the early spring and back to the city in the late fall. As the car approached a chunk of pink granite sticking out of the ground, surrounded by tall black spruce, her parents would shout: "We're almost home now."[11] Home was provisional. It was wherever they landed. In her memory, childhood included the tar smell of heavy canvas tents and the smoke from campfires, or the rancid smell of fish in the bottom of the boat, where she sat as her parents rowed. And there was the eternal taste of Klim, the powdered milk of those years.

The landscape of childhood provides the foundation layer of our psyche. Margaret's landscape was the north woods. For a young child there would have been terror in the bush, and Margaret acquired a healthy sense of terror — of lightning, bears, forest fires, even rivers. And yet, it was also home, with adults moving adeptly through its labyrinth. For it had its own potent magic. The northern woods, for anyone who has spent time in them, seem alive, almost like an animistic presence. At your back, they seem to sit like the unconscious mind — something is always watching. This, too, would layer Margaret's psyche. She would say, looking back:

> I'm most at home in an airplane, a thousand feet up, skim-
> ming over the taiga at one remove. Lake, lake, lake, swamp,
> sprinkle of low hills, twist of river; ice creeping out from the
> shores. It has to be big, though; rocky, sparse, a place you
> could find yourself lost in easy as pie, and walk around in
> circles and die of exposure. . . . Out the window, way down
> there: desolation, instant panic. With a view like that you
> can feel comfortable.[12]

And it delighted her that she had the right name for such a landscape. Atwood comes from "Atter wode," and means "pearl of the woods." "It's an English name," she would say with pleasure, "quite old, probably fourteenth century or earlier."[13] One also thinks of Nathaniel Hawthorne's Pearl, that sprite of the forest, who may not be that far removed from the child Margaret once was.

Life in the woods had its own regularity. During the day Dr. Atwood would set out by motorboat for work at the research station where he studied his insects. Sometimes there would be field trips when he would be gone for several days and, occasionally, even longer trips. In her story "Hurricane Hazel," Margaret fictionalizes those memories from a child's perspective:

> All the time we were going through our daily routine . . .
> he was flying in bush planes into valleys with sides so steep
> the pilot had to cut the engine to get down into them, or

trudging over portages past great rocky outcrops, or almost
getting upset in rapids. For two weeks he was trapped by a
forest fire which encircled him on all sides and was saved
only by torrential rains, during which he sat in his tent and
toasted his extra socks at the fire, like weiners, to get them
dry. These were the kinds of stories we heard after he came
back.[14]

During these excursions to remote regions when he was working and
the family couldn't follow, his wife held the fort. She must have felt
anxious at times, without telephone, electricity, or running water — or
easy access in emergencies to hospitals or help of any kind. The only dire
emergency her daughter publicly recorded occurred when Margaret was six
and they were living in a cabin north of Lake Superior. Margaret's brother,
Harold, also remembered that incident.

Their father had bought land on the St. Mary River, outside Sault Ste.
Marie. As his son remembered it, "Father single-handedly built a road in,
including a bridge over a swamp that was in the way, and constructed a
cabin in two weeks. He had to go off on a research trip. We were parked
out in the cabin, and our food supply was in a nearby tent. Mother heard
something outside. She looked out the window and a bear was sneaking
up to the cabin. The door had only a string and a nail to hold it shut." Mrs.
Atwood yelled "Scat" and the bear fled, but not before devastating the
food supply. In Harold's memory, his mother had sent him and his sister
down to the beach to attract the attention of passers-by who could get
word to the research station that they needed food.[15] In Margaret's, her
mother sent them to scavenge the woods for anything salvageable, and
managed to round up enough potatoes for breakfast. They had sat down
calmly to eat. The bear returned and her mother ran at it, yelling "Scat."
The bear fled. "If my mother had had a rifle handy," Margaret remarked,
"she probably would have shot the bear. She wasn't a bad shot."[16]

Both Harold and Margaret remember those occasions when they were
taken out of school early in the spring, or would be returned late in the
fall, and Mrs. Atwood gave them their lessons. No one seemed to object
to this. In those days there were no theories about the child's need to be
with a "peer group" or about the value of "socialization." And, in any case,

Mrs. Atwood had taught school in Nova Scotia. Margaret believed this method of learning was excellent training; it gave her "self-regulation." She would do the work she had to in order to be free to do what she wanted: draw and paint. More important, Margaret thought, she escaped that peer pressure on girls "to be dumb," as she put it — the idea that it wasn't chic to be intelligent.[17]

Her father taught them informally as well. A walk in the woods with him whistling Beethoven, wearing the hat he always wore to keep falling insects off his head, would be a lesson in nature lore. "We learned by observation. We spent considerably more time with our father than other children would because he didn't go to an office. . . . He'd put a rubber sheet under a tree, hit the tree with the back of an ax, and the caterpillars and other insects would fall down onto the rubber sheet. Then everyone would pick them up."[18] This kept her from being squeamish and gave her a certain power edge over the boys, who expected to be able to frighten girls with spiders and such. She, instead, could calmly identify the genus and species. Her father would also teach them about plants, usually adding embellishments. He might point to hemlock and say: "This was the stuff, by the way, that Socrates used to commit suicide." You were never allowed to say, That's a tree. You had to know what tree and how to distinguish it from other trees. He might give a series of thin, eerie barks, and then grin. He seemed to know every bird and most animals by their calls and could mimic them. This kind of training in naming and in precise and disciplined attention is invaluable for a writer.

As children we enter a fixed universe; it is the prescriptive ground we are given. All we can do is battle to find our place in it. For Margaret this meant being second in a family of three children, two and a half years behind her brother, Harold. What does it mean to be second? For one thing, the second child learns quickly, by imitation, so deep is the pressure to catch up. But there is also a fierce craving for independence in order to slip out from under the shadow of the older sibling. A second child develops a strong will, and fierce personal boundaries that can't be crossed. Of course, such formulations are simplistic. But Margaret did develop an extraordinarily strong will. Her mother could say: "No one guided Peggy. I don't think anyone could guide Peggy."[19] Being second was a lucky placement for a young girl who would turn into a writer. She had an ally in her brother, since, over those long months in the woods, she was the only one he had to play with. It might also be fair to speculate that he was a rival to whom she was continually having to prove herself, which was also good training.

Margaret was very close to her brother, but there is a family story that gives an added dimension to her attachment to him. When he was three years old, Harold fell into a lake and almost drowned. Margaret's mother claimed that, because it was a calm day, she had been able to hear the sound of his bubbles emerging from the water. Margaret remembers the devastating impression that story of near tragedy made on her: her older brother became suddenly vulnerable. She took to following him about anxiously, her vigilance earning her the title within the family of "the little shadow."

After their mother's formal lessons in the morning, for the rest of the day Margaret and Harold were free to invent their own play, and the amusements Margaret remembers were imaginative. In the bush they had to make their own fun. Together they read comic books — *Captain America* and *Blackhawk* — and Harold wrote his own, peopled with science fiction characters, with notes and detailed drawings describing all the species of plants and animals living on his imaginary planet.[20]

There was, of course, no television, but occasionally there was a radio connected with the research station, though at that distance they were lucky if there was any reception at all. Like most children, Margaret learned the singing commercials by heart: "You'll wonder where the yellow went when you brush your teeth with Pepsodent."

Harold was an amateur naturalist (he would grow up to be a neurophysiologist): "My brother did take worms to bed and hid snakes under his pillow," Margaret remarked. Once, when their aunt Joyce was visiting, Harold had taken a snake to bed and it got away, crawling into the wood stove, where it was warm. When Mrs. Atwood opened the stove to light the fire in the morning, there was the snake. She said casually: "I think the snake would be happier outside." Years later Margaret would collaborate with her aunt on a children's book titled *Anna's Pet*, based on this anecdote.[21]

It was from Harold that Margaret says she first learned to read, and she fell in love with the idea of the book. At the age of five, she created her own book: cutting pages from her scribbler and sewing them together, copying into it all the poems she had memorized and then adding her own. She remembers it as a "totally satisfying object." She wrote a novel at six, about an ant floating down a river on a raft. She and Harold also wrote plays that they would perform on an improvised puppet stage.

For pets she and Harold had frogs, snakes, crayfish, and jays that would eat out of their hands. When they got older they built a birch-bark tepee and made maps of the woods, inventing names for the unnamed lakes and rivers.[22]

As they grew up together during those summers in the woods, Harold's range of skills increased, and these were passed on to his sister, from swimming and canoeing, to scaling and gutting fish, and shooting bows and arrows and rifles. Eventually, he also taught her how to play chess, and a little perfunctory Greek. In "Hurricane Hazel," one of four quasi-autobiographical stories in *Bluebeard's Egg*, written years later, she conjures up those Greek lessons, describing how the brother taunted his sister with Greek:

> The Greek was something he himself was learning; he was two grades ahead of me and was at a different high school, one that was only for boys. He started me with the alphabet. As usual, I didn't learn fast enough for him, so he began leaving notes about the house, with Greek letters substituted for the letters of the English words. I would find one in the bathtub when I was about to take a shower . . . (*Turn off the shower*, the note would read when translated). Or there would be a message taped to the closed door of my room, which would turn out to be a warning about what would fall on me — a wet towel, a clump of cooked spaghetti — when I opened it. . . . I didn't ever learn much real Greek, but I did learn to transpose quickly.[23]

Harold remembers that, in grade eight or nine, he did learn the Greek alphabet in school and, with his friends, had taken to using it as a secret code. He had taught his little sister as well. The anecdote corresponds to fact, but his sister's embellishments are fiction — delightful to be sure, but her own. He was never, he believes, quite that much of a tease.

Mrs. Atwood, like all mothers, had her favourite anecdotes about her children. One was of Margaret squirming into her pyjamas and saying: "Hurry, Mummy. I'm telling myself a story and I can't wait to find out how it turns out." She also remembered her brief anxiety when Harold started kindergarten and she wondered if Margaret would be lonesome without him. After they'd returned from delivering him to school, "Peggy went around doing her little chores, putting her piles of junk here and there — and humming like a contented hen. I said: 'Peggy, you are having a nice little time singing,' and she said, 'Oh yes, I have lots of little hums like that running around inside my head.'"[24]

When asked once by an interviewer if there were signs of what Margaret would become, Mrs. Atwood replied: "There were no signs." Except that Margaret started writing as soon as she could print, using phonetic spelling. In grade two and "crazy about cats," she wrote a book of poems which she called "Rhyming Cats." She also wrote a play in grade one or two. "Shall I tell you what I thought was the best line?" Mrs. Atwood asked the interviewer. One character said: "If I am telling a lie may the moon fall down." The next line was CRASH.[25]

Mrs. Atwood recalled the time she was invited to a government tea in Ottawa, when teas were official functions attended by the wives of civil servants. Unable to afford a babysitter, she had brought the children, though they might have secretly been her reinforcements because these were social functions Mrs. Atwood disliked. Bunny-rabbit cookies, iced with little-boy pants and little-girl skirts, were reserved for the children. Telling the story to an interviewer, with her daughter sitting nearby, Mrs. Atwood remarked: "You chose one. You went off to a corner with it, by yourself. Mrs. X noticed you and went over. 'Aren't you going to eat your cookie?' she said. 'Oh, no,' you said. 'I'll just sit here and talk to it.'"[26]

Mrs. Atwood's anecdotes about Margaret, at least those recorded, all seem to be about the imagination of a child who would become a writer. (It is possible that these are edited memories, but it is more likely that this is an accurate portrait.) However much we may pretend otherwise, we do not have access to our children's inner lives. Margaret was an imaginative and resourceful child, already autonomous in her private inner world. Mrs. Atwood was a gifted mother in that she knew how to encourage without intruding on her children's privacy. She allowed Margaret to discover things for herself. Wisely, she seems to have understood that respect for her autonomy was exactly what her daughter needed.

This portrait of the artist as a young girl is, of course, not that different from the portrait of the artist as a young man. A necessary motif of isolation seems characteristic in artists' stories of childhood — the child alone, building his or her own fantasy world. Margaret's isolation came, not from being different within a dysfunctional family, but from the family's being different in what her father might suggest was a dysfunctional world. He was an early environmentalist and something of a pessimist where human beings were concerned; indeed, at that moment the world was engaged in global warfare.

Books became essential companions in Margaret's childhood. When she was six, her parents sent away for a volume of *Grimm's Fairy Tales* from a mail-order catalogue. What they got, rather to their dismay, was the unexpurgated 1944 Pantheon edition with Josef Scharl's Gothic illustrations of skulls, hangmen, witches, ogres, and other wonderful grotesques. Her parents were a bit worried that she and her brother weren't ready for "the barrels of nails, red-hot shoes, removable tongues and eyes, cannibalism and various forms of open-heart surgery that abounded." "They thought we'd be frightened by these," Margaret remembers. "They forgot that children like being frightened." "On a life-time count" of reading, as she would put it, *Grimm's Fairy Tales* was the book she read most.[27]

Those she liked best were "The Juniper Tree" and "Fitcher's Bird." She had picked two of the most gruesome. "The Juniper Tree" is a story of a little girl whose brother is killed by a wicked stepmother who serves him as dinner to his father. In the end, the boy is resurrected as a magnificent bird to tell his story. Surely Margaret identified with the little girl who loves her brother and saves his bones. "Fitcher's Bird" is an archaic version of the Bluebeard story, a story that would haunt her, to the extent that its motifs can be found throughout her mature writing.

These sinister little stories are accurate records of the child's inner life, of the turmoil the child inevitably feels in the sweep of often incomprehensible emotions. A child's world is made up of exaggerations. We are more joyous, more fearful, more convinced of magic in the raw world of childhood than we can ever be again. The world is mysterious because we cannot see its motives.

Margaret would later say that what she loved was the magic, the assurance, the fairy tales offered "that anyone might turn out to be someone other than you thought they were . . . and that even at the bottom of a pit courage and faith could prevail."[28] But the Gothic elements also satisfied her imagination — like many children, she loved the fear the stories instilled. There was also real fear in her own forest world: you could get lost in the bush and never come out. In those stories, which so often take place in forests, animals could talk. And in her own world there was mystery, even in the way the rising sun must have hit the black spruce in the morning or the loons cried over the water at night.

She didn't find it exceptional at the time, of course, but in the unexpurgated versions of the Grimms' fairy tales, which were the ones she read, little girls often had the magic powers. The princess rescued as often as did the prince, by using intelligence, cleverness, and perseverance. Margaret remarked: "The women in these stories are not the passive zombies they would later become in the sanitized versions." As a child she took it for granted that girls were powerful too.

Those Gothic fairy tales layered her imagination with haunting images that would become part of her way of seeing the world. They were as real as anything else in her childhood. They "sank to the bottom of my mind," she has said, "and still send shoots."[29]

Like most writers, Margaret became a reading addict — she soon fell into that familiar habit of using a flashlight under the bedcovers at night. She read all the girls' books — Cherry Ames, Junior Nurse, and the Bobbsey Twins — and the boys' books — Treasure Island, Gulliver's Travels, and the animal books of Charles G.D. Roberts and Ernest Thompson Seton.

In addition to books, there were other narratives in the Atwood family. Margaret calls them "kitchen stories," and they, too, would provide nourishment for her young mind.

I keep noticing that, in her accounts of growing up, she is listening to the seductive voices of the adult world, eavesdropping on family secrets. These are tantalizing, exciting; they contain the forbidden knowledge. She listens, unaware of the adult rules of censorship. The stories provide a notion of lives themselves as stories that fold in easily with other written narratives. And very early it becomes clear that she identifies the storyteller as the mother. Mrs. Atwood would provide the model for her daughter's muse, the first storytelling voice. Once asked whether her muse was male or female, Margaret replied: "Oh, she's a woman."[30]

Not every girl who hears stories at her mother's knee will become a novelist. But, as Virginia Woolf said, "a woman writer thinks back through her mother." For many women this connection is blocked. At about the same time we discover that fairy stories aren't real, we discover that mothers have no power. But Margaret's world was not a conventional one. There was little sex-stereotyping in her family. Margaret could not have known at the time how unusual this was.

There was, of course, as there is for all young girls growing up, a separate mother's and father's world. These were discrete, and each had its own priorities. What makes Margaret's experience remarkable is that these two worlds were equally powerful.

The young girl who surfaced from those months spent in the forest was an outsider to female conventions. Margaret speaks of herself as someone who was introduced too late to the conventional social roles assigned to women ever to mistake them for natural states of being.

When the family returned to Ottawa in the colder months of the winter, Margaret watched her mother put on "a whole other identity than the one she wore in the north woods." As a child in the forties she could see that, when her mother came to the city and put on dresses, she put on much more as well. "And I suppose from that I got the idea that the thing wasn't set, wasn't determined, you could rearrange yourself, you could change your presentation. Nor did it have anything particularly life-threatening to do with your essence. You could do several things, be several things, have several appearances and remain the same person."[31]

The discovery that women were quick-change artists was more fascinating than disturbing. As she approached adolescence, Margaret began collecting women's fashion magazines, studying them and decorating the walls of her bedroom with pictures of the costumes and disguises available to her. The fact that women are malleable creatures isn't the problem. Looking back, she would say: "The problem is the pressure to believe that the mode of behaviour that is required *is* the essence, *is* what you are. That's what we all have to resist."[32]

Like most children with happy childhoods, she never questioned her mother's life. But her mother did have other possible versions of how she might have lived. In an interview for a book titled *Mothers and Daughters*, Mrs. Atwood remarked: "If I have a reincarnation, I want to come back as an archaeologist. Just the other day I found a prehistoric arrowhead when I was picking stones out of my garden."[33] Margaret records this fantasy in her story "Significant Moments in the Life of My Mother."

> "In my next incarnation," my mother said once, "I'm going to be an archaeologist and go around digging things up. . . ."
>
> This statement of hers startled me. It was the first time I'd ever heard my mother say that she might have wanted to be something other than what she was. I must have been thirty-five at the time, but it was still shocking and slightly offensive to me to learn that my mother might not have been totally contented fulfilling the role in which fate had cast her; that of being my mother. What thumb-suckers we all are, I thought, when it comes to mothers.[34]

Margaret understood, however, that, on balance, her mother was content with her life. She was a practical woman. Given the alternatives — in her youth, a married woman didn't work after the birth of her first child — the bush had provided a flexible life. She had always been cheerful and productive, the virtues she valued above all else.

By 1983, when she was forty-four and a mother herself, Margaret decided to make gestures towards recording her own autobiographical account. She was already wary of the way a writer's life is the subject of speculation and invention. Determined to lay claim to her own narrative, she wrote several quasi-autobiographical stories about her childhood years. The fictional mother in her story has a Mrs. Dalloway quality: hers is a subversive world in which women are strong, and men are often fragile, protected by a female conspiracy of silence.

> There were some stories which my mother does not tell when there are men present: never at dinner, never at parties. She tells them to women only, usually in the kitchen, when they or we are helping with the dishes or shelling peas, or taking

the tops and tails off the string beans, or husking corn. She tells them in a lowered voice, without moving her hands around in the air, and they contain no sound effects. These are stories of romantic betrayals, unwanted pregnancies, illnesses of various horrible kinds, marital infidelities, mental breakdowns, tragic suicides, unpleasant lingering deaths. They are not rich in detail or embroidered with incident: they are stark and factual. The women, their own hands among the dirty dishes or the husks of vegetables, nod solemnly.

Some of these stories, it is understood, are not to be passed on to my father, because they would upset him. It is well known that women can deal with this sort of thing better than men can. Men are not to be told anything they might find too painful; the secret depths of human nature, the sordid physicalities, might overwhelm or damage them. For instance, men often faint at the sight of their own blood, to which they are not accustomed. For this reason you should never stand behind one in the line at the Red Cross donor clinic. Men, for some mysterious reason, find life more difficult than women do. (My mother believes this, despite the female bodies, trapped, diseased, disappearing, or abandoned, that litter her stories.) Men must be allowed to play in the sandbox of their choice, as happily as they can, without disturbance; otherwise they get cranky and won't eat their dinners. There are all kinds of things that men are simply not equipped to understand, so why expect it of them? Not everyone shares this belief about men; nevertheless, it has its uses.

"She dug up the shrubs around the house," says my mother. This is a story about a shattered marriage: serious business. My mother's eyes widen. The other women lean forward. "All she left him were the shower curtains." There is a collective sigh, an expelling of breath. My father enters the kitchen, wondering when the tea will be ready, and the women close ranks, turning to him their deceptive blankly smiling faces. Soon afterwards, my mother emerges from the

kitchen, carrying the teapot, and sets it down on the table
in its ritual place.[35]

Margaret herself would never be able to live in such a world: it
belonged to a different generation. Her own generation would feel that too
much of one's own authority was lost in this fiction of the need to protect
men, which of course led to disguising one's own power. But, in the order
of things she describes, it is the world of women that she sees as most
powerful.

Certainly the one thing Margaret was assured of was the genuine affection between her parents and the comfortable understanding between
them. In her story the parents seem innocent, and there is a nostalgia and
protectiveness in the way the narrator regards them, as if these two stood
fixed in a picture and she must defend them from the future world
"hurtling into chaos behind them." It is always dangerous to confuse a
fictional narrator's voice with the author's, but one might see something
of Margaret Atwood here. This stance of needing to be strong enough to
protect others, even her capable parents, may have been one of the particular legacies of her childhood. Her friends would call this the "girl scout"
part of Peggy Atwood.

3

PRELUDE: THE BUSH

The bush was a constant in the Atwoods' lives, but the cities changed. In 1945, the family moved briefly to Sault Ste. Marie, where they rented a house while Carl Atwood helped to build a Forest Insect Research Laboratory for the Department of Lands and Forests. That was when he bought the small piece of land on Lake Superior, one of the spots to which the family returned over the years. In November 1946, they moved to Toronto. Margaret's father had gotten a job as a professor in the Department of Zoology at the University of Toronto.

Toronto was a winter city when they arrived in November. Margaret would say later that her first experience of Toronto was throwing up on it. In the woods in summer, they were never ill. Illness came with the city, where they had no immunity; her memories were of mumps and endless colds.[1] She remembers hating Toronto as a child. It was associated in her mind with "standing in slush with dampness seeping through my boots, itchy bloomers, grey muggie skies, old ladies who hit your knuckles with the metal edge of the ruler if you didn't know the words to 'Rule, Britannia.'"[2]

Toronto in 1946 had far more people than it could comfortably accommodate now that the soldiers had been demobbed. The war had ended the previous August, and the men returning from the front were demanding their jobs back. According to the young journalist Doris Anderson, who had just arrived from the prairies expecting a cosmopolitan city, Toronto was a disappointment. It was "provincial, smug, and dull."[3] The event of the summer was the Orange Parade, 12 July, which wound its way through the downtown core, led by the mayor in his ribboned finery.

Sunday was sacrosanct. Eaton's department-store windows had curtains and, following the founder's edict, these were drawn shut on Sundays. Timothy Eaton was typical in believing "the piety of the populace should not be contaminated by commercialism" on the Lord's Day. In 1946, public restaurants were an oddity. The most popular one on Bloor Street had the appetizing name of "The Diet Kitchen." There was one theatre, the Royal Alexandra, but no professional drama company. (The first Toronto company, at The Crest Theatre, was established in 1954.) There was only one concert hall, Massey Hall. Even though Toronto was a city on a lake, one did not slip down to the beach to bathe in its debris-filled water.

To be fair, there was an undertow of a different sort — the young could go dancing at the Top Hat, Casa Loma, or the supper dance at the Royal York Hotel. All these places were "dry." Toronto's first cocktail bar, the Silver Rail, didn't open until 1949.[4]

There was a jazz scene. You could go down to the Coliseum at the Canadian National Exhibition to hear Bix Beiderbecke and Gene Krupa when they were in town, and the CBC always broadcast the bands that showed up at the Palais Royale on the Lakeshore. Mac Reynolds, a painter and sculptor, remembers when Count Basie played there in 1946. He also remembers that blacks weren't allowed into the dance hall.[5]

Some might point to the Toronto Symphony, under Sir Ernest MacMillan; the Art Gallery of Toronto, where there was a small and lively arts scene; and the visits of New York's Metropolitan Opera every summer, to say that Toronto was not a dull town. But it wouldn't wash. Toronto was politically conservative and quintessentially WASP.

The city kid's life centred on comic books or listening to radio programs like "Inner Sanctum," "Jack Benny," "Fred Allen," "Fibber McGee and Molly," and "The Great Gildersleeve." Or if the children were sick at home they might listen to their mother's programs: "The Happy Gang," "Ma Perkins," or "Helen Hunt (Can a woman find happiness after forty?)." In the city streets, in the autumn twilight, one played games of ring-a-lievio and, in the winter, staged snowball fights. Kids didn't take lessons outside school much, except sports for boys and ballet and tap-dancing for girls. Art was considered sissy, or perhaps pretentious. The only theatre for children was the Toronto Children's Players, with productions at Eaton's Auditorium. (It was there that Glenn Gould gave his first public performance in December 1945.)

After living in the north part of the city, in 1948 the Atwoods moved to a house in the Leaside district of Toronto, near the southern end of Bayview Avenue. They had to wait while it was being built, staying until mid-November in the bush, and living briefly in a motel. This would be the only Toronto house they would own.

One block to the north was the elegant two-hundred-acre Mount Pleasant Cemetery, opened in 1876, where many of Toronto's elite are buried. Just a short walk behind the house, at the end of Heath Street, was a footbridge. There Margaret could climb down through dense underbrush into the Moore Park Ravine, which snaked through the east side of the city. If she followed the creek, which eventually hooked into the main trunk of the Don Valley (the expressway was not yet built), she'd reach the Don Valley Brickworks, and the old Todmorden Mills, built in 1827.

Though it would later become a district of trendy boutiques, at mid-century Leaside was on the edge of downtown and decidedly middle class. The Atwoods' house was a modest brick bungalow with a spacious yard for gardening. To visitors recalling it later, the house seemed spare but warm, the living room decorated with durable tweed and Naugahyde chairs around a blazing fire. On the mantel stood the cherry-wood carvings made by Grandfather Killam. Historical maps of England and Scotland hung unframed on the wall.

Only select images, anecdotes, and landscapes survive the amnesia of childhood. Spotlighted in our memory, they can be called up at will. The city that Margaret began to walk as a child of six would layer its landscapes in her brain, and years later she would be able to conjure up those images to give rich texture to her fiction. Examining them and the memories they instilled, we can begin to watch the growth of the writer's mind.

In writing her novel *Cat's Eye* in 1988, Margaret would say that she had "wanted a literary home for all those vanished *things* from my own childhood — the marbles, the Eaton's catalogues, the Watchbird Watching You, the smells, sounds, colors. The textures. Part of fiction writing is a celebration of the physical world we know — and when you're writing about the past, it's a physical world that's vanished. So the impulse is partly elegiac. And partly it's an attempt to stop or bring back time."[6]

What is a city for a child? It's an unruly patchwork: certain resonant landscapes, buildings filled with mystery, moments that catch the imagination. Margaret's Toronto included what the journalist Robert Fulford playfully calls the "Hidden City," Toronto's green underside, the hundreds of ravines that provide its subterranean life. As Fulford says, "No other big city has so much nature woven with such intricate thoroughness through its urban fabric."[7] Built on six rivers, from Etobicoke Creek on its west side to the Rouge River on the east, Toronto has been called "San Francisco upside down." Streams that flowed from the northern Oak Ridges moraine after the last Ice Age carved the landscape into an intricate network of wooded, steep-sloped ravines that are like deep cuts, almost invisible from the surface. Once you are inside these ravines, the city seems to vanish. The ravines are the breeding places of raccoons and wild foxes, of birds like the yellow-bellied sapsucker, and of ferns and wild flowers and eccentric vegetation like the scarlet pimpernel and the spotted touch-me-not. In the snags (standing dead trees) are holes made by woodpeckers and used by cavity nesters and endless families of squirrels. For a child, of course, these could be places of terror and adventure. "To go down into them," Margaret once wrote, "is to go down into sleep, away from the conscious electrified life of the houses. The ravines are darker, even in the day."[8]

Before the Toronto Parks Department tamed the ravines with nature walks, they were wild, scary places where a child could slide down the muddy slopes and track the meandering streams; and the dilapidated bridges became tests of nerve for those who had the guts to cross.

Margaret's house was on the edge of one such bridge. The upper part of the ravine was in the cemetery; going south across a road, you would follow a small river that ran through a culvert. As the river swelled in spring, children in rubber boots dared each other to walk through that culvert — because it was dangerous, full of old bottles, old tire parts, and the occasional dead animal. The river led eventually to the brickworks. You could ride a sheet of cardboard down its spiralling pit.

The children of her fiction sometimes enter that magic world, in defiance of parental prescriptions — little girls were warned of the dangerous men who lived in the ravines like trolls; they probably existed, but one rarely saw such men, and this only added to the thrilling danger. So deeply had this labyrinthine network of cuts in the city's underside embedded itself in her mind that it would become an obvious topographical metaphor. It's where Elaine in *Cat's Eye* undergoes her ordeals at the hands of Cordelia, and where the bag men of the poem "In My Ravines" live out their days.

The Atwoods were obviously aware that they had extremely bright children, and they clearly sought ways to keep those minds busy. The Royal Ontario Museum (ROM) had a Saturday Morning Club, and Margaret was duly enrolled when she was nine. She went with her friend Meg Graham, whose father, Dr. Walter Graham, was head of the Greek Archaeology department. The building they went to would have been the original old Gothic structure at the corner of Bloor Street and Queen's Park, inaugurated in 1914 with Charles Trick Currelly as its director. Currelly had amassed an unusually good collection from the days of his field work in Egypt, Crete, and Asia Minor in the first quarter of the century.[9]

The children of the Saturday Morning Club would gather in the appointed meeting place in the basement, and be issued wooden folding stools — Margaret remembered these particularly since they were apt to fold on you as you tried to sit. They would be led upstairs to one of the displays, where they would sit while the adult in charge explained some exhibit encased behind dusty glass. It could be a ceremonial mask, a suit of armour, a stone statue of an Egyptian god, which they would attempt to draw. Then they would return to the basement, where, with paint and glue, buttons and feathers, they would construct their models.

Before the days of renovation, trick lighting, and video displays, the ROM was a delightfully cluttered museum. It was famous for its domed-glass entranceway, and this feature, too, seeped into Margaret's mind subliminally. Years later she would describe that space as a "crazed man-made brain," a "golden cranium" where she wandered among fragments of gods and skeletons, dragged through human history to the "mind's deadend."[10]

To a child, the museum seemed dramatic, like a time capsule: "Down in the cellar, for instance, there were whole tribes of Indians made out of plaster, squatting around a crepe-paper fire, and up a couple of flights of stairs, an Egyptian mummy case, open, with a real dried-up body inside, done up in Band-Aids. There were also a good many weapons — swords, blunder-busses, crossbows — and, most exciting of all, a whole room devoted to dinosaurs, at that time my favorite variety of wildlife, with a sort of panorama of a bunch of sabre-toothed tigers being trapped in a tar pit."[11]

The best time came after the art class, when Meg Graham and Margaret would meander back to Dr. Graham's office on their own. Dodging the custodians, they would explore the museum.

> The space seemed endless, labyrinthine, empty of living people, populated by statues and gods and clothing worn by invisible people, and strewn with the kinds of things I had otherwise encountered only in adventure stories: crossbows, blowpipes, necklaces dug up from tombs, cave bears, skulls. Our favorites were, of course, the Egyptian mummies, which we approached with a queasy and delicious fear — would they start to move?[12]

She would call the ROM her "First Museum Love." It would surface in poems and novels decades later. In *Life Before Man*, the museum is almost a character in its own right.

Another of Margaret's magic places was her father's building, since torn down, on the University of Toronto campus, where the Department of Zoology was housed. The back windows of the building overlooked University Avenue and the provincial Parliament Buildings, which loomed like "an outsized pudding mold." It was there they would go to watch the Santa Claus Parade wind past Queen's Park. She and her brother, Harold, and whatever friends had been invited would sit on the windowsill, above the hissing radiators, totally entranced. When she looked back at these moments to recover them for the purposes of her fiction, Margaret would note the bizarre juxtaposition of microscopes on the black oblong tables, and pickled ox eyes and snakes and greyish organs floating in jars of formaldehyde in glass cases, while the fairies and ice palaces passed in parade outside.[13]

Margaret started school at the age of six. She went briefly to the Duke of York School in North Toronto, an area not yet developed and which she remembered as practically farmers' fields. When the family moved to Leaside, she was enrolled at Whitney Public School, and then at Bennington Heights. She skipped grade seven, which, in those days, was not uncommon for bright kids. But her eighth-grade class had only eight students in it. That was unusual.

Clearly the training students received was good, but those schools had one peculiarity that stood out only in retrospect. In their pedagogy and their attitudes, they were still colonial outposts of "the British Empire." One learned to recite the names of all the kings and queens of England, draw the Union Jack, and sing "Rule, Britannia!" while the kings and queens stared down from the classroom walls. A complacent racism was buried in the school texts. The school reader, for instance, contained this couplet: "Little Indian, Sioux or Cree, / Don't you wish that you were me." Loyalty to Britain was instilled in songs such as "The Maple Leaf Forever": "In days of yore, from Britain's shore, / Wolfe the dauntless hero came, / and planted firm Britannia's flag / on Canada's fair domain."[14] It was the British connection that was important at these schools. Children collected parcels for poor British families suffering through the aftermath of world war.

But, after school, the cultural pull came from another direction, the United States. The kids read comic books featuring superheroes like Captain America. In those comics, the bad guys were Germans and Japs, and the good guys were always Yankees. Of course Margaret could joke about it in retrospect: "We learned that all Japanese die by going 'Aiieeee, whereas Germans die by going 'Aarrgh."[15] But there was no acknowledgement of one's own national history, or even landscape. A child was offered little sense of his or her Canadianness. As she would later put it:

> The truth about the universe was contained in comic books traded and re-traded till their covers fell off: Batman, Blackhawk, the Human Torch, Plastic Man, Captain Marvel. We knew these comic books were American, because occasionally a grey and white Canadian imitation of inferior quality would turn up. Canada for us was not-America, the place where popsicle bag offers didn't apply and everything was ten cents extra; the comics were news bulletins of the action going on across the border which we could watch but not join.[16]

For a writer, this sense of exclusion would prove a double-edged legacy. In retrospect, it would be a source of anger, but also a catalyst: that vacuum of identity needed to be filled, and Margaret would set out, along with other writers of her generation, to do exactly that.

In the Protestant schools Margaret attended, there was a "religious knowledge" teacher who came once a week. A Bible passage was read aloud at the beginning of each day, and psalms were sung in choir practice.

Not wanting to be excluded from what her friends were doing, Margaret staged her first rebellion. She insisted that her family allow her to go to Sunday school.[17] Her father was very much against this, but gave her permission anyway. She attended a Presbyterian–Methodist Sunday school, where they would read the Bible and write essays. (Her essay on temperance won a prize.) The Methodists put out a Sunday-school paper with an icon depicting little children from all over the globe dancing in a circle. Clearly, this was part of their missionary propaganda. Later, when she came to write *The Circle Game*, Margaret would recall this as a sinister image. But, at the time, this tight world allowed her a momentary sense of belonging and, despite the negatives, she would come to believe that those high-minded Sunday-school days fostered a kind of idealism that would be useful in later life.

In fact, as is true for most children, religious concepts had their fascination. Sometimes this was purely playful. She recalled how, later in high school, she challenged a girlfriend with the following conundrum:

> If Heaven is a good place and preferable to earth, why is murdering good people bad? Wouldn't you be doing them a favor, since that way they'd get up there sooner? Only murdering bad people should be bad, since they weren't about to go to Heaven anyway. But if they were bad enough, surely they deserved to be murdered. So murdering both good people and bad people was actually quite good, all things considered; to the good people you'd be giving a helping hand, to the bad ones their just deserts.[18]

Margaret learned early to be provocative, to establish her own place, not to disappear. She was a fast mind at play, wanting to be deliberately outrageous, picking out the schoolteachers who would and wouldn't enjoy those righteous murders. Her point to her friend, of course, was that religion could get out of hand. Her friend had replied: "God is the good in people," to which she retorted: "Like vitamins in milk?"

Later, between the ages of fourteen and twenty-one, Margaret would visit every type of church she could. This was characteristic. If anything took her interest, she needed to know it first-hand. She had the writer's instinct for research, and these visits would come in handy later, in crafting her fictional characters. The Jordan Chapel in *Lady Oracle*, whose members dabble in spiritualism, is loosely based on one such church she encountered, a version of the kind of church we have since come to identify as Charismatic Pentecostal. There she received a message from a white-haired lady who said: "I have a message for someone in the audience whose name is Margaret but whom everyone calls Peggy." She was briefly impressed. The enigmatic message was: "Everything will be all right in nine months."[19]

The impulse to be like her girlfriends was growing in Margaret. There had been many summers without girlfriends. Now she joined the Brownies, meeting winter nights in those damp church basements, sitting around imaginary campfires, singing summer songs. And earning all those badges in woodlore, which of course was something she herself could have taught the adult leaders, or Brown Owls as they were called. But the desire to belong, not to appear eccentric, grows in the imaginative and isolated child. She started to attend Brownie camp in summer. To her small friends, she must have seemed to be the one who knew everything.

In a project she did in public school, it is clear how precise her knowledge of woodlore was. She divided her twelve-page essay into chapters: chapter I was devoted to animal tracks; chapter II, to insects. She carefully illustrated her descriptions with drawings.

Chapter I   ANIMAL TRACKS

THE COTTONTAIL RABBIT

The tracks of the cottontail rabbit always seem to be going
in the opposite direction than they really are. This is due to
the fact that he runs or jumps using his front legs as a "lever"
to swing his back legs forward, and thus places the back legs

in front of the front legs, (hard to describe, but it comes
naturally to the cottontail). [She included a detailed drawing of the cottontail's tracks.]

Describing the white-tail deer, she explained that "the pettallike
[Margaret would always be a bad speller] track is very dainty and beautiful. The Deer is put in the class of 'Toenail Walkers' for it does truly walk
on its toenails."[20]

In her mind, Margaret had already intimately tied woods and books
together. To the Atwood house would come many of her father's friends
who shared his interest in science and with whom he went on canoe trips.
There was Sigurd Olson, who wrote *The Lonely Land*, about a trip on the
Churchill River in Saskatchewan, and Paul Provencher, a forester and
artist, and author of *I Live in the Woods*, a book of personal recollections
and woodland lore. He had accompanied her father on one of his expeditions in search of budworm outbreaks on the north shore of Lake Ontario.
Provencher was Margaret's favourite. Over dinner, the Atwood family
would be falling off their chairs laughing as he recounted his northern
adventures, such as eating fermented moose stomach when he stayed with
the Montagnais. An impressionable child, Margaret was absorbing the fact
that these men who shared her father's passion for science were also adven-
turers. The life of the mind was not academic. Knowledge was a passion
to be applied experientially.

The house was full of books about the woods, a number by men her
father knew. When she was twelve, she became so obsessed with Ellsworth
Jaeger's *Wildwood Wisdom* that she practically memorized it.[21]

Five hundred pages long, *Wildwood Wisdom* was intended as a book for
adolescents, and offered precisely detailed instructions, with illustrations,
on how to become an expert woodsman. (Not the usual obsession for a
young girl.) Jaeger explained that the best woods-wear was buckskin; it was
rainproof, warm, and good protection against brambles and thorns. And
he instructed his young readers how to make it. All you needed to do was
to skin a deer and then "Indian tan" the hide. "To do this," he wrote, "you
will need the deer's brains, and perhaps its liver, as well as its skin." He
explained how to build winter and summer shelters: "Do not camp under
large trees." (There was always the danger of lightning.) "In the winter

build your shelter facing the cliff." (The cliff would reflect heat into your tent.) He included instructions about how to make fire, offering at least seven ways, using a variety of hand-made instruments, from a bow drill fire stick and a pump fire drill to a fire saw. He identified bird and animal "voices," and described how to call moose, deer, muskrat, and beaver. And then he explained how to trap them using pieces of rawhide and stone. If you were lost and starving and had no rawhide, you could dig holes to snare them. Best for Margaret, the book contained a long list of forest edibles, including nuts, roots, and "starvation foods." There was a chapter titled "Lost," which began: "Remember, you're not lost. It's your camp that is lost."

While the closest that most of her city girlfriends came to the forest was a summer cottage or summer camp, Margaret spent months in the bush with her parents, and one of her passions became to identify and dig up, or catch, cook, and eat many of the varieties of natural edibles Ellsworth described. She rated them: "Puffballs and Indian cucumber got an A, cat-tail stew and Rock Lichen a D. Lake clams were muddy. Crayfish were good, though you would have to eat a lot of them to make any difference."[22] She and her brother made pancakes from cat-tail pollen, and would have tried porcupine, but couldn't catch one. Getting lost in the wilderness was obviously something she took as a real possibility, but, with *Wildwood Wisdom*, as she once remarked, she would know what to do.

She was satisfied by Ellsworth's message on the value of improvisation: "Don't panic. Look around you. Use what you've got." This lore would find its subterranean way into her writing years later. The unnamed narrator in *Surfacing* is an expert canoeist, knows how to read the bush without a map, understands weather patterns, and clearly identifies more easily with the animals than the humans who abuse them. And she does not sentimentalize nature.

In my mind's eye, I watch this young girl and am impressed by her thoroughness. I also think of the mother who could let her children be, off in the woods cooking their concoctions. But Mrs. Atwood didn't have to worry. Her children had been woods-proofed. As well, for this young girl, books were real — she tested them, acted them out. The young Margaret obviously felt a deep need to be self-sufficient and to exert some control in the woods, because chaos was just around the corner. She once said: "I learned to be adept at not being cornered."[23]

A second writer who helped to shape her young imagination was the nineteenth-century author Ernest Thompson Seton. Born in 1860, Seton was essentially a Victorian, with that strange temperament that is both practical and mystical. He was fascinated by myth and legend, but was also a trained naturalist, a term that, for him, had a visionary as well as a scientific resonance.[24]

He grew up in Margaret's world. His family emigrated from England in 1866 and soon bought a house in Toronto beside the Don Valley, then an unclaimed wilderness. He trained as an artist at the Ontario College of Art, and later at the Royal Academy in England; worked as a science illustrator (*Studies in the Art Anatomy of Animals* came out in 1896); and wrote travelogues (*The Arctic Prairies: A Canoe Journey of 2,000 Miles in Search of the Caribou*) and dozens of books of animal stories. But he had a singular passion: he wanted to train children to be "Woodcrafters." He was instrumental in founding the Boy Scouts of America in 1910, though he was expelled from the organization when he levelled charges of militarism against it in 1915.

It was his *Wild Animals I Have Known* that the young Margaret fell in love with. The book contained biographies of animals, told from the animal's point of view. In his 1898 preface, Seton wrote: "Since, then, the animals are creatures with wants and feelings differing in degree only from our own, they surely have their rights. This fact, now beginning to be recognized by the Caucasian world, was emphasized by the Buddhist over 2,000 years ago." He added that all the stories in his book were true. "The fact that [they] are true is the reason why all are tragic. The life of a wild animal always has a tragic end."[25]

Seton described the "private life" of animals by attempting to understand their thinking. The adolescent Margaret must have been intrigued by his method of patient observation. Watching his black collie, Seton explained how he discovered Bingo's complicated system of signal stations for getting and giving the news. To a canine, smells were a precise, telegraphic language. Or there was Redruff, the Don Valley partridge, who, almost a century earlier, had explored her world: the Rosedale Creek, then lined with silver birches, and Castle Frank and Chester Woods, now subway stops on the route to east-end Toronto. Years later, when Margaret came to write her poem "The Animals in That Country," she might have been remembering Seton's tragic animals: "Their eyes / flash once in car headlights / and are gone. / Their deaths are not elegant. / They have the faces of / no-one."[26]

Margaret was entranced by both Seton's and Jaeger's books. With her own scientific bent, she could easily have claimed Seton's title "Woodcrafter." She and her brother certainly spent time testing some of Jaeger's instructions, including how to make clay pots from river mud. But she had another interest: it must have struck her that telling stories could be both magical and practical.

For she was discovering that it was in the world of books that she could most be herself. Her reading was omnivorous and seemingly without prohibitions. In the children's library at school, she terrified herself with Edgar Allan Poe. And she would slip down to the basement at home and raid her father's shelves. She was not reading girls' books. She once said: "I grew up with a lot of history. My father is a history nut. The basement is full of it. So I read the biography of Rommel when I was twelve. I read Winston Churchill's five volumes on the war when I was fourteen or fifteen."[27]

And there would have been models for her industry. Her father was always engaged in some research, and he must have sat up some nights correcting his students' assignments. Margaret would later write her first early poems on the back of his mimeographed lecture notes and exams. Down in the basement, her brother had constructed his experimental lab. Those were the days when poisonous substances could be bought over the counter, and he could be found down there making all kinds of stuff, with horrible smells and burning sulphur.

Moments from childhood sit like holograms in a writer's mind, to be used at will. Of course such moments will be variously reinvented as they break free from the bedrock of autobiographical realism to follow the dictates of art. I am particularly fascinated by one such moment that appears in a number of Margaret's poems and novels. One summer her brother, Harold, built himself a laboratory in the swamp so that he could investigate moulds. Moulds grow best in sunless damp. He raised the cultures on pieces of bread he kept in jars, dating the containers and arranging them in orange crates. When the mould was in full bloom, he would open the jar and perform his experiments. The sight of her brother crouched among the black spruce and mosquitoes, brooding over his mouldy jars, stuck in Margaret's mind. I wonder why that moment, among so many, resonates so strongly that it was reinvented in her first unpublished novel, *Up in the Air So Blue*, in *Surfacing*, and in the poem "The Laboratory."

Sometimes her brother invited her into the inner sanctum of experiment. She was aware that, as a girl among adolescent boys, this was a privilege. Being the little sister, trailing two and a half years behind, she must have felt both her election and her exclusion. With her brother, she would have felt a healthy competitiveness; she would have wanted to earn a place in his esteem and, paradoxically, to distinguish herself as separate. When she wasn't invited into the swamp, she would say she preferred swimming.

The ways we learn to establish our own autonomy and authority are subtle. As it turned out, Harold was a benevolent sibling to knock up against as she tried to define herself. One message was clear: she would have nothing to do with the world of female subservience.

Later she would think about scientific passion, that "exact fury" of the nascent young scientist to discover the secret of life in his dark swamp. It was a theme to be found in many of the books she was reading, such as Mary Shelley's *Frankenstein*. In her later fiction and poetry, Margaret would become critical of the world's tendency to separate science from art. In her father, as well-read in the humanities as the sciences, she had a model that made it clear such rigidity was not necessary.

Who was this young girl, then, growing up in the safe suburban world of Leaside, but who spent long summers in the northern bush, where suburban complacency was knocked on its ear by wildness?

"I'm interested," she would say, "in edges, undertows, permutations, in taking things that might be viewed as eccentric or marginal and pulling them into the center."[28] She would become someone who was always looking for a space to stand — on the borderline between city and bush, between reason and feeling, between fear and empathy. She was someone who learned from that wild world what she would call "the gaping moment" — "a sense of the hole in the sky." She would say that, for her, the city world was the fearful place where she had to learn the mysterious codes of behaviour that everyone else took for granted.

But she was, after all, a girl, growing up in the 1940s and 1950s. At the age of ten, she already thought she might become a writer or a painter, even though she was momentarily traumatized by the propaganda of girl-hood, and by that film, *The Red Shoes*. She understood its message: that a girl could not be an artist without great suffering, without, in a sense, being unnatural. You could be either an artist or a woman, but if you tried to be both you would have to jump in front of a train. What might have distin-guished her was that she instinctively understood the message of the film in the first place. Not many girls did.

This lesson was, however, what society taught. She didn't learn it at home. What distinguished Margaret's family was the absence of gender stereotypes, which had its downside, of course, because it left her unpre-pared for the real world. She would say in retrospect:

> In my family I was never threatening to men. They aren't
> noted for self-doubt. I could do whatever I liked. I wasn't
> forced into the role of being female, though I never had any
> doubts about being a girl. . . . When one is brought up in a
> family where men aren't exactly lacking in confidence, such
> as mine, the realization that some men are afraid, anxious
> and shaky is a shock. It was a terrific shock to discover men
> were vulnerable. What did I say?[29]

Confidence, she would explain, depends on whether the child is appre-ciated as a human being. A lot of people never pursue their passions past the first flush of enthusiasm because they don't have the confidence. Girls in particular are trained to please, and when somebody doesn't like them they think the fault is their own. Margaret was shocked to discover that most parents weren't as benevolent as hers, that the more familiar arche-type was hyper-critical parents attempting to mould their children. What Margaret received was an unshakable, totally realistic faith in her own abilities, and a confidence to do what she wanted to do. The Atwoods might have been middle class, but they had invented their own version of what that meant.

What most fascinates me about this young girl is that she inherited none of the female guilts. She once said: "My parents never used guilt as a weapon on me and consequently I missed out on it growing up. To me it's always been a useless emotion."[30] What is female guilt? It is certainly the sense of being watched — what will others think? — the legacy of which is probably repressed anger. It would take her a while (she would have to pass through the morass of teenage-hood), but as a young woman she could be straight-dealing, and compassionate when compassion was called for. But she certainly didn't need to be nice. Margaret was not trained to please: she could say humorously: "If you're not annoying someone, you're not really alive."[31]

When Peggy Atwood had become Margaret Atwood, the writer, a Canadian film-maker, Michael Rubbo, attempted to do a documentary titled *Atwood and Family*. Setting his film at the family cottage in the heart of Canadian Shield country, he lingered on shots of her, alone in her canoe, executing a perfect J-stroke through dark choppy lakes. Rubbo was looking for the romantic artist — the one who must have had tragic beginnings, who must be haunted, a tortured soul. He was thinking of Margaret Atwood as a mystery to be solved, and he was looking for the clue. She wasn't helpful. She soon realized it seemed almost a fault that her parents appeared so benevolent. Surely they were repressively benevolent.

We are addicted to a pathological interpretation of childhood, perhaps because so many childhoods are pathological. The truth, however, may be that our interpretation of reality is so imbued with psychological ramifications because we remain romantics in our hearts — there is an ideal and everyone fails, but it can be achieved if we work at it.

But the Atwood family appears pragmatic. Their way of dealing with things was with stoicism and humour. In the film, Margaret puts a bag on her head, and the family interviews her. Asked who this woman in the bag is, her father replies: "Someone masquerading as Margaret Atwood." The anonymous woman in the bag was the writer the world had invented. The real Peggy was hidden underneath. What is fascinating about this moment is how little allowance is made for the ego of Mr. Rubbo. He was being made fun of. Family solidarity was powerful, but this was not a family in which a lot of time was spent protecting vulnerabilities. If you stuck your neck out, you had to be prepared to take the consequences. And you also had to be prepared to fight back. Not bad training for the writer.

4

THE THENNESS OF THEN

It was the early fifties, the decade of schizophrenia. Five years after the conflagration of world war, everyone, at least in North America, seemed bent on pretending that order had been restored. But underneath that illusion, it was a dark, complex decade.

In 1951, 500,000 Chinese and North Koreans took the city of Seoul, South Korea, and the Korean War began. General Douglas MacArthur was dismissed by the American president, Harry Truman, after publicly demanding the right to bomb Chinese targets in Manchuria. The war would last until 1953. Joseph Stalin died in March 1953, and people in the tens of thousands began to stream out of the Stalinist prison camps. Lavrenti Beria, head of the Soviet secret police, was murdered in the ensuing power struggle. *Coups d'état* and military dictatorships had become the fashion in Latin America, occasionally with American support — Haiti (1950); Cuba (1952); Bolivia (1952); Colombia (1953); Guatemala (1954); Paraguay (1954); Argentina (1955). These local conflicts were overlooked as hemispheric anomalies, but they would surface to haunt North America in later decades.[1]

The early 1950s was the era of McCarthyism, which ended only in 1954, when thirty-six days of televised Army–McCarthy Hearings exposed and disgraced the witch-hunting U.S. senator. He survives in films, his truculent brawling and sneering villainy making him seem almost comical now, though he once terrorized America. He had his more dignified equivalents in Canada — those who also stirred fears of creeping communism, who shared the idea that China was lost, and soon

Europe would be lost, too, because Western governments were full of trea-
sonous pro-Soviets.

The real nightmare backdrop of the decade was, of course, the nuclear
arms race. In 1951, the American army had begun atmospheric nuclear
weapons–testing at the Nevada Test Site, 75 miles northwest of Las Vegas.
More than a hundred above-ground nuclear tests were conducted from
1951 to 1958, and the resulting radioactive fallout contaminated hundreds
of square miles. The approximately 100,000 people living downwind from
the test sites were never evacuated, or even warned of the hazards. In 1959,
Canada entered into a treaty with the United States, constructing the
DEW (Distant Early Warning) Line, some fifty tracking, warning, and
control stations across the Arctic, from Greenland to Alaska. As part of
the continental-defence system, air-raid sirens were erected in public
parks, and underground bomb shelters became the rage. Everyone wanted
one in the back yard. Perhaps this, more than anything, characterized the
schizophrenia of the decade: the almost-universal desire for a suburban
back yard and a bomb shelter.

For, in the 1950s, when Margaret was growing into an adolescent, the
dream of suburbia had taken over. The adults of her parents' generation
had spent their childhoods in the threatening instability of the Depression and had seen their youth sacrificed to six years of war. The men back
from the front, and the 33 per cent of women who had worked in factories and offices for the war effort who were now back in their kitchens,
were determined to resurrect the dream of home. And the propaganda
machines, from church to commerce, from advice columns to fiction,
were there to encourage them. From 1945 to 1960, the values of marriage
and family took on mythic proportions.[2]

Suburbia was created to house this dream. Industries that had recently
fed on the war machine were converted to the construction of cheap,
prefab houses on little patches of land that spread out from the cities' skirts
in standardized pleats. Thousands moved in, often with government grants
in the form of Soldiers' Compensation. Uniformity was the rule.

The age of brand names, miracle synthetic products, and the clutter of
consumerism had begun. Functionalism defined modernism. Arborite,
Formica, Congoleum, and Marboleum replaced wood, and sofas were
covered in vinyl. The kitchen was cluttered with appliances — pop-up

toasters, electric frying pans, and Mixmasters. It was the age, not just of the newly invented television, but of TV stacking trays, and reclining chairs with built-in footstools. Design magazine articles counselled: "Don't be a Colour Coward. Give your House a Splash of Colour." The palette of the age was pink, aquamarine, and turquoise.[3]

Roads, too, were transformed. Toronto's Gardiner Expressway was built in 1955 to get through the city without having to see it, and the Don Valley Parkway was opened in 1964, slicing through Margaret's secret ravine world. Cars became success symbols; with V8 engines and wide, swept-back fins, they were powerful and absurdly unsafe.

By 1955 many Ontario households had televisions. Fads hit and then disappeared: yellow rain slickers, open galoshes, Hula Hoops. Barbie dolls arrived in 1959 and stayed. The notion of the peer group was invented, and everyone participated in peer-sanctioned consumption.

Lewis Mumford called the suburbs "an asylum for the preservation of illusion." Pundits were busy trying to name this new phenomenon. They came up with the word "Populuxe" "to refer to 'America [having] found a way of turning out fantasy on an assembly line.'"[4] The 1950s were a time of conformism and standardization, propelled by an idealism that was built on insecurity: world war had happened twice; it mustn't happen again. And all that insecurity was centred on creating a myth of marriage and family.

Such was the ideological world that surrounded Leaside High School when Margaret enrolled in 1952. The cosmopolitan kids went to Jarvis Collegiate, and the rich ones to Forest Hill Collegiate, and both sneered at middle-class Leaside. Having skipped a grade, Margaret was younger than the other students. From her home each morning, she walked the fifteen minutes it took to get to Leaside High on Eglinton Avenue. Her walk led past Woolworth's where notions were sold, past the I.D.A. Drugstore, and past the local cinema where kids went to see films about war and romance. The "fast" kids from Leaside hung out at the Sunnybrook Shopping Plaza, which was one of the first of its kind in the area.

The principal of Leaside, Norman McLeod, ran his school as if it were an extension of his Scottish clan, with the McLeod tartan as the school's official colours and a Gaelic saying on its crest. The school yearbook was called *The Clan Call*. Mr. McLeod's claim to fame was his visit to Dunvegan Castle in Scotland, where he'd had luncheon with the Queen, the Duke of Edinburgh, and Princess Margaret. He'd been the Princess's luncheon partner.[5]

The kids at Leaside wore uniforms: for the girls this meant square-necked black tunics, white blouses, knee-socks in spring and fall, and black stockings in winter. There was an official regulation that tunics had to be no shorter than seven inches above the knee, since girls tried to hitch their tunics up above the belt to raise the hems. The school had a chaplain, Dr. Maura, who taught Latin and led the Scripture readings and prayers at assembly in the gymnasium. That was also the place where students sat for exams. It was an odd and rather menacing structure, since an iron catwalk ran the length of the four walls, about ten feet above the students' heads.[6] Years later, as a kind of private joke, Margaret would dig out the memory of this gymnasium with its catwalk for the sleeping quarters of the handmaids in her sinister novel *The Handmaid's Tale.*

The school also had an indoor rifle range, a long narrow passage running down one side of the second floor, which students and adult members of the Leaside Rifle Club used for target practice four nights a week. Anyone entering the school on those nights might hear the eerie sound of gunfire. The club eventually vacated the school premises when one of the participants was accidentally killed.

Canadian public high schools were overtly Protestant and still schools of the Empire — students studied Ancient Greece, Ancient Rome, Ancient Egypt, Europe in the Middle Ages, England, and the United States. Canadian history was reserved for grade thirteen, by which time many students had dropped out. Margaret would always remember her high-school Canadian history book, *Canada in the World Today*, which had an airplane on the front cover: "It was about who grew wheat and how happy we were with the parliamentary system. Not much, in those days, about possible French-speaking malcontents or the fact that Indians might have come out the losers in a few forced land deals."[7]

The Earle Grey Players, which consisted of Mr. and Mrs. Grey and a few other adults, came round every year to put on a Shakespeare play in the auditorium, usually the one set for the grade-thirteen exams. Students could bring their own bed sheets and be in the crowd scene for *Julius Caesar*. The school chorus, to which Margaret belonged, did musicals like

Oklahoma! and *Brigadoon*, and the Dramatic Society did Broadway plays like *Time Out for Ginger*.[8]

Brainy kids, like Margaret, took French, though the teacher spoke with a Parisian, not a Québécois, accent. Literature was British, Shakespeare and after; it stopped short of the United States and Canada, except, again, for those brains who made it to the optional grade thirteen, when they read E.J. Pratt, a living Canadian poet. The only live poet who visited Leaside was the elderly Wilson MacDonald, who came each year and read "The Song of the Ski" and "The Scarlet Maple Tree." In high school, students simply took in stride this absence of things Canadian, believing that real history and real literature were made abroad.

Margaret began at Leaside as a "scrawny, unprepossessing" twelve-year-old. It took time for her to find a way to fit in. In the ditty under the photograph of the ninth-grade class in *The Clan Call*, the school wits wrote: "Marie is fond of a dark-eyed boy. Peggy likes to study. John B. aims to catch flies professionally."[9] One of her teachers in those early years, Miss Smedley, later noted cryptically that there was nothing about the young Margaret Atwood that would lead you to anticipate what she would become.

Margaret got 100 per cent in algebra and did brilliantly in botany. Like all teenage girls, she had the familiar anxieties. She was self-conscious about her hair, which was wiry and unruly, a style that would become wildly popular two decades later. She cut it short and sometimes took to hiding it under a kerchief. Like all kids, she must have looked longingly at the fuchsia nail polish and orange lipstick that the older girls bought at the Kresge's cosmetics counter.

Her eccentricity surfaced in other ways. One of her pets at this time was a praying mantis called Lenore (after Edgar Allan Poe's heroine), which she kept in a large jar, feeding it insects and sugared water from a spoon. Lenore led to one of her most embarrassing moments. She was fourteen and it was the early days of television. The woman who lived next door and for whom she babysat, had become producer of a show on CBLT called "Pet Corner." She invited Margaret to appear on her show, which, like many in those days, was broadcast live, with just one camera at the crew's disposal. Margaret dutifully described the habits of the praying mantis — among other things, the female's habit of eating the male after copulation.

Presumably impressed by her way with animals, "Pet Corner" asked her back, this time to assist with another pet performance. A guest was bringing a tame flying squirrel onto the show. It was duly introduced and set to fly, but being a nocturnal animal and terrified by the studio lights it immediately looked for dark shelter and shimmied down the front of Margaret's tunic. The camera watched the travelling bulge slither above the belt of her school uniform, heading downwards, until the pet owner fished it out from the back of her garment. Luckily the program was shown during school hours; Margaret's main anxiety was that her school friends might see it.[10]

Her parents might have been brilliant in the woods, but they were not much interested in the city, nor for that matter in the new suburban ideal. There was no TV in the Atwood household; Margaret did not discover restaurants until she went to university. She earned her own pocket money. She started with the inevitable babysitting, but she was more enterprising. When she was twelve, she and a friend had attended a class and learned to make marionettes. Soon, they had a "puppet business," doing puppet plays for children's birthday parties.

It had started casually enough. A neighbour, whose little daughter had her heart set on a puppet show for her birthday, had been unable to find a professional puppeteer, and approached Margaret. Margaret was completely captivated by the idea. The two girls made the puppet heads from strips of newspaper dipped in a flour-and-water paste, then dried them and gave them life with tempera paints. The puppets were "green-faced and gruesome." They made a collapsible stage, which had a nasty habit of falling down, and managed to simulate night lighting by using a long black stocking to cover the bulb clipped to the back of the stage. The scripts Margaret wrote were usually based on fairy tales — "The Three Little Pigs," "Hansel and Gretel," or "Sleeping Beauty" — but dramatized with sound effects that would make your hair curl.[11] Later, her father delighted in teasing friends by telling them that Margaret used real blood in her shows.[12] The two got so good at puppetry that they were soon being asked to give performances at company Christmas parties.

Under the grade-twelve photos in the school yearbook, the editors identified their fellow students satirically, using the style of a bird watcher's guide to rare specimens. It's not surprising they described Margaret as: "The Peggy Atwood: Plumage — Corrugated head-feathers. Call — Let's do something original!!!"[13]

To earn money, Margaret also took a job, briefly, at the Canadian National Exhibition, a collection of pseudo-Romanesque buildings and arches on Toronto's waterfront where various (usually trade) shows were launched. Every August this became the site of "the Ex," the event for which the exhibition grounds were famous. Margaret had not been to the CNE before because she had been up north every summer, and, anyway, with the polio outbreaks of the early fifties, parents kept their children away. Terrifying stories of children paralysed and entombed in iron lungs, with photographs of small bodies encased in huge metal cylinders, hit the newspapers with every outbreak, until the horrendous epidemic of 1953 that ended when the new experimental Salk vaccine was used for the first time. One of the most famous exhibits at the Ex in the early fifties was of a patient in a huge iron lung. Only the person's head was visible, resting on a leather pillow; he was gazing into the bit of the world reflected in the mirror above his head. The machine made a terrifying breathing noise. Thousands lined up to see the display.

To get to her part-time job at the Sportsman's Show, Margaret caught the bus in front of her high school and then the streetcar down Bathurst Street to the CNE. Her job was to rent out arrows for the archery range. She describes this in retrospect:

> They wanted a girl, and one that could help the customers get the arrow on the string and pointed the right way. What they shot at was balloons pinned to straw targets, and sometimes, by mistake or for a joke, me, when I was up there collecting the arrows. The worst moment was when you turned your back. On my break I would drink Honey Dew and eat hot dogs and watch Miss Outdoors, in her hip waders and checked shirt tucked in tight, doing a few casts, or wander into the arena to hear Sharky the Seal play the national anthem on a set of pipes, which calmed the nerves.[14]

Margaret always thought she would have a career. At first she had wanted to be a painter, and then a dress designer, but, in high school, she got hit, as she put it, with the concept of having to earn her own living. This was a concept, incidentally, that did not "hit" all young middle-class girls, who often took the more familiar route of collecting a trousseau for the marriage that would provide their role in life.

The problem was that there were only five careers listed for girls in the Guidance textbook. (Margaret invariably remembers this textbook as grey, representing the reality principle.) A girl could be a nurse, teacher, airline stewardess, secretary, or home economist. Margaret decided to major in Home Economics since that career promised to pay the best. In her courses, she was taught that "every meal should consist of a brown thing, a white thing, a yellow thing, and a green thing, that it was not right to lick the spoon while cooking, and that the inside of a dress seam was as important as the outside."[15]

But even here, her originality surfaced. While ripping out all those zippers in home economics class, she designed her own skirts. Other girls were using flower-patterned fabric, but on hers she painted troglodytes and newts in orange and blue.

At Leaside, Margaret soon put on her pragmatic persona. The year-books portray her as the well-rounded all-Canadian girl: she played on the basketball team, was a member of the U.N. Club, and was on the editorial staff of *The Clan Call* in grade twelve. She belonged to the "Triple Trio" that went around to the Rotary luncheons, singing songs like "Come and Trip It as You Go."

The U.N. Club was for the more studious. The students attended meetings in the cold drafty rooms of Upper Canada College to prepare for the third U.N. Model Assembly and then went to the Parliament Buildings downtown for the big debate. Leaside's delegation of sixteen represented Belgium.

In 1956, the club became involved in relief work for Hungarian exiles. When Russian president Nikita Khrushchev delivered his "secret speech" on the massive crimes of Joseph Stalin, triggering huge defections in the Communist movement, riots swept through Eastern Europe. The most visible consequence was the Hungarian Revolution. When the Soviets arrived in tanks, almost 200,000 people fled into exile, and many came to Canada. The Leaside U.N. Club netted close to $200 for Hungarian relief, a large amount of money in those days.

Clearly, Margaret already wanted to be part of the larger world beyond Leaside, and the moral imperative of commitment that would define her as a novelist was already evident. The U.N. would have been particularly popular in Canada. It was in 1956 that Canada's prime minister, Lester Pearson, won the Nobel Peace Prize for suggesting that U.N. peacekeeping forces be mobilized to occupy the Suez Canal during the Sinai–Suez (Arab–Israeli) War, staving off a multipronged invasion of Egypt by British, French, and Israeli forces.

In grades twelve and thirteen, Margaret took to writing columns for the school newspaper, *The Home and School News*. Her column, "High Headlines," kept her fellow students up-to-date on what was happening: she covered the school assemblies, the initiation rituals, the school elections, and the activities of the various clubs, including the U.N. Club, and gave info about the upcoming dances and the sports activities. She would later say that publishing in the school newspaper certainly brought her up against some of the problems she would eventually face as a writer — "mainly people thinking you're nuts." You knew you would be better off to "keep it to yourself and never have to face anybody else's reaction."[16]

The fifties in Canada were largely an innocent and earnest time. Kids at Leaside danced at Hallowe'en Hops and Spring Stomps to the music of bands like the Sateen Bandbox. Girls agonized over finding the right prom dress and dyeing their satin shoes to match. There were no drugs. Occasionally students died in car accidents involving alcohol, and girls got pregnant and disappeared from school, but it was an insular, safe, and protected world.

Intelligent girls did well at Leaside. In her "High Headlines," Margaret noted the girls who'd won prizes: Jean Matthews and Karen Whytock won prizes in the Botanical competition sponsored by the CNE and *The Toronto Daily Star*, and Eleanor Cobbledick won the Imperial Oil Scholarship. Among the chief delegates to the U.N. Model Assembly in 1956 were four girls and one boy. There were even girls' athletic awards, though in writing about recipients Margaret assured her readers that they didn't look at all like "the popular conception of the muscle bound female athlete." Of course, a paragraph in each of her columns focused on the boys' football team.

There was sexism in the structure of school institutions then, but it was largely unconscious and went unacknowledged. Perhaps the best illustration of how sexism worked comes from an anecdote Margaret offered years later, describing how she and a friend participated in the Consumers' Gas "Miss Future Homemaker Contest." They'd been chosen as entrants from their Home Ec class. The contest involved three feats: ironing a shirt with a gas iron, cooking a dinner on a gas stove, and a third thing with gas that she couldn't remember. The point was who could do the triple task fastest.

She and her friend, wearing the requisite aprons, set about getting the wrinkles out of a shirt and cooking the dinner of meat loaf, frozen peas, and baked potatoes. They lost the contest, but got a compensation prize of a charm bracelet with little golden bells. It never occurred to them that this had anything to do with them. They weren't going to be homemakers; they were going to have real lives. Even then Margaret saw the absurdity of the fantasy scenario: the husband arrived home from work, and his happy homemaker produced his pressed shirt and his meat loaf. But she tried, dutifully, to win the contest.[17]

The fifties was the age of contests: Miss Teen, Miss Wool, Miss Vodka, Miss World. It wasn't obvious then that the whole purpose of such contests was for Consumers' Gas and their ilk to promote their products. Nor was the condescension towards girls — those compensatory charm bracelets — transparent. The myth was too strong to know how to question it. Now the image of the teenage Margaret Atwood maniacally ironing up on that stage brings only disbelief and guffaws.

In her mind Margaret would always locate Leaside "in the middle of the middle class in the mid-fifties . . . in mid-century," and this bland middle-class world was not where she belonged. The world she belonged to came from books. She was avidly reading the classics: *Wuthering Heights*, *The Mayor of Casterbridge*, *The Mill on the Floss* (which she practically memorized), and *Tess of the D'Urbervilles*.

In grade twelve, she found the English teacher all young writers crave, Miss Billings, who revelled in the literature she was teaching, and who had style. Margaret discovered she could possibly pursue a literary life without "necessarily turning into a bedraggled frump."[18] She turned away from those sewing classes and from biology.

She described how, in 1956, she suddenly became a poet:

> The day I became a poet was a sunny day of no particular
> ominousness. I was walking across the football field, not

because I was sports-minded or had plans to smoke a cigarette behind the field house — the only other reason for going there — but because this was my normal way home from school. I was scuttling along in my usual furtive way, suspecting no ill, when a large invisible thumb descended from the sky and pressed down on the top of my head. A poem formed. It was quite a gloomy poem; the poems of the young usually are. It was a gift, this poem — a gift from an anonymous donor, and, as such, both exciting and sinister at the same time.

I suspect this is why all poets begin writing poetry, only they don't want to admit it, so they make up explanations that are either more rational or more romantic. But this is the true explanation, and I defy anyone to disprove it.

The poem that I composed on that eventful day, although entirely without merit or even promise, did have some features. It rhymed and scanned, because we had been taught rhyming and scansion at school. It resembled the poetry of Lord Byron and Edgar Allan Poe, with a little Shelley and Keats thrown in. The fact is that at the time I became a poet, I had read very few poems written after the year 1900. I knew nothing of modernism or free verse. These were not the only things I knew nothing of. I had no idea, for instance, that I was about to step into a whole set of preconceptions and social roles that had to do with what poets were like and how they should behave. I didn't yet know black was compulsory. All of that was in the future. When I was 16, it was simple. Poetry existed; therefore it could be written. And nobody had told me — yet — the many, many reasons why it could not be written by me.[19]

She began to type on the right-hand corners of those early efforts "First North American Rights Only."[20] She wasn't sure what these rights were, but the writing magazines she had begun to consult told her this was what one did. Having learned from the nineteenth-century masters like Brontë and Poe, and wanting to write poems that would make the toenails curl, she began to haunt the cemetery across from her house. She wrote poems about snow, despair, and the Hungarian Revolution.

When she announced to her female friends in the school cafeteria that she was going to be a writer, it was a conversation stopper. Nobody said a word. Only years later did a friend explain to her that they had all been astounded, not because of what Margaret had said, but because she had had the guts to say it out loud.

Her parents were dismayed: how was she going to earn a living as a writer? They had been through the Depression and knew people needed proper jobs just in case. But even though they thought her decision economically unwise, they certainly didn't stop her. "No one guided Peggy. I don't think anyone could guide Peggy," her mother explained.[21]

Her father would elaborate to an interviewer years later: "We didn't intentionally raise Peggy in any specific way. The marriage market just didn't make sense. Independence and freedom rate very high with us. One of the reasons we liked life in the bush so much was that it presented problems we had to settle without outside aid. We were on our own a lot."[22]

Margaret had to brook the complacency of those who thought she would get over this writing idea. A friend of her mother's remarked: "Well, that's nice, dear, because you can do it at home, can't you." In the face of such comments, she found taking the offensive the best defence. Once asked whether her fellow students took her seriously as a writer, she remarked: "Everybody was so terrified of me anyway. They didn't not take me seriously. I had a smart mouth. People usually didn't mess around with me."[23]

After she decided to become a writer, Margaret found Home Economics increasingly pointless. Wanting to turn her hand to every form of writing, she wrote singing commercials for the school dances, which were announced over the school PA system; her "Reindeer Romp" was noted in *The Clan Call*. And soon she found an ingenious way to subvert her Home Ec class.

The Home Ec teacher, Miss Ricker, had proposed a special project. She suggested the students make stuffed bears, but, unwisely, she invited a democratic vote on it. Margaret persuaded the class that, instead, they should put on a Home Ec operetta. Miss Ricker acquiesced, but insisted that at least the subject matter must be relevant.

Margaret decided to write an operetta about synthetic fabrics. She called it "Synthesia: Operetta in One Act." She set the scene in the Palace of Synthetics where King Coal, his queen, and their daughters — Orlon, Nylon, and Dacron — sit around a table, sipping tea. As the parents discuss the merits of Dreft and Tide with a warm-water sauce, iced cleaning fluid, and a bottle of carbon tetrachloride, the children squabble about who is the most mature, complaining that their parents treat them like children even though they've been around a long time. Sir William Wooley arrives like Prince Charming. However, he has a terrible problem — he shrinks when washed. It is proposed that he marry Orlon. Together, as Fabric and wife, the two produce Gabardine.[24]

The play was performed in the school auditorium, with Margaret as director. Already, at sixteen, she was writing satire. While other teens might be writing romantic love poems, she preferred to make fun of the "Populuxe" world that surrounded her.

Looking back on it, Margaret believes that deciding to be a writer took a particular toll on a young girl. First, it was always a gamble whether or not she would prove to be any good, and, second, at that time she fervently believed that she couldn't get married, have children, and be a writer too. She had seen *The Red Shoes*. This was a heavy acknowledgement for a sixteen-year-old.

> When I started to write poetry I had no audience, nor could I imagine one. . . . The year was 1956, the proper stance for girls was collecting china and waiting to get married, and although my immediate friends broke this mold — one wanted to be a doctor, one a psychiatrist, one an actress — none of them wanted to be poets. . . . I had some vague notion that I wanted to write, but no idea that I would ever be read by anyone. . . . It was awful starting out without qualifications. . . . But at the time I thought it was the answer to everything; I thought it was wonderful.[25]

When Margaret said that she felt the pressure to get married and it cost a great deal to resist it, she wasn't exaggerating. Growing up in the 1950s, one was subjected to the cult of marriage.

In a colourful book that encapsulates that decade, the historian Doug

Owram describes just how pervasive the obsession with marriage was. "By the mid-fifties, girls, starting at the age of fifteen, had begun to focus on the prospect of marriage and children." Sociologists, psychologists, and the lifestyle gurus of the fifties created a propaganda of marriage; in some American colleges after the war there were even "Departments of Marriage." Head "Marriage Instructor" at St. Stephen's College, Henry Bowman, produced manuals on marriage that became best-sellers in the United States and Canada. Books like *Successful Marriage: A Modern Guide to Love, Sex, and Family Life* appeared in 1955. (More than 1,000 such books were published in North America in the decade after the Second World War.)[26]

According to Henry Bowman, those who failed to marry were narcissists, predators, or simply immature. They were victims of parental fixations or of deep-seated inferiority complexes. Sexual roles suddenly became an obsession. Medical experts began to talk about the pathologies of bachelors and spinsters. "The unmarried were afflicted, like the victims of disease or mental illness."[27] Those who didn't get married risked sexual disorientation. They might become latent homosexuals. Anyone could tell that bachelors were fussy, and spinsters were masculine.

Experts were backed up by opportunistic advertisers. The consumption of household items, from stoves to mouthwash, was connected with romance, intimacy, and fulfilment of dreams. "An amazing number of products could, with a little imagination, be associated with a successful marriage. . . . 'She's engaged! She's Lovely! She Uses Ponds!' said one soap commercial. 'Another man just slipped through my fingers!'" was a nudge to buy mouthwash.[28]

It was, of course, the girl whose job it was to get married, who had to tie the noose around the wayward male, and advertising products were targeted at female consumers, and magazine fiction at female readers. A young girl was told she must marry between the ages of twenty and twenty-four, and have at least 2.4 children; but it was something she began to aim at from the age of fifteen. A popular book — *Win Your Man and Keep Him* — that appeared in 1948 offered consolation to those still unmarried by the age of twenty-three, desolate because Mr. Right had not yet surfaced. When Barbie, the symbolic queen of "Populuxe" for the preteen market, came along in 1959, with her perfect pink breasts and tiny waistline, she was certainly a bizarre toy for a pre-pubescent girl, but it was as if she summed up the decade.[29]

In Canada, the magazines of the day were *Ladies' Home Journal* and *Chatelaine*. *Ladies' Home Journal* specialized in gracious living — etiquette and table settings were important (when Margaret said her girlfriends were collecting china, she meant it). All married women in its pages were jubilantly happy, and marriage was the happy ending of almost every *Chatelaine* story.

Young women journalists at *Chatelaine*, such as Doris Anderson and June Callwood, were trying to break out. In the early fifties an obstetrician, Dr. Marion Hilliard, was persuaded to put her name to a series of articles on women's health ghost-written by Callwood: "Sex — a Woman's Greatest Hazard" and "Fatigue — a Woman's Greatest Enemy" duly appeared and the issues sold out, suggesting that women were not as monolithic in their thinking as the conspiracy of their contentment would suggest.[30] But conformity was the rule and the resisters kept silent. When Doris Anderson won a magazine prize in 1957, her boss, Floyd Chalmers, said: "What I like about Doris is that she looks like a woman, acts like a lady, and works like a dog."[31]

Anderson's portrait of a young girl's education is a little more realistic. According to her, the conventional advice that mothers like hers gave their daughters was to marry a man who would be a good steady provider, and not to expect too much. Any career they might undertake (teaching was the usual one) should be considered a stop-gap measure. Since only beauty could serve in the matrimonial sweepstakes, if you weren't a stunner it was best not to be too ambitious. Every relative felt free to comment on a young girl's appearance. "Better put a brick on her head," they would say; "she's growing too tall for the boys." Or "Don't encourage her to be too smart. You catch more flies with sugar than salt."[32]

In the high-school texts Margaret was reading, especially those in Mental Health and Hygiene, females were defined as the equals of, but not the same as, men. The stereotype that girls were weak and frail creatures was fading. The sixteen-year-old swimmer Marilyn Bell had swum Lake Ontario in October 1954, and become an instant celebrity. But jobs for women still had to instil the virtues of the future homemaker — you worked, and then got married and quit. The ethos declared that there could only be one job per family.

Margaret felt isolated in this world. Years later, obviously referring to herself, she remarked: "You didn't feel that there was anybody else who agreed with you. [You were] regarded as crazy, peculiar, eccentric, queer, and brainy." It would be almost fifteen years before feminism began to change things. "I'm very tough now," she added, "but I wasn't always then, and I would have appreciated some of that support, at that time." Margaret had not bought the cult of marriage. She believed that getting married would be a kind of death. But society didn't offer alternatives. "There was no women's lib telling you you could do both."[33]

Equally devastating in the fifties was the new cult of the female body that developed along with the fetishizing of marriage. It was in January 1954 that the first issue of *Playboy* surfaced on the newsstands, featuring the naked Marilyn Monroe. The magazine was meant as a handbook for the young single urban male and was a rebellion against the moral conservatism of the fifties. Boys bought it, but it wasn't much use to young girls. What most of them learned from its stereotypes was that they fell short of the perfect measurements: 36/24/36, grotesque by today's anorexic standards. Young girls secretly took out their tape measures. The ones with breasts learned how to clutch their school books to their chests, so that the bust could be pushed up to advantage. The ones without went on the sly to Kresge's to buy padded bras in the Ladies' Wear department. Though she would later be described as pre-Raphaelite, Margaret did not have the kind of beauty that would have worked in those days. She was the young girl about whom the neighbours would say: "If she would only do something about herself, she could be quite attractive." This hurt, of course. She was at the age when people's opinions mattered to her.[34]

In her quasi-autobiographical story "Hurricane Hazel," she describes how young girls looked at boys in those days. They were "alarming if vaguely exciting." There were the "drips" and "pills" and the others who were either "cute," or "a dream." The most popular girls wore fuzzy pink sweaters with little pom-poms hanging from the collar and were cheerleaders at the football games. They went out on dates. The best was with a boy who had one of those fish-finned cars, usually his father's, and they went to drive-in movies and necked in the back seat after popcorn. The girl was meant to stop the exploratory hand; it was her responsibility to keep the boy from going all the way, since boys had no control. There would be long, inarticulate telephone conversations of pauses and mono-syllables, with both sides embarrassed, and incapable of ending them. Eventually the girl got pinned, or wore the boy's identification bracelet, like an army dog tag.

Margaret's world was being shaped by the teen culture of the mid-fifties. That was the time when dark melancholy figures suddenly surfaced on the movie screens. *The Wild One* with Marlon Brando came out in 1954, and James Dean's *Rebel Without a Cause* in 1955. In 1956, Elvis Presley appeared on *The Ed Sullivan Show*. The amusing thing was that these films were really the product of the new obsession with psychology; they were about boys who felt powerless and purposeless in an adult-dominated world. Elvis offered no new space for girls in his retinue. Scandal hit when it was discovered that the fiancée of Jerry Lee Lewis, one of the rock 'n' roll kings, was his cousin, a girl of thirteen. But in the uniform culture of the fifties, rock 'n' roll felt like liberation. It took over the school dances, where being distinctive meant dressing like everybody else. Boys started wearing jeans and leather jackets, and sported a dangling cigarette, and girls wore saddle shoes and crinolines — they weren't yet allowed to wear jeans.

But the coded world of sex remained confusing since, despite those dramatic icons, ordinary teenagers still lived within the expectations of their safe fifties world. Margaret catches this perfectly in "Hurricane Hazel." As she remembers it, the boys were as confused and vulnerable as the girls. In fact, in her story, her fictional Buddy is more trapped than the narrator — trapped by the expectations of a mother whose narrowed life would embitter his own, by a paternalistic society that expects him to get a job and earn a living, and by the mysteries of sex, at which he is totally inept. He is hoping for a girl to take over his identity and protect it, along with his "identity bracelet," since he can't imagine how to define himself. Margaret will escape this world, mostly because she expected more from it, but the "Buddys" get stuck.

In her story, she makes dramatic use of a traumatic moment in Toronto's history to provide the emotional metaphor for the ending of the narrator's relationship with Buddy. It's an ingenious gesture.

In the early morning of Saturday, 16 October 1954, just before Margaret turned sixteen, the worst natural disaster in Toronto's history, Hurricane Hazel, hit the city. In the suburb of Etobicoke, sixteen brick

houses, sitting beside the floodplain of the Humber River, were swept away
by waves six metres high, killing thirty-six people. Across the Toronto
region, eighty-three people died.[35] Margaret described this October morning some thirty years later, mixing memory and invention:

> After we had listened to the news, cars overturned with
> their drivers in them, demolished houses, all that rampaging
> water and disaster and washed-away money, my brother and
> I put on our rubber boots and walked down the old pot-holed
> and now pitted and raddled Pottery Road to witness the
> destruction first-hand.
>
> There wasn't as much as we had hoped. Trees and
> branches were down, but not that many of them. The Don
> River was flooded and muddy, but it was hard to tell whether
> the parts of cars half sunk in it and the mangled truck tires,
> heaps of sticks, planks, and assorted debris washing along or
> strewn on land where the water had already begun to recede
> were new or just more of the junk we were used to seeing in
> it. The sky was still overcast; our boots squelched in the
> mud, out of which no hands were poking up. . . . two people
> had actually been drowned there during the night, but we
> did not learn that until later.[36]

The previous night, the narrator of the story had broken her date with
Buddy because of the raging storm. She reports: "He said if I wouldn't go
out with him during a hurricane, I didn't love him enough." The line brilliantly carries all the poignancy of the world of teenagers, and particularly
their intractable solipsism. The debris that surfaces the morning after the
hurricane is not just the result of a natural disaster, nor simply a symbol of
the break-up of the relationship. It represents Buddy himself, the look of
him: "the ordinary-looking wreckage, the flatness of the water, the melancholy light." Buddy, who worked in a garage, would marry a typist and fit
into the cult of marriage that the fifties dictated, not because he might
have wanted to, but because he had never been led to think there were
other options. There is great compassion for Buddy in this story.

But Margaret herself was learning a new law: not to get trapped. The thing not to do was to have an accident (a euphemism in those days for getting pregnant) in the back seat of one of those fish-finned cars. The nightmare had become ending up with a baby and a washing machine in the suburbs.

Margaret would go to university. It was already a tradition in her family that women received university educations. Her aunt had gotten a Master's in History at the University of Toronto when she was nineteen. When Grandfather Killam made it clear to Margaret's mother that he felt she was too frivolous to be sent to college, she earned the money to send herself. Using one's intelligence was a moral injunction. Margaret was expected to get a scholarship; her parents would have felt disappointed if she hadn't. While other daughters were urged to collect china, become cheerleaders, and prepare for marriage, Margaret was encouraged to be independent. Her parents weren't feminists. The term hadn't been invented. They simply believed it was incumbent on their daughter to become as educated as possible.

Margaret would say that, at Leaside High School, she learned two things which were not necessarily on the curriculum: flexibility and lateral thinking. You needed to know how to shift and change gears when you had to.[37] In *The Clan Call* of 1956–57, in the section devoted to photographs and bios of the graduating classes, Margaret appears, looking rather demure in her high-collared white blouse and short-cropped hair. Her fellow students write: "Peggy's not-so-secret ambition is to write THE Canadian novel — and with those English marks, who doubts that she will?"[38]

5

PEGGY NATURE

When Margaret entered the University of Toronto in the autumn of 1957, like all young students she would have walked innocently into its complicated power structure. At the time, in addition to its professional schools, it contained four liberal-arts colleges which were still divided by their religious affiliation or lack of same. There was St. Michael's College, or St. Mike's, which was Catholic and sat off in exile in a far corner of the campus. Students not registered at the college ventured there only for Classics, taught by an Irish priest who, as Margaret remembered him, always said "Hairy-stotle." Trinity was Anglican, the college of the Anglo-Canadian Establishment, and its students wore their academic gowns. University College had no religious affiliation and attracted students from different ethnic backgrounds and from the mobile working class. Victoria College was United Church, middle class, and polite.[1] It was founded as a Methodist institution, but, unlike Trinity or St. Mike's, it never required a faith test. (And, unlike some of the other colleges, it had never had a quota on the number of Jews admitted.)

Begun as Upper Canada Academy in 1836, Vic was housed in a Romanesque, domed monstrosity of faded two-tone stone across the road from Queen's Park and the Parliament Buildings. Above its door, carved in Gothic lettering, was the college's motto: "The Truth Shall Make You Free." For four years, Margaret passed through its portals, flanked on both sides by plaques erected in memory of the 154 students who had died in the two world wars.

Vic was reputed to have the most high-powered English Department on campus, its most famous luminary being the critic Northrop Frye. Margaret remarked: "I did know for a fact that Vic was supposed to have something called Northrop Frye and that if I knew what was good for me I should go there to absorb some of it."[2] She was as naïve as most young eighteen-year-olds starting out, and her plan might have been fuzzy, but her instincts were excellent. If one was to write, this was a place to start.

"Being in many ways from the sticks," as she characterized herself, "not only Leaside High but before that the real sticks (upright, known as 'trees')," she was thrown by her sudden exposure to campus life. "I was intimidated by almost everything at University. Red lipstick and pearl button earrings intimidated me; so did black turtleneck sweaters . . . I always suspected there was something, some secret, that other people knew and I didn't."[3]

By the late fifties, the Beat movement had filtered up from the United States and hit Canadian campuses, dividing the students like the proverbial Red Sea. On one side were the preppies, though the word hadn't yet been invented. These were mostly the high-school students from the middle-class district of Lawrence Park. The boys wore jackets and ties, and the girls wore lamb's-wool sweaters and red lipstick, with cultured-pearl earrings, high heels, and nylon stockings with seams. They could be found in the student common room playing bridge over coffee, or at the football games under bear rugs, waving the student colours and swigging from the silver flasks hidden under college sweaters. On the other side were the disaffected males and females in black turtlenecks who carried copies of Jean-Paul Sartre's *Nausea* and Samuel Beckett's *Waiting for Godot*. Instead of bridge, they played existential mind games.[4] Margaret put on the requisite black stockings, pulled her hair back in a bun, and gave up lipstick. As she put it: "Gloom set in."[5] She drank her coffee in the bowels of Wymilwood, the new students' union building. Nothing would have indicated to her that thirty years later the coffee shop would be named "The Cat's Eye" in her honour.

She continued to live at home, but she wasn't allowed much angst around the house. In her fictional account of student days, her character remarks: "I had to indulge it in the cellar, where my mother wouldn't come upon me brooding and suggest I go out for a walk to improve my circulation. This was her answer to any sign, however slight, of creeping despondency.

There wasn't a lot that a brisk sprint through dead leaves, howling winds, or sleet couldn't cure."[6] This was certainly Mrs. Atwood's ethic.

To someone of Margaret's potential, no other place on the University of Toronto campus could have been quite as congenial as Vic. The college was full of brilliant eccentrics. And it hired women professors. Even the free-thinking University College did not do that.

Victoria College had been admitting women students since 1884. In fact, Annesley Hall, an odd-looking, turreted structure on the edge of the Vic grounds, had been erected in 1903 as a residence for women. Its intention, as its dedicatory plaque announces, was to "provide for the daughters of Methodism a home of high tone in an atmosphere of refined social culture." It seemed natural that women could also teach at Vic.

Margaret would realize only in retrospect the value of walking into an English Department where she could find women who were considered capable of thinking, and who supported themselves. The right of women to work outside the home was still a controversy that raged in the Canadian press throughout the 1950s. Not before 1951 did a woman sit on a jury in Canada. In 1958, two seats in the House of Commons were occupied by women. It wasn't until the Liberal government of Lester Pearson set up the Royal Commission on the Status of Women in 1967 that the legal rights of women were even discussed. In the fifties, in most universities, women were still expected by their male professors to metamorphose back into housewives after they got their degrees.

But even Vic, which may have hired women, did not readily promote them. One of Margaret's teachers, Kathleen Coburn, would become a world authority on Samuel Coleridge, but it took years before she was promoted to full professor.[7] It was a different kind of Red Shoes moral: If you wanted to be a woman and a professor in those days, you might as well jump in front of a train. Luckily, Margaret already knew she didn't want to become "an expert on Coleridge."[8]

Still, Victoria College had a quality of tolerance and eccentricity that was nurturing. There was little of the intellectual one-upmanship that usually characterizes university life, and its English Department afforded a place to Canadian writers, a thing unheard of in those days. On entering the august foyer of the college, one encounters a huge portrait of E.J. Pratt, Canada's first epic poet, who had been a student at Vic and had taught there until his retirement in 1953. By the time Margaret arrived, Pratt could still be found at High Table in the dining room, where a chair was permanently leaned forward, waiting for him to occupy it. And stories attached to him. In the old days, it was said, when someone was being considered for a job at Vic, he would be invited to Dr. Pratt's for dinner. After retiring to the study for cigars, the young candidate would be asked to light the fire with a page from Dr. Pratt's doctoral thesis. If he baulked, he didn't get the job.[9] That was the side of Vic that was self-deprecating. Nobody was allowed to have pretensions. It was curiously comforting and quintessentially Canadian.

There were only seven freshmen, five girls and two boys, in the English Language and Literature program in 1957. Margaret had been afraid that concentrating on English courses might narrow her outlook, and so she took Philosophy. However, she took her English courses with the Vic group. (She would officially join them in her second year.)

They were an extraordinary bunch, though they didn't yet know it. Many would end up with distinguished careers in academia. Sandy Johnston, who would become a Medieval scholar, and eventually principal of Vic, described it as a wonderful, very protected hot-house environment, where a young woman could feel "empowered." "We all came from backgrounds where you were expected to succeed. We learned from each other. We bounced off each other. We were treated as if we had minds."[10]

She remembered Margaret's air of intense scholarship, and how she seemed to live in two worlds. Though she was living at home, Margaret never spoke of family. (Johnston was vaguely aware that Margaret's father was a scientist.) Those first years, it was as if she had split her life into two parts, as if she were living behind a barrier of her own making, which undoubtedly came from a sense of insecurity. Clearly, at this stage, camouflage was necessary if she was to protect herself as the poet she intended to become. Johnston also felt she might have been a bit embarrassed by her own middle-classness, since it didn't fit the current stereotype of the poet.

She was shy and her insecurities were familiar. Years later, Margaret and Sandy Johnston would joke about hair. Johnston had had long dark brown hair, which she wore in a French twist, and it was absolutely dead straight. Margaret explained how envious she had been of that hair as she tried to keep her own unruly curls under control by clipping them close to her head. In those days, Johnston found her remarkably generous and antic. Though occasionally she would crash at the residence to avoid the trek back to Leaside, mostly she could be found in the coffee shop, writing poems and doodling sketches in her notebook.

Dennis Lee, who would become a well-known poet, was one of the students in English Language and Literature. His reputation had preceded him to Vic. He was the kid from Etobicoke, one of the blander Toronto suburbs, who was rumoured to have gotten 99 per cent on his high-school leaving exams and won the Prince of Wales Scholarship. (He'd gone to the University of Toronto Schools, where the standards were so rigorous that, of five hundred elite applicants, only ninety were accepted.) Margaret remembered being awed. They first met at the freshman mixer. As they danced, "foxtrotting crabwise across the floor," their horn-rimmed glasses locking, he informed her that he intended to be a United Church minister. But she soon learned he had a shadowy second life; he had had an equally ardent desire to be a magician. As a sixteen-year-old, he had gone down to the CNE to watch magicians like the Great Manzini to learn their magic tricks. Dennis had his zany side, which would come out in the kids' books he later wrote that became mantras for children in Canada: "There are midgets at the bottom of my garden / Every night they come and play on violins. / One is named Molly, and one is named Dolly / And one has diarrhea and grins."[11]

For both of them, Vic that first year was an exciting intellectual challenge. It was the year Frye published *Anatomy of Criticism*, and seemed to become instantly world famous. And Jay Macpherson brought out her remarkable collection *The Boatman*. Students thought of her as a more amiable Emily Dickinson as she scuttled by, her waist-length hair trussed up in a bun. She was enormously good-hearted but skittishly shy. As don, she lived in the college dorm, and students in residence might find her delivering their term papers to their doors at midnight in her dressing gown.

Classes that first year were on a human scale, from two to fifteen students studying Anglo-Saxon, American Lit, and at least a dozen Shakespeare plays. They read everything in the course and rarely missed a class, because it was a challenge. There was a sense of young minds straining at the leash in those English classes. Dennis Lee remembers being aware of Margaret's mind; he recalls her as being intelligent, though not overpoweringly so, with a kind of determination whose source and scale he didn't completely understand. She had bite and a capacity to think for herself.[12] They soon found themselves working together on the student literary magazine *Acta Victoriana*, and in the drama club.

The social world that Margaret entered after classes was decidedly tame, in the fifties sense. She studied with other students in the Vic library, a stone room with stained-glass windows like a pseudo church, with sepia-toned portraits of eminent Victorians lining its walls. Green-glassed desk lamps lined up on the study tables like sentinels. She was frequently asked out for beer by the male students, but she suspected they only wanted her as a passport into the King Cole Room, the beer parlour beneath the Park Plaza Hotel on Bloor Street where the students went to drink. Dennis, too, remembers that place. The "Men Only" side, where women were not allowed to enter, was dismal and smelly, but, under Ontario's baroque ordinances, men needed a female to get into the more congenial "Ladies and Escorts" side. There they would go to play chess and drink ten-cent draft beer, shaking a little salt on it to cut the foam.[13]

Like most students, Margaret needed summer jobs to support herself at school. She had already worked at summer camps, first as a counsellor at a camp for physically challenged children, and then, in 1958, as a wait-ress at Camp Hurontario on Georgian Bay. (John Sewell, a future mayor of Toronto, remembers how he and Margaret wrote lyrics for the camp revue.)[14] These experiences would later provide background details for stories in her book *Wilderness Tips*, stories about waitresses, pulp magazines, sex and betrayal, or the drowning of a child in the lake.

At the end of her sophomore year, she found a job through her next-door neighbour, Dr. Kronick, a dentist whose daughter was a close friend. Dr. Kronick's brother, Joe, ran a summer camp for Jewish children called White Pine in the Haliburton region, northeast of Toronto. Its slogan was: "Camp White Pine where the sun always shines in beautiful Haliburton." There were at least six hundred people at the camp, including staff, and forty-two sleeping cabins for the campers. Margaret was hired to set up the nature program.

White Pine was a Reform Jewish co-educational summer camp more interested in fostering social awareness in its campers than in swimming marathons, hiking, or canoeing. In this, it was very much a product of the fifties. The fear that the Second World War and its immediate aftermath had brought to the Toronto Jewish community was gradually tempered by the enormous economic prosperity of the decade. Many who had grown up in the sweat-shop factories of the garment district of Spadina in the downtown core were able to make the flight north to the affluent Jewish district above Eglinton Avenue. The mood was assimilationist, and Jewish people were merging into the general social culture in ways that hadn't been possible before.

A lot of the kids at White Pine came from the Reform synagogue, Holy Blossom Temple, on Bathurst Street, south of Eglinton. Among them was Charlie Pachter, who would become one of Canada's most prominent visual artists. But he was a fifteen-year-old kid, going on sixteen, when he was hired as an assistant to the camp's arts and crafts director. And there he met Peggy Atwood.

At camp, Margaret was called "Peggy Nature." She worked out of "The Nature Hut," a dank little shack, on the edge of a muddy, mosquito-filled bog, that had once served as a tool shed. Charlie remembers their first encounter: "She was dressed in rubber boots and a little cocky outfit with her hair covered with a *shmata*. She was sitting there with a circle of kids at her feet, trying to get them to touch the toad she held in her hand. The lesson was: touching a toad doesn't give you warts. The kids were all going 'Ew, ew, I don't wanna,' and she called me over. 'Here, you do it,' she said." He reluctantly obliged. "There was something so quirky about her then," he remembers. "All the other girls at camp were trying to imitate Annette Funicello from the Mouseketeers, or Natalie Wood from *Marjorie Morningstar*, and here was Peggy with this beautiful skin and those clear blue eyes. She was like Jane Goodall."

He discovered she had an incredible capacity to answer any question he needed answered, "like what happens to the string on the tent pole when it goes in and how do you fish it out," and Margaret would very quietly explain how everything was done. They'd sit on the dock, slapping mosquitoes, and he'd talk about his frustration with his high-school art teacher who'd given him a D– and she'd say: "You'll be painting God's murals in the sky and the teacher will be roasting in hell." She offered him wonderful adolescent fantasies of revenge.

It felt like instant osmosis, she was so supportive, almost as though she were a muse. He found just being around her triggered ideas. And he made her laugh. "She was like a schoolgirl with me, with those lethal peals of laughter. She would scold me if I was going over the edge: 'You don't do that,' and of course I would go out of my way to do *that* all the time. We were a bit like Groucho Marx and Margaret Dumont. Something symbiotic."[15]

Years later he would do a serigraph image of her as Peggy Nature, sprouting capillaried pink wings and insect-eyed sunglasses, holding out a caterpillar with a seductive and slightly sinister smile.

Margaret herself describes her role at White Pine as "nature counsellor." She spent a lot of time with snakes, snails, lizards, frogs, and worms. The kids would catch them and come to her and say: "Look what I caught" and "there it would be all over their hands." She spent her time "rescuing creatures from kids who clutched them too tightly." To keep the kids interested, she ran "What is it?" contests. The prize was a cake decorated with frogs, spiders, newts, and so forth, which she made with the assistance of the pastry chef in the camp kitchen.[16]

But the camp itself was like a cultural microcosm. There were several generations of Jews at White Pine: the adults who ran the camp and who were heirs to populist Depression politics; the counsellors; and then the kids themselves, mostly from quite rich areas of Toronto. The older people taught the kids to sing songs from the Spanish Civil War, which, of course, they had no way of understanding. Margaret herself didn't know the tradition behind them and thought they were just songs, but their impact filtered into her mind, layering her political sensibility. The memory would be there when the anger that drives her fiction and poetry surfaced: who gets hurt, who gets abused?

At the camp many of the programs were quasi-political. Joe (Jo-Jo) Kronick organized lectures once a week as part of his Institute for Living. Speakers were imported from the city to talk about everything from the philosophy of non-violence to existentialist theology. Jo-Jo had a lot of what his young staff called "sociological sound bytes" to describe the camp: it was supposed to be, as its letterhead attested, "a unique experience in small group living." The themes of its five-day special programs were likely to be earnest variations on the Brotherhood of Man.

For Charlie, the memories of White Pine are mainly comic anecdotes. As he tells it, Joe had decided that the young boys should have female counsellors because it was too soon to take them away from Mom. Grouped by cabins, they were called the Kiwis, Koalas, and Dolphins and so on. Margaret was put in charge of the seven- and eight-year-olds. She came home one night to find a turd in the middle of the cabin floor. She suspected whose it was but couldn't prove it. This was a job for the section head, so she cleaned up the turd and told him what had happened. "Let me handle it, Peggy," he said. He went into the cabin and lined up the little boys. He addressed them: "Men, you all know what I'm talking about. It's very important in life to achieve respect. I'm going to go around and ask each one of you quietly who did this and I'm going to respect the person who tells me he did it. And I want that person to 'fess up." Margaret had retreated to the porch, and when he emerged she asked: "So, was it Edward?" Her fellow counsellor looked at her, sheep-faced: "They all said they did it. They all wanted respect."

White Pine seems to have been a kind of Mel Brooks camp, with bright young counsellors delighting in mockery, skits, and outrageous jokes. "We would do these diabolical things," says Charlie.

Each year the counsellors organized a camp-wide program during which the usual routine would stop for three days and the camp would go slightly crazy. The program had to start with some exciting, dramatic event. One year they decided this would be an alien invasion. One of the counsellors, Phil, a big jock from Michigan whom everybody loved, went to the Fire Department in Haliburton and managed to rent asbestos suits. When they told Joe Kronick what they were up to, he was worried that they might frighten the kids. He insisted that, if they were going to tell them their parents had been murdered by aliens, they had better make sure the kids felt safe.

Sirens went off in the middle of the night, and the campers were hauled out of their beds in bathrobes and slippers and brought to the main field. Counsellors ran around announcing: "The Martians have landed." From a big bonfire they had built and doused with kerosene, two men emerged, wearing the asbestos suits: "We're from Planet So-and-So," they said. "We've decided that the Earth is behaving badly and we give you seven days to make peace." A voice over the loudspeaker announced that Toronto had been captured and they'd been in touch with the Haliburton police, but not to worry. If they learned to live in peace and harmony for the next few days, everything would be okay. Some of the smaller children started to cry, but then one of the kids, Charlie Harnick (who would later become Attorney General of Ontario), shouted: "It's only Phil."[17]

Beneath the antics and the earnestness was a hidden side to the camp that Margaret recognized. There was a man who peeled potatoes for the kitchen. He did nothing but peel potatoes. And he had a number on his arm. Everyone knew he was there, but nobody talked about him. He was the "forbidden man." The war and concentration camps were still too close in time to be spoken of. The emotions that circled around the man were complex: awe, reverence, and even fear — the fear that a person who had survived such horror might really be mad.

Margaret was also aware of the anti-Semitic prejudice in Ontario. Charlie tells the story of the guy who came up to White Pine to test kids for their Red Cross swimming badges. "He was a raving WASP elitist." As Margaret lined up the youngsters, he remarked: "You can always tell who's Jewish." And she said: "Oh really? They're the ones who get nervous before the test? The ones who try to find excuses so they don't have to take it?" And he replied: "I can always pick them out." "Just by looking at people you can tell whether they're Jewish or not?" she asked. She lined a whole group of kids up on the dock: red-haired, freckled jocks, fat and thin, every variation. And said: "So how do you do it?" When he picked several, she said: "No. You're wrong. They're all Jewish." Her refusal to let such prejudice pass was, according to Charlie, "part of her girl-scout persona," and he admired it.

The friendship between Charlie and Margaret continued when they returned to Toronto. He was delightfully arch and funny, but she, three years older, had also identified him as a boy on the verge of recognizing his vocation as an artist, and she obviously delighted in the metamorphosis. Charlie had discovered a hole in his closet that led to the attic where he made his hideaway. He had to climb through his mother's clothes to get to it (she hung all her clothes in his closet). He was a pack-rat and had draped his "pad" with silks and would bring friends up there and light candles. One of the first things he painted on his wall was the landscape from a two-dollar bill, much to the bewilderment of his mother.

There was nothing self-conscious about their friendship, but underneath there was a mutual recognition of what it meant to want to be an artist in Canada, where painting or any artistic pursuit, particularly in a middle-class household like Charlie's, was not considered a suitable occupation for anyone, and certainly not for a male. If art was done at all, it was done elsewhere by dead Europeans. One needed defensive armour. Margaret delighted in Charlie's instinct to enter and possess forbidden territory. He shared her mind. She would later write:

> This is the environment in which Pachter grew up, then; a Canada noted for its niceness, a bland surface which concealed a wildness, a Gothic weirdness, even a menace. Any Canadian looking at Pachter's seemingly pastoral sunbathers on a beach, their backs turned to the viewer, their eyes fixed on an endless blue expanse of water, knows that under the surface of the lake there's someone drowning; as indeed there is, every summer.[18]

But they also made hilarious buddies. Charlie soon graduated to being in charge of the art program at Camp White Pine. He used to organize slide shows of the paintings of the Group of Seven, and the weirdness of placing those celluloid images of trees and skies against the backdrop of the real thing delighted him. He was also given his own drama hut, called "Pachter's Equity," and was expected to organize skits like "Counsellor on a Hot Tin Roof."

During the year, he and Margaret would go to the Hadassah-WIZO Bazaar in search of costumes for his shows and would buy up all the tulle gowns and ratty stoles for five cents. Margaret, too, loved dress-up and would laugh gleefully as she tried on the outfits and hats and wigs. They'd cart them back to Margaret's house in Leaside, where her aunts from Nova Scotia might be having tea with her mother. "In would come this madman," as Charlie puts it, "shouting: 'Can you believe this dress for five cents?'" Margaret said that her aunts had never forgotten that. They always commented: "What an unusual young man!"

Charlie loved going to Margaret's house because, in his version of his own family, there was so much chaos. (He immediately launches into a parody of his mother browbeating the kids.) "'I just bought those doughnuts and you're eating them. Leave them alone. They're fresh.' And I'd

say: 'What are we supposed to do, wait for them to go stale and eat them?'
I'd go over to Peggy's and everything was please and thank-you and milk
and cookies, and there was rhythm. People spoke only when they were
spoken to." To Charlie it seemed sheer magic. He'd never seen anything
like it. In his house you couldn't get a word in edgewise because "everyone was clamouring for attention, desperate not to be put down."

Margaret's father was an endless source of information. "Whatever you
mentioned," Charlie recalls, "he had piles to tell you about it, whether it
was the sewage system in Rangoon or the War of 1812. He was very gentle
and pleasant about it, and it was always lovely listening to him. He was
like a sage." Charlie thought of him as a happy pessimist, if such a thing
is possible. "He knew humans had screwed up, yet he had built his cabins
and cultivated his wonderful gardens out of little brown patches of earth."
Although he was a professor, he was never pompous or academic. To Charlie he was almost out of *Hee Haw*: you expected him to be wearing
suspenders and smoking a corn-cob pipe. But he was very, very erudite.
The image Charlie held in his mind of him and Mrs. Atwood was of adults
doing Scottish country dancing. They had a very lively interest in others
and there was not a whit of racism about them. "If you were Jewish," Charlie remarks, "it didn't mean a thing."

Occasionally Charlie tried to shock Margaret, but it didn't work. She
was unflappable. Once he took her to visit a call girl he knew. His mother
used to rent a room in their house to a woman from Oshawa named Stella.
"Stella," Charlie recalls, "was Ukrainian and gorgeous. She looked like
Snow White." When he was ten or eleven, he used to watch her painting
her lips red with a lip brush, and he remembered the time she was ironing
her bra with the point of the iron and he'd gotten a little frisky and she
smacked him with a towel. After she moved out, Stella had changed her
name to Stacey and become a call girl, living in a coach house on Prince
Arthur Avenue, next to what would become the Innuit Gallery. Margaret
didn't believe Charlie knew a real call girl with red lips, and so he took
her for a visit. Mischievously, he introduced her as "M.E.," the initials she
was using beneath the poems she had begun to send out for publication,
and Stacey replied: "Oh. Amy. Nice to meet you, Amy."

Charlie and Margaret became lifelong friends and occasional collabora-
tors. What impressed him most was that, from the beginning, she had such

a tremendous sense of self-worth. He felt he and others had to deal constantly with self-doubt, but she always had a very healthy sense of herself. "Perhaps that was her father's influence," he remarks. "I had ultimate trust in her. It was really and truly a joy watching her grow as an artist."

By her second year, Margaret had found her way into many of the college's social activities, including singing and acting in student revues. At Vic there was a tradition called "The Bob Revue." Bob (Robert) Beare was hired as a janitor at Vic in the nineteenth century and served the college for nearly forty years; the face of the clock in Vic library has a Latin inscription dedicated to him. In his honour, the first Bob party was held in 1874. It developed into "the Bob," a variety show satirizing freshmen and faculty alike. Being targeted was called "getting Bobbed."

In 1957, Donald Sutherland, the future actor, was in the revue. In 1958, the show was called *Guys$ and Dollars$*, and Margaret played Gertrude Wimple, a starry-eyed young freshman wandering around and blundering into the various campus activities. Margaret and Dennis Lee were credited on the programme for their "blood, sweat, and tears" during the revision of the script, though Dennis remembered he felt intimidated by the original writer and shrank from advising her that the script was execrable. The next year the Bob produced *The Big F*, with a skit by "Peggy Atwood" called "Portrait of the Poet as a Young Goat." She also did the graphics for the programme cover.

By her third year, Margaret had become visible on campus, not only because she had been publishing her stories and poems in the college magazines, *Acta Victoriana* and *The Strand*, but also because she had started her own silk-screen business. Suddenly her very startling posters for college plays and theatre programmes began to appear. She also played in drama-club productions. Jay Macpherson remembered her in Ben Jonson's *Silent Woman*. She had a small part, but her sense of comic timing was memorable.

The University of Toronto was populated by brilliant eccentrics in those days. There was Frye himself, and Marshall McLuhan at St. Michael's College, and, along with Donald Sutherland, among the students, was Teresa Stratas (then Anastasia Stratakis). Born, as she used to say, in 1938 on her parents' dining-room table in an apartment above a Chinese laundry at the corner of George and Dundas streets, she had made her informal debut at four, singing "Pistol-Packin' Mama" on the counter of her father's restaurant. In 1958–59, when Margaret was in second year, she was completing a degree in the Faculty of Music.

At Vic, Northrop Frye was the *éminence grise*, and most fled at his approach. A rotund man in a grey suit, he had the look of the lay United Church preacher he moonlighted as on weekends. He was shy, and notoriously uncomfortable with small talk; a ride on the elevator with Dr. Frye could be excruciating. He rarely fraternized with students. But, in his classes, the remarkable generosity of the man became evident. Behind his back, students called him "Norrie." In her third year, Margaret took his Milton course and remembered his impact long after:

> Frye taught Milton. "Taught" isn't exactly the word. Frye
> said, "Let there be Milton, and lo, there was. It was done like
> this. He stood at the front of the room. He took one step
> forward, put his left hand on the table, took another step
> forward, put his right hand on the table, took a step back,
> removed his left hand, another step back, removed his right
> hand, and repeated the pattern. While he was doing this,
> pure prose, in real sentences and paragraphs, issued from his
> mouth. He didn't say "um," as most of us did, or leave
> sentences unfinished, or correct himself. I had never heard
> anyone do this before. It was like seeing a magician produc
> ing birds from a hat. You kept wanting to go around behind
> Frye or look under the table to see how he did it. . . .
>
> It was hard, though, to be completely intimidated by
> anyone as easily embarrassed as Frye. . . . Frye, when he'd had
> the bad luck to come face to face with one of his students
> outside the lecture hall, would lapse from perfectly-punctu-
> ated prose into a kind of reassuring and inarticulate mumble.
> "They're just as frightened of you as you are of them," my
> parents used to say of things like bumblebees. The same
> could be said of Frye.[19]

Frye was unconventional and gargantuan in his range. With his dead-pan delivery and a certain impishness, he could travel from the Bible to Blake, making tangential references to comic strips and pop songs. He had read everything, including *Acta Victoriana*, some reference to which he might slip in as an aside in his lectures.

Margaret made the astonishing discovery that Frye took Canadian literature and young writers seriously. For years Frye would write "Letters in Canada" for *The University of Toronto Quarterly*, and review Canadian poetry in *The Canadian Forum*. Though someone of his calibre was expected to leave a provincial city like Toronto, he stayed at Vic because it was congenial. Also, he believed that it was best for an educator to be rooted in his own community, a decision Margaret would come to feel applied to the artist as well, for she would never permanently leave her native city.

Frye's mind, like Margaret's, was also magpieish; it must have been thrilling to realize her professor had a mind in some ways like her own. She, too, had read all of *Grimm's Fairy Tales*, knew the cultural icons from Wonder Woman to Batman, and could recognize the biblical quotations. She also delighted that he was a Maritimer from New Brunswick. She knew that "deadpan delivery," that ironic, monotone voice concealing impish and sometimes deadly jokes, that discomfort in social rituals: they were her own family tradition as well.[20]

Frye did not separate high and low literature or succumb to the ivory-tower syndrome. He insisted that the way human beings understand themselves is through their stories. And all plots resemble other plots, whether they come from *King Lear* or soap operas. These are the raw material out of which we construct our cultural mythologies. Margaret instinctively understood that we are myth-driven, an understanding that would shape the way she would later write her books.

Margaret held to one of Frye's comments in particular. In speaking of Emily Dickinson, he dismissed the common orthodoxy that she was neurotic and hid herself away in a New England garret. "Maybe we should be looking at it the other way round," he advised. "These were the conditions that enabled her to write poetry. It was the only way she could create the conditions to write." That made perfect sense to Margaret. "Instead of assuming there was something wrong with you that caused you to write, he assumed that writing was a good thing in itself, and if you had to rearrange your life in order to make it possible, that's what you would do." When she published in *Acta Victoriana*, it was exciting to realize that the great Frye was reading her; he made it clear that all writing was valuable.

As she remarked: "In a provincial society where writing was either immoral or frivolous, [Frye's affirmation] was protection indeed."[21]

Still, having artistic pretensions was an act of defiance even at Vic. Among the students, few had the temerity to claim the ambition to write. Those who did quickly found themselves allies. Soon, Margaret was involved in it all. "I impressed the hell out of myself when I got a story published in *Acta*. . . . [it was] as I recall, a story of medium awfulness." "It's hard to recall any piece of publication which [gave] me greater satisfaction."[22] Unlike her scripts for "the Bob" and her stories, she published her serious stuff, the poems and reviews, under the name M.E. Atwood.

There was a simple reason for this. The bland initials, a vogue in the days of T.S. Eliot and W.B. Yeats, were also a way to disguise one's sex. And she still needed two versions of herself — the serious one under which to hide Peggy Nature.

It was complicated working out one's version of oneself if one was a young woman wanting to write. When she had walked across that high-school football field and had been hit on the head by her first poem, writing had seemed a divine gift, something given. She was a purist. Art was personal; it would be pursued privately, and recognition meant immortality, which came after one was dead. In 1958, one didn't think one could become known as a writer. "I'd thought that my future would be to be published in little magazines. . . . If I was very lucky I might be able to publish a book. I didn't have in view ever being able to support myself as a writer, and that was probably good for me. In other words my goals were idealistic and writing-centered. I wanted to be a great writer" was how she put it.[23]

She was reading nineteenth-century literature and so it had never occurred to her that a woman couldn't write; George Eliot, the Brontës, and Jane Austen were at the centre of the tradition. At that point it seemed only that Canadians couldn't write poems and novels, since she had encountered so few of them. That seemed much easier to overcome.

She would say about those early university days when she published her first poems:

> I was not conscious of my woman's audience but I realize
> now that my writing and my gender met at two points. I

published with initials, because I feared rejection as a lady writer, which everyone knew was about as bad as a lady painter; and I was convinced I would never get married. The biographies of women authors were very clear: you could write and be classified as neurotic or you could get married and be fulfilled. Being fulfilled sounded very dull.[24]

It was complicated. The put-downs for one's sex were subtle. "Women's weeds" was a phrase that had annoyed her from her high-school Shakespeare. "It suggested vacant lots, rank with random and negligible but persistent flowers."[25] Presumably, one's own experience was just too trivial to be included in the canon of art. She didn't want the label "lady writer," and yet, as a woman, how could she keep women's weeds out of her writing?

Margaret's response to this pressure was fascinating. She was too deeply directed by her desire to write to feel ground down by this. She might have felt annoyed sometimes, but not seriously inconvenienced. But it did mean that she developed a sharp tongue as a defensive strategy. Decades later she would look back at her own younger self: "I was very intolerant as a youthful person. It's almost necessary, that intolerance; young people need it in order to establish credentials for themselves."[26]

But more complex was the question of how to be a writer at all, since the model for the poet was still romantic, and romantic geniuses died before they were thirty. She had caught the romantic disease from John Keats and Emily Brontë. She wasn't sure she would go mad, but she was sure she would be dead by thirty. She could laugh about it later:

> I used to think it was a disadvantage to have such nice parents, because here there are all these books about people's dreadful childhoods, so I would have to use other people's dreadful childhoods. . . . For men there was the tubercular-genius idea and for women there was the idea that they were somehow damaged or warped or suicidal and if they weren't that, then they weren't real writers. It was almost, die and prove yourself.[27]

More immediately pressing was the need to determine why there were no writers in Canada. When Margaret began her investigations, reading A.J.M. Smith's *The Book of Canadian Poetry*, it turned out there were Canadian writers, they had been there all along, but the colonial culture of Canada remained indifferent to their presence. Even at Vic, in the Twentieth-Century Fiction and Poetry course, it seemed a risky concession when even one novel or one book of poems by a Canadian was squeezed onto the reading list. Like many other young Canadian writers, Margaret would spend years trying to fathom Canada's indifference, if not contempt, for its own cultural productions.

At the time, it was important that she could meet practising writers who had actually published books.

Jay Macpherson was an influence by the mere fact that she was there. They became friends: "I don't remember whether Peggy was called 'the Beetle,' or if I just thought of her as a beetlish character," Jay remarks. "She wore a brown winter coat which she rarely took off. It was a kind of disguise. And she had a stooping walk, like a scuttle, designed to be inconspicuous, which of course made her conspicuous." Even then Jay thought Margaret had "the Sibylline touch. She had such healthy instincts." "Those last two years of university," she felt, "were extraordinarily creative for her. She was on a writing streak. Sparks were coming off her."[28]

The poet James Reaney also became a friend. He was considerably older than Margaret and had already been teaching at the University of Manitoba when he came to Toronto in 1956 to do a doctorate under Northrop Frye. Reaney was an original. A small, energetic man from southwestern Ontario, he had somehow managed to retain the playfulness and genius of a child savant. Everything was possible in Reaney's ebullient world. As a teaching assistant, he liked to give seminars on teaching poetry. "There is an iconography of the imagination," he would say. "Dreams and myths are the most peculiar shortcuts to reality." He would retell the myth of the Robber Bride and ask: "Who is the Robber Bride in your life?"[29]

Reaney remembers Margaret as very shy and very bright. When she showed him poems, he was intrigued. He could feel the beat and rhythm of the poems, but there was always something going on underneath. "Those poems had roots," he says. It was already clear to him that poetry needed something new. "The male figure on the scene, the poets propelled by the *Esquire* image of the male, was exhausted." He expected those new things from Margaret.[30]

Margaret was determined to be a writer and, with the resilience she had learned from her family, she just did it. As early as March 1958, in the spring of her freshman year, she had submitted a story to the student magazine *Acta Victoriana* and it was published. *Acta* was a sophisticated, well-produced little magazine, with articles and creative work by professors and students. It surfaced two or three times a year from a tiny office in the basement of Emmanuel College.

Margaret titled that first story "The Glass Slippers." Two pages long, it is an amusing little vignette in which a young woman stands at a bus stop in a pair of glittering high heels, while two stern matrons watch her disapprovingly. "She sauntered slowly back and forth, turning her glittering arched feet ever so slightly, eclipsing the two bulky sober matrons sagging on the bench, rendering them drab and dull. They were solid society and she wore their disapproval like a crown."[31] The invective is amusing in a young female undergraduate: there was an enemy, "solid" middle-class propriety, and weapons, high-heeled shoes, to shock them. And she already had the writer's instinct to get the most out of imagistic details.

The power that was still latent in the young writer can be seen in a single line in the next story she published, in December 1958. "The Pilgrimage" is about a young girl who returns to visit the primary school teacher whose indifference she felt had sabotaged her confidence as a child and destroyed her life. The old teacher exudes an aura of lavender perfume: "Her elegant, surprisingly young hands might have lain for years neatly folded in the cool bottom of a cedar drawer."[32]

In a third story, published in February 1959, a young girl on a bus meets a neighbour whose daughter has had a shotgun wedding: "Your smile reminds me vaguely of a halitosis ad, she thought, or one of those little back-pages-of-the-newspaper ones about false teeth."[33]

By the fall of 1958, Dennis Lee had become one of the managing editors of *Acta* (that year they would produce four issues) and Peggy Atwood is listed on the masthead of the November issue, under "Drawings." She had done the cover design. It is an evocative graphic of Vic, looking rather sinister and Gothic in black silhouette with a ghost-white outline of a tree, the base of which turns into the path leading to the college steps. The Vic trustees would not have been flattered.

According to Dennis, until they worked together at *Acta*, he and Margaret had been skirting each other very carefully, each intimidated by the other. "Peggy spent a lot of time walking around without several layers of skin, with a terrible sense of exposure. I think we both enjoyed the discovery that we could work together — both of us being reasonably tied up in ourselves, inhibited, really mixed up about our futures and all those tensed-up and fraught questions: 'Can you be what you want to be?' Neither of us had a whole lot of social savvy. And we discovered we could both plug into something goofy and infantile and silly."

She was the other half of "Shakesbeat Latweed," a pseudonym that combined their surnames, under which they wrote satirical pieces. She called it a "demented literary joke that grew out of a sophomoric sense of humour." Margaret loved mischief-making and the tongue-in-cheek. Their first effort would explore the fashions in modern poetry, including the Cola school and other facetious trends.

By her third year, with her usual pragmatism, Margaret started to send out work. She had discovered that there was an audience for poetry. It was small, but it bought and devoured the same "little" magazines she did. There were only eight that accepted poetry and had any kind of national distribution: *Fiddlehead*; *The Canadian Forum*, edited by Milton Wilson; *Tamarack Review*; Louis Dudek's *Delta*; *Queen's Quarterly*; *Prism*; George Woodcock's *Canadian Literature*; and James Reaney's newly founded *Alphabet*.

In November, Milton Wilson, at *The Canadian Forum*, accepted her poem "Small Requiem," telling her: "We thought it had a rather grim charm."[34] They had already published "Fruition" in September. It was her first professional publication.

The latent power was there. In drafts written on the back of her father's biology assignments, where he might be asking his students to examine the head of a horsefly, are the beginnings of Margaret's authentic voice. There were lines in individual poems: "Soon the hysteria will be in bloom." Or the poem titled "A Detective Story":

> My love, inside
> Your skull are many

Secret predators
(And I among them)[35]

The kid who read the *Grimm's Fairy Tales*, who kept a praying mantis
as a pet, began to appear. It would be the Atwood vision. Under the still
surface of the water a body was drowning. She had made the discovery that
ordinary lives are, as Alice Munro once so wonderfully put it, "deep caves
lined with linoleum." She was going to look in the deep caves.

After the first two columns with Dennis, she wrote Shakesbeat
Latweed on her own and, in a little piece titled "The Expressive Act," took
on clichés about writing. The academics said poetry was allusive. She
wrote a poem composed of footnotes. The romantics said: "Write from
Life." She took the advice of "the Prophet from Montreal" (presumably
an allusion to Irving Layton) and went to a coffee shop with a pencil and
a scrap of envelope and wrote what she saw. She learned that "the Artist
was concerned neither with Literature nor with Life; he was concerned
only with himself." "My self was about to express itself." She burnt the
poem.[36] Margaret seemed to delight in challenging. She even wrote a literary parody of Northrop Frye in which she applied his archetypal theory of
literary criticism to the current Ajax commercial. "I did not fear retalia-
tion," she recalled. "I expected Frye to find it almost as funny as I did."[37]

As Women's Don at Vic, Jay Macpherson lived in the residence, but
in the summer of 1960 she bought a tiny house four blocks from campus.
Even though it would be a year before she would be able to occupy it, she
was too poor to forgo such a bargain. Aware that Margaret was finding
home a little small for someone of her age, and that, with all the night life
on campus, she was tired of hiking up to Leaside, Jay suggested that
Margaret caretake her house.

The house was practically empty. Jay bought a few sticks of furniture
from the Salvation Army, but when Margaret moved in in the spring of
her final year, she was virtually camping out. She stayed after graduation,
and, through that summer, Jay came to fix up the house. She remembered
them scraping off the horrible wallpaper of wild horses that seemed to fill
the kitchen (together they called it "the vanishing prairie").

Sitting at the kitchen table over endless cups of coffee, they would talk
books. Jay stored some of her books in the house, and of course Margaret had

permission to read them. Jay remarks: "I think she chose the Jung part of the shelf and Graves's *White Goddess*, and all the modern Canadian poetry."

There was a wonderful creative symbiosis between them. Jay became one of Margaret's early readers, seeing drafts of a novel she had started titled *Up in the Air So Blue* and reading the manuscript of *Double Persephone*. Jay delighted in the poems' Gothicism: "When you're young," she remarks, "you want to do something that gives you power."

In fact they shared an instinct for the Gothic. Margaret introduced Jay to Béla Bartók's *Duke Bluebeard's Castle*, and also gave her a watercolour she had done called *The Robber Bridegroom*. Jay understood the power of the Gothic for Margaret. It provided machinery to get at disturbing reality. For Jay, the essential archetype of the Gothic is the story of Cain and Abel, of the man who kills his brother and is eternally exiled. That fratricide is reflected in the human psyche: the divided halves of the self are locked in eternal struggle. The Gothic has a sense of soul fragmentation, of parts of the self that need to be reclaimed. "The dark shadows come back in under the skin and tend to be more vengeful for being exiled and denied" is how she puts it. "I think of Blake: 'My spectre round me night and day.'" Margaret's direction as a writer would always be towards those sinister shadows, towards what is under the skin, under the page.

Dennis Lee would say that, for himself and Margaret, this last year at university had been a time of wrestling with doubts and confusions, of determining what could stop them. They didn't want to waste their talent. Sometimes they would lament they had chosen the more staid Vic college, instead of University College, where the really radical stuff was happening. They had no idea — of course one never does when one is in the thick of it — that people would look back at the late fifties at Vic as a golden time.

6

THE SIBYLLINE TOUCH

By 1960, the city Margaret had grown up in was beginning to change. Toronto had always been called "Hog Town"— ostensibly because of the slaughterhouses that filled its west end, but in fact because it was a rather small-minded, puritanical little city of just over 700,000 inhabitants, still frozen in the permafrost of colonialism. "A sanctimonious icebox" was how the British artist Wyndham Lewis, who had lived there in the 1940s, put it. According to the journalist Robert Fulford, it was a private city devoted to order and cleanliness, a city of silence. Sidewalk cafés were illegal and there were few public festivals. Municipal laws prohibited its citizens from drinking beer in their own back yards. As Fulford remarked, many mistook Toronto's reticence for virtue, but it worked for those in power.[1]

There was only one place in Canada where things happened, and that was Montreal. Torontonians had a massive inferiority complex in relation to that city; they believed culture was possible only in Quebec. It was certainly not possible in Hog Town.

In the decades leading up to the sixties, Montreal was "a jaunty, rakish church-and-nightclub town," as William Weintraub described it in his enthusiastic eulogy, City Unique.[2] It was there that the stripper Lili St. Cyr made her reputation in the forties at the Gayety Theatre with her props of a Chinese temple, incense, and a Buddha, and the large key with which she removed her chastity belt. Her "Suicide" piece always reached its climax when, at the end of her pantomime of unrequited love, she would threaten to jump naked from a windowsill prop, bringing the devastated crowd to its feet, shouting: "Lili! Don't jump!" She was a good tourist draw.

Montreal had its puritanical prelates, like Cardinal Léger, who complained that the city had more nightclubs than churches, and its notorious mobsters, like Frank Petrula, friend of Lucky Luciano, who ran the heroin trade; it had vice probes and crime-busting lawyers, and goon squads smashing windows on election night.

And it was only in French Montreal that English poets could become famous. Frank Scott, a law professor at McGill University and a well-known poet, became a public hero when, in 1957, he challenged the government of Premier Maurice Duplessis in the Supreme Court over the notorious Quebec Padlock Law — and won, ending the right of the police to padlock any house on the suspicion that it was a source of communist propaganda (what constituted communism was never clarified). Scott was greeted in triumph on the McGill campus with student banners that read: "Knight F.R. Scott Vanquishes Night Duplessis."[3]

And there was Irving Layton, the priapic poet of Montreal, a bohemian rather than a Beat, whose lyric poems celebrated the poet as social prophet and Dionysian lover. There were espresso bars and coffee houses where the poets met: the Colibri, the Carmen, the Pam Pam, and the Coffee Mill in the university district, or El Cortijo on Clark Street. Those coffee houses would become synonymous with a young bohemian, Leonard Cohen, who emerged from their midst in 1956 with the publication of Let Us Compare Mythologies. He was then twenty-two.

In Montreal, poetry was a blood sport. You could be on the side of Irving Layton, Leonard Cohen, and Louis Dudek, or you could be on the side of those Torontonian formalists, Jay Macpherson and the young Daryl Hine. It was mostly rhetoric and shadow-boxing, since Macpherson and Hine were unaware of being a side, but it meant the poets felt that poetry mattered.

Many believed that the extremes of political life in Quebec under the corrupt, authoritarian regime of Maurice Duplessis, supported by a reactionary clergy, fostered an intellectual fierceness in young minds like that of Pierre Elliott Trudeau from Outremont or René Lévesque, which English Canada's bland politics could never hope to emulate. Others envied the rich Jewish tradition in Montreal that, in the downtown ghetto of St. Urbain Street, nurtured the colourful Layton or Mordecai Richler, and, uptown, the likes of Leonard Cohen.

Toronto picked away at its inferiority complex with regard to Montreal, but, by the late fifties, here, too, a cultural revolution was under way. The city's Presbyterian veneer had begun to crack when new jazz clubs opened like subversive improvisations. In the late fifties, the cultural escapees could be found in the House of Hamburg on Bay, and the First Floor Club, in an old coach house on Asquith. And then the folk-music phenomenon started at places like the Village Corner, where Don Francks played with his young back-up guitarist, Ian Tyson. Finally, the Bohemian Embassy opened on 1 June 1960 in a warehouse west of Yonge Street, off Wellesley, at the end of what was then a cobbled lane, St. Nicholas Street.

This was the heart of the Gerrard Street Village, about four square blocks, Toronto's only bohemia, the place you went to find relief in Hog Town. The Village dated back to before the war, when artists' studios occupied its back alleys, and artists, like the Group of Seven's Fred Varley, could be found at Malloney's cocktail bar. But the Village had only begun to be a scene in the early fifties when the painter Albert Franck and his wife moved to a ratty little house at No. 94 Gerrard Street, which also served as Franck's shop. Dutch by birth, Franck restored paintings to make money and was affectionately called "Old Dutch Cleanser." From Gerrard, he made his treks into the back yards and alleys of Toronto to paint his chronicle of the city.

The young painters came to the Village like filings to a magnet to see Franck — Harold Town, Walter Yarwood, Kazuo Nakamura. In 1956 the painter Barry Kernerman opened the Gallery of Contemporary Art on Gerrard Street, and it set the style of the art boom that was to follow: it featured a black egg-crate ceiling, displays of pre-Columbian art, Hokusai drawings, and champagne openings. The area had its characters, who were characters because, as Harold Town said, they were "totally unaware of eccentricity as a commodity" — Willie Fedio, the lamp maker; Madam Alice, who read tea leaves; Nancy Pocock with her pet skunk, famous for her painting of a naked lady who ran past her door one day and later told the judge she was invisible.[4] There was always something doing, and joining the Village was easy.

When the Bohemian Embassy opened at 7 St. Nicholas Street, it was a modest affair. In his late twenties, Don Cullen was working as a copy clerk in the Television News department at the CBC, rewriting stories for the Sunday night national news. People were looking for an alternative to the

Celebrity Club on Jarvis Street, where the CBC types gathered for three-hour lunches and to drink and play darts. Cullen's idea — he was still enough involved in his Fundamentalist past to think it would work — was a liquorless night club. A group of five from the Television News department put down a hundred dollars each and the Bohemian Embassy was born. Cullen bought two fourteen-cup aluminum percolators and a hot plate at Eaton's on College Street and churned out advertising flyers on a Gestetner. He would go up to the football games at Varsity Stadium to hand out his flyers, saying, "Would you like some subversive literature?"[5]

The Bohemian Embassy was up two flights of narrow, banisterless steps, on the second floor, a barn of a room with walls painted black. The building dated from the days of horses, with a pulley outside to haul up goods through a hole in the wall, now boarded up. Whoever was available collected the cover at the door (membership was $2.25 a year). There were little tables, covered with red-checked tablecloths and candles stuck in Chianti bottles, and chairs for about 120 people, with a stage at the back and a sound system of sorts. The washroom was a cubicle that opened directly onto the main room. It had no lock, and you had to learn to pee with one hand on the door if you weren't to find yourself, pants down, staring into the audience under the glare of the naked bulb swinging above your head.

The Embassy was run as a private club, and the police — they didn't like the after-hours part — often tried to close the place down. If there was a drug bust at a coffee house in New York City, not to be outdone, Toronto's finest would come calling. Or perhaps some alderman's daughter would come home at 3:00 a.m. and say, "I was at the Bohemian Embassy." The Embassy was threatened with closure so often that a judge advised them to counter-charge with police persecution. The plainclothes officers were readily identifiable in the audience, but there was not much for them to do since the Embassy never served alcohol and frowned on drugs. Cullen was adamant about this. He felt that certain kinds of talent, unleashed too early into the rough-and-tumble of the local bar scene, could be destroyed. The Embassy nurtured the new. It was anti-bourgeois — Cullen was hugely amused to get the occasional letter from people who, thinking it was a real embassy, inquired about visas. There was an ingenuousness about the place. Looking back, Cullen thinks of it as curiously "sincere and kind of dear."

The week had a set schedule. The club opened at 10:00 p.m., when most of the city rolled up its sidewalks, and could stay open until 6:00 a.m. Monday was an open evening; for a while there was an acting teacher who gave lessons, and later there were fencing lessons. Thursday was the literary evening; Friday was folk music; Saturday, jazz. Regularly the Embassy would put together a social and satirical revue and comedy improvs. Their strength was that they would do anything. The North American première of Jean Genet's *The Maids* was done at the Embassy, and the first plays of David French and David Freeman opened there.

Soon most people had found their way to the Embassy. Sharon and Bram from Sharon, Lois, and Bram played there; Denny Doherty from the Mamas and the Papas; and Zal Yanovsky from the Lovin' Spoonful. And a young black comic up from the United States called Bill Cosby treated the place like home. Those who dropped into town, Leonard Cohen or Harry Belafonte, for example, wound up at the Embassy. The audience, Margaret would later say, were all those kids who were looking to music and poetry as an exit from "the lumpen bourgeoisie and the shackles of respectable wage-earning."[6]

Dennis Lee remembers reading about this very un-Torontonian place that was getting a lot of press in the local papers, and telling Margaret about it. It was she who took him to the Bohemian Embassy. It was part of her sniffing things out. "I don't think I would have ventured over there," he remarks. Away from the middle class in their camel-hair coats and two-piece suits, they listened to jazz and folk and poetry. For twenty-one-year-olds, it was intoxicating stuff.

The Embassy was the first to provide a venue that made a kind of collegiality possible among writers in Toronto. The scene was small, and there was a sense of being together on the fringe. Most people were writing poetry. You could count on the fingers of one hand the number of novels published in Canada in 1960 and 1961. In those days, it did not seem that Canada could support a professional writer. The novelist Mordecai Richler exiled himself to England because the cultural fabric of the country was too thin. The real activity was in poetry, because it was cheap to publish and one could publish one's own.

It was at the Embassy in November 1960 that Margaret gave her first public reading. She remembered it as a terrifying ordeal. She had acted in the Vic revues without suffering stage fright, but here she felt exposed. "There was nothing to hide behind." People kept going for cups of coffee, working the espresso machine, and talking. On stage she felt green and queasy. She remarked, "If you could survive the Embassy, you could read anywhere. Just as you reached your most poignant point [in a poem], someone would be sure to flush the toilet or turn on the espresso machine." For years, readings would give her those writerly nightmares of finding herself on stage, opening her notebook, and discovering everything in it was written in Chinese.[7]

But, as soon as Margaret read, most people were aware that here was somebody to be reckoned with. Who was this young woman behind the horn-rimmed glasses who read with such intensity and such intelligence?

In a context outside the university, Margaret would meet many of the people who would become close friends, and it was nurturing. The older generation would show up — James Reaney, Jay Macpherson, Phyllis Webb, Al Purdy, Margaret Avison — as would the younger poets, such as David Donnell, Gwendolyn MacEwen, and Joe Rosenblatt. There were almost as many women as men. The community was small and seemed to be permeable to anyone with talent.

Yet there was a subtext to the Embassy that was less attractive. It was hard to talk about because no one had quite figured out how it worked. There was no language yet to describe the subtle undermining. Attitudes towards women were still paradoxically, if not intentionally, hypocritical. All the propaganda still insisted that creativity was male. Thinking back, Margaret remarked: "Not even the artistic community offered you a viable choice as a woman."[8]

It was all very slippery and hard to get right. What was bohemia after all? In its flyer, the Embassy invited its patrons to "Relax in an Invigorating Atmosphere of Decadence. In aid of the almost lost causes of: Culture in Toronto, Intelligent Conversation, Informality, Inter-Galactic friendship, General Subversion and etc. etc. etc."[9]

It seemed like an extraordinary rebellion, and of course, after the conformity of the fifties, it was. But a woman would have to negotiate her way very carefully if she was not to find herself consigned to the role of female groupie.

The presiding genius of the Embassy was decidedly, if unconsciously, misogynist. Milton Acorn, a poet from Prince Edward Island, later to be called "the People's Poet," dominated the Embassy as if it had been created especially for him. Acorn would march into the Embassy and at first glance seem like a caricature — the lumberjack, working man's poet — always in plaid workman's shirt, jeans, running shoes or rubber boots, the butt of a stogie between his stubby fingers. His face was a craggy rock, made asymmetrical by a nervous tic, and seemingly anchored only by heavy-ridged eyebrows. He was a maverick who drank hard and played hard. With his bravura persona of the primal man, antediluvian and durable, an evening with Acorn deep in drink could be outrageous. He cultivated the edge. Margaret, while respectful of the talent, was more ambivalent about the man's aggressive arrogance: "He was from the kind of red-blooded truck driver school. 'If you want to be a poet, you can't go to college. You have to be a truck driver.' And I would think, 'What gender does he think he's talking to?' And the message seemed, you can't be a poet, which is what it probably was. Well, I'd been a waitress. Will a waitress do? I used to think. There was quite a lot of inverse snobbery going on."[10]

What was Acorn talking about anyway? There were remarkable women poets who came to the Embassy. Webb, Avison, Macpherson were impressive writers. And yet, how were they viewed? Margaret could remember a dinner party with Irving Layton, who had the largest reputation among the poets. Layton had declared that Margaret Avison had a "furtive look" because she knew she was invading male territory. To Margaret he seemed to be suggesting, not that women couldn't write poetry, but that they shouldn't.[11]

Layton's wife, Aviva, remembers the first head-to-head encounter between her husband and Margaret, which would have been about 1969.[12] It was at one of the endless parties that were common in those days. Aviva remembered that, when she first saw Margaret, she was stunned by her beauty. Dressed in a dark velvet dress and with that nimbus of hair and porcelain skin, she looked like a pre-Raphaelite heroine. (Margaret must have been indulging her love of costume.) As soon as Layton saw her, his hackles rose. He instinctively sensed dangerous territory. When he attended her first poetry reading, he made a point of reading his own poetry from the audience in an audible tone while she read on stage, and then he promptly fell asleep, snoring loudly. Aviva said that Margaret appeared unfazed.

There was a discrepancy between Layton's public and private personas. In private, he could be kind, but in public he had a reputation to maintain, and Margaret's strength seemed to threaten him. Irving Layton described to his son years later his strategy for dealing with women. "You have to undermine their confidence and then you build it up," he explained. "So that they became dependent on you."[13] Those were the days when, to be an artist, you had to be a hard drinker and a womanizer. Harold Town, the avant-garde painter who dominated the art scene, was the model of the consummate male artist, with one mistress on Centre Island in the heart of Toronto's harbour and one in the city.[14]

How did it work? The early part of the sixties was not a time of liberation for women. The sexual liberation that those years brought had nothing to do with female liberation. If anything, the world of bohemia had been invented for men.

In the United States, the presiding voices of those days included those of Jack Kerouac and Norman Mailer. Their vision of rebellion focused on the icon of the writer as the hard-drinking, priapic male. Having stabbed his second wife, Mailer was famous for his remark that it took a great deal of love to do it with a knife. There was a frenzy about it all, as if maleness were under threat, as if they already sensed the icon was dying.

Margaret was beginning to understand there was little place for women in this sexual revolution. Thinking back, she would say: "It was 1960, when *Playboy* was very big amongst men. That male liberation thing started with spitting on women. If you go back and read *The Ginger Man*, it's all there, or *On the Road*. The perfect woman in *On the Road* is a woman who lets her man come and go as he pleases and smiles all the time. Now that's a woman. Who could be that? Or who wanted to be that?"[15] Only by the 1980s, when books were being written by the women of that set, did we begin to see what was up. In 1990, Carolyn Cassady, wife of Neal Cassady, the model for Jack Kerouac's hero in *On the Road*, finally published her own memoir, *Off the Road*, and the absurdity of the position of the woman in that bohemian set became apparent. Cassady herself had been an aspiring artist when she met Neal Cassady, but she turned into the "wife as groupie." Attracted by his bohemian extremism, she became its victim, destroying her own chances at art as she tended the home front with the children, while Cassady roamed through his drug heaven and multiple mistresses in the name of raw experience. Both were destroyed in the process.

Margaret was a young woman who wanted to be part of the artistic world, but the sexual politics between male and female remained a central problem.

Women could only look at this issue privately, among themselves, and, even then, could discuss it only elliptically. The language to understand it had not yet been explored. And society at large was certainly not going to help. In 1960 the CBC network cancelled the airing of an interview with Simone de Beauvoir because she approved of divorce and argued that women were equal to men.

One of Margaret's close friends at the Embassy was the young poet Gwendolyn MacEwen. The hardest thing for her and Gwendolyn, she has remarked, was to find a space for female creativity in what was essentially a male world.[16] The troubling questions were: What was creativity for a woman? Why were there no great women painters or great women writers? Was creativity different for men and women? Could women create? That long, exhausting dialogue of the sixties had just begun.

But there was also a personal question. How were you going to live your life? The older women writers at the Embassy, such as Phyllis Webb, Margaret Avison, and Jay Macpherson (who, though only twenty-nine, was already an established poet), conformed to the model that said that, if a woman were to write, she would have to pursue her art alone. For whatever personal reasons, they had not married. They did not live with someone. They did not have children.

The subject that everyone at the Embassy was obsessed with in those days was mythology. It had filtered down from Robert Graves's *White Goddess* and from Northrop Frye's lectures at the University of Toronto. And everyone had read Leonard Cohen's *Let Us Compare Mythologies* (1956). Jay Macpherson's *Boatman* had come out in 1957, Margaret Avison was publishing *Winter Sun* (1960), Gwen MacEwen was writing *Julian the Magician*, and Margaret was working on *Double Persephone*.

The White Goddess had appeared in 1946 and, as Graves explained, was intended as "a historical grammar of the language of poetic myth." His argument was that the language of poetic myth "anciently current in the Mediterranean and Northern Europe was a magical language bound up with popular religious ceremonies in honour of the Moon-goddess, or Muse. . . . this remains the language of true poetry." It was a revolutionary book since he was one of the first poet/critics to break out of the Judaeo-Christian and unrelievedly classical tradition. He insisted that the language of poetry had been tampered with when patrilineal institutions were substituted for matrilineal ones. At first glance, this seemed good. Poetic myth, he was suggesting, came from matrilineal cultures. Classical poets, in particular, had turned their backs on "the Moon-goddess who inspired them and who demanded that man should pay woman spiritual and sexual homage." But it was obvious, in fact, that it was a brilliant elaboration of an old misogyny. Graves writes:

> The Goddess is a lovely, slender woman with a hooked nose, deathly pale face, lips as red as rowan-berries, startlingly blue eyes and long fair hair; she will suddenly transform herself into sow, mare, bitch, vixen, she-ass, weasel, serpent, owl, she-wolf, tigress, mermaid or loathsome hag. Her names and titles are innumerable. . . . the test of the poet's vision, one might say, is the accuracy of his portrayal of the White Goddess and the Island over which she rules. The reason why the hairs stand on end, the eyes water, the throat is constricted, the skin crawls and a shiver runs down the spine when one writes or reads a true poem is that a true poem is necessarily an invocation of the White Goddess, or Muse, the Mother of All Living, the ancient power of fright and lust — the female spider or the queen-bee whose embrace is death.[17]

As Margaret remarks wryly: "Ah, yes, the moon-goddess: Man does / Woman is" (the title of another book by Graves). Women were still, by definition, not poets but muses. The Moon-goddess had three phases: lover/mother/hag. And in that triad the only place for the independent woman was as bitch (as Margaret would herself discover as she increasingly received that epithet when her work became better known). Margaret elaborated: "Not only did [a woman] have to be a goddess, she had to be a man-destroying goddess. Because what the white goddess did was to bite off your head. Every spring and fall, I forget when — this head biting took place twice a year. Do away with one and you have another."[18]

Margaret and Gwen became increasingly obsessed with sorting out the nature of the muse when the writer was female.

> I myself always thought the muse was female. . . . If the muse is a woman for the woman poet, unless the poet is a lesbian, the sexual connection gets removed, and it's more like a second self, a twin, a mother, a wise old woman. It can be any of these things. I did a survey of people and their muses, which was very revealing, and most muses, for both men and women, are women. So it turns out. Probably if you want to be psychological, it is the voice, and the voice is the mother's voice. That's how we learn to speak, usually from our mothers.[19]

The female voice that Margaret heard through her mother had always felt powerful and autonomous, and she instinctively saw herself within this female tradition. This, of course, would provide a kind of freedom.

Gwen, by contrast, thought of her muse as male. But then, this created problems. She kept seeing the men she met as muses. Women had been serving as muses for centuries. They usually accepted the projection easily, and served willingly as handmaids to male artists. It was flattering, though they were always shocked to find how easily they were replaced. But, for a woman, a man was a complicated figure onto whom to project the muse since most men wouldn't suffer the projection gladly. It diffused the power they had been taught to believe they needed over a woman. This made the territory of sexual politics — the power games of erotic love — even more complex for someone like Gwen. Margaret would listen patiently to her sagas of anguished relationships. But she herself had too much self-possession for such romantic extremism. If she were going to have lovers, they would be simply that. Still, she began with some very confused notions of what might constitute the female writer's life. Looking back, she parodied the scenario she had set for herself:

> I'd read the biographies [of women writers], which were not encouraging. Jane Austen never married Mr. Darcy. Emily

Brontë died young, Charlotte in childbirth. George Eliot never had children and was ostracised for living with a married man. Emily Dickinson flitted; Christina Rossetti looked at life through the wormholes in a shroud. Some had managed to combine writing with what I considered to be a normal life — Mrs. Gaskell, Harriet Beecher Stowe — but everyone knew they were second rate. My choices were between excellence and doom on the one hand, and mediocrity and coziness on the other. I gritted my teeth, set my face to the wind, gave up double-dating, and wore horned-rims and a scowl so I would not be mistaken for a puffball.

It was in this frame of mind that I read Robert Graves's *The White Goddess*, which further terrified me. Graves did not dismiss women. In fact he placed them right at the center of his poetic theory; but they were to be inspirations rather than creators, and a funny sort of inspiration at that. They were to be incarnations of the White Goddess herself, alternately loving and destructive, and men who got involved with them ran the risk of disembowelment or worse. A woman just might — might, mind you — have a chance of becoming a decent poet, but only if she too took on the attributes of the White Goddess and spent her time seducing men and then doing them in. All this sounded a little strenuous, and appeared to rule out domestic bliss. It wasn't my idea of how men and women should get on together — raking up leaves in the backyard, like my mom and dad — but who was I to contradict the experts? There was no one else in view giving me any advice on how to be a writer, though female. Graves was it.

That would be my life, then. To the garret and the TB I added the elements of enigma and solitude. I would dress in black. I would learn to smoke cigarettes, although they gave me headaches and made me cough, and drink something romantic and unusually bad for me, such as absinthe. I would live by myself in a suitably painted attic (black) and have lovers whom I would discard in appropriate ways, though I drew the line at bloodshed. (I was, after all, a nice Canadian girl.) I would never have children. This last bothered me a lot, as before this I had always intended to have some, and it seemed unfair, but White Goddesses did not have time for children, being too taken up with cannibalistic sex, and Art came first. I would never, never own an automatic washer-dryer. Sartre, Samuel Beckett, Kafka, and Ionesco, I was sure, did not have major appliances, and these were the writers I most admired. I had no concrete ideas about how the laundry would get done, but it would only be my own laundry, I thought mournfully — no fuzzy sleepers, no tiny T-shirts — and such details could be worked out later.[20]

Margaret did try cigarettes — that lasted a mere six months — but it soon began to occur to her that maybe Robert Graves mightn't have the last word on female poets.

Clearly this was a time for sorting out doubts and confusions, and asking the question: what could stop you? Margaret had enormous energy; she would just get on with it. With the aid of a friend's flatbed press, she designed and printed her own first book of poetry, *Double Persephone*, in 1961. It was seven pages long. Each page had to be printed separately and the type redistributed, as there were not enough a's for the whole book. The cover was done with a lino block. The print run of 250 copies was sold through bookstores for fifty cents a copy. So scarce were poetry publications in those days that *Double Persephone* even got reviewed, and CBC Radio, whose arts producer, Robert McCormack, was always looking for new work, eventually bought the rights to air it. And paid Margaret forty-five dollars.

In *Double Persephone*, Margaret took the conventions of the courtly love poem — the questing knight and his lady — and modernized them. The poems are parodies, and the idea behind them is quite brilliant: the heroine is not the knight's pliant mistress. Rather she is the "girl with the gorgon touch." Margaret took Robert Graves quite literally. Her Persephone is double — both sinister and seductive; she is Graves's bitch goddess, though probably one he never wanted incarnated in real life:

His true love, never one to pine,
Smirks as he dwindles down to spine
And dawdles on the snow alone,
Fiddling a tune across his bone . . .[21]

The dancing girl's a withered crone;
Though her deceptive smile
Lures life from earth, rain from the sky,
It hides a wicked sickle; while
Those watching sense the red blood curled
Waiting, in the center of her eye . . .[22]

The bright feet bleed upon the grass
    Freezing motion as they pass
As gathering words as cruel as thorns
    She wanders with her unicorns . . .[23]

When she read the poems, Gwen MacEwen wrote to Margaret to express her excitement:

> With the onslaught of Persephone, both of them, I at last struck that very subtle and rather vicious vein of authenticity under the sometimes innocent skeleton caging it . . . like it very much is what I mean — partly because I like to strip away rose petals and find insects underneath — not insects for their own sake, but put there to emphasize the flower by their contrast to it. Forget the metaphors, but I did see in "persephone" a kind of half-sister to Marie-Claire Blais (if you've read her in trans. or otherwise) who also sees the other, less pleasant, side of the mirror. This must be essential . . . possibly the female poet has to emphasize the anti-primrose and candyfloss business more than the male . . . hair ribbons and all that — can be hampering, I think. To achieve that clean-cut, uncompromising slant on things is an achievement. (what a sentence that was) . . . — Gwen[24]

How to eschew hair ribbons and all that stuff, to get at the real business of being female, without acceding to the romantic codes that required women to be beautiful, compliant, non-threatening? If one risked that persona, what would be the cost to one's private life? Who would have the courage to do it? In a story "Insula Insularum," published in *Acta* in her last year as an undergraduate, Margaret had begun to confront these questions. It might not have been that she was particularly brave; it was just that she had no other way of seeing the world. Despite its undergraduate title and its debt to Samuel Beckett, "Insula Insularum" is a remarkable story, the first story that has her own particular voice.

In the story, the unnamed central character goes canoeing in the city harbour with a young man. Little happens, but the mastery comes from the juxtaposition of the present with flashbacks from the main character's childhood.

> People are buried under the sand, she thought. They are buried thickly, one beside another, and the long weeds are their hair which grows up through the sand and keeps growing although they are dead. The driftwood is bones . . . no, the driftwood is nothing; it is.

When they stop to rest on a beach, the young man and woman encounter a dead seagull, and the woman thinks: "All red things are death and then the dead become white like bone or smoke or broken water." The young man wants an intimate moment, at least some necking on the sand. "He slides his bare arm around her waist." But she is stuck in her vision of the emptiness at the core of things.

> the crickets are the voices of the dead people in the water.
> my own voice is like that inside my throat, small and hard with a surface like the shined back of an insect, the sibilance of legs rasped against wing-cases; the whisper of death rises like sand around our heads . . .
> The crickets in the august flowered air go on pulse on pulse . . .[25]

The girl withholds herself without explanation. She has her own vision, but there is no speech to communicate this to the boy. A Freudian analysis would see this as a story about repression. A more intelligent reading would be that this is a young woman caught in the throes of her own vision, for whom the man is, for the moment, peripheral.

Margaret once said that, growing up in the bush, it seemed to her that it was human beings that were strange, mysterious, even dangerous. Sometimes she could look at them, male and female, with fascination, almost as aliens: so this is how they behave. Most men were not used to such scrutiny from a woman.

Like any young woman, Margaret was looking for a companion. She and Gwen talked of their one nightmare: it would be marriage in the suburbs, complete with washing machines. They wanted to be out there doing things, to be artists. Within a year, Gwen would be married to Milton Acorn. She had followed the pattern of marrying the mentor (Acorn was almost twenty years older), but soon this turned into disaster. He proved mentally unstable, and she used the occasion of a casual infidelity on his part to break with him. But it was painful. While at graduate school, Margaret would become engaged to Jay Ford, a young philosophy major at the University of Toronto and a family friend whom her father knew and liked well. But the prospect of a conventional marriage, as it loomed ever more real, was impossible to tolerate, and the relationship ended in 1964.

While she was living in Jay Macpherson's house, Margaret had access to Jay's library, and was reading madly. In that library, she was able to read the poetry of P.K. Page, Anne Hébert, Margaret Avison, Phyllis Webb, Anne Wilkinson, Jay Macpherson, Elizabeth Brewster, Miriam Waddington, Kay Smith, Gwladys Downes, and others. She confirmed what her earlier reading of pioneer writers like Susanna Moodie, Catherine Parr Traill, and Marie de l'Incarnation had already told her: you couldn't read Canadian literature and overlook the women. And she read her first two experimental Canadian novels that year: Sheila Watson's *Double Hook* and Marie-Claire Blais's *La Belle Bête*, books whose dark symbolism might possibly have given her the nerve to write "Insula Insularum." The women were there. Women could write. For the moment, she would leave aside the question of their biographies.

In Canada, it was the Canadian component, not the female, that appeared to be the hurdle. Though there were writers, the culture itself was indifferent to Canadian talent. Canadian subjects were dismissed as boring or provincial. Novelists were advised to set their novels in cosmopolitan (which meant European or American) locales. Poets could expect to sell books to their friends. At least the men and the women were in the same bind.

As her fourth year came to an end, Margaret considered her options. She thought of a career in journalism, but the danger was that most women ended up writing the society or obituary columns, something to do, she would quip, "with their ancient roles as goddesses of life and death, deckers of nuptial beds and washers of corpses."[26]

It was Northrop Frye who helped her to decide on graduate school. One of her other professors had asked her: "Wouldn't [you] rather get married?"[27] But Frye was encouraging. She remembered the encounter as follows:

> "What do you think you might do?" [Frye] asked while we were standing, for some reason, in a hallway, both gazing at the floor.
>
> I said that I was going to do the thing that was considered appropriate for young Canadian writers in those days: that is, I was going to go to England and work as a waitress, so I could write masterpieces in a convenient garret at night.
>
> He said he thought it might be more productive to go to graduate school, as I would have more time to write.
>
> I said, Would that be ethical?
>
> He said he thought so. Anyway, he thought maybe a scholarship might be a less exhausting way of nurturing one's great works.[28]

At graduation, she walked away with prizes: the Victoria College Alumni Award and the E.J. Pratt Medal, which was the university's major prize for poetry. She sent Pratt a copy of *Double Persephone* as a gesture of thanks, and his wife wrote back to say that "Ned" felt she had real promise.

The students in English Language and Literature had a tradition of exchanging graduation photos, but Margaret hated her photo. Instead, she drew herself as a little troll with wiry hair, and handed out that.[29]

Armed with a Woodrow Wilson Fellowship, she would set off for Harvard in the fall.

While she had enjoyed her years at Vic, she had become somewhat ambivalent about academic life. A few years after graduating, she had a dream: "I dreamt that I had died and had been buried, and had resurrected through the Victoria College lawn. I walked into the library, covered with mud and half-decaying, but nobody noticed."[30]

7

THE CANADIAN CLUBBERS

In the fall of 1961, the twenty-one-year-old Margaret arrived in Cambridge, Massachusetts. She moved into Founders' House, the women graduate students' residence at 6 Appian Way, a rambling New England clapboard house (since torn down) in front of Radcliffe Yard. Her room was in the garret; she had to haul herself up to it using a banister made of rope.

She headed out those first days to explore on foot, refusing to buy a bike because she believed Cambridge and Boston traffic would finish her off. One route took her along Appian Way to Garden Street, which, in 1630, had been called Great Swamp Way. This ran smack into Cambridge Common with its plaque to General George Washington, who on 3 July 1775 had assumed command of his army of volunteers, named that day the Continental Army. A bronze Abraham Lincoln stood in the centre of the Common, commemorating the Gettysburg Address. She then passed Christ Church, built in 1756. This was the church of the defectors, which, for her, gave it a special significance. At the time of the American Revolution, most of the congregation fled with the British when Boston was evacuated. Many ended up in Canada. Margaret's father always joked that the United States never quite recovered from the brain-drain of 1776. Given her penchant for graveyards, Margaret occasionally took the detour across the Old Burying-Ground, also known as "God's Acre," where the headstones dated back to the seventeenth century. How strange the chance of history. Her own ancestors, the Atwoods and the Killams, had left before the Revolution, but had they stayed she would have been American, and what would that have meant?

She eventually made her way to Harvard Yard. Its double quadrangle encapsulates Harvard's history: confident and yet withdrawn, holding in tension the old and new, a monument to the mind. At the south end of the New Yard, she walked up the steps and through the twelve Corinthian columns of the Widener Memorial Library (Harvard students quipped that its architect, Horace Trumbauer, had an edifice complex). The library was named after Harry Elkins Widener of the Harvard class of 1907. His mother had donated the funds for its construction in memory of her son, who died on the *Titanic* in 1912. One of the great libraries of the world, its collection includes a Gutenberg Bible and a First Folio of Shakespeare's plays. Margaret was impressed. She wrote to Charlie Pachter that the library was fantastic. She couldn't resist commenting, however, on the John Singer Sargent paintings that hang at the top of the main stairs: "they are the most grisly things you ever did see. Victory triumphing over death in pastels, our sons choosing glory in the first world war." Even modern guidebooks call them the very worst works of public art done by a major American painter. "By the way," she added in her letter, "big bomb shelter controversy down here."[1]

While Margaret was still preparing to leave Toronto for Harvard, East Germany built the Berlin Wall virtually overnight, on 12 August 1961, closing the border between East and West Berlin, and entrenching the cold war firmly in the global imagination. A November issue of the student newspaper, the *Crimson*, led with the headline "Should Harvard Have a Bomb Shelter?" and *The Harvard Lampoon* did cartoons of an Alice-in-Wonderland caterpillar sitting on a mushroom-shaped nuclear bomb–cloud, smoking a hooka. In all, 1961 wasn't a good year. It was the year President John Kennedy promised direct military aid, in the form of advisers and supplies, to support the government of South Vietnam in its civil war with the north. It was the year of the disastrous Bay of Pigs Invasion of Cuba by anticommunist Cuban exiles in Miami. The Sandinista guerrilla war began that year in Nicaragua, and, in South Africa, a year after the Sharpeville Massacre, the African National Congress, too, embarked on a guerrilla war. In fact, the sixties would be the decade of guerrilla war, from Vietnam to Montreal. Initials became popular monikers among revolutionary cadres: the FLM, ANC, PLO, FLQ. Nineteen sixty-one was also the year the London-based human rights organization

Amnesty International was founded. The world was heating up, and Margaret was about to enter the power centre of what was routinely called the First World.

But, being a female student, her position was odd. Another headline in the *Crimson* — "Cliffies Seek More One O'clocks" — tells the story. The women undergraduates in residence at Radcliffe were lobbying to change their curfew. They wanted unlimited eleven o'clocks, and their current number of one o'clocks increased to thirty. They were also demanding the elimination, during exam periods, of the six o'clock formal dinners, with the china place-settings, the dress code, and the after-dinner coffee served in demitasses. They baulked at the arcane signing-in and signing-out rules, particularly the "Charred Body Book" — if a girl was visiting any resident overnight, she had to be signed in so that, were the dorm to catch fire, the extra body could be accounted for in the charred ruins. The students were challenging the administration's assumptions of what was to be expected of young women. It must have been irksome. While the "boys" were allowed to play with the big issues, the girls were bogged down in battles over trivia.

In walking from Radcliffe Yard to Harvard Yard, it wouldn't have taken Margaret long to register the distance she had travelled. Harvard University was founded in 1638. (Intriguingly, there was an Austin Killam, possibly one of Margaret's ancestors, on the contributors' list of 1653.) It had always been a very male university, and had survived as such for almost two and a half centuries, until 1878, when Radcliffe, a female college attachment, was established. Women students, or Cliffies, were exiles at Harvard. In the early days, they were required to go to Harvard Square wearing hats and gloves, in order to avoid "unseemly cross-infection" (as a Harvard grad of 1934 put it).[2] Harvard professors trudged across the Cambridge Common to Radcliffe to repeat lectures delivered the previous hour to the male students. Any woman using the Widener Library, where women were generally forbidden to tarry, was thought to be a bit wild and dashing, if not downright provocative. Radcliffe women were told they should consider themselves pioneers simply by being at Harvard in the first place. They were advised by their housemothers not to be ungrateful. The novelist Alison Lurie, who graduated in 1947, wrote that, "for Radcliffe students in my time, the salient fact about Harvard was that it so evidently was not ours. Our position was like that of poor relations living just outside the walls of some great estate: patronized by some of our grand relatives, tolerated by others and snubbed and avoided by the rest. Almost every detail of our lives proclaimed our second class status."[3]

Years later, those women who wrote memoirs would be most shocked to recall how easily they had accepted it all. Heather Dubrow, a graduate of 1966, wrote: "In my nine years as an undergraduate and a graduate at Harvard, I was taught by exactly one woman."[4] In 1962, there were no female announcers on WHRB, the student radio station, because "women's voices were considered distracting." Even the journalist Linda Greenhouse, who would eventually cover the Supreme Court for *The New York Times*, felt only mild regret when her fellow *Crimson* editors gathered *en masse* in the all-male dining room of Adams House. She wasn't allowed to join them and ate her solitary hamburger in Harvard Square before they regrouped to discuss the next day's edition.[5] In those days, no one was preoccupied with the status of women at Harvard. It was simply part of the fabric of life, one thread among many. Only in retrospect was it viewed as an issue.

The American novelist Faye Levine arrived at Harvard at the same time as Margaret, in the golden fall of 1961, when Harvard was Kennedy country. She wrote: "One looked about Harvard Square and saw amazing reflections in the population of the President's confident walk, his manly jaw, the Yankee wit in his eyes." There were five males to every female. Campus politics was an amiable, gentlemanly sort of activity. A Global Disarmament Committee called Tocsin (referring to an old French country warning bell) was established, with the polite slogan "Unilateral Initiatives."[6] The revolutionary sixties, with their vehemence for social change, wouldn't begin until mid-decade.

Levine described the women at Radcliffe in her 1962 article for the *Crimson* "The Three Flavors of Radcliffe." "Peach" was the flavour of the girls who had "gone to fancy private schools and valued social grace and sociability." They wore silk stockings and high heels, majored in Fine Arts and English, ran the dorm committees, and favoured "charming" as an adjective. They had a dread of being seen as overly conscientious and of being called "dogs, or ugly charmless grinds." "Chocolate" were the girls from the big-city public schools, of "Midwestern and/or Jewish background," who studied government or science, and for whom everything was "interesting." "Lime" were the girls with "Continental, bohemian, or déclassé life-styles" who had gone to progressive preparatory schools. They were the most sexually sophisticated. Only limes used the word "sympatico." Though being Canadian left Margaret an enigma, she probably belonged with the chocolates.[7]

Levine baulked at the elaborate "parietals," the rules that prohibited boys from having girls in their dorms, except at certain hours and with the doors ajar. Females weren't allowed in the male Houses even for public lectures. When she declared it unfair, she was warned that she would forfeit her female privileges, such as having the door opened for her, assistance with her coat, or her meals paid for. She'd heard about the careers of luminaries like Thomas Wolfe and Teddy Kennedy, their all-night binges in crummy cafeterias and then sleeping through classes. Boys flauted the rules and made good. "Girls took the legible class notes boys would copy." Even when they made token gestures of rebellion, girls stayed "neat, clean, and stylish." "Girls, particularly Radcliffe girls, are the pillars of civilization, the rock without which the destructive male force would undermine society. In short, they are finks."[8]

Another novelist, Beth Gutcheon, arrived in 1963. She remembered the importance of being one of the guys and recalled that, when she was told, "You think like a man," she blushed and said, "Thank you." Fresh from a boarding school, she expected college to lead to marriage, ideally to a Harvard man. She wasn't happy about it, but she certainly believed it.[9]

In those days, elaborate machinations were required if a boy and girl wanted to live together off campus. The journalist Anne Fadiman put it best: "Females at Harvard — possibly excluding grandmothers and maiden aunts — belonged to the same category as liquor and marijuana: fun, but not to be used in public."[10]

The "Cliffie" label probably did not matter a great deal to Margaret personally, since she was a graduate student, which meant that there were no sign-out books and no curfews. By the early sixties, women graduate students were at last taking their courses along with the men on the main Harvard campus. Still, she walked into the "Cliffie" prejudice in other ways. She remembered in particular the occasion when Radcliffe was looking for a dean. A sociologist friend explained that the candidate would have to be a good role model. "What's that?" she asked. "Well," he replied,

From left to right: Joyce, Margaret (Margaret Atwood's mother), and Kathleen Killam

Margaret's mother and father, circa 1948, in Nova Scotia

Margaret Atwood

Margaret's father, Carl Atwood, cleaning fish.

Peggy Atwood:

Peggy's not-so-secret ambition is to write THE Canadian novel - and with those English marks, who doubts that she will? Notorious for those Hallowe'en Hop announcements, she surpassed herself by writing a singing commercial for the Reindeer Romp.
Next year — U. of T.

Clan Call: Leaside High School yearbook, 1956-57

Victoria College, the University of Toronto

The E.J. Pratt Room, Victoria College, 1964. Northrop Frye is third from right.

Dennis Lee as a freshman, 1957

The Bohemian Embassy, early 1960s. From left to right: Marie Kingston, Margaret Atwood, unidentified, Lawrence Stone. Sylvia Fricker (Tyson) performing.

Gwendolyn MacEwen, early 1960s

Margaret and Sue Milmoe in their apartment at Harvard, 1966

Jim Polk and Sue Milmoe, Harvard graduation, 1967

Margaret Atwood, circa 1968-69

Margaret and Charlie Pachter at the opening of Pachter's exhibition at the Canadian Art Galleries, Calgary, 1970

Jim Polk and Margaret in Northern Quebec, 1971

"the future dean would not just have to have high academic credentials and the ability to get along with students, she would also have to be married, with children, good-looking, well dressed, active in community work, and so forth." Margaret knew she would be a terrible role model. She wanted to be a writer. But the conversation gave her a life-long distaste for the phrase "role model."[11]

With references from Northrop Frye, she had come to Harvard to study under a Canadian professor named Jerome Buckley, an eminent Victorian scholar, who had himself been an undergraduate at Victoria College and in the very first class that Northrop Frye had taught there. Coming from Vic, Margaret was not prepared for the sexism at Harvard. There were just two women professors in the whole university, neither teaching English Literature. It was commonly accepted that professors were easier on female students than on male students because women would never compete to teach at Harvard. Such condescension irked Margaret. She didn't like double standards: "I always felt a little like a wart or a wen on the great male academic skin. I felt as if I were there on sufferance."[12]

Her real interest, though, lay in her apprenticeship as a writer. Writing was her vocation; university was her day job. But she discovered that the best strategy was to fortify herself through anonymity. When she blithely announced to her fellow women graduate students that she was going to be a writer, there was a kind of collective gasp. She remarked that "it was like saying you were going to pee in the men's washroom: either daring or in bad taste." "Fancying oneself a poet" was "a fancy it was death to admit."[13] Doing so was either pretentious, frivolous, or self-deluded, especially if you were a woman. She was beginning to discover that women writers were viewed as freaks, oddities, suspicious characters. No women protested. Who wanted to sound peevish or shrill? Those were the days when men found it humorous to say that women, writers included, were good for only one thing.

It was all, of course, a matter of perception. At that time in the United States, from the perspective of the academy at least, *real* writing was done mostly by men. The popular female writers who sold well, such as Mary McCarthy, Katherine Anne Porter, Lillian Hellman, and Dorothy Parker, didn't count because they weren't considered serious writers, and the few who were included in High Literature, such as Flannery O'Connor, Marianne Moore, and Gertrude Stein, were treated as honorary men. Margaret concluded that being a woman writer in the United States was the obverse of being a woman writer in Canada. Young American women aspiring to write could feel they counted for something as Americans, but not as women. By contrast, in Canada nationality rather than gender was the problem. Nobody had actually said no to her as a woman, but who cared about Canadian writing?

Well, for instance, she and Gwen MacEwen cared. They had begun a correspondence in which they often wrote about their work. Gwen sent Margaret her new pamphlet *The Drunken Clock*, which she had self-published under the imprint Aleph Press. She was writing her sequence "Adam's Alphabet," which refused to complete itself, and she joked that she "revised regularly, like taking regular pills for a chronic stomach ache."[14] They discussed the merits of free verse and its diffuseness: it "dripped" all over the page. They traded advice on where to "plunk down" their books for maximum exposure and sales. They talked about who they were reading: Marie-Claire Blais had a new novel, *Tête blanche*. Margaret was reading Edgar Allan Poe.[15] His "faded lily" quality made her wince. They traded news about the interpretation of the Tarot cards. The intellectual and playful collaboration between these two women poets was a luxury. And in this world of male writers, their mutual confirmation of artistic seriousness was helpful.

Margaret's version of her life at 6 Appian Way included afternoons spent in the bathtub on the third floor reading Dickens, scribbling "dismal poems," and "listening to the rain and the pitter-patter of sexual perverts as they scampered up and down the fire escape."[16] She wrote to Charlie Pachter that they were like aphids infesting the outside of a house. The residence had a problem with voyeurs. In fact, the first week Margaret was there, a man entered the building through an unlocked window and walked straight into her bedroom. Her room-mate awoke and frightened him off. On one occasion a man was actually apprehended, having somehow gotten trapped on the roof long enough for the police to arrive. Though he had an extensive record of violence, he was let out on bail. When Margaret and her fellow residents went to court to testify, the man never showed up. There were so many obscene phone calls that the residence eventually bought a dog whistle, which the girls would blow into the phone. Margaret later remarked that Cambridge was her first experience of urban violence.

Margaret's room-mate was a girl from North Carolina, Mary Irving Carlyle, whose Southern drawl delighted her. Mary's father was a liberal lawyer who had run for public office supporting the integrationists, which, as Mary put it, "just finished him off." He couldn't even get a lift with the garbage man. She was thinking of teaching at a black college after she got her doctorate, even though she knew it would mean being socially ostracized.[17]

Margaret wrote to Charlie that Cambridge was a dreary town where it rained every Friday. She was going down to Winston–Salem, North Carolina, because Mary was getting married, and she intended to participate in the civil-rights sit-in strikes there before going on to New York for Thanksgiving. Why didn't Charlie ever come to Boston? There were so many top-notch museums that made "Toronto's little wayside station look sick."[18]

She'd only been at Harvard a month and was enjoying the English Department. The library was the problem. All the modern poetry was locked in the Lamont Library, accessible to male students only; "studentesses" were not allowed in. Legend had it that some unbreakable codicil in Thomas Lamont's will barred their entry. But the truth was that many still felt the presence of women would be distracting to male students. "Getting out a book of modern poetry from Lamont," Margaret later remarked, "required somewhat the same procedures as those needed to extract a book of pornography from the X section of Widener Library, and, being of a retiring nature, I didn't want anyone to see me doing the former under the mistaken impression that I was doing the latter." The Canadian poetry section was not kept with the real poetry, but was housed in the bowels of the Widener with the Canadiana, catalogued with Ethnology and Folklore, and "freely accessible to students and studentesses alike."[19] She was finding that, in the United States, saying you were Canadian was about as interesting as saying you had mashed potatoes for lunch. "Am I really that boring?" she would wonder.

Her professor Jerome Buckley remembered her that first year: "She was very, very shy, recessive, observant. She would sit in my seminar of fifteen students saying little. I had no idea she intended to be a writer since she seemed to be making no gestures in that direction."[20] Because Frye had sent her to him, he took an interest in her, inviting her, along with several other students, to Thanksgiving dinner at his house.

Beneath the shyness, Buckley found Margaret could be bold and quirky. He remembered her coming into the hundred-year-old clapboard building that housed the English Department and showing the secretaries a tablecloth that she had bought in a discount store and intended to make into a dirndl skirt. But Margaret would remember herself as practically mute. A university is a dangerous place for a young writer. Everything has been studied, has been said, and any original, personally arrived-at insight risks seeming banal. One has to have a strong ego to get through it. Margaret would later call Harvard a "hell-hole of fierce competition; there were always a few suicides, people throwing themselves into the Charles River every spring off the bell tower."[21]

As an MA student, Margaret was required to live in residence for two years. She had to take four and a half courses each semester, and for her PhD to demonstrate a reading knowledge of three languages: one classical and two modern. Before she could start her doctoral thesis, she would be required to pass a general oral exam, adjudicated by five examiners. She didn't take any courses in creative writing, even though there was always a Boylston Professor of Creative Writing in residence. Obviously she didn't have time. But neither did she seek out Robert Lowell, who came to teach there in the fall of 1962. Distant and private, he was once described as "Heathcliff played by Boris Karloff."[22] Struggling writers who had heard of his famous seminars at Boston University with students like Sylvia Plath and Anne Sexton approached him with awe. Margaret was a Canadian and had no interest in becoming a young acolyte writer at Harvard. She did not join the *Crimson*, the *Advocate*, or the *Lampoon*. She had done that sort of thing at Victoria College, and, anyway, these were considered undergraduate preserves.

Everyone who met Margaret would describe her as observant, a listener. She seemed not to need to establish a persona as a writer. She would say that, in the United States, and even in Canada, young male poets ran in packs, whereas young female poets tended to be loners. There were "schools of poetry, like schools of fish. These schools were male."[23] She was biding time until she herself was ready.

At Harvard she was having to think a lot about what it meant to be Canadian. She hadn't thought that much about Americans before. She would joke that, in her childhood, Americans were the ones who arrived in the bush with the best equipment but then got lost and didn't burn their garbage.[24] Changing countries had seemed no more drastic than changing cities.

A month after arriving at Harvard, however, she found herself in name-calling arguments with Americans about the draft, missiles, Communists, education, always in sentences that began "In Canada, we . . . ." She checked herself for symptoms of an American accent, "as though it were measles." Soon she was socializing with a group of very bright, very articulate young Canadians who formed almost a subculture at Harvard. She noticed how quickly these mild-mannered Canadians turned into rabid maple-leaf nationalists. One new friend from Kenora, who had spent summers guiding American tourists on fishing trips, confessed that, finding himself in the United States, he discovered "they're so much nicer in America, and we seem to get so much nastier."

To explain these transformations to herself, she came up with the notion of "The Great Canadian Lie." The most urbanized Canadians, who might have spent no more than a week in, say, Algonquin Park, once south of the border reinvented themselves as Great White Hunters. When Americans dropped allusions to "grey" or "faceless" Canadians, she casually related horror stories about man-eating polar bears in northern wastes and intrepid lumberjacks. When an American acquaintance challenged her about the lack of a typically Canadian food, she brought back from her next trip home a dozen bottles of spruce beer, telling him, as she gulped down the bitter brew with practised flair, that it was the national drink, with "True Northern Flavour."[25]

This posing seemed a little absurd, and she decided to examine what she and other Canadians were up to. In her Harvard notebook she described a party she attended with a friend, Dave Wood, at "The Canadian Club," the name a group of ex-pats at the Harvard Business School had adopted.

The young business students at the party were enormously polite. The first question was invariably: "Where are you from?"; the second, "How do you like it down here?" Then the comparisons started. One person assured her that he wasn't at all prejudiced; some of his best friends were

Americans. Another remarked with gloomy satisfaction that the graffiti in the men's washroom were much dirtier than any he'd seen in Canada. The few Americans at the party whom she managed to flush out left early, driven away when the Canadian chauvinism got too much for them. The French Canadians were fearsomely polite and avoided the subject of politics; they, too, left early.

She wrote: "I'd been in the country long enough to identify my own reactions as a general pattern characterizing the phases Canadians went through, like a disease." As she sardined her way through the party, she tested her "phases theory," determining, by the relative amounts of hostility and guilt, which phases the Canadian Clubbers were in. According to Margaret's theory, the first phase was a "deceptive euphoria."

Then the second phase set in. As a Canadian, one felt invisible, like having no reflection in a mirror. "Something, some ectoplasmic, metaphysical quality, which eluded you every time you tried to define it, was uncomfortably different. . . . It wasn't the American national identity that was bothering us; nor was it our absence of one. We knew perfectly well we had one, we just didn't quite know what it was. We weren't even insulted that 'they' obviously knew nothing about us; after all, we knew nothing about ourselves."

A kind of rank, hot-house nationalism was a symptom of this phase. "We sufferers would hunt for differences with the minute and random attention of robins on a worm-scarce lawn." That's when the lies were invented about shooting rapids in birch-bark canoes or living with the Eskimos.

The transition to phase three came with the first trip home, when the Canadian adopted "a soggy but supercilious internationalism, somewhat like the country's foreign policy."

At the party, to terminate further conversation, Margaret came up with a non sequitur. "Canada," she would remark to the expectant Canadian Clubber, "is a zipper in a continent of buttons."

As an afterthought in her notebook, she wrote: "Every country has its national mania. The American is megalomaniac and his fear is of subversion from within; the Canadian is paranoid, fearing invasion from without. Every good American believes he is Napoleon, whereas every good Canadian believes every American is Napoleon." "The beaver," she added, "is an animal that spends most of its time constructing earthworks and swampy but protective bomb shelters. It chews off its own testicles when attacked. The eagle, by contrast is a bird of prey."[26]

Of course, in this piece she was trying her hand at satire, but it was typical of Margaret that she was less interested in defending Canada than in unmasking the hypocrisies of both countries. Like a mock scientist, with her satire of pathologies she searched for the symptoms of disease.

Margaret was not the only one to experience this kind of culture shock in her first encounter with the United States. It happened to another young Canadian, the Québécoise writer Marie-Claire Blais. Blais arrived in Cambridge just after Margaret left, and the two did not meet until a few years later. But, for both, coming across American versions of themselves triggered a need to define their own cultural identity.

Marie-Claire Blais arrived in Cambridge on a Guggenheim fellowship grant one sunny afternoon in June 1963. The city was wonderful. Cambridge for her meant bicycling beside the bucolic Charles River, past the morning runners and the cheerful families picnicking on its banks with their dogs, and watching the young boys in red jerseys bobbing mechanically over the water in their racing shells. But in her *American Notebooks: A Writer's Journey*, she described the shock of running into what she characterized as "American insensitivity" in the person of an MIT student. When she told him she was from Canada and had written several novels that had been published in the United States (she was then only twenty-four), he replied that she was very lucky to have a publisher in Boston, because "Canada isn't known in our country, Canada is nothing. Just nothing." In the same imperious tone he added: "What would you be without us, nothing, right, nothing?"[27] Paralysed by shyness and a language she had barely mastered, she could not defend herself. His questions, spoken with such aggressive confidence, inspired only anger.

Observing the layering of classes in Cambridge, Blais would rage against all exploitation, whether in Harvard or in Quebec. And this anger would also be fed by her sense of exclusion as a woman. She had arrived as the protégé of Edmund Wilson, an erudite man with an elegant mind whose some twenty books she could read standing in any Cambridge bookstore, but whose condescension towards women appalled her. He recommended Virginia Woolf's *Orlando* as an avant-garde masterpiece, but added: "the book is all the more surprising because it was written by a woman."[28] She had come to recognize this rigid, smug, proprietorial tone that male critics adopted when talking of women writers.

So it seemed that exclusion as a Canadian fuelled one's sense of exclusion as a woman. Both forced an examination of the reality of power and powerlessness. No doubt this was one of the reasons why Canada produced so many women writers. National identity and gender were both predicated on second-class status. Women didn't have to feel like outsiders to the national culture; they were its definition.

As she was trying to sort out her Canadian nationalism, Margaret found an unexpected source of inspiration. She hadn't studied American literature before and, to fill her gaps, she took Professor Perry Miller's course on American Romanticism. Miller was an audacious, larger-than-life character. He was known to show up for his morning classes already "well-oiled," but he was brilliant and students were devoted to him. (Margaret would dedicate her novel *The Handmaid's Tale* to him, after his death.) In his seminar, she made a number of discoveries.

In the early sixties, a debate was raging in Canada in the small literary magazines about why Canadians suffered from an inferiority complex. Northrop Frye had described Canada as having a "garrison mentality" (an anglophile culture in an alien wilderness) and lamented that the legacy of colonialism was like frostbite withering the culture's creative roots.[29] Propaganda developed that the purpose of literature was to give a national identity to the culture. Why was there no great Canadian literature? Where was the great Canadian novel? There were fierce arguments about whether such a novel would be nativist, or international and eclectic. Young writers believed they had to become great artists. How did one go about being the great Canadian novelist?

Reading Perry Miller's *The Raven and the Whale*, Margaret discovered the Americans, too, had had their own period of colonial insecurity and their search for national identity. *The Democratic Review* of 1849 ran articles on the subject: "Have we national traits sufficiently developed to mark an epoch in literature? We have Negro music and Southwestern tall-tales, but while we do have Niagara Falls, we have no customs or habits of thought peculiar to ourselves."[30] Walt Whitman lamented: "As long as we wait for English critics to stamp our books and authors, before we presume to say they are very good or very bad; as long as British manufactured books are poured over the land . . . as long as an American society, meeting at the social board, starts with wonder to hear any of its national names, or any national sentiment mentioned in the same hour with foreign greatness . . . so long shall we have no literature."[31] With a slight alteration of rhetoric, this could have been a Canadian speaking.

Now Margaret had found a new perspective from which to judge the debate. It was clear that a hot-house nationalism was an inevitable part of the attempts at self-definition that every ex-colonial culture seemed doomed to undergo. It had happened in the United States one hundred years earlier, and Canada was, after all, a century younger.

Margaret believed that a writer must write out of his or her physical and cultural landscape. Canada still had a physical environment out of sync with its cultural development, and the job of the writer was somehow to reconcile this. Landscape and perception had to be welded together in a way that would be indigenously Canadian.

But perhaps the most important insight she derived from Miller's course was his contention that all writing was political, not in the ideological but in the generic sense. "It was a big eye-opener to me," she said.[32] Literature, she discovered, had to do with how people relate to power structures and are shaped by them. Margaret had been brought up in the romantic tradition that claimed literature was self-expression. She now saw that the classics were imbued with political vision; the writer, simply by examining how the forces of society interact with the individual, was seeking to change social structures.

Margaret passed her general exam and was duly awarded her Master's from Radcliffe in the spring of 1962. The degree didn't help her get a job in Toronto that summer. She worked as a cashier in a coffee shop in what is now The Venture Inn on Avenue Road. The cash register kept getting stuck and she spilled the coffee, but she persevered. She needed the money. She was back in Cambridge that fall.

At Harvard Margaret's true focus was always her own writing. Among her early papers are at least a thousand pages of drafts of poems. She was trying multiple forms: rhymes, ballads, pastoral poems, allegories, sometimes using medieval and Greek myths to give them resonance. Everything became a potential subject for poetry, from skating in the morning on Cambridge Common to "A Contemplation of Trunk Murders":

All women can be divided
Into two basic categories
Trunkable
And untrunkable[33]

In a Harvard copybook she also jotted ideas for prose fiction. She might put down a single thought, an anecdote, or a brief conversation. One such note was a paragraph on the mystery of sexual relationships:

It was hard to go to bed with a person. You wanted to go to bed with an idea and you did, but the idea crumpled in your arms; but when you woke up in the morning there was not even a person. There was only a jumbled collection of idiosyncrasies and flesh and hair and fingernails. Then you got away from it as soon as you could.[34]

This was still the early sixties, before the subject became popular, and she was beginning to train her acerbic eye on the dynamic between men and women; she already understood that the bed was the locus of sexual politics.

Her methods often seemed to be a kind of freewheeling play. Thinking about how a novel is structured, she made notes: "dynamic vs static characters; those who learn, those who stay the same."

Snakeman

little girl   old man

dynamic   static

7 days of creation (will have to use nine days)

island (ark)

9 characters/ 9 narrators

Little girl begins with the myths of resistance. . . . She gives in but in 21st [*sic*] she returns to resistance even stronger.

She drew fish and jotted down thought associations: "starfish, moonfish, planetfish, earth fish? He is inside the goldfish bowl. Saturn fish, Venus fish, Mercury fish, Mars fish, Pluto fish, Jupiter fish, Uranus fish."[35]

She was improvising, circling ideas, using all the strength of her imagination to focus.

She needed a rationale, her own aesthetic, to find a place for herself as a woman. If the tradition of writing excluded women, there had to be something wrong with the tradition. In one of her notebooks, she wrote notes for a piece she called "Metaphors for the Poetic Act: Muse vs Malthus," in which she looked at where the poems were coming from.

Up until Milton, she concluded, poetry had appropriated the metaphor of birth. "The poet, impregnated by the muse, gave birth to the poem." He thought of himself as making a contribution to society, much as a woman did bearing children; both were fulfilling a necessary social function. Fertility was the prerequisite and the poem/child a blessing.

The Romantics represented the turning point, and Thomas Malthus (the nineteenth-century essayist who predicted that human populations would exceed the means of subsistence) was the catalyst. In an overcrowded world, the poet became isolated, cut off from everyday society. He began to think of the muse, not as the begetter of the poem, but as the "arouser of the poetic erection that allows for orgasm."

"All modern metaphors for art are orgasmic," Margaret wrote. Sterility and narcissism were its specific modes of expression: "Abstract expressionism. The Beats. The splatter-forms. The artist is sterile, lots of splash, but nothing fully formed, no new human being." She added a crucial coda: "We must not become enslaved by the metaphor and think anything not produced in this pseudo-sexual way is no good."[36]

"We," of course, referred to women in particular. Where, she wanted to know, did the female poet come in? She needed to know. And, characteristically, she confronted the problem head on. She had been through the machismo at the Bohemian Embassy and remembered Layton's assertion that women should not write poetry because they were invading men's territory. She needed to attack the source of the heresy that made writing male. It was an impressive rebellion for a young woman of twenty-two.

From the beginning Margaret wanted to write fiction as well as poetry. Jay Macpherson remembered seeing early drafts of a novel she was writing when she was a student at Vic. Margaret was using her Harvard notebooks, as a writer would, to learn how novels were made. They were composed of factual details, which might come from research, or from one's own life, but the details had to ring true.

She was studying nineteenth-century novels: William Thackeray's *Vanity Fair*, Jane Austen's *Pride and Prejudice*, and George Eliot's *Middlemarch*, and examining their construction. The essential question was how a novel moved in space and time. She made charts and diagrams about the books: cycles of the seasons; of action, psychological and physical; of the interweaving of destinies; of architectures. Where did money come into those novels? she wondered. She noted that Victorian society was one in which everyone had to be paid, yet in which the gentlemanly ideal of doing nothing remained. Manners, etiquette, and deportment were central. And what was the physical environment? There was no electricity, and long-distance transport was by railway, which had just come onto the scene in the 1830s and 1840s. She thought about the women in those books. The way a woman established herself then was through marriage (which meant that the Victorians' prudish morality was really a matter of economics and self-protection). Even the genteel poor had servants. Women, except servants, were not expected to devote themselves full-time to children. The concept of the housewife had not yet been invented. A woman's days consisted of leisurely breakfasts, tea at 5:00, and formal dinners at 8:00 or 9:00. There was no effective birth control, though abortions occurred.

Margaret had begun to see the novel as a vehicle not only for self-expression, but also for social observation. She was not interested in the confessional mode that often characterizes first novels. She would follow the Victorian tradition of the social novel in which she was being trained.

This would always shape the way she saw fiction. She would find it necessary, in order to write about a place, to have actually been there, or at least to a place resembling it. Where she had been, what she had done, would provide the space in which her characters moved, but the characters themselves would be hybrid inventions. In her later fiction, like Alfred Hitchcock she might make a cameo appearance as a kind of private joke. For instance, she was the female graduate student dressed in black who appeared at the party and talked about Death in *The Edible Woman*. "It's an impulse towards whimsy," she explained, like the "Gothic cathedrals where the carvers put imps under the skirts of angels."[37] But her main characters always began as hypotheses: what if? Novels, she concluded early, did not have to be romantic confessions.

In a graduate seminar in the fall of 1962, Margaret met a young man named Jim Polk. He had arrived at Harvard in 1961 as a scholarship student from Miles City, Montana. "I had seen her around," he remembers, "but had been quite put off by her. She seemed extremely bright and conscious of it. She was at the time very oddly dressed, I thought. Lots of curly hair and cat-eye glasses, and she had a sort of fang tooth which she later had chiselled off. She always wore a rust-brown corduroy jumper, and no make-up, and didn't seem to care about anything but English Literature. I would hear her in the hall expounding theories. I thought: This is not for me."

In Jerome Buckley's Alfred, Lord Tennyson seminar, she "seemed a star, giving reports about early Tennyson on this and that," while Polk wondered what he was doing there: "Was Tennyson really worth it?" He had had a devastating first year. His father had died and his family life had disintegrated alarmingly. He had returned to Harvard only because he had thought he might be drafted. (Even in 1962, Vietnam was percolating, and only student exemptions kept the draft board at a safe distance.)

Polk found himself next to Margaret one afternoon as they read Tennyson's narrative poem *Enoch Arden*. Buckley had put him on the spot with a casual "How do you like it?" Polk had turned to Margaret and pointed to a line that said: "A bill of sale gleamed through the gloom." They both got the giggles, shattering the academic decorum.

He soon discovered that the cool, single-minded girl in the brown jumper was a disguise, one of many.

> What I found was a very funny, very quick woman who, on some level, was a kid (as I was) playing with this big toy set called Harvard. I think that Peggy and I got on well because we both considered ourselves savages from bizarre places in the world, and here we were in the middle of the Ivy League Capital of whatever. She was the wild Canadian girl. What she saw in me was this haunted stranger from Montana. She said: "When I heard you were from Montana! Nobody's from Montana." She saw western skies and starlit whatnot. When she said she was from Canada, I saw the same, only colder

and more northern. Harvard was not where either of us should have been. What were we doing in this extremely stuffy, extremely sexist place?

They became very close friends. They went to movies all the time. It was the age of the great black-and-white films, and the Brattle Theater was always running some Fellini or Bergman or Truffaut festival. Margaret had been on her own to Salem, Massachusetts, to visit the Hawthorne museum, and had come back with rubbings from the local tombstones. She was quite proud of them. She was fascinated by the Gothic cast of the New England mind, and, besides, she had an ancestral link to the seaport. Salem was where the witch trials of 1692–93 had taken place. She visited Witch House, the home of Judge Jonathan Corwin, who was a member of the court who had condemned nineteen people to death. She and Jim returned to Salem, and went up to New York when they could to visit the art galleries and see the shows. "For graduate students, we goofed off quite a bit," Jim remarks. He remembers long walks along the Charles River and making snowmen on the Common (one was of Queen Victoria). On a visit to the Museum of Man, he remembers Margaret being fascinated by "The Illuminated Woman." It was a plastic mock-up of a female body. You pressed a button and her various organs individually lit up. For Jim, it was Atwood country.

Jim was living with two room-mates from the Deep South, one a D.H. Lawrence expert and the other a T.S. Eliot expert. Margaret, they thought, was "a disaster." "In the opinion of Southern gentlemen, women were supposed to know their place, carry parasols and so on, but she had opinions and was so definite about her tastes and needs." His room-mates did come round, though never entirely. But Margaret got her own back. Jim recognizes them, transformed into Canadians, as minor characters in The Edible Woman. "Duncan was based on me," he remarks, "although I did have a little more going for me than Duncan. I did go to the laundromat a lot, and I did watch the clothes go round and round." Jim likes the idea that Duncan is a bit farouche, a bit wild and shy, as Jay Macpherson called him. But the portrait was never intended to be factual. Rather, Duncan serves as an amusing caricature of a graduate student in a novel that was satirizing, among other things, intellectual consumption. The idea that people might read fiction as autobiography seems to have come as a surprise to him. When he published his own novel, *The Passion of Laureen Bright Weasel*, in 1981, he was dumbfounded to discover that what he had intended as a comic romp through a small Montana town was assumed to be based on fact. One of the locals from his home town of Miles City made charts listing the people he thought were in it. One person even told him he'd bought more than one copy in order to cross-check so that he didn't miss anything.[38]

Because Margaret was still engaged to Jay Ford, whom she had met when he was a philosophy major at the University of Toronto, there was little question of the relationship between her and Jim getting more serious. They remained friends. Jim remembers the delight they took in making fun of Margaret's graduate residence, Founders' House, which seemed to be run like a rigid theocracy. In the hot-house atmosphere, where women were living together, trapped in the tension of the academic regimen, jokes about Women and Bondage came easily. (Jim would say that, when he came to read Margaret's *The Handmaid's Tale*, with its harem of women, he thought back to Founders' House.)

To lighten things up, Margaret and Jim gave a costume party at Founders' House, which they announced as a Roman orgy. Margaret came as Cleopatra's breast, wearing a bird cage covered in a flesh-coloured towel, while Jim came as the asp. He also remembers the iguana that lived under her bed in the residence. She had inherited it from some biological experiment gone awry. It was ejected from the house after the maid who discovered it had a mild heart attack.

When Jim learned that Margaret was a poet, never having met one before, he was delighted. She started showing him the magazine *Alphabet*, and he was impressed, particularly by the work of Eli Mandel and Jay Macpherson.

He'd always thought Canada was a bit superior. In Montana, he'd been able to listen to the opera on CBC Regina, which also aired live dramas such as *Brave New World*. Listening to "Anthology" in the middle of barndance music and "Grand Ole Opry" had already convinced him that Canada had a sophisticated literary culture.

Margaret had begun to publish in Canada with some frequency. Luella Booth, a friend from the Embassy, wrote in January 1962 that she had been invited to be a guest editor of a special issue of *Evidence*. She was in charge of the women poets, who had been assigned sixteen pages, which, she commented ironically, was "fair" for the ladies. That same March, Fred Cogswell of *Fiddlehead* agreed to publish "The Siamese Twins." *Tamarack Review* accepted "What Happened to the Idiot Boy" and "The Cold Philosopher," and *Alphabet* and *The Canadian Forum* were taking poems. Later, in 1963, twenty poems under the title "Gorgons and Idiots" were broadcast by CBC Radio. Margaret wrote to Charlie that the poetry business was flourishing and the markets were good, adding that she had his paintings up on her wall and everyone was commenting on how good they were. One of these days he would be rich and famous, and she'd write him an ode.

Each of the previous four years, she had put together a collection of her poems and submitted it; each year, to her dismay, and then relief, it was turned down. She once explained that she was so eager to publish because, like all poets in their early twenties, she thought she would be dead by thirty.

There's a notable evolution in these Harvard poems as Margaret became increasingly assured of her own voice. She was learning how to bring her mythologies and her sideways vision into the present. She was discovering that the trolls under the bridge and the terrors they evoked had human faces.

In June 1962, the infamous Boston Strangler had begun to terrorize Boston and Cambridge. His signature was always to leave the instrument with which he'd strangled his victim, usually a stocking, tied neatly in a bow. Frightened women emptied the dog pounds of Boston and raided the locksmiths' shops. By July, the Strangler had already killed his first four victims. His eighth victim, a twenty-three-year-old student from Cambridge, was murdered in late spring 1963, just as Margaret was preparing to return to Canada.

Because of the new pervasiveness of television, the Boston Strangler was the first in the long line of media-hyped serial killers who have become common fare today. Terror spread far beyond the local boundaries of where he stalked his prey. All women knew of the Strangler. Finally, after he'd killed thirteen women, he was apprehended for molestation in another city, where he'd gained the moniker "the Green Man," presumably from the green maintenance uniform he wore. Forensic experts had profiled the Boston Strangler as an unmarried paranoid schizophrenic, or possibly a homosexual. It turned out he was a mild-mannered family man from the suburbs who'd gained entrance into women's apartments posing as a maintenance worker. He was convicted in 1967 as the Green Man and given a life sentence, but he was never tried as the Strangler. Finally, in 1973, he was stabbed to death in his cell for selling speed below the market price.

Margaret was fascinated less by him than by a society that could have produced him. She wrote several poems to him, including "The Green Man," in which she wondered what no-face he had that women never recognized him in advance. But her most intriguing poem on the subject was "The Cliff Dwellers in the Heart of the City," though she never published it. She did not feel it was good enough to be included in her first collection, *The Circle Game*, which would come out in 1966.

Because they have fear
the streets are no longer safe:
something carnivorous has come
from the forest, attracted
by the smell of panic.

Even in our apartment
courtyard, where there used to be
peacocks and a moat with goldfish
we have discovered wolverine
footprints in the flowerbeds, and
yesterday
we found the last peacock
with its throat cut.

(When the woman screamed
we didn't even
turn on the lights, but lay pretending
to be asleep, waiting for her
to die or go away.)

In the mornings we find
blood on the sidewalk, smashed bottles
gleaming in sunlight,
vomit in the pond (the goldfish
floating bellyup among the
lilies), occasionally
a collapsed white rubber
finger or two (indicating
that the scuffle in the dark
was love, not murder).

The janitor cleans the sidewalk
shaking his head as he collects
the glass and goldfish; we
ask him to check the locks

but with all that
spilled red fear
poisoning the plant-
roots, who can repair our gardens?

It is the victims' fault, we say;
their terror makes it
happen;
if only they
were fearless as angels, how
freely we could walk, we say
cowering behind the drawn
venetian blinds
and safe cement-block tenth-floor-up
walls, clenching our teeth till dawn.[39]

There were other fears that winter of 1962. At Harvard, the steam
tunnels that threaded the bowels of the campus were stocked with food,
and the campus was dotted with new orange-coloured signs indicating the
location of bomb shelters. The Cuban Missile Crisis brought the world

within a hair's breadth of nuclear war. Margaret remembered huddling in the front parlour of Founders' House on Appian Way, drinking tea and wondering whether the world was about to end.

From October to December, television pundits deployed maps, first showing a flotilla of Soviet warships winding its way through the Caribbean Sea, and then President Kennedy's blockade of Cuba.

It is difficult, today, to tap the dead weight of fear the crisis produced. Fear doesn't travel well. What terrifies one generation is likely to bring only puzzlement to the next. During those several months, people really did feel that the end might come. On 2 December, a deal was finally brokered, and the Soviets withdrew their warheads. A writer's mind is like a palimpsest. One layer in Margaret's, certainly confirmed by her experience at Harvard, would be her rage at humanity's lust for violence.

Margaret headed home in the summer of 1963. She'd run out of money and needed a job. In Toronto, she felt she could find the time and space she needed for her own writing.

She would come back to Harvard to continue her doctorate, but the Harvard she knew would be gone. A few months after she left, President Kennedy was assassinated and the old political and moral reality that Harvard personified melted, as one journalist put it, "like a Dali watch." Kennedy had been Harvard's man, and his loss was felt like a personal blow. For many "the sixties" began on that 22 November in 1963, in Dallas.[40]

In retrospect, Margaret could say she enjoyed Harvard in a nervous sort of way. It was "like anchovies, an acquired taste. But in my case, one that I could never truly acquire."[41] She had enjoyed its libraries, its professors, and its eccentrics, like the man rumoured to have broken into the Houghton Rare Book Library in order to expose himself to the Gutenberg Bible. But she also recognized that Harvard was very important. It was the place where she started thinking of Canada as a country with a shape and a culture of its own. And it was the place where she discovered that writing was a political act, the assertion of the individual against the social structures that confine.

8

"A DESCENT THROUGH THE CARPET"

When Margaret returned to Toronto that summer of 1963, she began to look for work. She was pursuing the fantasy that she could find some menial and mindless, though lucrative, day job, while she worked at her art in her garret at night. She applied to the Publicity and Promotion Department of Oxford University Press, McClelland and Stewart, and Bell Telephone, but was rejected by all three on the grounds that she was overqualified. She would later say that this produced in her "that state of joblessness, angst and cosmic depression which everyone knows is indispensable for novelists and poets, although nobody has ever claimed the same for geologists, dentists or chartered accountants."[1] Her irritation came from the fact that in her application she had made the mistake of saying she wanted to be a writer. She could be witty about this in retrospect, but at the time she was flat broke. "Living on a diet of coffee and fingernails," she desperately scanned the daily "help wanted" ads in The Globe and Mail.

When she was finally hired by Canadian Facts, a Toronto market-research company that farmed out and collected interviews on clients' products, she was grateful. Her job was to read the questionnaires "concocted," as she put it, "by the shrinks higher up in the totem pole, and render them grammatical and comprehensible."[2] This meant that she sometimes had to go out onto the streets and walk her way through those questionnaires to determine whether they worked, since the questions had to be shrewd enough to ensure that the intended respondent/housewife wouldn't slam the door in the market researcher's face. Margaret concluded that the woman in charge of the researchers, Mary Sims, had hired her because she thought she was off-beat and eccentric, and might "juice things up." Soon after Margaret got the job, one of her tasks was making a wax voodoo doll of the company's Montreal branch manager that could be stuck with pins every time he got obstreperous. Sims thought this effective therapy. She asked to read Margaret's poetry.

Market research was a perfect job for Margaret at this time. One of her gifts as a writer is her capacity never to lose sight of what is usually called "the real world." Fresh from six years of academia, she plunged into the loony side of the business world and, beneath its staid conformity, discovered its absurdist aspect. And she found the craziness enchanting. She participated in the first Pop-Tart test, in which housewives were sent Pop-Tarts and the requisite questionnaires. The Pop-Tarts exploded and toasters had to be replaced. She was also involved in the test for canned rice pudding and the bran-breakfast-cereal-with-raisins test. The flies that had gotten into the cereal boxes along with the raisins were sent back in the mail.

Margaret was trying to fit into this world, but not quite pulling it off. She kept her hair in the then fashionable bubble cut, an effect created by using monstrous wire rollers each night (though, because her hair was curly, the results were often questionable). She still wore her horn-rimmed glasses, and bought the clothes she thought a business girl would wear. The effect was not quite what she had in mind. One of her fellow office workers remarked: "I don't think the new girl is very bright."

At her desk, with phone and typewriter, she could complete the day's assignment in record time. Even when she dawdled, she couldn't stretch it out, and she would then slip her manuscript into her typewriter and work on her novel. At lunch or coffee break, she could indulge her amusement in office gossip. Her gift for empathic listening, indispensable to all novelists, drew the personal stories her way. Someone told her about the Underwear Man, an individual who used the company's name to phone women, saying he was doing market research in lingerie. When his questions got increasingly intimate, the enraged women would phone the company, and Mary Sims would have to explain he was not an employee.[3] Market research would prove wonderful material when Margaret was ready to use it in her first published novel, *The Edible Woman*.

Years later, invited to give the after-dinner speech to advertising executives, she told her business audience that, if they wanted to discourage artists like her from turning their companies into fiction, they could keep them out of their offices by supporting grants for writers.[4]

Living in a small rented cupboard in a rooming house on Charles Street, cooking on a one-burner hotplate and storing her macaroni and cheese in a dresser drawer, Margaret was working on her novel and writing short stories (she wrote "The War in the Bathroom" at this time). She worked at night, directing the light over the desk. She used to say she felt like a literary dental surgeon. The novel in manuscript was *Up in the Air So Blue*. Set in a modern city, it was about young people finding their lives were circumscribed in various ways. At the end, the heroine is in a swing, suspended ambiguously. Margaret would later joke about it as a "document of unrelieved gloom which ends with the heroine trying to decide whether or not to push one of the male protagonists off a roof."[5] She had *Up in the Air So Blue* finished by May 1964.

Margaret sent Jim Polk the manuscript. He, too, had run out of money and had left Harvard to return to Miles City, Montana, the previous summer. Almost as soon as he arrived home, his draft-board rep sprang on him in the street and asked when he was planning to serve Uncle Sam. He replied that he had a teaching job and, by pure luck, did find one at Idaho State University, in Pocatello. This gave him a year's grace. He spent it teaching seven hundred hours of English composition, which, in fact, he thoroughly enjoyed.

Polk was impressed by *Up in the Air So Blue*: "It was so haunting to me, her vision of a surreal city where you look down and everything seems drowned in those ravines; at eye level, you see the tops of trees."[6] He suggested to Margaret that she consider identifying the city as Toronto, though she hesitated, thinking perhaps that the city should remain unnamed, unreal.

She sent the novel to the New York publisher Abelard-Schuman, and waited. The reply came in August from the associate editor, Kay Grant: "Your book simply fascinated me, as a mood piece and for the story; but I'm afraid we're not going to be able to use it. . . . There is so much good writing in it, and the underlying idea is so good, that I can't resist trying to tell you what I think it needs." What it needed was greater character development. Grant wrote encouragingly: "I hope we shall hear from you again."[7]

The Canadian publisher she sent it to, Clarke, Irwin & Company, was more officious. They sent a synopsis of the readers' reports, which were almost uniformly dismissive. One reader's report was précised with a single line: "The use of the continuous present throughout the story is particularly irritating."[8]

A fascinating proposal did come her way. The Canadian composer John Beckwith was commissioned by the CBC to write a piece of music for the quatercentenary of William Shakespeare's birth. He agreed to the commission as long as the text did not have to be by Shakespeare. He could see no point to a new setting of "Where the Bee Sucks." He had a chat with Jay Macpherson, who had just collaborated with him on a cantata called *Jonah*, and Jay suggested she had a brilliant young colleague called Margaret Atwood who might be interested. The three of them talked, and in two weeks Margaret had a first draft ready. The piece, twenty minutes long, was called *The Trumpets of Summer* and had its first performance in November with the Montreal Bach Choir and Le Petit Ensemble Vocal, under conductor George Little. Margaret got $150 for the commission. It must have seemed like a fortune.[9]

Leaving behind her novel and a rejected poetry manuscript, Margaret quit her job in order to make the mandatory pilgrimage to Europe. Charlie had just returned from a year in Paris, studying French and Art History at the Académie de la Grande Chaumière in Montparnasse, and was pressuring her to go. Besides, the trip was something every student did in those days, setting out with a copy of *Europe on Five Dollars a Day* and a Eurailpass, suitcase in tow (backpacks had not yet been invented). She borrowed $600 from her parents and, on 13 May, boarded a plane for England. Earlier that year a psychic in a tea shop had read her cards and told her she would be in Europe in May. "No, I won't," she had said, but there she was.[10]

Her life, she said, was of "Gordian complexity." Her parents were (understandably, she felt) increasingly uneasy about her impecunious status as a writer. She had ended her engagement to Jay Ford, which hadn't been easy. Jim Polk explained: "The break-up took a long time, and is part of *The Edible Woman*."[11] Margaret decided "the viewing of various significant pieces of architecture" would improve her soul, "would fill in a few potholes in it."[12]

She had three months ahead of her. The England she encountered on her budget had a "Graham Greene" kind of tawdriness: rooms-to-let in

Victorian row houses, gas heaters fed with endless shillings, cold water, dingy furniture, and clammy bed sheets. The English in the early sixties knew nothing about the culinary arts, and restaurant food was mainly eggs with bangers and peas, or fish and chips. Undaunted, she set out in her grey-flannel jumper and suede Hush Puppies to get some culture.

In those days, student travellers went to Canada House on Trafalgar Square to read the Canadian newspapers, and found their fellow ex-pats in the local pubs. Luckily, Margaret learned that a Toronto friend, Alison Cunningham, was in London studying dance and living in a flat in South Kensington. Against the rules of Lord Cork and Lady Hoare, who owned the flat, Alison offered her a bed. Occasionally, though, she had to disappear for a few days on her rail pass to maintain the pretense that she had not taken up residence there.

Her tourist itinerary was the one every aspiring young writer from the colonies followed: Dickens's London, the Lake District, the Brontës' Heath. Her eye, though, was original. She liked the Brontës' gloves and shoes. They were child-sized, and reassuring: she, too, was of tiny stature. Of all the places she visited, she liked Stonehenge best because, as she described it, it was "pre-rational, and pre-British, and geological. Nobody knew how it had arrived where it was, or why, or why it had continued to exist, but there it sat, challenging gravity, defying analysis."[13] She was the daughter of a scientist and knew about the geology of stones, but she always preferred their mystery.

At the end of his teaching stint in Pocatello, Jim had headed off with his current girlfriend to England. She had gotten him involved in an archaeological dig at Winchester Cathedral as part of a college course through the University of North Carolina. He remembers the dig as a disaster. "I found myself in a trench all day, and then I went back to an abandoned army base and ate bad English food. I never knew what we were looking for and, as it turned out, we were working in the wrong excavation. They found the Roman baths farther away, and the medieval stuff even farther, and it was endless labour. Maybe I was naïve about what a dig was, but I certainly found out what it wasn't."

He broke with his girlfriend and, much to the displeasure of the archaeologists, left the dig. He went to London to see Margaret and they decided to do the youth-hostel tour of the sites of England. They mostly ended up in odd places like Clacton-on-Sea and Walton-on-the-Naze, quaint British bathing towns with tea shops that overcharged. Their England was comic rather than sublime, though that also suited their temperaments.

Along with Alison, they decided to visit France. They hiked dutifully to Notre Dame and the Eiffel Tower and did the Louvre (Margaret liked Rouault), saw the mime artist Marcel Marceau, and rented a car to visit the *châteaux* in the Loire Valley. They stayed in cheap *pensions*, the kind with paper-thin walls and light switches that turned themselves off before you got up the stairs. On their subsistence fare of baguettes, cheese, and oranges, Margaret got dysentery. As she lay moaning on a park bench, Alison read her Doris Lessing's *The Golden Notebook*. Of course, they loved it all. Paris was wonderful, like a novel by Proust.

Alison had to return to England, and Margaret and Jim journeyed on to Luxembourg. "Where we broke up," as Polk puts it laconically. "Whatever it was we were doing and being together, she was going back to Canada and, for some reason, we weren't ever going to do this any more. I was going on to Vienna to improve my German. Who knew what we were doing when we were young?

"We parted forever in the Luxembourg train station. I remember it as a huge, early upper-High-German construct, a gloomy place, and it was then that Peggy began "The Circle Game." Later, she told me. 'I had to make your eyes blue because they had to be like thumbtacks, but they're not. The man is not really you, but a combination of people.'" Polk recognized a lot in the poem. games on hillsides, paper-thin hotel walls, the single sweater drying on a towel (who had two dimes to rub together?). For him the poem was a moving and accurate portrait of the end of an affair. And of course not just their personal affair, but one highly compounded and transformed.

Jim, too, headed back. He had tried Vienna and Denmark, but Europe was too expensive. He secured a place at Harvard for the fall to continue his PhD. "All roads kept leading back to Harvard," he remarks, "in part because I was draftable."

The previous fall, Margaret had applied for a position as a lecturer at the University of British Columbia, and much to her astonishment she had gotten the job. As she prepared to set off for Vancouver, she visited the poet Doug Jones at his summer cottage on Paudash Lake, near Bancroft, Ontario.

Doug Jones, a fine poet, was a professor at Bishop's University in Lennoxville, Quebec, and then at the Université de Sherbrooke. He was ten years older than Margaret. As a student, she had reviewed his second collection, *The Sun Is Axeman*, for *Acta Victoriana*, describing it as having a wonderful feeling of space, a "summer" book. They had become friends. Jones was an original, handsome in a lean athletic way which also managed to be aesthetic: one could imagine him leaning against a tree in a David Milne landscape, with a provocative air of humour and a slight whiff of decadence. He was one of the few Canadian poets who crossed cultural lines and wrote in English and French. Women were intrigued by him, and, obviously, Margaret was too.

There were other guests at the cottage: the poet Al Purdy and his wife, Eurithe. It was the first time Margaret and Purdy met, and the meeting made such an impression on him that he later called it the "Atwood–Purdy incident."

When Doug Jones returned from the train station with Margaret, Purdy was a bit nonplussed: "A small girl, wearing horned-rimmed glasses for what I presumed was short-sightedness, she could have seemed mouse-like. I hasten to add she was not mouselike. Her personality was electric."[14]

As they sat by the lake, drinking beer and discussing Shakespeare as a vaudevillian comedian at the Mermaid Theatre, Purdy managed to provoke Margaret (he liked to provoke) by referring to her as an academic. She detested the label. She grabbed her beer, shook it vigorously, and aimed it directly in his face. A beer-swizzling fight ensued, and both ended up in the lake, with Doug and Eurithe watching bemused from the sidelines.

They would become good friends. Purdy always included Margaret on his short list of important Canadian poets, though he would continue with his provocative assessment that she was too intellectual (he liked to call her "Intellectual Lady"). She, on the other hand, saw him as a permanent fact of the literary landscape, a kind of escarpment, jagged and impressive. He was well on the way to becoming acknowledged as one of Canada's finest poets. One might say that, between them, they changed the shape of Canadian writing.

There would always be an element of self-parody in Purdy's public persona. It might have been that poets of his generation (he was twenty-one years older than she), coming as they did from a colonial context unused to poets, felt the need to prove they weren't fey, that they were men's men. Or it might simply have been the pressure to conform to the requisite Henry Miller model of the writer in those days. Purdy was a hard drinker. He was known to keep down the page of his book at a poetry reading by placing his foot on it, which often involved considerable acrobatic skill if the podium was tall. The gesture implied that he was not precious, that poetry was not cut off from mud and footwear. Beneath the bravura and rough exterior, Margaret saw the gifted writer and the intelligent and perceptive man. She would later sign one of her books for him: "To Awful Al from Perfect Peggy."[15]

It had been a year of consequence for Doug Jones and his family. His marriage had disintegrated earlier. He was attracted to Margaret, whose good humour might have been exactly what he needed to get him through.

Margaret wrote to Jim about her visit. Although they had split up and it was, ostensibly, all over, neither Jim nor she would forgo the friendship. As Polk put it, "Our letters continued over the year, a 'roman' in letters." Margaret set out for the University of British Columbia.[16]

She found an apartment on the top floor of a house at 3886 West 11th Avenue. It was a large place, with a living room and two bedrooms, one of which she used as a study. Most important, it had a spectacular view of the city and bay, with the mountains looming in the background. She scoured the shops for cheap furnishings. A friend found her a marvellous old-fashioned barber's chair in a junk shop, and she bought the requisite fifty-cent frying pan and seventy-five-cent tea kettle for her kitchen collection. She wrote to Charlie Pachter that she wished he were there to help her decorate. The wallpaper was grotesque, and the bathroom was done in mauve and haemorrhoid pink. "I have a satin green bedspread that just demands black satin negligées split to the navel," she joked.[17] Charlie responded that, if she wanted to cover the haemorrhoid pink, she could do it in "Yellow Pages Provincial." She could just get some wallpaper paste, cut up the Yellow Pages into squares, jumble them up, and lay them side to side on the wall. "The effect is quite surprising, in fact, astonishing. You'll never be the same."[18]

The beauty of Vancouver immediately overwhelmed her. She found it a "strange, raw, unfinished, slightly hallucinatory" city. "I like it," she told him, "but it constantly escapes me."[19] The mountains, however, were worth everything. The university was turning out to be fine, and the students more responsive than she expected. She was teaching grammar in a Quonset hut to engineering students at eight-thirty in the morning, and the early schedule gave her plenty of time for her own writing. She made the engineers write imitations of Kafka, which, she told them, might help them in their chosen profession.[20]

People were friendly. She met chums of Charlie's called Larry (who wore cowboy boots and owned a Hudson Superjet) and Steve (a painter who kept a pet monkey). For Steve's birthday, she and Larry bought him a giant fungus and a fifteen-pound birthday watermelon, which they covered with candles. She became friends with many of the West Coast artists and writers: Takao Tanabe, Roy Kiyooka, Jane Rule, and George and Angela Bowering. Through Jane Rule, she found herself a literary agent with the British firm of John Farquharson in London, which she hoped might sell her novel. It was a relief to hand over the confusing business of selling her work to an agent. At the time, of course, there were no Canadian agents looking to take up young writers.

Margaret found it wonderful living on the ocean. One of the first things she did on arrival was to go down to the beach and dip her hand in the Pacific. The university had its own beach out on a point reached by a long precipitous climb down through scrub and trees. She described the spectacular beauty of that walk to Al Purdy:

> Last week it was really blowing & about 10 pm I and friend took off to the university beach: . . . pitch-black path for a long time; fitful moon, high wind, a few lurid stars, and the sea coming in like hell. We walked & walked, past an old bunker built during the war; lighthouse flashing across the bay. Really it was like the end of the world. There just didn't seem to be any place at all one could go from there. Just walking & walking between the cliffs & the sea.[21]

It was usually the drama of the landscape that caught Margaret. With friends she went skiing in the mountains above Vancouver as often as she could. She described to Purdy the eerie experience of skiing in fog, the landscape effaced by white on white, and then the fog settling just enough to bare the tops of the peaks. The fear, and possibly exhilaration, of moments like these, when the self fractures and disappears, seemed to hold endless fascination for her.

She walked Vancouver and came to know it well. It was still a provincial city and seemingly empty, but it was a good time to be there. As the last stop of the cultural escapees in their flight west, Vancouver had always had an off-beat feel, but now a literary revolution was just beginning. Small magazines seemed to be sprouting up out of nowhere. *blewointment*, one of the most experimental, had come out with its first issue in October 1963.

bill bissett and his friends Lance Farrell and Robert Sutherland tramped the damp rainy streets of the Kitsilano district of Vancouver, frustrated because there was no place to publish their poems. And so they decided to do it themselves. Riffling through the dictionary in search of a name, they stopped at "blue ointment." They liked it. It sounded medicinal and medieval; the story would circulate that it referred to a Victorian cure for venereal crabs. Starting with a Gestetner, they eventually got hold of an old 1903 A.B. Dick mimeo machine, and cranked out the pages. Sometimes their paper stock was liberated from the garbage out behind the local printing shop.

bill was one of Canada's first literary hippies. He had left his home town of Halifax in the late 1950s and hitchhiked across the country to "escape Western civilization." Living communally in a cold-water house, unheated except for the sawdust burner in the basement and a fireplace where they burned parts of the neighbouring houses, bill and his friends set about "changing modern consciousness." They wanted to break out of all the boxes and cages. With the Dadaist impulse in their bones, they followed the new fad of reinventing orthography: *blewointment* dropped capitals and played games with words and spelling "to let th pome b a map for th mood statement show n tell uv feeling."[22]

The psychedelic movement that Timothy Leary had started at Harvard in 1963 was filtering up to Canada, and bill soon acquired its trappings: the Volkswagen van, the pot, and the parole officer. He would make his way through the sixties by occasional ditch digging, picking beans in Arizona and Mexico, and staring at the sea. Vancouver was not happy to be the venue of the new psychedelic consciousness, and bill bissett soon found himself harassed by police and in and out of court for possession of the herb.

He was accused of everything from political subversion to pornography (he had, in fact, never written any, but thought the form might be interesting). Those were the days when confrontational politics were just beginning. Readings started everywhere, and clubs mushroomed: the Advance Mattress coffee house on 10th Avenue, the Trots Hall behind Vanguard Books on Granville Street, and the Flat Five Jazz Club. By 1965, there were open-air readings on the hills near Vancouver, raising money for poetry presses. *blewointment* would last for two decades. In its heyday, the mid-sixties, it was zany, experimental, and always open to new stuff. You could find anything in it: pages torn from other magazines and interleaved at random, making each copy unique. Sometimes you even might find a small square of wood bound into the magazine's spine, presumably a gesture of gratitude to trees.

A native of Vancouver, the poet bp Nichol explained why so esoteric a figure as bill would have such a profound impact. When he first read bill bissett's work in *blewointment*, he realized two things: (1) that bill had no antecedents; he was completely himself, going in his own direction. And (2) that it was a Canadian who was doing this. "I didn't have to go gazing south of the border or across the sea for that hit of adrenaline that really new writing gives you. It was happening right there in the first issue."[23] bill made it clear that it was time to create a native, home-grown writing scene. bp took bill's revolution east in 1964, starting Ganglia Press and the GrOnk series of pamphlets, and at the end of the decade making sound-poetry with the group the Four Horsemen.

By 1964, while Margaret was in Vancouver, the experimental mags were finally getting their wings, and the scene was exciting. In addition to *blewointment*, there was *TISH*, started by George Bowering, Frank Davey, and Fred Wah in 1961. It billed itself as the avant-garde magazine devoted to "right" writing, not the "aw-shucks Canadian thing." And, in 1964, there was *Imago*, Bowering's solo effort. Small presses sprang up, like Patrick Lane's Very Stone House, and later, in 1967, David Robinson's Talonbooks. The small magazine wars that developed between the West Coast and the East (by which was meant Toronto) made things colourful.

blewointment appealed to Margaret's sense of fun, and she published several poems in it. In 1966, she reviewed the magazine: "It expresses its region [the West Coast] and its own point of view while managing an astonishing range and flexibility. It can print poetry so awful you'd have to be high to appreciate it, and poems so good they create their own high." She affectionately referred to its editor as the "polyinspirational Bill Bissett."[24] One of the first of the poems in her sequence *Power Politics* appeared there, as well as, over time, a number of her drawings. Pushing from behind, all this energy was a catalyst for her own writing. She was quickly invited to be part of the scene.

Those first months in Vancouver, she was writing at full tilt. She'd sit down to revise and retype the old stuff and would find herself producing new poems. "It's getting to be a bore; how do I turn off?" she asked Charlie.[25]

She was writing poems about family. Sometimes, when she thought about it, she believed the function of coming to another city was to "fortify" oneself through anonymity, evading the known expectations of family. She knew she had to leave behind that benevolent family if she were to write. They had the ability to keep the world at a distance — her mother with her admirable code of optimism and backbone, her father with his scientific commitment to reason — but that ethic was not where the poems came from. In her poems, she began to play obsessively with the metaphor of underness, the plunge downward into the psyche. The point was "how to get down where it hurts without feeling self-pity."

She could imagine being stretched out on her carpet, looking out at the bay, and almost like a hypnotic trance the process would take over. And she wrote poems like "A Descent through the Carpet." The sea water became like "depthless glass," while the patterned living-room carpet, with its brittle fronds and petals, invited penetration:

> . . .
> It makes the sea
> accessible
> as I stretch out with these
> convoluted gardens
> at eyelevel,
> > the sun
> filtering down through the windows
> of this housetop aquarium

and in the green halflight
I drift down past the
marginal orchards . . .[26]

Down beneath, in the undercarpet world, beneath the human, reptilian brain, she confronted fear, what she called the "cold jeweled symmetries / of the voracious eater / the voracious eaten."

She was drawn compulsively by the discovery that the false part of life happens openly, while, underneath, the unappeasable needs in the self lie hidden and unspoken. She was working on a book that she would call *The Circle Game*. Metaphors of underness are threaded through it. Each house recoils from its cellar; each life from its own darkness. Life performs its strange dance between the feeling of threat and the need for refuge.

The poems of *The Circle Game* accumulated: "This is a Photograph of Me," a poem describing a photograph in which she is the drowned body under the surface of the lake, threatening to devastate the gentle landscape once she is discovered; "In My Ravines," a poem to her childhood ravines, in which old men, the world's homeless, dream "of slaughter," "of (impossible) flight." In "Man with a Hook," a man recounts how he blew his arm off making a bomb to destroy the robins on his lawn; "glittering like a fanatic," he says his hook is an improvement over the human instrument. It can hold fire.

It is a mad, tense world she discovered, one that holds so desperately to an artificial order that it seems about to explode. In this world people are fed on myths "like tapeworms." A simple drive through a pleasant Vancouver suburb on an August afternoon becomes a nightmare vision:

> . . .
> But though the driveways neatly
> sidestep hysteria
> by being even, the roofs all display
> the same slant of avoidance to the hot sky,
> certain things;
> the smell of spilled oil a faint
> sickness lingering in the garages,
> a splash of paint on brick surprising as a bruise,

a plastic hose poised in a vicious
coil; even the too-fixed stare of the wide windows

give momentary access to
the landscape behind or under
the future cracks in the plaster

when the houses, capsized, will slide
obliquely into clay seas, gradual as glaciers
that right now nobody notices. . . .[27]

She had seen enough of voyeurs, and the mentality of war and bomb shelters, to know that the prim suburban reality was a camouflage. But it was also anti-human, since the human includes strange appetites, the acknowledgement of death, and the recognition of time's relentlessness. To hide the truth so absolutely was to allow it too much sting when it inevitably invaded. In that world, she is the outsider, itinerant, her own life a train station, and she is "hunched on the edge of a tensed suitcase." The world is turning her into evening and she lives "on all the edges there are."[28]

But there were also the love poems. Poems are not mere autobiography. The "I" in a poem is a fiction, compounded from various emotions, various selves, and various experiences beyond the self. Still, Margaret was now becoming increasingly involved with Doug Jones. They corresponded. In December she was going to visit him in Quebec.

With that clarity of vision that was her gift, Margaret began to look at the nature of love. What the world called love was a sanitized myth, a romance of treacle. Paraded above the streets in billboard advertisements, the body, both male and female, was sold as a cardboard perfection. People look for this ideal in the real world of flesh. Meanwhile men and women remain separated by "sheer cavernous inches of air."

And what is the truth? In a poem titled "A Meal," Margaret describes what we all know something about: the voraciousness of love.

. . .

but something is hiding
somewhere

in the scrubbed bare
cupboard of my body
flattening itself
against a shelf
and feeding
on other people's leavings

a furtive insect, sly and primitive
the necessary cockroach
in the flesh
that nests in dust.

It will sidle out
when the lights have all gone off
in this bright room . . .

: how it gorges on a few
unintentional
spilled crumbs of love[29]

She created a symbol for this hunger, the sibyl in the self: "with her safely bottled / anguish and her glass / despair."[30]
But there are tender poems that describe the sinking into love:

Again so I subside
nudged by the softening
driftwood of your body
tangle on you like a water-
weed caught
on a submerged treelimb

with sleep like a swamp
growing, closing around me
sending its tendrils through the brown
sediments of darkness
where we   transmuted   are

part of this warm rotting
of vegetable flesh
this quiet spawning of roots

released
from the lucidities of day . . .[31]

Margaret needed a new language for the affirmation of love. By conjuring up the swamp world of her childhood, she caught perfectly that sinking into the other in the timeless darkness of erotic love where new life spawns. And we wake from this, newly shocked at our separateness. In the world of daylight, she wanted to know the other, not to be exiled to the guarded surface. "There are mountains / inside your skull," she wrote, "gardens and chaos, ocean / and hurricane; certain / corners of rooms . . . your deserts; your private / dinosaurs; the first / woman."[32]

The title "Letters, Towards and Away" catches perfectly the way we are all tentative before the profound exposure of love: are we courageous enough to be known?

i)

It is not available to us
it
is not available, I said
closing my hours against you.

I live in a universe
mostly paper.
I make tents
from cancelled stamps.

Letters
are permitted but
don't touch me, I'd
crumple

I said

everything depends on you

staying away.
. . .

v)

You collapse my house of cards
merely by breathing

making other places
with your hands on wood, your
feet on sand

creating with such
generosity, mountains, distances
empty beach and rocks and sunlight
as you walk
so calmly into the sea

and returning, you
taste of salt,

and put together my own
body, another

place

for me to live
in.
. . .

vii)

. . .
Now
I'm roofless:

the sky
you built for me is too
open.

Quickly,
send me some more letters.[33]

As a writer, she lived in a universe of paper. Another's entry into that world would change it. And yet, like everyone, she wanted love. Perhaps the difficulty for her was that she saw things too clearly to be able to talk herself into them.

Margaret was thinking seriously about a relationship with Doug Jones, but the difference between her and, say, her friend Gwen was that she was willing to weigh what was at stake. After the disintegration of her marriage to Milton Acorn, Gwen was courting passion, the tortuous love affair with the demon lover. At about this time she was involved in the painful break-up of a two-year relationship with a strange painter called Bob Mallory who was famous on Toronto Island for his séances with candles and organ music, and who became the model for the novel she had been working on, *Julian the Magician*. Gwen had turned Bob Mallory into her muse, her route to magic.

Margaret was thinking more directly about the consequences of entering the life of somebody else. She was deeply attracted to Jones, who, she told Al Purdy, was a beautiful man. But she was wondering what would happen to the privacy, the wanderings-about at odd hours, the improvised life that she felt was necessary for her work. What about those blank spaces, those blank times, necessary for writing?

Was it coldness to think this way?

Purdy had suggested there was something hard about Margaret's emotional centre. She agreed. If being emotional involved throwing oneself over the nearest metaphorical cliff for the sake of love, then she wasn't prepared to do that. She felt that you had to look out for yourself; no one else could and, more important, no one else should.

Years later, Margaret would say: "Many people thought I was really quite cold and perhaps I am in a very specific way. . . . I felt that if I was going to marry or form a permanent relationship then that individual had to know, from the beginning, who I was and what I was doing. I wasn't going to conceal it."[34]

What moved her about Jones was that he seemed to allow her autonomy. Her fantasy was of two people meeting in balance, maintaining their differences, rather than the old romantic metaphor of the couple as two halves destined from eternity to meet and merge. In that model one of the halves always seemed to be in control. She was not a romantic.

But she would have had to pay for this. There must have been a part of her that was tempted by Gwen's romanticism. The world said there was only one kind of love, and that love involved the total risk of the self in an ultimate intimacy. Was one at fault for not believing in it?

Margaret told Purdy that she was tired of living out of an emotional suitcase, but she knew she probably wasn't ready to settle for a while. For whatever personal reasons, the relationship ended. She and Doug Jones remained friends.

As she was writing the poems for *The Circle Game*, Margaret was discovering that poetry was personal and dangerous. She described it as the search for a verbal equivalent of an emotion or, sometimes, of an emotional ordeal. Once she commented: "My own theory is that poetry is composed with the melancholy side of the brain, and that if you do nothing but, you may find yourself going slowly down a long dark tunnel with no exit."[35] She felt that being ambidextrous and writing novels as well provided her with some balance.

This was not a casual observation. She also remarked:

> By the time I got round to actually being a writer [she was speaking of 1964], I began to notice that women with vocations were considered rather odd, that biographies of famous women writers tended to point out how warped and/or sexually stunted or childless they were . . . but it was too late by then. I could see the disadvantages of being a

woman, but somehow they didn't impress me as fatal or final.

There were certain conventions attached to women poets; they might have to shut themselves up in a cupboard (pace Emily Dickinson) or look at life through the wormholes in a shroud (pace Christina Rossetti) or drink or kill themselves in order to be real poets.

For a while there, you were made to feel that, if you were a poet and female, you could not really be serious about it unless you'd made at least one suicide attempt. So I felt I was running out of time.[36]

Something very strange had been happening to American poetry ever since the Beats appeared on the scene in the late fifties. It became inextricably entwined with madness. It had begun with Robert Lowell's *Life Studies* (1959), a largely autobiographical portrait of growing up a Boston Brahmin. The book explored mental breakdown and the disintegration into madness and attempted suicide. Following Lowell, many poets wrote about suicide and mental breakdown: W.D. Snodgrass, John Berryman, Anne Sexton, Sylvia Plath. So many that, in retrospect, those poets became typed as "the Confessional School." Even poets like Theodore Roethke and his disciple James Wright felt a compulsion to explore madness. It was so widespread and singular a phenomenon that it isn't enough just to say these poets were individually mad. The *Zeitgeist* of poetry was driving the poets to the edge, since it was encouraging them to explore this dark territory. Lowell was their spokesman. He believed that the spiritual inheritance of the Second World War, with its genocide, concentration camps, and atom bombs, revealed a warping of the human psyche so profound that health could be recovered only by going into that nightmare territory in the self — the poet must explore his own darkness. And women poets like Plath and Sexton went into personal dark spaces of anger and revenge that led to dead ends, that led to actual suicide and death.

Margaret was right to be wary, but her imperative was different. Everyone who knew her spoke of her secure sense of self that fortified her in these underground journeys. As she wrote poems like "Journey to the

Interior," it was not personal exorcism she was after, but rather an under-standing of why humans behave the way they do: why the self is a mystery even to itself; why we crouch on the edge of the psyche unwilling to enter the depths below.

While Margaret was in Vancouver, Charlie Pachter was studying for a Master of Fine Arts at the renowned Cranbrook Academy of Art near Detroit, Michigan, doing everything from book design to painting. He was making paper out of old clothing and asked her to send what she had. She did have some old blouses she wanted to get rid of, but she thought the idea a bit unsavoury and added, humorously: "there is something sort of magic-spell about giving away anything that's belonged to one; how do I know you won't use them to put a hex on me?" She remarked that he sounded "engrossed, immersed, challenged, and all those nice things that CREATIVE people ought to be," and sent the blouses.[37]

Casually, he asked for something she'd written to illustrate. By the end of September she sent him "The Circle Game," the sequence of seven poems she'd begun in August. She thought it might work for him because it was full of images and moods: "it's got people, patterns, buildings, maps too, and even a few birds, & some mirrors and rooms if you want them." She explained that the sequence got "its 'generating' image from 'The Family of Man,' all those pictures of little kiddies going around; though of course it was about other things entirely."[38]

The sequence might have grown out of her experience in Luxembourg, but, in the writing, it became something other than a confessional story of a broken relationship. It became a deeper search into what happens between a man and a woman: what are the rituals and myths that prescribe how we relate to each other? Maps of how we will behave have been seared into our minds from childhood. "He" plays the orphan game, "the game of the waif who stands / at every picture window"; "she" tends "to pose . . . outside other windows."[39] Each builds a defence against intimacy. All this is framed within a description of children playing a game reminiscent of "Ring Around the Rosie." They are drawing a circle of safety to keep out anything that threatens from the unknown world. She wants the circles broken; she wants to enter the wilderness of self and of other.

Charlie found "The Circle Game" wonderful material, but he had questions. "As for those questions: darling," she replied, "you know perfectly well that I can neither type nor spell. Look up Anenomes in the dict. Argueing should be arguing . . . Pice? A typo. I can't think what it might be; have just read through both poems & still don't know. Perhaps you could send me the line and tell me which poem."[40]

When his first illustrations arrived in mid-December, she was thrilled. For a painter he had a wonderful verbal dimension, and the interaction between text and image was ingenious. He elaborated the phantasmagoric, introspective mood of the poems. She felt the poems came out a little more horrific when filtered through his mind than they did through hers, but that the effect was wonderful. (He would eventually do other series, including "Speeches for Dr. Frankenstein," "Kaleidoscopes Baroque: A Poem," and *The Journals of Susanna Moodie*.)

The Circle Game was Pachter's first limited-edition folio. He printed up fifteen copies and decided to charge $150 each. By March, he and Margaret were in full gear, sending them to galleries they hoped would buy the book. Both felt funny about peddling, but it had to be done. Margaret thought of trying the National Gallery, the Isaacs Gallery, the Vancouver Art Gallery, and of sending it to *Canadian Art* and the American magazine *Art Forum*. In the end they easily sold all fifteen copies.

At the same time, Margaret was beginning to receive requests for poems. John Robert Colombo published ten poems in his anthology *Poetry '64/Poésie '64*. *Kayak* from San Francisco was sending inquiries. Its editor, George Hitchcock, seemed keen on her work and she couldn't figure out why. But she was obviously delighted. No Canadian magazine had yet been quite so enthusiastic. "Why the STATES?" she wondered. To her, her work seemed so obviously part of the Canadian "matrix."[41]

Early on, Margaret had made a distinction in her mind. She had two lives: her work and her personal life, which she sometimes referred to as her "Other Life." It was not easy in those days for a woman writer to figure out how to shape her personal life. Unlike male writers who had a role to hide behind, women writers were exposed. The novelist Joan Didion put it best: "When I was starting to write — in the late fifties, early sixties — there was a kind of social tradition in which male writers could operate. Hard drinkers, bad livers. Wives, wars, big fish, Africa, Paris, no second acts. A man who wrote novels had a role in the world, and he could play that role and do whatever he wanted behind it. A woman who wrote

novels had no particular role."[42] The male writers often fell into two categories: the priapic lovers who drew young women to them like a harem
pool (a strategy that energized the body and fed the ego), and those in
permanent relationships who often found a woman who could take care
of them or play the muse. Many of the women poets of the sixties seemed
still to be caught in a fantasy of romantic obsession, looking to a man as
a life solution. They did not understand how emptying this could be. Bed-
hopping didn't really work for women (you could do it, but usually it
meant giving away, rather than gaining, power). The puzzle remained: how
to be with a man and not lose yourself?

Margaret still seemed to be a mystery to many men. An amusing anecdote is told by the West Coast poet Patrick Lane. He had been visiting the
poet John Newlove, and they had been drinking together for ten hours,
surrounded by the domestic debris of the Newlove household of children.
John had carved out a five-foot circle in the centre of the room where he
wrote and into which the children weren't allowed to penetrate.
(Whether you're male or female, it's never easy to be a writer. The luxury
of privacy requires the kind of money few poets earn from their work.)
They were talking about starting a new magazine, which John Newlove
wanted to call *The Singing Head*. Patrick Lane writes: "We are very drunk
with the steady drunkenness of hours, each word coming slowly with what
we think is grace and is only the careful cadence of the very drunk."
Margaret dropped in. This was the first time Lane had met her (although
he had heard there was a poet around called Peggy):

> Peggy accepts a beer. She knows there is no point in playing
> catch-up, not with two men who have been steadily drink-
> ing all day. We talk along, but as we do Peggy becomes more
> and more irritated at these two men who are no longer capa-
> ble of entering her world or any world other than their own
> twilight dream. She puts her beer down on the table and
> interrupts what to her is silence and to us is the struggle to
> continue. *Just what do you two want? What's your ambition?*
> she asks. *What do you two want out of all this?* For a moment
> both John and I try to understand what she means by *this*.
> We are at the stage of drunkenness that is akin to a steer just

after he's been hit by a ball peen hammer. John looks up from his beer. *I don't know*, he says. *Win a Governor General's Award, I guess. . . . I agree*, I say. *Me too.* Peggy looks at us both. There is no sense of derision, no judgment I can see. Frustration, perhaps disappointment. . . . there seems to be a clarity in her, a toughness I don't fully understand. She isn't the usual woman-poet. I look at her, trying to think my way into her, who she is, what she wants. She's slender, dressed in quiet clothes, strange in this time, this place. She is not angry with us, she's angry at something else, the complacent stupidity of men, their drinking, their self-mockery, their self-pity. *Is that it?* she asks. We both nod, pleased somehow with ourselves. I'm pleased one of us had any idea at all. John stares down into his bottle with his left eye. He is trying to sense what is left in the bottom under the foam. *And you?* John asks, not looking up from his beer. *The Nobel Prize! Jesus, you two!* she says. She drinks her beer, puts it down and walks out of the room.[43]

Lane had a version of what the "usual" woman poet was like, and Margaret didn't fit. She was too direct, too clear-minded, and yet she had nothing of what Lane calls "male self-mockery or self-pity." It was Newlove who came up with the idea of prizes. In her reply to them, was she expressing ambition, or mocking their Canadian provincialism?

Margaret's schedule was dictated by the university. She taught in the daytime, ate canned food and Kraft Dinner for supper, and stayed up until 4:00 a.m. writing. She wore the housecoat Charlie had bought her at Honest Ed's Discount Store in Toronto. He had sent it because it was labelled "The Princess Peggy." It matched her wallpaper. "You certainly have a natural eye for the ugly," she complimented him.[44]

She told Al Purdy: "Here it's spring. Green things almost ready to bloom, crocuses already out. . . . Me feeling slightly frazzled around the edges, restless as I am every spring. . . . That slightly unearthed-worm sensation in the sun."[45] She was writing *The Edible Woman* in blank UBC exam booklets.

The book was rooted in her loony experience working for the market researchers at Canadian Facts. She created a neurotic young heroine, Marian, who gives up eating altogether when she perceives the consumerism around her to be a form of cannibalism and can't help identifying with the goods consumed: her employer is feeding on her energy; her fiancé is feeding on her sexuality. "Hunger is more basic than love," she comments. "Florence Nightingale was a cannibal." When she bakes a cake of herself and offers it to her fiancé, she is at last freed from her role as a consumer item.

For Margaret the fascinating struggle was not plot but technique: how to write it. In the end she decided to write the book by following the story, and using flashbacks when necessary. The cake image emerged gradually. She thought of having the heroine give her fiancé a doll. But then, "while gazing at a confectioner's display window full of marzipan pigs," she came up with the title scene. "It may have been a Woolworth's window full of Mickey Mouse cakes, but in any case I'd been speculating for some time about symbolic cannibalism. Wedding cakes with sugar brides and bridegrooms were at that time of particular interest to me."[46]

Margaret wrote this book as an anti-comedy, and was rather annoyed when the publisher billed it as one of those serious books that treat modern life and female problems, rather than as a send-up of the genre. She complained that they were "treating a soufflé as though it were a steak."[47] The jacket copy she approved describes the novel this way:

> off-beat and diverting . . . a cool look at the articulate, inwardly bewildered members of the generation freshly hatched from college — not the hippies, but the other ninety-five percent who are trying to opt, not out, but in. Her heroine is concerned less with discovering herself than with deciding what kind of world she must inhabit. And modern society, when viewed through her witty and relentless eye, is indeed far stranger than fiction.[48]

The novel wouldn't be published until 1969, but when it was written, in 1964–65, the newly emerging hippie rebellion was only just beginning. In the story, Marian's characteristic feature is her wish to be average, to fit in. As Margaret explained in her summary of the novel for prospective publishers, Marian is meant to be a young woman "attempting to be normal, but failing despite herself." She views her incapacity to adapt as a consequence of her own stupidity, and until the end of the novel is "unable to trust her own perceptions about other people and about society." It is a satire of the world of consumption: the intellectual consumption of symbols and ideas, the emotional consumption of people, and physical consumption.

In answer to the question what next for Marian, Margaret wrote to Marge Piercy after the novel's publication that Marian's life would be circular, one more time around. "Obviously one can work out personal solutions or semi-solutions; social ones are much more difficult, not only to bring about but to imagine. . . . I could see in 1965 . . . no 'out' for her provided by society."[49] She would also say to Joyce Carol Oates that, if there is any autobiographical element to *The Edible Woman*, it is her own recognition of the trap of marriage just for the sake of being married.

By July, Margaret had 180 pages of her novel finished. She was living in that strange, misty reality where her fictional characters, with whom she spent so much of her time, were more real than real people. When she wasn't writing, she was consuming books, including Francis Parkman's *The California and Oregon Trail*, *The Decameron*, and Ford Madox Ford's four novels about the First World War. She would sometimes read a chapter of each until she got bored. She wasn't having much luck with her books. She'd collected rejection notices from three publishers for *Up in the Air So Blue* and her manuscript of poems called *Places, Migrations* had also been rejected. She decided it was time to return to Harvard to complete her doctoral thesis and enrolled in a summer course in German at the University of British Columbia, knowing she would have to write her German language exam. She had already said goodbye to her engineering students, of course, and had put them through the ritual of exams. Her antic side is clear in one of the tests she set them:

Logic

III. Examine the following for inductive or deductive fallacies:

a)   A man got drunk one night on scotch and soda, the next

166 / *The Red Shoes*

night on rum and coke, and the third on rye and ginger-ale. He decided to swear off carbonated beverages . . .

d) A bull will always charge a red cape; bulls must hate the colour red.

e) Everything in the world is obviously there for a purpose: cows to give milk, vegetables to be eaten, houses to be lived in. Man himself must have been put on the earth for a purpose too.

IV. Cope, somehow, with the following:

a) There was a faith-healer of Deal
   Who said, "Although pain isn't real
   If I sit on a pin
   and it punctures my skin
   I dislike what I fancy I feel."
                                    Anon.

b) Pincer Martin, marooned on an island, saw a red lobster scuttle into the seaweed. Later, he reflected on the fact that lobsters are red only if they have been boiled or otherwise killed. What did he conclude?

c) I put my hand upon my heart
   And swore that we should never part;
   I wonder what I would have said
   If I had put it on my head.
                                    C.D.B. Ellis.

d) A beautiful but not exactly brilliant young woman once said to Bernard Shaw that they should produce a child together, because it would have her looks and his brains. He questioned her premise. How?[50]

The year in Vancouver had been a good one. While teaching full-time, she'd completed *The Circle Game*, which would come out in 1966 and would be her first published book. She'd finished her second novel, *The Edible Woman*. And she'd managed to write two scenes for a new novel that would eventually become *Surfacing* (the section in which the mother's soul appeared as a bird, and the first drive to the lake, though the character was older than in the final version, and this draft of the novel was written in the third person). As well, she'd written several short stories. "It was an astonishingly productive year for me," she would later say. "I looked like *The Night of the Living Dead*. Art has its price."[51]

Her friend Jim Polk decided to visit from Montana. When he arrived in Vancouver, he encountered a small provincial city; the setting was gorgeous, and the city itself seemed quiet and composed, almost surreal. Everyone he met seemed creative and very bright. Margaret, he felt, lived in a kind of charmed circle. Yet, he also had a sense that she was portaging through all these places. "She was really from the bush, and with her background, she could look at things as if from afar, as it were, and seemed to see everything through her special lens. She could make a comedy of it when it was her mood, or see ordinary things in an odd, surreal, hushed, Gothic way."[52]

Together she and Jim set off by train to Toronto. It was a stunning late August for a trip across Canada. In those days, train travel was still a romantic adventure. The dining cars had linen tablecloths, with single roses on each table, and one could sit in the observation car, watching the country unroll at one's feet. Jim couldn't get over the beauty of it all: "mountains and prairies, and old towns with huge Canadian Pacific hotels. It was a revelation. Who knew it was up here?"

When they arrived in Toronto, the city seemed to Jim as if hushed and under water. "I was seeing it through Peggy's eyes," he remarks. He immediately picked out Mrs. Atwood and Margaret's sister, Ruth, on the platform by their clear, frosty-blue eyes. Mrs. Atwood was reserved, polite. They got on the subway and went to Leaside.

Though he had known Margaret for three years, he had never thought about what her family would be like. He'd expected a Gothic house with lots of chambers and turrets, and discovered, instead, a nice suburban house with a beautiful garden, though inside it was stark and spare of furnishings.

Mr. Atwood was an extremely formidable presence, very friendly but intimidating because he seemed to know everything. For Jim's benefit, he would quote great reams of Robert Southey and Shakespeare, with the comment: "Well, you must know this one, Jim." Jim was invited into the basement to see the plant and insect experiments. There seemed to be enormous energy in that house. In the background stood Mrs. Atwood, with her twinkling eyes and her tea. He says fondly: "She was a very smart cookie." Ruth, who was then thirteen, was there, but Harold no longer lived at home.

Jim was most impressed when, the next morning, the whole family was roused to go out. A migration of flying ants had come through in the thousands. He was given a paintbrush with some kind of sticky substance and had to pick up the ants and put them in bottles. Mr. Atwood was doing an experiment. He thought: "I like this family."

The Atwoods took Jim to their property in the North. The late August weather was beautifully serene. He was astonished to see moose climbing out of the water, and baby foxes playing in the scrub. Mr. Atwood was still working on the log house he had been building inch by inch for the previous thirteen years. When they weren't stuffing oakum into the cabin walls, they were canoeing. Mrs. Atwood's standing joke became her imitation of Jim learning the J-stroke in the canoe, turning round and round in circles. When they went fishing, he was shocked when he caught a fish, and, more so, when he understood he was supposed to hold it and kill it. At night, they read nineteenth-century literature by the light of the kerosene lamp on the mantel and he was instructed in various points of nature lore. "It was a very interesting, Victorian kind of family," he remarks, "like the Huxleys or the Woolfs, or Darwin's family, a giant tribe of people. There were relatives too. Peggy had an uncle who worked at Chalk River who was an expert on atomic energy. Everybody seemed really vigorously interested in culture and science and the arts, and were doing things. I was used to a very different kind of model: 1950s Americans with money who were interested in golf and parties and BBQs. This was not what this family was about."

He was later to find this same quality in other Canadian families he met, like the Dewdney tribe, whose son Christopher would become one of Canada's most erudite poets. Margaret told him that Canada was a nineteenth-century country, like a Victorian woodcut. He hadn't expected anything like it.

9
—

THE WALL

W hen they returned to Harvard in the fall of 1965, Jim found accommodations on the bottom floor of a house with his old room-mate
Mowbray, the D.H. Lawrence specialist. His second room-mate had gotten
married, and was replaced by another Southerner who'd grown up in
Oxford, Mississippi. As a boy, he'd delivered prescriptions from the drugstore
to Mr. William Faulkner. Margaret had left the search for a place to live too
late and had had to spend the first month in an anthropologist friend's front
parlour. Jim and she had not yet determined their status together.

She found a large room, kitchen at one end and a desk at the other, in
a three-storey clapboard house at 340 Broadway, next door to a funeral
parlour. It was about ten blocks east of Harvard Yard. Apart from the
university and the luxurious nineteenth-century residences south of the
Yard, much of Cambridge was blue-collar. It was common in Cambridge
for families to buy up the large houses and rent out rooms. The noises of
the landlady's family carried through Margaret's paper-thin walls.

The house at 340 Broadway might have suggested a story. One of her
fellow tenants was an Arab student. She wrote to Charlie: "Oh paranoia
and misery. There was a fantastic scene here Monday night."[1] Though the
young Arab student had seemed quiet and reclusive, like most of the visa
students, one night he held an uproarious party with music and dancing
girls. The landlady called the Cambridge police, and as she screamed
insults the young Arab was carted off to jail. He was evicted the next day.

In the story "Dancing Girls," Margaret invented a poignant fictional
narrator, a graduate student studying urban planning, whose fantasy is to

build a Romanesque aqueduct in the middle of a shopping centre to revitalize the urban sprawl. The narrator has only a fleeting contact with the Arab student, who is alone and isolated, unnerved by Boston's strangeness. The obtuse fictional landlady, with her "Noah's Ark of seedy brilliant foreigners," becomes a focus.[2] The story is about racial fear. In the green urban spaces she hopes to create, the narrator imagines a world where human harmony might be possible. It will, she knows, never happen.

The Harvard Margaret and Jim returned to in the fall of 1965 had altered. Opposition to the Vietnam War was mounting, and the city of Boston was heating up. The draft was widening, and young men were returning from Vietnam. Those lucky enough not to be sent back in body bags came back spaced out by guerrilla war.

In April, 50,000 people had marched from the black section of Roxbury to Boston Common to protest against racial inequality in the North. Martin Luther King Jr. spoke at the Common, warning that Americans must not become a nation of onlookers. The fight for equal rights and integration had, he said, only just begun.

By 1965, radical students were taking on the Establishment they believed was responsible for racism and the war, and while the majority of the students remained apolitical they could be counted on to sympathize with the radicals. Soon protests against the Vietnam War began to include university issues. The students wanted the Reserve Officers' Training Corps (ROTC) kicked off campus. They wanted a Black Studies program on the curriculum (in 1965, of the more than three thousand students enrolled at Harvard, only twenty were black). And they wanted the hierarchy of administration and faculty brought down. They just didn't know what they wanted to replace it.

Margaret was still at Harvard in the fall of 1966, when the first mass demonstration against the war occurred. Students erupted in a spontaneous protest against Secretary of Defence Robert McNamara, who had come to speak at Quincy House. As McNamara left the hall, they encircled his car, rocking it back and forth. McNamara's shocked and woeful expression could be seen through the window, and on his face was also imprinted the anger that would define the divide between students and the Establishment for the next half decade. That October, students began burning their draft cards, and protest sit-ins were followed by more sit-ins.[3]

The following fall, of 1967 (after Margaret had left), this momentum reached its logical conclusion. When a group of about 150 students occupied Harvard's administration building to protest the university's tacit support for the Vietnam War, the university's president, Nathan Pusey, called in four hundred state and local policemen. In their bright blue riot helmets with Plexiglas visors, wielding clubs and shields, they broke down the front doors of University Hall with a three-foot battering ram, and forcibly ejected the demonstrators. Similar assaults had happened at Columbia and Berkeley, but this was not meant to happen at Harvard. Harvard was a liberal institution.

In a painful, retrospective memoir, writer and journalist Roger Rosenblatt speaks with anguish about those years. He had first come to Harvard as a graduate student in 1962 and, by 1966, had rocketed from being a teaching fellow like Margaret to being appointed a full-time lecturer in the English Department. In those days, he writes, "at Harvard, and in the country for which it believed it stood, nothing was working — not the army, not the classes, not the cops, not the soul, not poetry, or the teaching of poetry."[4]

The university was run by what was called the Corporation and, rather eccentrically, the Board of Overseers, and it prided itself on its New England Puritan tradition of service. Harvard, everyone knew, was reserved for the ruling class. Yale might contribute the diplomats, and Princeton, the Wall Street lawyers, but Harvard produced the men who governed the country. Now that assurance was cracking from within. Students felt trapped in a terrible situation of moral bad faith. There had always been a divide between town and gown in Cambridge, but now it was out in the open. It was the blue-collar class, not the students, who were being sent to Vietnam.

Margaret was not a political activist. Jim remembered that she went on a few of the peace marches, but they lived like postgraduate students, absorbed in their studies. Yet her mind was like a sponge. She already believed that the writer's function was to bear witness, and she was absorbing Harvard's world. Calling on her memories years later, she would use Harvard as the fictionalized headquarters of her band of fundamentalist dictators in The Handmaid's Tale. Her book is a terrifying vision of patriarchy: sterile, unable to reproduce itself, it turns murderous and enslaves the young men and women under its control. When the novel was published in 1987, she gave a copy to Jim Polk, suggesting that he would get a kick out of the echoes. "Some things," he remarks, "were recognizably Harvard." He recalled the wall where the novel's executions occur (it was located across from the restaurant where they went for cheap meals), and the red gowns worn by the handmaids were like those donned by Harvard students at convocation. But what struck him was the clarity of Margaret's vision. He, too, had felt the oppression behind the walls of Harvard. But it was Margaret who penetrated the hypocrisy and exploded it into nightmare.

Now that she was back at Harvard, Margaret began working on poems for *The Animals in That Country*. She had again plunged into her private obsessions: her fascination with the fiction of reason, particularly with the pretension that science can give us control over the chaos of the mind; the anthropomorphic myths used to give the raw world a human face; the armature of language that blocks us from knowing each other. She wrote poems about her landlady; poems about "the Green Man" (the Boston Strangler); and about the Royal Ontario Museum. Under its dome, its "ornate golden cranium," she wandered among "fragments of gods."[5] She was again moving at full tilt, sending off sparks. Her energy was enormous.

The Animals in That Country contains poems to dying species. The giant tortoise was becoming extinct, becoming one of the brittle gods, one of "the relics" we have destroyed, our "holy and obsolete symbols." Margaret, at twenty-six, was already looking for the deeper causes of our self-destructiveness. She wrote a war poem, but it was not like other protest poems that came out of the Vietnam War. Something has gone fundamentally wrong with the human brain, and now she sees that war has been the backdrop to her entire childhood.

It is dangerous to read newspapers

While I was building neat
castles in the sandbox,
the hasty pits were
filling with bulldozed corpses

and as I walked to the school
washed and combed, my feet

stepping on the cracks in the cement
detonated red bombs.

Now I am grownup
and literate, and I sit in my chair
as quietly as a fuse

and the jungles are flaming, the underbrush is charged with soldiers,
the names on the difficult
maps go up in smoke.

I am the cause, I am a stockpile of chemical
toys, my body
is a deadly gadget,
I reach out in love, my hands are guns,
my good intentions are completely lethal.

Even my
passive eyes transmute
everything I look at to the pocked
black and white of a war photo,
how
can I stop myself

It is dangerous to read newspapers.

Each time I hit a key
on my electric typewriter,
speaking of peaceful trees

another village explodes.[6]

Her capacity for image had grown to an intensity that could almost be described as hallucinatory. It is evident in her remarkable poem "Speeches for Dr. Frankenstein." Those years when she was an undergraduate, she had sat with Jay Macpherson in her kitchen, discussing *Frankenstein* and the meaning of Gothic symbolism — that, wrapped in our loneliness, we contain the destructive shadow self within us. "I pull around me, running, / a cape of rain," Frankenstein says, and denying that he himself has let loose the rage for destruction turns to his monster: "Blood of my brain, / it is you who have killed these people."[7]

"Backdrop Addresses Cowboy" is a comic meditation on America's obsession with violence. Margaret later said it was inspired by the era of Lyndon Johnson, whose insignia was his stetson and cowboy boots.

> Starspangled cowboy
> sauntering out of the almost-
> silly West, on your face
> a porcelain grin,
> tugging a papier-mâché cactus
> on wheels behind you with a string,
>
> you are innocent as a bathtub
> full of bullets . . . [8]

There were also poems about loneliness.

> My shadow said to me:
> What is the matter
>
> Isn't the moon warm
> enough for you
> Why do you need
> the blanket of another body
>
> Whose kiss is moss
>
> Around the picnic tables
> the bright pink hands hold sandwiches
> crumbled by distance. Flies crawl
> over the sweet instant

You know what is loose in those baskets

The trees outside are bending with
children shooting guns. Leave
them alone. They are playing
games of their own.

I give water, I give clean crusts

Aren't there enough words
flowing in your veins
to keep you going[9]

Margaret was driven by her own momentum. She wrote to friends in
Canada, to Gwen MacEwen, to Jay Macpherson, to Charlie. And sent out
poems for publication. She did go to the occasional poetry reading at
Harvard (once to hear John Berryman, who was drunk and incoherent,
but she liked what she managed to hear). Anne Sexton lived in the area
and gave frequent readings, having assumed Sylvia Plath's mantle. The
Canadian poet Daryl Hine visited, and they went for long walks through
Cambridge. But Margaret was not seeking the company of other writers.
She once said: "I don't care if anybody down here reads my stuff."[10] She
was too busy writing.

Like Jim, she was working on her thesis and her language exams. She
was also teaching a seminar as one of Jerome Buckley's assistants. He
would meet his section leaders over lunch at the faculty club once a week
to talk over the course. When he and Margaret met to discuss her thesis,
she told him she was doing a novel with her left hand, the devil's hand,
and her thesis with her right.[11]

It was customary at Harvard for PhD students to select obscure minor
figures as their subject. She would later say that, because she was female
and wasn't allowed into the Lamont Poetry Room, where all the good
poetry was kept, she had spent many hours in the substrata of the Widener
Library, reading Victorian authors like Edward Bulwer-Lytton. (He
suffered from her favourite Victorian madnesses. He believed he was invisible.)[12] She chose to write her thesis on the novelists H. Rider Haggard,

George Macdonald, and W.H. Hudson, Victorian practitioners of the Gothic romances she had read in childhood.

Haggard's novel *She* already had a cult following. It is the story of a young man and his mentor who return to central Africa in search of a mysterious white queen called Ayesha, whose dreaded title is "She-Who-Must-Be-Obeyed." Ayesha has discovered the secret to immortality in a strange fountain in the depths of a mountain. Haggard, drawing on his knowledge of Africa and of Egyptian mythology, had created a woman of ethereal beauty and unlimited power. A demonic figure, she is the embodiment of one of the most potent and ambivalent archetypes in Western mythology: the *femme fatale*, who is both monstrous and desirable, deadlier than any male. Many have interpreted this novel as a fable of imperial decline and male dread. Margaret, however, wanted to understand the male obsession with the supernatural female.

Margaret was not ironic about the supernatural. It was a long-standing preoccupation of hers. In a third-year essay written at the University of Toronto for Jay Macpherson titled "The Uses of the Supernatural in the Novel," she speculated that "the supernatural may extend the levels of human consciousness into a fourth dimension that has its possibilities for existence within the human imagination."[13] She would later say the supernatural is a valued and necessary part of human mentality.[14]

In her thesis she was wonderfully cocky. She wrote: "The psychologically-minded may disagree with the assumption that it is the *Zeitgeist* rather than the author's own warped psyche that is primarily responsible for the configurations of fiction. This objection we will sidestep as gracefully as possible: if we are putting the cart before the horse, it is because for the purposes of this study it belongs there."[15] But beneath the artifice of the thesis, Margaret was doing something quite fascinating. She was looking at how woman was being used as an archetype in fiction.

That year she published an excerpt of her thesis in James Reaney's *Alphabet*. In the metaphysical romances of Rider Haggard and his ilk, she found embodiments of the triple goddess Robert Graves had identified: the Virgin Goddess, the Demonic Sorceress, and the Domestic Woman. When it came to choosing, these novelists preferred even the demonic woman over the domestic woman, exoticism over normalcy. She concluded the essay: "The true enemy of the hero's salvation and spiritual fulfillment proves to be The Angel in the House; the only good woman is a dead woman, preferably swathed in the grave-clothes of mystery."[16] In these bachelor novels, the men got away from the women as quickly as possible. Ordinary women were boring, shackled in domestic virtue as the "Angel in the House." (Margaret had picked up Virginia Woolf's phrase long before it gained common currency.) Only the supernatural females were allowed to be sexy. And they were deadly. What were the men afraid of? It was puzzling.

This wasn't an abstract issue. At Harvard, women were still being punished for any display of sexuality. At about this same time, Margaret's friend Ilze Sedricks was told she was going to be kicked out of graduate school. She was a Renaissance scholar and her grades were better than many, but she had rather flamboyant red hair and the habit of wearing fuschia mini-skirts. Jim claimed that Margaret had a hand in uncovering the real explanation for her threatened expulsion. Apparently, Margaret asked the Dean of Women why this was happening to her friend, such a bright student, and the Dean had finally admitted that Ilze's flamboyant dress was not suited to one who was a Harvard graduate.[17] Ilze promised to wear black and tie her hair up neatly, though the black she chose was tight and décolleté.

That autumn of 1965, Margaret's letters to Charlie made glancing references to her Vancouver novel. She told him that she had just finished typing the manuscript of "horrid novel shriek, shriek." When he later referred to it as *Shriek Shriek*, she was amused, but informed him the title was *The Edible Woman*. "For me," she added, "the agony of creation is all in the fingers. When I'm rich I'm going to buy an electric typewriter and when I'm really rich, an electric secretary."[18]

In October, she asked Charlie if he would consider doing the cover for her new collection of poems, *The Circle Game*. It had been accepted by Contact Press in Toronto. It surprised her that they even wanted the book since she knew one of the editors, Louis Dudek, didn't much like her work. (He'd rejected an earlier manuscript in 1963.) But she'd been writing for ten years, and it was time for an officially published book. Contact editor Peter Miller wrote: "We cannot afford (as we make no profit, and indeed invariably lose, however good a book is) to pay cash to the author; instead, we would send you 12 copies. You can also buy an unlimited number of copies at trade discount (40% off list) for whatever purposes you wish, including resale."[19] Though the book was accepted in September 1965, production was slow. It would not come out until October 1966.

Contact, one of the best of the small Canadian presses, had been founded in 1952. Financed in large part by the editors themselves, Contact saw its role as bringing along talented young poets until they could make it with the larger commercial publishers; or publishing older poets whose work was too uncompromising for conventional houses. It managed to publish sixty-one books in the fifteen years before its demise in 1967. Margaret's would be one of the last of the Contact books.

Charlie did send a cover illustration, but the publishers wanted something more typographical. So Margaret did her own cover with Letraset and dots ("cretinous," she called it, "but it would pass").

Charlie was having a hard time. He wrote to say he'd just been turned down for a Canada Council grant. Margaret reassured him: "Looks like the Can. is up to its old tricks of kicking worthy merit in the teeth via unworthy merit, but never mind. One has encountered similar discouragements oneself and the main thing is to keep working."[20] In another letter, she wrote: "Forget about the critics and follow your own intuitions. If the critics approve, fine, otherwise they just aren't plugged in to what you're doing. Critics are specialized, just like artists. You simply have to wait til the right one comes along." "Fortune," she consoled him, "will smile on you with teeth, however false."[21]

In the public world of art, she advised Charlie not to be cowed. It was the stance she adopted. In a world where people had a quick characterization for "the usual woman poet" and where one could still be told women poets were invading male territory, it wasn't a bad idea to stake out one's defensive boundaries.

Among those who were closest to her, Gwen and Charlie, Jay Macpherson and Jim, Margaret offered loyalty and generosity. But when the relationship involved her professional life, she adopted a witty persona that packed a sting. Nothing slipped by. She wrote to Al Purdy to congratulate him for winning the Governor General's Award in 1966:

Dear alpurd,
Hadn't heard
isolated as I am down here among Chicago murd & race
riots that you'd got the govgen
Golly gee that shore is nice, couldn't have gone
to a nicer. Didn't find out till avidly reading my Prison
[*Prism*]. Why don't you ever tell me anything?

But you are rather awful anyway. Whaddya mean writing
me a crappy letter like the last? Knocking my poems, my ego,
my personality etal, and into the bargain feedbacking from my
previous letter (I can't even remember what I wrote) . . .[22]

In fact, Margaret was being playful. She and Purdy joked about their alter-
nating nasty and friendly letters to each other, and they traded manuscripts
and comments about poetry. But on this occasion he must have crossed a line.
From their first beer-swilling encounter, Purdy had a fixed idea of Margaret.
She was academic and had a temper. She challenged him on both grounds:
"As for my temper: I'm afraid it's a figment of your imagination . . . but given
a choice between a henyard and a thunderstorm, I'll choose the latter most
of the time (which is a way of saying that I don't like being pecked at; if you
behave like a chicken who's just found a worm, get yourself a new worm)."[23]
    There were few young women who would have challenged Purdy in
this way. Her tone was clearly a measure of the strength of the friendship.
Still, behind the playfulness, she was clearly telling him she wasn't someone to mess with.
    Among friends, she and Jim were by now regarded as "an item." His
antic side often got them through the trying days of student life: the cheap
accommodations, endless deadlines, surviving day by day on the wretched
salaries of teaching assistants. Once, tired of other graduate students
endlessly talking about their cats, he bought a pet mouse for seventy-nine
cents at Woolworth's. It lived in a fishbowl in his room and was called "the
Singing Nun." In her room, Margaret hung a mobile that featured surgi-
cal instruments and an enema bag. It was a gift from a friend. If she
favoured the Gothic imagination, so did he. She had become an excellent
reader of the Tarot. He could read palms.

Referring to the comment of a critic who said that the figure he becomes in certain of her early fictions is a Jungian archetype of some kind, Jim remarks: "This is silly. We were just having a good time. We travelled a lot on the East Coast, and went up to New York to see the art exhibitions and the theatre." On one New York trip they crashed at Rick Salutin's tiny apartment (Margaret knew him from Camp White Pine), and managed to see *Juliet of the Spirits*, *The Royal Hunt of the Sun*, *Marat/Sade*, and *Hogan's Goat*. And Margaret cooked a dinner for seven.

Jim adds:

> We were culturally omnivorous. We went to movies at the Brattle Theater at student rates [1966 was the year of Antonioni's *Blowup*, Truffaut's *Fahrenheit 451*, and Mike Nichols's *Who's Afraid of Virginia Woolf?*]. We had tickets for the Boston Symphony Open Rehearsals. That was the time of the Great Blackout, when the electricity went out on the whole East Coast. We put wicks in bacon grease and lit them as candles (that was when you still ate bacon), and played bridge and told ghost stories. In fact, we had a great time together. We had troubles — our grades, the draft looming — but it was the best and worst of graduate-student life: lots of ideas, lots to do, no money.

By January, Margaret was studying Latin (her language exams were coming up in May and she was jittery). Her spare time was spent writing poems, brooding, and "deep thinking" about another novel. "As for me," she told Charlie: "I write, weep, eat, sleep, and read bad novels in German and platitudes in Latin. . . . Oh for a return to tactility. Roger, over and out. P."[24]

It is remarkable that she could keep the pace of it all going. Certainly, one of the things driving her was the comparative poverty of the graduate student, and the need to make money to survive. (As W.H. Auden used to say, money is one of the best incentives for writing.) The Hudson's Bay department store, in a promotional gesture of support to writers, decided to buy space in Canadian literary quarterlies. They published poems with the company logo at the bottom of the page. The Bay bought Margaret's "Carved Animals" for fifty dollars.

As she pasted up huge flowcharts made of shelf paper on her walls with the relevant dates for the publication of *The Bride of Abydos* and *The White Doe of Rylstone*, she often wondered what she was up to. She jokingly complained to Charlie that she'd been reading millions and millions of fantasies and they were affecting the content of her dreams, which were all about strange beings, severed heads, fights with Natives, and so on. "What I'm really worried about," she added, " is I'll lose my self-control and insult people."[25] She told Al Purdy: "It will be a race between me & incipient blindness & senility & and of course my ever-dwindling bank account."[26]

That summer Margaret and Jim stayed in Boston. She found a summer sublet, and Jim stayed on in his old place. The city was brutally hot and sticky. She would spend the morning in the Widener Library, and then emerge into the glare of the July sun, stop perhaps in Harvard Square to read the headlines on the Vietnam War, and then return to her apartment to work on her new idea for a novel. This would be her third novel, though she was still an unpublished writer. Looking back years later, trying to reconstruct her state of mind then, she would say that panic set in easily.[27]

The novel was to be called *The Nature Hut*, and was to be based on her "summer camp" experiences. As she invented her fictional camp, she drew maps to scale, indicating various buildings: the staff house, boat house, rec hall, kitchen, and baseball field, locations through which her characters would move. The story was to be set in Georgian Bay, three hours by train from Toronto, twenty miles from Parry Sound. She made a summer calendar with the days marked off, and set up the incidents for each chapter. The novel was to be told from the point of view of eight characters, whose lives and stories would intertwine. One of the novel's openings began with the camp's owner awaiting new arrivals. He was a victim of shell shock from the war and, in this bucolic setting, she accorded him surreal intrusions of violent memories. The man with numbers on his arm, who used to sit on the kitchen steps peeling potatoes at Camp White Pine, would also be fictionalized in the novel. She actually got through the first eight chapters, twice, before she bogged down. She would later say that she'd taken on something too large for her. At the time, she didn't know enough. It was the man on the steps, his story, that was the core of that novel, but he remained silent.[28]

She went back to Canada for a couple of weeks that summer, and visited Jay and Charlie. Charlie had just acquired what had been an old bicycle shop in the Portuguese section of Toronto and he intended to set up his own studio and printing press. People kept coming to the door asking him to fix their bicycles. She also spent ten days in northern Quebec with her family. She canoed the "ancestral" lake and helped her father, who was still hammering oakum into the log-cabin walls. She needed those renewals of roots. They were a necessary drug.

Susan Milmoe, a young graduate student, was looking for a room-mate. Before going back to Canada, Margaret had answered her ad in a Cambridge paper. They met and agreed to move in together. (Sue's first impression of Margaret was that she looked daunting and had ghastly shoes.) But that fall, when Margaret got back to Cambridge, she found Sue homeless. The landlord had given what should have been their apartment to someone else. Sue's mother threatened lawyers and exposure of Cambridge's notorious real-estate racket, so they were given another apartment at 333A Harvard Street. As Sue remembered it, it was a mess, with slime and grease covering every available surface, but with a cleaning they thought it would do. Sue had already decided that Margaret was an aged graduate-student frump, but when she showed up with her suitcases and boxes, assisted by three handsome young men — Mowbray, Chuck, and Jim — Sue was impressed.

Number 333A was one of the rundown, once-elegant old apartment buildings that line the rolling brick sidewalks of Cambridge. Its steps were flanked by white pseudo-Corinthian columns, and the foyer was oak and glass, but, inside, the narrow iron staircase had seen better days. Sue and Margaret used the living room of their apartment as an entrance hall and mixed up all the other rooms.

Soon a third girl was living with them at 333A: Karen, from Wisconsin, who had done an undergraduate degree in Chemistry and had spent a year in Germany before coming to Harvard. Sue called her a delightful greenhorn from the farm who was always saying: "I can't believe it; I can't understand it." Sue was studying psychology and was considered the sophisticate.[29]

Jim would come Friday nights and stay over. "This was part of the fluidity of the times," he remarks, "and of our own kind of backing into what would turn out to be a commitment. Marriage wasn't on my agenda. At the time Vietnam was my *bête noire*. The student deferrals were being stopped. But that year my draft-board man died and the new draft-board man never bothered me. When I finally got another draft-board card, I discovered I was exempt. Of course, I didn't ask why. In those days, lives and a lot of PhDs were shaped by U.S. military history."

He and Margaret took on the role of house parents, the old married couple. Sue remembered that, most of the year, "Peggy listened patiently to narratives of our broken hearts." She soon found that, lurking in Peggy, was a secret girl scout with all the homely, old-fashioned virtues. She was as "sweet as honey," and had an "insatiable need to solve problems presented to her." Which they were, endlessly. This brought out her practical side, her take-charge competence. Sue was also amused to discover Margaret could be killingly rude. Sue's beau from the Midwest used to say things like "Hot dog" and "Fantastic." Once Margaret asked: "How many of those do you have?" And she had a habit of predicting disaster for her room-mates' love affairs when she read their Tarot cards.

According to Sue, Margaret was extremely domestic, making a little home in which to hold all their lives. As a group they ate dinner together each night, though not on weekends. Margaret invested a lot of energy in daily life, and there were rules. For instance, there was a running debate about whether to hang the bath mat on the tub or lay it on the floor. Margaret wrote a hilarious "chapter and verse" directive that she taped up on the wall. She was an imaginative cook, too. When her brother, Harold, visited, she made a cake with artificial creepy-crawly critters in the icing. Visitors were always somehow squeezed in, sleeping on a broken-down sofa that had been liberated from the sidewalk outside.

Sue explained: "Karen and I were focused on our lives. Had I known who Margaret was, I would have paid more attention." She had no idea Margaret was a writer. When she found out she wrote poetry, Sue naïvely suggested she submit some to the student *Harvard Advocate*. Over the year Margaret made comic strips for the household, featuring them all as characters.

They were on strict budgets, particularly Margaret, who was on a Canadian visa and had no work permit. When they ate out, they ate at Mr. & Mrs. Bartley's Gourmet Burgers (the kind of student restaurant with long wooden tables and plastic chairs and Humphrey Bogart posters on the walls). Directly across the street was a brick wall, built as a gift to Harvard by the class of 1880 with a dedicatory plaque. This would become the wall where the executions occurred in *The Handmaid's Tale*.

That fall, Margaret wrote to John Newlove to congratulate him on his remarriage and said she was waiting for *The Circle Game* to come out. She had moments of wanting to cancel the whole thing, but it was too late anyhow. She wrote to her publisher: "Don't worry about sending me reviews when they come out. I'd sort of rather not know, at least till after Jan. 5 [the date of her PhD orals]. I have a full-sized persecution complex already."[30]

For all writers, the publication of a first book is traumatic. Margaret wrote in retrospect: "I suppose any person, but especially any woman, who takes up writing has felt, especially at first, that she was doing it against an enormous, largely unspoken pressure, the pressure of expectation and decorum. This pressure is most strongly felt, by women, from within the family, and more so when the family is a strong unit. There are things that should not be said. Don't tell."[31] Margaret was "dreading disapproval." She worried about her family, though she knew they had survived other of her eccentricities; she worried about her Nova Scotia aunts, who, she thought, might be scandalized. To her surprise, her aunts came through "with flying colours." Her aunt Joyce thought it was "a wonderful book, a real book." Her aunt Kathleen said "that there were certain things that were not said and done in her generation, but they could be said and done by mine, and more power to me for doing them." Margaret commented:

> This kind of acceptance meant more to me than it should
> have, to my single-minded all-for-art-twenty-six-year-old
> self. (Surely any true artist ought to be impervious to aunts)
> . . . perhaps it was a laying-on of hands, a passing of some-
> thing from one generation to another. What was being
> passed on was the story itself: what was known, and what
> could be told. What was between the lines. The permission
> to tell the story, wherever that might lead.[32]

In her mind, Margaret kept a photo-album portrait of her mother and her two aunts. Now, instead of three women, there were four. She felt she was taking up her inheritance in a family of female storytellers. She was being "allowed into 'home.'"

She need not have worried about the book's reception in the larger world either. The reviews were excellent. Letters of congratulation came from friends everywhere. Doug Jones wrote to say that *The Circle Game* was a very fine book: clear, clean, strong, and beautifully produced.[33]

On 5 January both she and Jim took their PhD oral exams. Hers proved to be an anti-climax. She wrote to her friend Daryl Hine:

> Ours were farces, of differing kinds: my board chivalrous (cause I'm a GURL & they don't hire such at Harvard, I guess) and were delighted and one suspects surprised when I displayed a knowledge of hard words like "decorum" and things like the structure of Beowulf ("well, it comes in two parts . . .") Jim's savage & sadistic, asked irrelevancies like "Tell us about the rise of Methodism in the 18th C." or "What Shelley scholar died of alcoholism?"[34]

Afterwards they went out and devoured lobsters and wept at the movies, both "purgative experiences." She joked to Hine that she had finally stopped having nightmares about Sir Walter Scott.

That March, 1967, she received a phone call from the Canada Council telling her she'd won Canada's most prestigious literary prize, the Governor General's Award for Poetry, for *The Circle Game*. The prize was $2,500. She was twenty-seven and the youngest person at that time ever to win it. Besides that, she'd won it for a first book. She was shocked. She'd thought it was Charlie playing a practical joke. She told Jim: "It's too soon, too soon. I've only one book. This isn't right." When she explained that the prize was the equivalent of the American Pulitzer, he'd reassured her: "But that's wonderful." She replied: "But I haven't anything to wear."

Sue and Karen took her in hand. Neither of them knew what a Governor General was, but they realized the event would be formal, and it was obvious as they went through her wardrobe that Margaret truly did have nothing to wear. The two tweed skirts, the dark cardigans with woolly balls on them, and the grey Hush Puppies just wouldn't do. Sue lent her a dress and earrings, and got her some brown high heels. She would say afterwards that the dress Margaret wore to the Governor General's dinner had been bought for $7.99 in Filene's basement and had been to dinner with Nobel

Prize winner James Watson, whom she had once dated: "Not a bad career for a dress." Sue and Karen set about working on Margaret's hair with hair spray. She'd also been trying out contact lenses, and these replaced her fifties cat's-eye glasses.

Margaret took the Greyhound bus to Toronto, and then flew to Ottawa. She was most concerned about meeting Margaret Laurence, who had also won the Governor General's Award, for her second novel, *A Jest of God*. (She had already published *The Stone Angel*.) Margaret's parents had sent her the novel for Christmas. She had studied the handsome, austere photograph of Laurence on the jacket flap, and had decided that "this was a serious person who would make judgements: unfavorable ones, about me. One zap from that intellect and I would be squashed like a bug."[35] She was in awe of Laurence's talent. Nobody else, except perhaps Simone de Beauvoir, would have had the power to reduce her to "a quaking jelly." Margaret Laurence, in fact, was feeling exactly the same thing. Her friend Jane Rule had told her of Margaret's fondness for fortune-telling with the Tarot pack, and Laurence wondered who this occult creature would be.

The ceremony at Rideau Hall on 2 June went well, but the new contact lenses made Margaret's eyes water, and while she sat in a frenzy of embarrassment the guests who flanked her thought she was crying with joy. Fleeing to the washroom, she encountered Margaret Laurence, who, although dressed in elegant black and gold, was even more of a dithering wreck than she was. Margaret Laurence was notoriously shy. It was "a moment of social awkwardness worthy of *A Jest of God*," these two remarkable writers comforting each other in the ladies' room of Government House. Margaret Laurence wrote to friends afterwards: "She was, I thought, very serious, slightly (to me) intimidating because so brainy, and then the next day she phoned me and said she was glad to find I wasn't as intimidating as she thought I was going to be, from my picture. How strange we all are and how vulnerable. Naturally I warmed to her enormously after that."[36]

When Margaret returned to Harvard, she found that Sue and Karen had incinerated her rubber-soled Hush Puppies, having decided these did not go with her new fame. They wanted her to have a more soignée, poetic image.

She had applied for a teaching job at Sir George Williams University in Montreal, and, to her surprise, it was offered to her. She was ready to leave the United States. She wrote to Al Purdy: "I really have to get out of this country. It gets to you after a while. Vietnam stories in the papers everyday."[37]

Jim's time at Harvard was also over. It was clear to him that his teaching contract wouldn't be renewed. "By supersaturation," as he puts it, he and Margaret decided to get married. "One day, I can't remember when or how it happened, we were getting married. It didn't seem to surprise anyone else because we were, in a way, married already, but it certainly surprised me."

When Margaret announced her and Jim's impending marriage to Al Purdy, she had to assure him that Jim had all the necessary defences to cope with someone as strong as she. "He is fully equipped to handle me, mostly by giving me enough rope to hang myself," she wrote, adding: "Do stop feeling sorry for my future husband. You make me feel like an ogre. He's doing very well — has won every spat so far & shows no signs of weakening — has a quiet obstinacy which is foolproof."[38]

It was not always easy for Margaret. It was the general wisdom in those days that a strongly directed woman would never find a man who could cope with her. And some friends did not make it any easier. Daryl Hine remembered, somewhat shamefaced, how he had overlooked Jim. "I spoke to Peggy. I tried to include him as a courtesy, but it was she I wanted to talk to. I suppose that happened with others." In that last year in Cambridge, Hine and Margaret would go for long walks through the environs of the town, while she listened to his anguished rambles about his relationship with his difficult lover. All relationships that are meant to last, he would remark, begin with difficult birth pangs.

His theory was that women like Margaret, if they marry their equals, fight all the time. (He had been a friend of Mary McCarthy's and Edmund Wilson's.) He believed that Margaret's self-confidence was totally unself-conscious. She moved forward like a ship in full sail. "Such women need a nice pastel young man: there must be two centres, one strong, one not so strong, when one of the two is generating the imaginative world."[39]

Margaret would not have been pleased to know of her friends' prescriptions. It was condescending to both herself and Jim. Why could no one in those days imagine that equals could marry? Why was it assumed that only the man could have the strong persona? That, if it belonged to the woman, she would inevitably castrate her partner, or else she would have to learn to diminish herself? Margaret believed it was possible to find a balance.

She wrote to the Department of Immigration in Quebec for information about what kind of visa her American husband would need. She and Jim thought of having the wedding in Miles City, Montana, but Jim's Catholic mother worried that it might alienate the town and the clergy. So they decided on Boston City Hall. This proved to be of "such extreme grunge and dinge" that Sue got all steamed up and, instead, weaseled a room in the Radcliffe Graduate Center on Ash Street.

In those days of ambivalence towards marriage, one married with as little fuss as possible. Jim found a justice of the peace by looking in the Yellow Pages. As it turned out, he was Chinese, and not what they had expected. He called himself Doctor Tehyi Hseih. (They called him Dr. Tee.) Jim wondered what was up when Dr. Tee asked them if they had cushions.

As Jim remembered it, the ceremony that morning of 9 June was bizarre. It was a blisteringly hot day. Mowbray, his best man, had forgotten the wedding was that day, and came flying in at the last minute. Margaret and Jim knelt on their cushions, and as Mrs. Tee struck a gong they pressed hands to each other's breasts. Dr. Tee, wearing his puttees, made up the ceremony as he went along, speaking of love lasting longer than the rock-rimmed mountains of New England. They had to pass their rings three times over a statue of the Buddha, at which point they were given a scroll with the message (as Sue remembered it): "Have each other for whatever you are and not for what you aren't."

Sue made the wedding cake. She had decided she had to be adventurous and make a special icing. It whipped up in swirls but wouldn't stiffen. When she brought the cake to the residence, the icing had slipped all over the place and the three layers had come apart in the heat. Margaret looked at it quizzically. "How interesting," she said.

The wedding party consisted of twenty-five or thirty people. Margaret's parents came, stopping by on one of their insect-collecting expeditions. Her brother and his wife were there. As was Charlie. Mr. Atwood was floored by the ceremony, though Mrs. Atwood found it hugely amusing. Jerome Buckley attended the reception, and was fascinated to see his graduate student wearing a white lace mini-skirt as her wedding dress. There were presents, including a sterling-silver telephone cover from some Montana relatives. After the bouquet was tossed, the youthful contingent of the wedding party made their way to a friend's apartment, where, in sixties style, they listened to music and some smoked pot.

Margaret and Jim waited until Monday to set off for Montana on their honeymoon. Jim doubted Dr. Tee was a legitimate justice of the peace, and didn't believe they were married. As it turned out, they were.

In Montana, Margaret's rather romantic version of the West was quickly shattered. Jim's stepfather, an old Montana banker, startled her with his deeply conservative political views. Their trip coincided with Jim's high-school reunion. At the party, cronies approached to say: "Well, Jimmy, that's sure a pretty little woman you've got there." Some of the young men took a great liking to Margaret and stepped all over her feet on the dance floor. It was a typical small-town reunion, and a rough-and-tumble Western crowd who liked to party. Margaret got the prize for being most recently married. An "old maid of the year" was elected, and the crowd encircled her, singing "Some Day Your Prince Will Come." It didn't help that, when Margaret was asked what she did, her reply that she was a writer occasionally elicited the response "Isn't it nice you have a little hobby."

In Toronto, Margaret's parents threw yet another party. The people at the garden party in her parents' back yard were formidable high Anglo-Saxons, including Northrop Frye. Suddenly it occurred to Jim how strange Margaret's cultural inheritance was. In his mind she was that girl standing at the edge of the bush, an outsider who had spent her childhood in the North. Now he realized she was also at the centre. Her father was a professor, and it seemed that many of the people who either were or were going to be important to the culture were part of her circle. She was outside and at the centre at the same time.

Finally, Jim and Margaret were able to escape up north for an extended stay. They went to the family cabin near Lake Simcoe, where Mr. Atwood had his tent-caterpillar farm. It was a relief to return to the quiet of Margaret's forest world, the world that was the source of much of her work.

Margaret's graduate-student days were over. She would later remark: "It was an excellent experience for me as a writer, as it allowed me distance from my own country while giving me a close-up view of another."[40] She was back in Canada, married, and with a published, prize-winning book. The Toronto she encountered, however, was transformed. In 1967, Toronto was on an extended fling, celebrating the "Summer of Love."

10

THE SUMMER OF LOVE

As the historian Doug Owram put it, the fifties didn't become the sixties until 1964, but then the counter-cultural revolution happened like a flash flood; it was the music that caused it. Yorkville Village, just north of Bloor Street, was the locus of the revolution in Toronto. In 1963 and early 1964, when Margaret had last spent time in the city, Yorkville was still a neighbourhood of cheap apartments and rooming houses, but as coffee houses and clubs like the Inn on the Parking Lot, the Mynah Bird, and the Penny Farthing opened up, the easy access to music and drugs made the area a magnet for the absconding young.

By 1966, there were forty clubs and coffee houses in Yorkville that featured live music. The best trip in town was at the Riverboat, a subterranean coffee house run by Bernie Fiedler. It was a long narrow room decorated with brass portals and lined with red booths where you could hear the best: Joni Mitchell sang "Nights in the City," her ode to Yorkville, and Phil Ochs sang "Changes," composed on the club's back steps. Neil Young's "Everybody's Rockin'" was his nostalgic tribute to the Riverboat. For the kids who sat and rocked at the Riverboat, being where the action was was a new thing.[1]

The novelist Matt Cohen remembered Toronto in 1966 as "an infinity of delectable possibilities, an adolescent theme park throbbing with folk music, jazz, drugs, protest marches, idealists of all ages, delusions of grandeur, delusions of wealth, delusions of righteousness — Toronto [was] a veritable fan dance of entertainment."[2] The hippie paraphernalia became the signature of street life in Yorkville: the beards and long hair, faded blue jeans, tie-dyed skirts and diaphanous dresses, sandals and Beatles boots, pendants on leather thongs and peace buttons, incense burners and water-pipes. That summer, the Grateful Dead, the Jefferson Airplane, and the Doors visited Toronto.

Continent-wide, the hippie movement had been building to a crescendo in 1967, and that crescendo was the "Summer of Love." The year was crammed with happenings, and nothing after it would be quite the same.

Canada, too, was on a hippie binge. In February 1967, the University College Literary and Athletic Society at the University of Toronto put on an event called "Perception '67." "Perception," in the Aldous Huxley tradition, meant drugs. *Globe and Mail* reporter John Allemang remembered the event.[3] He was then a fifteen-year-old student at the all-male University of Toronto Schools, where boys wore jackets and ties and where long hair was a subversive offence worthy of expulsion. He had been reading *Playboy*, the bible of psychedelics in those days, and so he knew all about "Perception '67's" big draw — Timothy Leary. Leary, it turned out, was a no-show, having been refused entry at the Canadian border, but Allen Ginsberg made it to Toronto, as did the Fugs, famous for their anti-war song "Rivers of Shit" and for "Boobs-A-Lot." Richard Alpert, Leary's colleague, was there, haranguing the crowd about consciousness. As was Paul Krassner, who pretended to urinate against the lectern. He was infamous for his article portraying Lyndon Johnson performing necrophilia on the dead President Kennedy during the plane ride back from Dallas. When an undergraduate at McGill University, John Fekete, reprinted Krassner's article that fall in the student newspaper, *The McGill Daily*, the outraged board of governors and the alumni called for his expulsion. The English faculty retaliated against their own administration by awarding Fekete the President's Medal at convocation, and the students gave him a standing ovation. The point of bad taste was, of course, to one-up the Establishment.

The battle between hippies and the Establishment was certainly not confined to Toronto. *The Vancouver Sun* ran headlines like "Psychedelic Scum Feared" and "Lice on Long-Haired Hippies? Man That's Just Lousy." In March, five thousand hippies attended the first Be-In in Vancouver's Stanley Park. (Regina had its own Be-In in Wascana Park that May.) In April, Canada's first underground newspaper, *The Georgia Straight*, was founded in Vancouver. One of its young editors, Stan Persky, characterized the tone: "We're totally repelled by the structure of the world. I think our objection to life on earth is probably total now."[4]

Just as in San Francisco's Haight-Ashbury, by the summer of 1967, tourists from the suburbs began to arrive in Yorkville by the thousands to gawk at the hippies. Newspapers ran reports of drug busts, and Toronto's *Telegram* warned: "these kids live for pure lust. They've lost touch with Christianity and all the meaningful values of life."[5] In Parliament, a Conservative MP issued the Select Committee Report on Youth, which urged work camps to deal with the hippie problem.

The Establishment, in the person of Toronto mayor Allan Lamport, responded by calling for a police sweep of the area to "ferret out rooms where boys and girls are living together."[6] The Yorkville community retaliated with sit-ins, demanding the area be closed to traffic. In mid-August, fifty Yorkville residents and supporters were arrested during a street-closing demonstration.

As illegal arrests became commonplace and illegal evictions became epidemic, a young lawyer, Paul Copeland, and a young law student, Margaret's friend Clayton Ruby, set up a free legal clinic. The point was to bring the law to the people. And so they did, literally, on the street. A coffee house donated a table and two chairs, which they set up in front of a convenience store, calling their sidewalk office "The Village Bar." It survived six months before City Council and irate parents closed it down, forcing the young lawyers to move their office into a Yorkville basement, though one suspects Toronto weather might also have been a factor.

To this day, it's hard to get the sixties right because there were so many threads to the story. The historian Todd Gitlin[7] describes the "Summer of Love" as the "Summer of Desperation." While the ethic motivating many of the youth was peace and love, there were also hard-core political radicals, and their images, too, became touchstones of that over-popularized decade.

In April 1967, 400,000 people marched on the U.N. Headquarters in New York to protest the Vietnam War. By September, 500,000 U.S. troops were in Vietnam, and President Johnson had approved a military budget of millions. Race riots erupted in the July heat in Detroit, Newark, and at least eight other U.S. cities. Detroit was in flames, with snipers shooting from rooftops, and 4,700 U.S. Army paratroopers occupied the ghetto, along with 8,000 National Guardsmen. Radical protest also made its way to Canada, aided of course by the increasing number of draft dodgers who arrived seeking safe haven. Peaceniks began picketing Safeway stores to protest the sale of Saran Wrap, made by Dow Chemical, who supplied the napalm in Vietnam. And there were other, international issues to protest. This was the spring of the *coup d'état* in Greece and the summer of the Six-Day War in the Middle East. Toronto became the country of choice for many of the Greek exiles who ultimately helped to transform the culture of the city.

Canada was as divided as the United States in its response to the sixties revolution. The draft dodgers were given safe haven, but they were often under surveillance by the RCMP.

And Toronto played a curious footnote in American politics. The Black Power movement was growing in the United States and it was not something the American public knew how to handle. One victim was the heavyweight champion Muhammad Ali. When he showed up at his 1966 draft hearing and said that he had no quarrel with the Vietcong, American cities that would have scheduled his next fight didn't want any part of him. So Toronto's Harold Ballard stepped in with the offer of Maple Leaf Gardens. The Toronto elite, who usually came to the matches in dinner jackets and furs, boycotted the fight that March.[8] Canada, too, had its racists. A young Torontonian, William John Beattie, grew a Hitler moustache and founded the Canadian Nazi Party in the mid-sixties. When he used Allan Gardens for his hate rally in 1966, he had to be protected by a cordon of police. Jews were his target, but the eight thousand blacks in the city also diluted racial purity.

Perhaps the single unifying characteristic of the sixties was energy. Whether you were a peacenik, a member of the radical left, a hippie, or just plain straight, there was an enormous sense that everything was changing, that everything could be changed. This wild freedom, so different from what appeared to have been the staid conformity of the fifties, seemed to be for everybody. But no one seemed to notice at the time that the one area that had hardly changed at all was sexual politics. Where were women in the sixties revolution? They were the same adjuncts they had always been in the past.

Had people been looking, they would have seen that the inevitable commercialism that would help to derail the sixties was also beginning to be evident in 1967. And young women were its target. Clairol's ubiqui-tous ad stared from city billboards: "If I only have one life to live, let me live it as a blonde."

In 1967, fashion was already taking over, and people who had perfected dressing down now began to dress up. A young designer, Pat McDonagh, fresh from a London triumph where she had been designing Diana Rigg's Emma Peel costumes for *The Avengers*, became the designer of choice. At the time there were only a handful of up-scale shops in Toronto selling mini-skirts and pantyhose, like Dollybirds on Bay, the Poupée Rouge, and the Unicorn. That summer, for her Yonge Street shop, the Establishment, McDonagh held a fashion show on the rooftops above Bellair Street with the models walking through searchlights, clad in vinyl mini-dresses and with iron balls chained to their feet. The audience, among them the famous anorexic model, Twiggy, stood in a parking lot across the street, drinking champagne. This was the hippest night Toronto had seen, until the police arrived and charged the audience with drinking outdoors with-out a licence. Their champagne glasses were confiscated.[9]

Around 1965, Rompin' Ronnie Hawkins, having picked up the trend in Los Angeles, began to hire go-go dancers as a feature of his rock 'n' roll band at Le Coq d'Or on Yonge Street. Soon girls in fishnet stockings, fringed mini-skirts, and shimmering white boots were dancing in cages at the second-floor window of the Mynah Bird in Yorkville. To the young writer Susan Swan, they seemed to be Ur-Women, "radiating a sexual charisma somewhere between the wholesome bounce of a cheerleader and the allure of a stripper."[10] This was what she wanted to do, but not in home-town Toronto. Because her mother didn't approve, she waited till she went to school in Montreal and then got herself hired by a French-Canadian nightclub. In the trademark boots, Cleopatra black eyes with false eyelashes, pale lipstick, and Clairol-bleached and ironed hair, she felt like a rebel. There was something of a show-biz allure about dancing the Frug suspended above the heads of night-clubbers. It would be a while before she, along with others, understood the manipulation of it all. She didn't know the bottom line, though Ronnie Hawkins did. He said: "There's something about women in cages men like."[11]

Most people got it wrong. "A-go-go dancing signifies to me woman's final break from man," a dancer wrote in the Toronto *Telegram*.[12] It would be another two years, almost the end of the decade, before even a few women began to see that the sixties liberation was really for men.

The Pill, first available in 1960, was only beginning to make its impact. Though there were doctors who disregarded the law, until 1969 it was against the Criminal Code to disseminate birth-control information in Canada. Many young women found themselves trapped between the conservative norms of mid-sixties sexual repression and the dizzying spirit of "free love." There was a new vocabulary: "one-night stands" and "cruising." Girls who had previously felt guilty for saying "yes" now felt guilty for saying "no." Like the soon-to-be-famous Joni Mitchell, a significant number spent the mid-sixties hiding out for nine months or, worse, had illegal back-street abortions. Teenage pregnancies were epidemic. Most such girls disappeared under a veil of secrecy, into walk-up flats in Yorkville or New York, or into homes for unwed mothers under assumed names where family members were banned from the premises to protect the identities of the other girls. Adoptions were executed with a finality akin to death.[13]

Even the radical New Left had found no accommodation for women's issues. As late as January 1969, when "Mobe" (the National Mobilization Committee to End the War in Vietnam) marked the presidential inauguration of Richard Nixon with a march and rally in Washington, a young activist, Marilyn Webb, took the stage under the circus tent and said: "We as women are oppressed." When she went on to denounce how the capitalist society viewed women as "objects and property," her fellow radicals greeted her with cries of "Take her off the stage and fuck her! Take her down a dark alley! Take it off!" Shaken, she finished her speech. A second woman, Shulamith Firestone, took over the microphone and went on the offensive: "Let's start talking about where you *live*, baby," she roared as people booed, "and wonder whether . . . capitalism and all those other isms just don't begin at home. . . . Because we women often have to wonder if you mean what you say about revolution or whether you just want more power for yourselves."[14] Women of intelligence were recruited by the movement and taken seriously, but then subtly got demoted to become girlfriends, wives, note-takers, and coffee-makers. And there were psychological penalties for women who resisted.

Margaret was now twenty-seven, married (however unconventionally), and about to take a job as a young assistant professor in Montreal. She had a published book of poems behind her and a novel in the works. She was not a member of the baby-boom generation, who seemed in the process of changing the world in the sixties. In fact, she preceded that generation by seven years. She was watching, of course, and the hippies of the sixties do surface in her novel *The Robber Bride* in the figure of the flaky, fragile vision-ary Charis, who lives on Toronto Island, believes in the power of numerol-ogy, reads people's auras, and recalls her days at the ashram. But Margaret was just old enough, and had had enough experience of the conformity of the fifties, to be able to watch the parade from a slight distance.

She did not believe that the world was transformed by the sixties gener-ation, as they themselves assumed. She was more sceptical, particularly with regard to the central issue that everyone thought had altered forever — the relationships between men and women. Younger women were caught up in the heady delusions of the sixties in ways that she escaped.

Margaret was not seduced by the rhetoric of "free love." Before most people were thinking seriously in such terms, she was taking a hard look at intimate relationships between men and women and concluded they were still all about power, and women were usually on the receiving end. But she wasn't interested in making women victims. Rather, she was sardonically amused by the way both men and women in relationships were acting out unconscious myths. In a 1970 issue of bill bisset's *blewoint-ment*, she published a poem from what would become her sequence *Power Politics*. Little did she know, then, how profoundly that sequence would fold into the *Zeitgeist*. She left the poem untitled:

> In restaurants we argue
> over which of us will pay for your funeral
>
> though the real question is
> whether or not I will make you immortal.
>
> At the moment only I
> can do it and so
>
> I raise the magic fork
> over the plate of beef fried rice

and plunge it into your heart.
There is a faint pop, a sizzle

and through your own split head
you rise up glowing;

the ceiling opens
a voice sings Love Is A Many

Splendoured Thing
you hang suspended above the city

in blue tights and a red cape,
your eyes flashing in unison.

The other diners regard you
some with awe, some only with boredom:

they cannot decide if you are a new weapon
or only a new advertisement.

As for me, I continue eating;
I liked you better the way you were,
But you were always ambitious.[15]

How astonishingly succinct she could be: in her parody she enfolds
Superman, romantic love, advertising, and weaponry, and punctures the lot.
Margaret understood, in a way that it would take many of the sixties generation some time to recognize, that the sixties hadn't solved the power
dynamic in sexual relationships. She would have to work that out for herself.

But the sixties did sweep her up in another way. As they did for everyone, they changed the entire cultural landscape. Beginning in 1966,
Canada entered a decade of enormous energy and optimism.

The city of Toronto, whose population had grown to 1.5 million, was
on the move. While the hippies and the protest movements had taken
over Yorkville, the Establishment was, concurrently, changing the city's

central core. The fifty-six-storey tower of the Toronto-Dominion Bank had been completed in 1966, altering the skyscape. Billed as the tallest building in the Commonwealth, it sat on King Street, on top of the first underground retail concourse. At about the same time, Henry Moore's much-vilified statue, The Archer, had been unveiled in Nathan Phillips Square, and the backlash was so great it helped unseat the mayor, Philip Givens, from office. In the summer of 1967, five thousand people gathered on Centre Island in Toronto Harbour for the first CHIN Radio picnic. With its Bathing Beauty contest, it would become a summer institution. In 1966, the Windsor Arms Hotel had opened its brand-new cosmopolitan restaurant extravaganza, Three Small Rooms, and was considered breathlessly avant-garde. Toronto Life magazine praised it in its first-ever restaurant review, calling it the best place in town, but expensive at $30 a head. That same spring, Winston's (after Winston Churchill) opened up for the business set. Though it did not quite have the feel of an international city, Toronto's version of itself was changing.

After a year spent in Copenhagen, the young film director David Cronenberg, sporting shoulder-length hair and a paisley shirt, returned to the University of Toronto to finish off his English degree. By the "Summer of Love," he had already completed his second film, From the Drain, a surrealist sketch in which two men, fully clothed, sit and talk in a bathtub. They are survivors of a futuristic holocaust. A mutant plant rises from the bathtub drain and kills one of them. Cronenberg remembers strolling through the hippified section of Toronto and seeing young people sitting on the sidewalks, screening films on bed sheets strung up on store fronts. He was thrilled to think his was one of the films they were watching.

Suddenly there was a new sense that things could happen in Canada:

> We wanted to by-pass the Hollywood system because it wasn't ours. We didn't have access to it. It wasn't because we hated it, but because we didn't have an equivalent, and we didn't have the thing itself. We didn't know people who distributed films; we didn't see Canadian films in the cinemas. Just as we didn't hear Canadian rock and roll on the radio in those days. I can still remember the first: The Ugly Ducklings. It was stunning to recognize yourself. Like any minority.[16]

Dennis Lee, Margaret's old friend from Vic, describes the same problem in publishing: "With few exceptions, notably Macmillan and Oxford, foreign-owned or branch-plant houses had a very bad track record in publishing original Canadian books."[17] The best solution was to subvert the system by becoming a publisher oneself. His first project was a chapbook titled *The Forms of Loss* by a brilliant young writer, Edward Lacey. Dennis asked for Margaret's help and she contributed a hundred dollars, a huge amount, considering she was still poor. (Margaret called her donation "giving blood." She felt there must be solidarity among writers.) Jay Macpherson also contributed. When Robert Fulford reviewed the chapbook, he remarked that it was intriguing to see such outlaw sexual material finally getting literary attention. At first, Dennis hadn't realized that Lacey was gay. Since most of the sex in the poems was either "gender-free" or coded, it had taken him several readings to recognize that Lacey was talking about men. "Shows where my head was," Dennis comments. "I missed all the puns. Edward was blowing guys on Philosopher's Walk."

In 1966 Dennis was teaching at Vic College, and Dave Godfrey, a young Winnipegger, was lecturing at Trinity. One day Dennis mentioned that he'd put together a manuscript of his own poems titled *The Kingdom of Absence*. After reading it, Dave said: "We ought to publish it." Dave found a guy to typeset it, and they printed 300 copies. Needing a name for it, Dave came up with "Anansi." (He'd spent time in Africa working for Canadian University Services Overseas [CUSO], and remembered the West African spider god who'd created the world and then degenerated into a Trickster.) They got the spelling of "Anansi" wrong on the first book.

Suddenly people started sounding them out about publishing manuscripts. Under Dave's direction, they put together a four-book package for the fall of 1967 and started operating as publishers out of Dave's basement on Spadina. The House of Anansi was to become one of the most important publishing houses devoted to Canadian writers.

But Dennis and Dave were more than Tricksters. It had slowly dawned on them that Canada was a *vendu* culture that rejected its own as second rate. "After ten years of continentalizing my ass," Dennis remarks, "[I realized] I was a colonial."

The insight had come slowly. In 1965, Dennis had attended a weekend teach-in on Vietnam held by professors and students at the University of

Toronto's Varsity Stadium. The place had been filled with radicals, and they were learning that the American government had been lying about the war. They also discovered that the Canadian media had been helping to spread the lies. Dennis did not believe that Canadian newspapers, radio, and television were being bought off directly by Washington. It was subtler than that. They were simply colonials adopting the imperial line. It shook him to the core to realize that he, too, was a colonial. In retrospect he could write:

> Canadians were by definition people who looked over the fence and through American windows at America, unself-consciously learning from its movies, comics, magazines, and TV shows how to go about being alive. The disdainful amusement I and thousands like me felt for Canadian achievement in any field, especially those of the imagination, was a direct reflection of our self-hatred and sense of inferiority. And while we dismissed American mass culture, we could only separate ourselves from it by soaking up all the elite American culture we could get at. . . . And we fell all over ourselves putting down Canadians. . . . The fact that we would never meet the Americans we admired from one end of the year to the next did not cramp our style.[18]

According to Dennis, one of the unheralded legacies of the Vietnam War was that it catalysed Canadian cultural nationalists to begin a movement that would change Canadian art. Young Canadian radicals had automatically taken on the American Vietnam War as their issue. Now a few among them suddenly realized that, while they sympathized with anti-Vietnam protests, they had their own agenda. They wanted to account for their tenuous sense of living here, their sensation of muteness and silence. They wanted a sense of home.

The mid-sixties were the foundation years of the literary nationalism that would dominate Canadian writing for the next decade. Some, like Dennis and Dave, had ideological underpinnings for their efforts to Canadianize Canadian institutions. But, as Margaret later said, "for most of us, nationalism didn't start out as something ideological; we were just writers and wanted to publish our books."[19]

There was an exciting sense of congruence as little presses started cropping up everywhere. In 1965, a Toronto printer and designer of books named Stan Bevington joined with a few other writers in a collective to found Coach House Press in a slum building on Bathurst Street. Their first book, *Man in a Window*, carried their pressmark: "Printed in Canada on Canadian Paper by Mindless Acid Freaks." This was printed in minute type under the logo of a beaver. Soon the press moved to a semi-renovated coach house off an Annex laneway south of Bloor. Over time, stories collected about the writers at Coach House. In a delightful memoir, Sarah Sheard describes how bp Nichol was the one who came up with the idea of taking out ads for books in the *Saturday Night* personals, as if the books were the ones looking for a good lay. A film of Coach House done years later would show Michael Ondaatje in a tuxedo washing books with soap and setting them to dry in the dish rack. This was a hands-on operation.[20]

From 1966, new presses began to spring up right across the country. Michael Macklem started Oberon in Ottawa in 1966, and David Robinson began Talonbooks in Vancouver in 1967. To the list would be added Barry Callaghan's Exile Press, Howard Aster's Mosaic Press, and Marty Gervais's Black Moss Press. By the mid-seventies there would be dozens of small presses. Everybody was making discoveries, leapfrogging into new turf independently, though in tandem.

Small theatres began opening, with the ambition to create venues for Canadian plays and Canadian actors. One of the best, Theatre Passe Muraille, was founded in Toronto in 1968. The name came from a story by a French writer, Marcel Aymé, about a man who has the ability to pass through walls. When he suddenly loses that ability, he is stuck forever in the middle of a wall. To the actors at Passe Muraille, Canada "felt like that thick wall, as thick as the Great Wall of China, thick enough to swallow up whole armies of artists."[21] Wanting to be current, hot, controversial, they produced John Lennon's satiric one-act play, *In His Own Write*. And they made headlines with *Sweet Eros*, a play in which a young man kidnaps a girl, ties her up, and undresses her as he tells his story. When he finally frees her, she is moved by his vulnerability. It wouldn't wash today, but then nudity on stage was exciting. It was a very sixties thing.

In retrospect, nationalism would be codified as a cultural movement, but it began with a bunch of artistic people trying to practise their art in their own country.

Offering an advance of $750, with a print-run of 1,000 copies, Dave and Dennis asked Margaret if they could publish a second edition of *The Circle Game*. The Contact Press run had only been 250 copies, and it was already out of print by the time Margaret won the Governor General's Award. She was still more or less unknown as a writer. She agreed and the new edition with her original cover came out in the fall of 1967.

Margaret and Jim were preparing to leave for Montreal, where she was to take up her teaching position at Sir George Williams University. That summer millions were suddenly flocking to the city to visit Expo 67, constructed on a slim peninsula and two islands in the St. Lawrence River, across from downtown Montreal. The country was a century old, and Expo was its birthday party.

Margaret and Jim went up to Montreal to visit Charlie. He had been in the city almost a year, working for Expo at the International Exhibition of Contemporary Sculpture on Île Ste-Hélène. Fifty-five sculptures, including works by Rodin, Matisse, and Giacometti had been shipped to Montreal from around the world, and his job was to build individual bases for them. As well, he was general dogsbody for Alexander Calder, then seventy-three, who was building his enormous ten-storey stabile on the Inco Plaza.

"Expo 67 was a decidedly sixties moment," according to William Thorsell, editor-in-chief of *The Globe and Mail*. He was then an enthusiastic twenty-one-year-old and fresh from university when he was hired to run the entire Western Canada Pavilion, with its sixteen hostesses. (No female candidates were interviewed for his job.) He recalls: "The whole world seemed to be reinventing itself and showing its modernity in Montreal. . . . [The city] was ablaze with idealism, adventure, money, sensuality, art, design, gin, parties, sunshine, and the manic urgency of knowing that Expo wouldn't last. . . . Canada was like an ebullient teenager."[22]

Some of the finest international artists, opera singers, and dancers came to the city to perform at Place des Arts. Buckminster Fuller's geodesic dome ballooned over the American Pavilion, and Habitat, Moshe Safdie's radical experiment in city dwelling, hung like a jigsaw puzzle over the harbour.

The Canadian Pavilion featured the latest in multi-media technology, and one of its guest speakers was Marshall McLuhan. He was already an international star, having appeared the previous summer on the covers of *Time* magazine and *Esquire*. Leonard Cohen, stoned, sang songs, including "Suzanne," at the folk pavilion.

After Expo, Canadians began to think consciously about themselves as Canadians, about the things that united and separated them. This wasn't a consequence of Expo; it was rather that Expo was itself a product of the groundswell of nationalism that swept Canada at the time of its centennial. Margaret summed up the general feeling: "Because of Expo, there was an optimism about Canada in the air, for the first time in living memory (mine)."[23]

In September, Margaret and Jim found a walk-up apartment at 17 avenue de l'Epée on the fringes of Outremont, a wealthy French district on the east side of Mount Royal. Lower down the mountain was the city's Greek district, with wonderful bakeries and restaurants. She and Jim shopped at Les Quatres Frères and lugged the groceries home by bus.

Jim loved "the idea of such a big Romanesque city up in Canada freezing under the northern lights."[24] Both he and Margaret felt self conscious about not being fluent in Montreal's predominant language, an inadequacy confirmed when a nun hit him with her umbrella for not speaking French. They both took classes one night a week to improve their French conversation. During the day he stayed at home and worked on his thesis, making the occasional foray down to Expo when he couldn't stand to look at another footnote.

Margaret commuted by bus and subway to Sir George Williams on the west side of the city. She was teaching two courses: Victorian Literature and American Literature, one in the daytime and one at night. She became a coffee addict, and her weight fell to 103 pounds. "I seem in retrospect to have been always running. . . . 'You look like a model,' my friends told me. 'Great cheekbones.' What they meant was gaunt."[25]

She was an inventive teacher. In her American Lit course, she offered the students a chance to be creative rather than continue their habit of writing everything down. She said she wanted them to be more interested in their own "self-development" and assigned 10 per cent for personal projects. At the end of the year the projects they submitted were ingenious:

. a scale model of Salem; a small, beautifully moulded clay whale; dolls dressed as Puritans; and some wall murals. One project included a slogan button that read: "MOBY DICK IS NOT A SOCIAL DISEASE."[26]

Social life was fun. George Bowering, whom she had met on the West Coast, was writer-in-residence at Sir George that year. Bowering was an original. Coming from a small town in the Okanagan Valley, he seemed to have made a commitment never to be unfaithful to his roots — his grandfather, he said, was a circuit rider. He detested pomposity and, though erudite, often posed as a clown. For George and his wife, Angela (whom Margaret liked immensely, she was so bright and sharp-witted), she invented Bowering Pie, a dessert made of "a meringue shell filled with a mixture of red things," berries, grapes, whatever, as long as they were red.[27]

She and Jim visited F.R. Scott. She'd received Scott's anthology of Canadian satiric verse, The Blasted Pine, as a Christmas present when she was a teenager, and she admired him as a Canadian pioneer. A constitutional lawyer, Scott moved among the elites. He loved to tell the story of his canoe trip with Pierre Trudeau and a number of other male friends in the Northwest Territories in 1964. He had taken an 8mm camera on the trip and had caught Trudeau after a morning swim cavorting in the nude. When Trudeau was elected prime minister, the Mounties arrived on Scott's doorstep to confiscate the film.[28]

Margaret and Jim also visited John (Buffy) Glassco in his basement apartment on Mountain Street, around the corner from the Ritz Hotel. He had not yet published his famous fictional autobiography, Memoirs of Montparnasse, recounting his meetings with Joyce, Stein, Ford, and scores of others during his youth in Paris in the late 1920s. He was an esthete, in the Baudelairian tradition, and delighted in referring to himself as a poet, novelist, and pornographer (in 1959, he had completed Under the Hill, the unfinished romance of the Victorian erotic artist Aubrey Beardsley). When visitors arrived at Buffy's, they would usually find him wearing his smoking jacket and cravat. Margaret delighted in his mischief making. And he taught her to eat hearts of palm.

The novelists Clark Blaise and his wife, Bharati Mukherjee, were also friends. Twenty-seven and fresh from the University of Iowa's Writers' Workshop, Blaise had been hired that year to teach Modern British and

American Literature, and creative writing, at Sir George. Mukherjee was teaching at McGill. Blaise was an expert linguist, and used to amuse Margaret by turning himself into a Russian, with appropriate facial expressions, as they drank coffee in the cafeteria. He remembers how his three-year-old son used to run down the hall of the English Department to her office, where she kept cookies for him in her drawer. She recalls babysitting his kiddies.

In his memoir of those days in Montreal, Blaise notes: "Over lunch one day she admitted that she'd also committed some fiction and asked if I would read the manuscript of a novel called *The Edible Woman*. She thought it might even get published if she could line up British and American publishers to go with the Canadian."[29] His suggestions proved helpful. Blaise and Muhkerjee often had Jim and Margaret to dinner. Jim recalls propping himself on their ottoman while being served rare and exotic Indian dishes. Incense burned in the background. He also remembers that Bharati was cultivating an interest in motorcycle-gang literature.

Michael Ondaatje visited, as did Doug Jones and his new wife, Sheila Fischman. And Margaret's friend Gwen MacEwen was in town. She had fallen in love with a young Egyptian graduate student at McGill and had pursued him to Montreal. Jim remembers visiting her:

> I was dazzled by the Canadian literary life, all these people who wrote poetry and were artists. It wasn't like anything I knew from my midwestern U.S. background, the doctor's son. And there was this exotic, sly creature trading amusements with Peggy about the poetry scene. I remember clearly how much we laughed. Gwen was living in a very inaccessible place that had no windows. She was, Peggy told me, hiding from her Egyptian friend. Entering her place was like entering an enchanted forest. Through numerous doors we came to a windowless room with her carved chest and her Oriental objects. She looked Oriental. She was learning Coptic, so that she could read the Coptic Bible. By then I had read her poetry and thought she was obviously an eccentric genius, an oddity in every way. And funny besides. I will always remember the weirdness of that evening, the beauty

of it. The room had candles, and the Coptic Bible made a deep impression. And the laughter.[30]

Margaret wrote to Charlie that, as it got colder, she'd taken to wearing her old Dale Evans shruggie as a hat. No one guessed it was really a sleeve. She'd cut up her old coat, and claimed that sewing was now her only recreation. She felt about to scream under the pressure of teaching and trying to write. There were too many social engagements and she wanted to be anonymous again.

> Soon oh soon I'll be ready to start working on poetry again, please the Lord. So carry on and when you have a minute you can burn a candle to me who am peaked, miserable, and not working as much as I'd like. Argh. Oh, those still small voices were right. Academia is no place for the artist. As for la belle langue, Jimmy speaks it in stores and they all love him because he is so inept but tries. I haven't improved any either. Ah cheri. Qui a le temps?[31]

In fact, despite the heavy teaching schedule, Margaret managed to work. She had begun to revise *The Edible Woman* for publication.

The manuscript had already had a bizarre history. Back in October 1965, she'd sent it to S. Totten, the fiction editor at McClelland and Stewart. She'd received an encouraging reply in February 1966, but then nothing. By March 1967 she sent a query to the press regarding the manuscript she'd submitted a year and a half before. Without results. Finally, back in Toronto that summer, she'd phoned and left her name, intending to retrieve her manuscript.

It was Jack McClelland, the head of the company, who returned her call. He explained, with considerable embarrassment, that he'd just read an article about her in a special centennial issue of *The Toronto Daily Star*, describing her as having won the Governor General's Award at the age of twenty-seven for her first book. McClelland had been "enchanted." He'd dictated a long, enthusiastic letter to her, asking to see the new novel to which she had referred in the article. Then, "struck by a terrible thought," he checked his files and discovered his firm had been "seeing the novel" for a year and a half. He told her she'd have a perfect right to tell them "to go to hell," but would she allow him to read it? In August they met for a long, involved lunch, and McClelland suggested that the novel needed revisions but that it should be published. The fall of 1968 would be a "judicious" time. When Margaret asked, "What about my agent?" he replied that it might be a good idea if the agent stopped sending it around any more. Margaret was wary, but decided to leave the book with M & S. It was a one-man company and she knew that, with Jack McClelland personally interested, efficiency would improve considerably.[32]

Margaret already knew the politics of publishing in Canada. To publish her book in her own country first would be the kiss of death. The previous summer, when she told her agent, Hope Leresche, that McClelland and Stewart and Clarke, Irwin might be interested, Leresche had explained the current environment to her:

> It is really not only in your interest but standard practice for books in the English language which are aimed at a wider public than solely a Canadian one to be placed first with an English publisher for U.K. and Commonwealth rights and a publisher in the U.S.A. for rights covering the United States territory (which includes its Dependencies and the Philippine Islands). It is also common practice for the publisher who first takes the book, whether he be English or U.S. to be given the Canadian market, although Canada is of course technically part of the Commonwealth market.
>
> Where a book has a special Canadian interest or the author is himself Canadian or has local Canadian contacts, then it is sometimes possible to arrange at the time of establishing a contract for British or U.S. rights to agree to a separate publication in Canada but this is done with the permission and approval of the English or American publisher, and with financial compensation. . . .
>
> As regards the two firms you mention, I would think that Clarke Irwin might be interested in arranging a Canadian edition when the book has been sold in England or America but, believe me, this is the way to do it and not the other way

round, which is putting the cart before the horse. I should also be chary of embarking on revisions for a small firm before awaiting reactions from the main market.[33]

As it turned out McClelland and Stewart did publish *The Edible Woman*, though it took yet another year and a half. (The book came out in the fall of 1969.) They bought world rights and were able to place it with foreign publishers. That same year, Andre Deutsch brought it out in England, and an American edition with Little, Brown came out in 1970. The cart had been put before the horse, and it worked.

That fall, as she taught at Sir George, Margaret was also working on proofs of *The Animals in That Country*. It was scheduled to be published in the spring by Oxford University Press under the editorship of William Toye. In Toye, Margaret had found the editor with whom she would publish most of her poetry over the next thirty years.

Their first contact had been fortuitous. Toye had received a phone call from his old friend A.J.M. Smith. Smith, who had edited a number of anthologies, including the well-known *Oxford Book of Canadian Verse*, had reviewed Margaret's *The Circle Game* and told Toye she was a young poet to watch. Toye immediately contacted her and said Oxford would like to publish her future work. Toye remembers: "She was not unsympathetic to this prospect, but naturally wanted to meet me if I was to be her future editor. Over lunch at the Inn on the Park, she asked me what sign I was born under. I'm a Gemini, she's a Scorpio. I know nothing about astrology, but she must have decided the combination worked well."

Letters passed back and forth about revisions and cover copy. Toye found Margaret was a consummate professional; she never missed a deadline, and his editorial input was reserved for the arrangement and selection of poems. There was never a need for a hands-on edit; her manuscripts always arrived fully polished. Toye would comment: "In my experience, exceptionally gifted writers are always the easiest for an editor to work with."[34]

But the work Margaret longed to get back to was *The Journals of Susanna Moodie*. Moodie was an obscure nineteenth-century poet who had emigrated to Canada from England in 1832, and who had then written two autobiographical memoirs: *Roughing It in the Bush* and *Life in the Clearings*. (The former was intended as a warning to prospective pioneers against coming to the god-forsaken wilderness of Canada.)

Margaret's sequence of poems had started mysteriously enough. She explains that one night, shortly after she had arrived back at Harvard in 1965, she had a particularly vivid dream in which she seemed to have written an opera about Susanna Moodie. Finding herself alone in a theatre, she looked up to see Moodie standing on the empty white stage, "singing like Lucia di Lammermoor." Later she realized it was probably the stage of Hart House at the University of Toronto where she'd seen James Reaney's *Night-Blooming Cereus*.

She had had only two previous encounters with Moodie. When she was growing up, it was her job to dust Moodie's nineteenth-century classic *Roughing It in the Bush* in the family bookcase. It sat among the grown-up books, and when her father had recommended it as a Canadian classic she'd given it a pass, since "classic" was synonymous with boring. Besides, as she explained, in her childhood log cabins and the bush were not exotic; she'd wanted castles and ray-guns.

Her grade-six reader included an extract from *Roughing It in the Bush* that recounted an incident in which Moodie's chimney caught fire and the log house burned down. Margaret was put off. Overworked chimneys that might catch fire had been a "bugbear" of her childhood.

But her dream was a "tip from the unconscious." She had rushed off to the bowels of the Harvard library where the Canadiana was kept, got out Moodie's two memoirs, and read them at breakneck speed. There seemed nothing there but Victorian prose and "Wordsworthian rhapsody," along with a "patina of gentility and class snobbery." Perhaps it had been "a bad tip." She made an abortive attempt to write a libretto, and promptly forgot Moodie.[35]

Yet, the poems gestated, and about a year and a half later she began her sequence. She had shown some early drafts to Jim at Harvard, and he remembers her remarking: "How intriguing that America had forefathers and we had foremothers." Before leaving Harvard, she found a daguerrotype of Susanna Moodie, "very moon-faced, greying and vague," in the Harvard library.

What resonance did Moodie carry for Margaret that, with such a slight history, she would surface in her dreams? Nothing other than that tip from the unconscious would have suggested that poems about an obscure, long-forgotten nineteenth-century pioneer writer would work. The American poet John Berryman, it's true, had written his sequence of poems about the seventeenth-century poet Anne Bradstreet, but at least Bradstreet was an American.

As she worked on the poems, Margaret discovered that Moodie and she were each other's obverse. Moodie was a kind of anti-self. A nineteenth-century Victorian lady thrust from the comforts of genteel British middle-class life into a pioneer's life in Canada, Moodie hated the bush. But, for Margaret, life in a log cabin in the bush had been normal. She was the bush that terrified Moodie.

In Margaret's poems, one can feel the thrill that comes when the writing surfaces from the deepest places within. She was occupied by Moodie:

> My brain gropes nervous
> tentacles in the night, sends out
> fears hairy as bears,
> demands lamps; or waiting
>
> for my shadowy husband, hears
> malice in the trees' whispers.
>
> I need wolf's eyes to see
> the truth.[36]

After seven years, when the historical Moodie left the bush to return to her comfortable antimacassars and china tea sets, she longed for the wilderness. But Margaret gives her a second chance. In *The Journals of Susanna Moodie*, as Moodie lies in her grave hearing the twentieth century bulldozing away her past, she refuses to be ploughed under. She returns as an old woman on a Toronto bus, to tell the city that it is also an "unexplored, threatening wilderness." Moodie, as Margaret explains, "has finally turned herself inside out, and has become the spirit of the land she once hated."[37]

By a kind of magic transference, Margaret found, in Moodie, a voice that spoke about her own doubleness. Because of her childhood spent in the woods, she could always look at people as odd creatures with eccentric habits and fetishes that seemed quaint (she loved to joke about her culture shock at flush toilets). This kept her at one remove. People and their habits were more terrifying than any wolf's eyes. When she wanted to, she could push this vision to a level of surrealism that was absolutely original.

Margaret was also intrigued by what she called the "hints and gaps" in Moodie's writing. Perhaps because she occasionally looked at people as aliens, Margaret had developed the habit, almost like an uncanny sixth sense, of listening, when people spoke, for what was said and what hovered, just unsaid, beneath the words. Moodie seemed to be saying one thing and feeling another.

Margaret was under contract to Oxford for her next book of poetry, but remarked to Toye that she had promised a book to Anansi. As soon as Toye read *The Journals of Susanna Moodie*, he phoned her and implored her to let Oxford publish it. Not only was he thrilled by the poems, but Susanna Moodie was something of a personal obsession for him. It was agreed that Oxford would do *Moodie*, and Anansi would get the next book (which proved to be *Power Politics*). Toye had one suggestion, that Margaret write an afterword. She obliged.

Back during her first stay at Harvard, she had formulated her theory about Canadian pathologies. In Margaret's afterword, Moodie became the embodiment of the Canadian national disease:

> If the national mental illness of the United States is mega-lomania, that of Canada is paranoid schizophrenia. Mrs. Moodie is divided down the middle: she praises the Canadian landscape but accuses it of destroying her; she dislikes the people already in Canada but finds in people her only refuge from the land itself; she preaches progress and the march of civilization while brooding elegiacally upon the destruction of the wilderness; she delivers optimistic sermons while showing herself to be fascinated with deaths, murders, the criminals in Kingston Penitentiary and the incurably insane in the Toronto lunatic asylum. She claims to be an ardent Canadian patriot while all the time she is standing back from the country and criticizing it as though she were a detached observer, a stranger. Perhaps that is the

way we still live. We are all immigrants to this place even if we were born here: the country is too big for anyone to inhabit completely, and in the parts unknown to us we move in fear, exiles and invaders. This country is something that must be chosen — it is so easy to leave — and if we do choose it we are still choosing a violent duality.[38]

Canadians were hungry for explanations of their own national ambivalence, their sense that they were part of a culture insecure in its own identity. They would latch on to Margaret's ideas, expressed with such definitive assurance, with a degree of fierceness that she did not anticipate. Since its publication in 1970, *The Journals of Susanna Moodie* has never been out of print.

While Margaret spent her time brooding on a Victorian English gentlewoman and revising *The Edible Woman*, there was a backdrop to life in Montreal that hardly impinged on her. That it didn't, disturbed her. In a French city, most of her friends and colleagues were English, and despite those French lessons she was taking, the cultural life in which she was involved was English. The French and English cultures truly were two solitudes, with little cross-over between them.

In the mid-sixties, Quebec was undergoing a process Quebecers called "the Quiet Revolution." A groundswell of nationalism was building, and politicians like René Lévesque and Pierre Bourgault, cultural heroes like the folk singers Gilles Vigneault and Pauline Julien, and writers like Hubert Aquin and Jacques Ferron were calling for Quebecers to be "Maîtres Chez Nous" (a phrase coined by Lévesque in 1962). When French president Charles de Gaulle leaned over the balcony of Montreal City Hall that July 1967 and shouted "Vive le Québec Libre" to the excited crowds (a gesture that led Prime Minister Pearson to compel de Gaulle to leave Canada), the nationalist cause found an international spokesman.

Though most Quebecers did not see it, the Quebec cultural renaissance had affinities with what was happening in English Canada. However, there was a dark side to the Quiet Revolution. The FLQ (Front de libération du Québec), inspired by underground revolutionary cadres worldwide, was dedicated to more violent tactics. In 1963 they had placed their first bombs in mail boxes and public buildings; in April of that year, Wilfrid O'Neil, a night watchman, had been killed in an explosion at the Army Recruiting Centre in Montreal.

Margaret now had first-hand experience of life in Quebec. She understood the historic roots of Quebec grievances, and instinctively knew what it meant to long to be masters in one's own house and have control over one's own cultural destiny. This would be helpful when she came to be involved, in later years, in the separatist debate. She also understood the dangers of ultra-nationalism, of the ideological squabbles within the family that led to violence and extremism. Her commitment would always be to the acceptance of a distinct Quebec culture in Canada. She read Quebec literature, and when she wrote of things Canadian she always included Quebec writers. She would write a screenplay of Marie-Claire Blais's *La Belle Bête*, and by the time she was well enough known to be interviewed on Quebec television she had learned to speak French.

In the spring of 1968, the Canadian Centennial Publications Commission awarded Margaret their Poetry Prize of $1,250. In March, she and Jim went down to Boston (one of several trips to Harvard related to his thesis), and she met Peter Davison, the editor of the Atlantic Monthly Press. He published Farley Mowat in the United States, and having become acquainted with her work through Jack McClelland had already bought one of her poems for *The Atlantic Monthly*. He asked if *The Animals in That Country* was being published in the United States, or if Oxford simply intended to send copies to Oxford, New York, for distribution. Offering an advance of $200, he said he would like to publish an American edition. Margaret wrote to ask Toye if this was possible, saying Davison appeared to be a "jolly, well-wishing type."[39] *The Animals in That Country* came out that fall with Little, Brown, which published Atlantic Monthly Press books. This was her first American publication.

Margaret and Jim spent time in Cambridge that summer while he put a few finishing touches on his thesis. She worked in the library and, for distraction, read *True Romance* magazines. When both felt they were going crazy, they went on excursions. "Watched the bargains in Filene's basement," she wrote to Charlie, and asked him whether he'd be interested in illustrating *The Journals of Susanna Moodie*. (He was, though it would take more than a decade before the illustrated book would appear in a limited edition of 120 numbered copies).[40]

Jim was awarded his Harvard doctorate. Margaret now knew that she didn't want to continue teaching, and he began to look for work. Sir George and McGill had no positions for a Victorian specialist, so he applied to Edmonton and Victoria, and was offered jobs in both places. He and Margaret chose Edmonton. He had the idea it would be a small bucolic town like Pocatello.

One evening, Gwen MacEwen read Jim's Tarot cards. He remembers that reading: "It was a nightmare disaster from hell. Everything upside down. Towers of destruction, death, you name it. And all of this really turned out to be the story of Edmonton. Dead on."[41] It was an inauspicious beginning. For Margaret and Jim, Edmonton turned out not to have been a good idea.

11

LEARNING TO MAKE FIRE

Edmonton was a shock. In 1968, it was still a provincial prairie town, but it was in the midst of an oil boom and things were changing fast. The postwar housing industry had scattered two-storey stucco houses through its suburbs, and new developers were quickly tearing down many of the remaining older homes. The downtown core was filling up with high-rise office structures and multiple housing units. Even the university seemed to be a huge cement monolith built by engineers. Edmonton was not the bucolic academic town Jim had imagined.

For an easterner like Margaret, the landscape was also a shock. She was used to the bush, to terrain that was tangled and up-close. The prairies and the distant mountains seemed huge and impersonal, impossible to assimilate.

Edmonton itself was unrelievedly flat, except where the North Saskatchewan River cut through its centre. What trees there were seemed stunted. In a review article she wrote at the time for *Poetry Magazine*, Margaret defined being Canadian as having "something to do with space, sensed as vast, open, unconfining, and oppressive."[1] It was as if she were standing in Edmonton, puzzled by why the city was there at all, isolated in a northern emptiness and disconnected from the rest of the world. The vast North Saskatchewan River had brought the fur traders to Fort Edmonton in the 1790s, but the impulse to celebrate its history had not yet arrived in Edmonton. The artists who would do so were just beginning to find their voice. For now its claim to fame was that it was Canada's most northerly capital city. There wasn't much in the way of urban entertainment. The only restaurants seemed to be pancake houses and pizza parlours. Films changed slowly, and though the local opera company was good and a theatre scene was beginning to develop, people suggested a visit to the zoo to see the buffalo if one inquired about entertainment in Edmonton.

Margaret and Jim found an apartment in the top half of a house on 107th Street, near the university. The house was small, with sloping gables, so that their space, though quaint, was like an attic. It was reached by an external staircase, which became increasingly hazardous as fall deepened into the inevitable winter blizzards. The tenant downstairs, Yetzke Sebysma, was a painter from Holland who taught art history at the university and could read palms, cards, and stars.

Jim was teaching in the Department of English, and Margaret was the accompanying wife. But her literary reputation was growing, and what to call her became a problem. She was asked whether she was going to be Mrs. Polk or Margaret Atwood. People were not used to women keeping their maiden names. She wrote to Al Purdy using two letterheads on her stationery, with each name followed by the full address, and told him to choose.

As they began to settle in, Margaret discovered that the city did have hidden resources. She liked to go down to Jasper Avenue to visit the tea-reading shops, and she scoured the second-hand stores. In one she found a pair of ladies' laced boots that the Chinese owner claimed were made in 1900; his grandfather had left a stock of them behind in the cellar. Few women had feet small enough to wear them. She bought a pair, feeling like Cinderella. Soon she and Jim began to find friends among the university professors. A number of exceptional academics and writers were there, including Diane and Frank Bessai, Morton Ross, Sheila and Wilfred Watson, Rudy Wiebe, and Sara Stambaugh. Often writers, such as Eli Mandel, Michael Ondaatje, and Alice Munro, came to attend conferences organized by the Department of English.

In fact, life was quite social. Diane and Frank Bessai always made a point of getting to know the new people. Diane remembers Margaret sitting in her living room that fall: "Margaret used to wear black Victorian boots, a black skirt, and a kind of up-to-the-neck and slightly decorated white blouse. And not an ounce of make-up. She'd found an old fur coat in a second-hand shop and was buried in it all winter. She was the first person I'd encountered who seemed to be cultivating a persona for herself, a Gothic persona (all of us were interested in the Gothic then). She looked a little different from the rest of us."[2]

The winter proved terrible: the temperature went down to 35 degrees below zero, with a wind-chill factor that made it feel like 75 below. The record-breaking cold stretches seemed to last forever. Margaret reported to friends that the cold was coming through the cracks in their apartment walls. They had hung blankets over the windows and wore thermal underwear, but still it felt like they were living in a farmhouse. During a cold snap, it was impossible to go out to buy food. At moments like these, they felt as if they were under siege.

The car they'd bought proved so unreliable that Jim had to walk to work, and injured his lungs running in the ice fog to keep warm. Margaret, too, was ill, with stomach problems. Her doctor had told her to slow down and recommended she abstain from alcohol and coffee. "It's a bit rough being the only sober person at the party," she told Eli Mandel. "Also it works like Sin; I know one day I'll be Tempted and Fall."[3]

The idea that going outside was a dangerous adventure (if one miscalculated, one could freeze to death) was certainly fascinating, but mostly Margaret stayed inside and worked. She kept a hot-water bottle under her feet as she typed. She told Al Purdy she was brooding and writing five pages a day about Power and Victorian Nature goddesses ("all those Victorians were just mad to return to the womb").[4]

To keep their spirits up in their small apartment, she bought Jim a harpsichord. He was a very good pianist and used to joke about how he'd played for quarters in Montana bars. Margaret was learning to play the recorder. Sara Stambaugh, from the English Department, was an excellent flautist, and so they had musical evenings together. For Christmas, Margaret got a book on astrology, with charts. She began to ask friends for their dates and exact times of birth so that she could cast their horoscopes.

That fall, Charlie sent Margaret his caterpillar portrait of her, done in lithograph and silkscreen. He'd titled it *It Was Fascination I Know*. He'd depicted her as "insectomorphic," with insect-like eyes hidden behind mauve sunglasses, and sprouting orange and pink butterfly wings. She is caught in the gesture of offering a caterpillar on a twig, presumably to the painter. To Charlie she was still Peggy Nature, with her gift for metamorphosis.

Margaret was initially a bit taken aback. She thought the painting was brilliant, yet the expression on the figure was one of wild, idiotic glee. "One's immediate reaction is 'gosh, do I look like that?' even though I know it isn't essentially me, or has ceased to be me or hasn't. I do look like that sometimes, that's what's scary."[5] But she was also amused, and began to sign her letters "Madame Butterfly."

For Charlie, she would always be something of a mentor, as she had been when they had first met almost a decade before. He continued to seek her help in clarifying confusing notions about being an artist. She seemed to be so clear-headed. It was not easy to be an artist in a colonial country. Of what use was art in Canada, where the artist was still largely ignored? Margaret had once said: "In this society poets live on a kind of cultural reservation, don't you think? (Having the rest of their territory invaded & annexed . . .)."[6] The only workable definition of the artist seemed to be a romantic one: the artist was a solitary genius fated to live alone in his garret, suffering.

Charlie had been puzzling over the question of creativity and suffering. He asked Margaret what she thought, and she wrote back at length. She knew that, for him, this was a very serious question:

> As for creativity and suffering, I think one goes through various stages. By "one", I mean me, as usual. I used to think age 18 to 23 that a) one had to suffer, b) ought to suffer being a poet, had to probably from the Byronic version of the tormented artist. Ought to, some guilty thing. Nice girls get married and have kids, they don't write poems. Therefore if you do write poems, you aren't a nice girl and deserve to be punished in some way. There's another version of that: artists suffer. Therefore if you don't suffer you aren't an artist. Therefore you deviously go about finding ways to make yourself suffer so you can write. I did some of that too. Have you? But basically I don't like suffering very much. So I evolved a rationale that permits less of it.
>
> Everyone has neuroses, granted. But the artist has a way of working them out in his art, not available to those who ain't. The latter have to work them out in their lives. Therefore, the artist is likely to be better adjusted to his own neurosis

than someone with-equivalent intensity of neuroses who isn't an artist. That's probably a lot of crap too, but I find it more viable than the suffering one. At least you don't feel guilty if you enjoy your life or have a good relationship with someone. And not all artists sublimate their neuroses anyway? Occasionally, when people tell me how sane I am, I feel I ought to be out there suffering. It's a hard habit to kick.

As for paying a price, I think there's a bit more to that. That is, if there are certain conditions under which you produce, and you have to make a choice between those conditions and something — marriage, a job, that would disrupt those conditions, then obviously you pay some kind of price. But that's different. You for instance have paid the price of doing without money, which isn't the same as suffering.[7]

Margaret made a distinction: personally, art was a vocation, a gift, which required all her imagination and commitment. But publicly, it was also a profession, with rights and responsibilities. Ironically, the romantic notion of the artist confronting demons alone in an attic freed society of any responsibility for art. The artist suffered, by definition, and was placeless in a culture where he or she had no social role. Margaret was beginning to see the artist as completely different from the romantic cliché. The artist was meant to actively shape society, and not be its victim. When the artist actually spoke out, though, society often felt threatened. In the poem "Spell for the Director of Protocol," Margaret put a hex on those who would muzzle the artist:

You would like to keep me
from saying anything: you would prefer it
if when I opened my mouth
nothing came out
but a white comic-strip balloon
with a question mark; or a blank button.

Sometimes you put it more strongly,
I can feel your thumbs

on my windpipe, you would like me to stutter,
I can feel you nailing STOP signs
all over my skin on the inside;
you would like me to sign my name, finally . . .[8]

By spring, life in Edmonton was assuming at least a modicum of domestic order. Jim and Margaret had acquired a small black cat, which they called Fedallah (after the sinister fire-worshipping Parsee in *Moby Dick*). That July, they drove down to Miles City, Montana, to visit Jim's folks. She wrote to George Bowering of their "hallucinatory drive thru mountains & Waterton Pk in early, chill dawn; great actually. On the road all day, injecting ourselves with cokes & tea etc to keep awake, thru wild territory; first mountains, then rolling grass-covered flesh-like hills, then thru jagged rock formations; often not another car in sight." The trip was an exhilarating high and would become material for poems. When they got to Miles City, they watched the launch of Apollo 11 on American television, and it wasn't lost on her that the broadcast was sponsored by Tang orange drink. "There was the earth, the moon, and the big bottle of Tang, in orbit."[9]

Margaret had been working for the past year on a new collection called *Procedures for Underground* (not, she warned Gwen, to be mistaken for a sewage manual or a handbook on revolution). She complained to Charlie that she wished it was ready, but that she kept rewriting: "Like the human bod. the cells keep renewing themselves, so it's almost all new material. But I'll finish it yet (clench fist, grit teeth)."[10]

"Underground," of course, meant the territory of the psyche, laced with collective mythologies and personal obsessions. Trapped in her winter isolation, she had undertaken underground journeys into dreams and myths. She wanted to know what makes us up. What is the self; what is the ego; what, indeed, is the unconscious? She wrote to Eli Mandel:

As for the ego — I wonder if it really exists? Perhaps instead of an ego-egg, shell containing things, one is simply a location where certain things occur, leaving trails & debris. I guess there must be something in one that organizes the random bits though.[11]

Margaret was fascinated by the bizarre fluidity of identity. It almost seems as if we can get a fixed sense of who we are only momentarily, in our encounters with others; alone, we slide back into the dark mystery that is ourselves. And for her this might have been even more marked. She was such a keen observer and had such capacity to enter the minds of others that there must have been times when she worried whether she had a self. She once told Al Purdy: "I am a different person (not even slightly but radically different) with each person I know. It is hard when 2 of them are in the same room. I feel as though I am being pulled apart."[12]

Margaret organized *Procedures for Underground* carefully. The first and last poems, which frame the book, are about her parents. Not the persons Mr. and Mrs. Atwood, but parental figures transformed into images in the psyche.

Eden Is a Zoo

I keep my parents in a garden
among lumpy trees, green sponges
on popsickle sticks. I give them a lopsided
sun which drops its heat
in spokes the colour of yellow crayon.

They have thick elephant legs,
quills for hair and tiny heads;
they clump about under the trees
dressed in the clothes of thirty years
ago, on them innocent as plain skin . . .

Does it bother them to perform
the same actions over and over,
hands gathering white flowers
by the lake or tracing designs in the sand,
a word repeated till it hangs carved
forever in the blue air? . . .[13]

She is describing how, in our unconscious, our parents remain fixed as if they were images in a strange and surreal cinema. We recognize them, though they only vaguely resemble people in the world. Margaret has caught our sense that a timeless drama, of which we are only sporadically aware, seems to unfold independently in our minds. The people in our lives have two realities: in the world, in real time, but also in the dramas we live inside our heads.

What is most moving about these images is that she has placed the parents in a safe Eden. It is the world, not the parents, who are dangerous. No wonder that people always remarked on her self-confidence. She had such simple affection for her parents and therefore such secure psychological ground to stand on. The problem for her may have been to construct her own world, apart from that insulated protected space.

In another poem, "A Dialogue," she writes again of dreams, and speaks of a sister. Her own sister was twelve years younger than she:

> My sister and I share the same
> place of recurring dreams
>
> (the lake, the island, the glacier-
> smoothed rock, the bay
> with low ground, spruce and cedar)
>
> though because we were born in different years
> we seldom see each other.
>
> > She says it is a swamp
> > at night, she is trying to get away,
> > her feet won't move, she is afraid
> > of the things that live under the water
> >
> > For me it is clear day
> > so bright the green pierces,
> > but in the distance I hear a motor, a chain-
> > saw, the invaders are coming nearer
> >
> > I passed her at evening, she was running,
> > her arms stretched out

in front of her; I called but couldn't
wake her

She watched me sinking
among the reeds and lily-pads;
I was smiling, I didn't notice
as the dark lake slipped over my head.

We talk about this in calm voices,
sitting at the kitchen table;
she is examining
her bitten hands, finger
by finger, I draw with a pencil,
covering the page with triangles
and grey geometrical flowers.[14]

Margaret has caught exactly how we can sit calmly in the kitchen by
day while we live in landscapes of nightmare at night. What does that say
about the mind? Even two sisters who share the same landscape transform
it so differently in dreams. Most moving are those dream figures, each
caught in her forest world, unable to help the other.

Margaret once said that what always terrified her was chaos. Did that
come in part from the forest world of her childhood? She believed that the
solid ground one stands on can suddenly buckle and give way; imperma-
nence marks the edge of everything. She sits in the kitchen, drawing
triangles for safety, imposing her own desperate sense of order.

That autumn, she sent Eli Mandel copies of her Susanna Moodie
poems. Deeply moved by them, he wrote back:

> I feel something like your Mrs. Moodie — coming out of
> the bus, (a slip: I meant to say 'bush') all those animals at
> the back of the bus (might as well leave it as 'bus' now)
> and I haven't really learned anything. There's snow today
> in Toronto. It's white. The roads are black. I don't seem
> to know very much else. But I'm grateful for your poems,
> the Moodie poems because they let me see. . . . Only I

wonder why you should trust objects and appearances so beautifully.[15]

She replied thoughtfully:

> No, I don't *trust* objects and appearances, quite: I believe that they exist (is that the same thing?) I don't believe they're permanent, but I do believe they're significant. Also — I suspect that some of the things in my poems which would be symbols for you are real things for me; or anyway real things which are in themselves symbolic. I know that Frye says once you put a sheep in a poem it becomes a poetic sheep, a sheep-in-a-poem; not sure I want that to happen. I think when I put a tree in a poem I want it to be a tree; which is a confusion between thing and word, characteristic, I believe, of autistic children, as well as a reason — or rather impulsive force — behind the writing of poetry. You create a poem so that it will be there, and then when it falls back into mere words you have to create another one.[16]

When she wrote of the bush, it was a real not a symbolic place, as were the creatures in it. Including the savage gods. In a poem called "Dream: Bluejay Or Archeopteryx," she conjures another dream image:

> in the water
> under my shadow
> there was an outline, man
> surfacing, his body sheathed
> in feathers, his teeth
> glinting like nails, fierce god
> head crested with blue flame.[17]

She would return to this image in her novel *Surfacing*, when the narrator meets the Manitou, the dark god of the forest. Margaret said she believed in the supernatural. It is a "valued and necessary part of the human mentality." She had no trouble believing we house strange, fierce, and powerful gods within us. In "Procedures for Underground," the title poem, she alludes to Northwest Coast Indian myths which offered rituals for going underground. Many cultures have myths of underground journeys to the dwelling places of spirits from whom human beings learn wisdom and power. These spirits must be acknowledged and placated. Unattended, they invade the psyche. Margaret's procedures for underground were, in part, strategies for entering the dark interiors of our psyches, haunted by ghosts we deny. This would, in fact, be one of the enduring obsessions of her life's work. What was the core of the story of *Alias Grace* except the portrait of a woman who has entered the dark impulses of the human mind — has known murder and violence, and been its victim? The young psychologist Simon Jordan stands at the edge of the psyche he thinks he can master and, when he sees his own dark uncontrollable impulses, runs in terror.

The underground was natural territory for Margaret. She'd always had a sideways way of seeing. Her world was clearly numinous and haunted. One has only to look to the poems where she imagines what animals dream, what language fish speak, or sees the brutal Zeus-faced horned god in the faces of the buffalo at the Edmonton zoo.

In Gwen MacEwen, Margaret had a friend with whom she could talk about such things. They could play with the supernatural by trading dreams and horoscopes. And they could also take it seriously. Gwen's new book, *Shadow-Maker*, came out in the summer of 1969. Margaret had been asked three times to review it. She refused on the grounds that Gwen was simply too good a friend; and she was anxious about the growing incestuousness of the Canadian poetry scene. "Why are they asking me?" she wrote to Gwen. "Is it because they think young lady poets should be reviewed by other young lady poets?"[18] But she was excited by the book and had decided instead to write an article on Gwen's poetry that would look at the figure of the male muse.

With her typical humour, Gwen said she had had a dream in which she and Margaret were required to deliver some important, seemingly political documents. "Now that I think of it," she wrote, "sounds like an exaggerated version of a literary mission, perhaps the search for the great Canadian couplet."[19] But in fact she was delighted that Margaret was examining her work, and began to send her reviews and other articles.

Margaret reported her progress to Gwen: "[Robert] Graves says there's no such thing [as the male muse], but it seems to me you prove him wrong. I would probably go into his triple nature — he comes through as God, Christ & Satan — or Ra, Osiris & Set — the Unchanging, & the 'bright' & 'dark' twins, both necessary, & their cycles. . . . Would this bother you? (Do I begin to sound like a graduate student nun?)"[20]

Gwen wrote back: "Does Graves really think the female poet has to be the goddess. How unfair! She'd then have to assume the enticing stance; but surely then all the poems would be about *her*, and terribly narcissistic, I think. Writing her poems would be like combing her hair or putting on her makeup or something; he would just fade away to nothing! Or so it strikes me. Also unfair because then she is assuming the role *he's given her*."[21]

Margaret's article "MacEwen's Muse" came out the following year. It was a deeply serious look at Gwen's effort to construct a myth of the muse, which Margaret described as "a creature half way between human being and supernatural power" who inspires language and is "the formative power of nature."[22] Gwen called the worship of the muse her religion; the muse was a metaphor for the unknowable mysteries both within and beyond the self.

Margaret and Jim were slowly discovering that they weren't cut out for Edmonton. "We didn't know it for a while," Jim says.

> We'd been children of the forties and fifties, and our stated goals were very conservative. I would teach in a college and she would write. Then she would teach and I would write. We would live somewhere in a small rustic cot or cottage. It was a kind of humble, nineteenth-century version of a life. It took me a while to realize that this version wasn't the right one for either of us. The world of Edmonton academia was fairly formalized. We went to dinner parties at the end of the week. But she wasn't a faculty wife, and though I published my ritual papers on Melville I wasn't the young academic.[23]

Margaret began teaching in the Department of English that September. In those days, women academics married to full-time staff were given sessional or part-time appointments, but Diane Bessai remembers that Margaret refused the "part-time" label. She insisted she be designated a visiting professor rather than as sessional. She was teaching a poetry class, and wrote to Gwen:

> Last night had them all thump on the table with their fists in different rhythms; one remarked:"I haven't had so much fun since Grade 2." Then they wrote Collective Poems by writing one line & passing the paper along, folding as they went so only one line at a time was visible. Now they have to transform the words so obtained into poems. (Such tactics avoid discussion of the Soul.)[24]

The Edible Woman came out at the end of that September, almost four years after Margaret had first submitted it to McClelland and Stewart. Andre Deutsch brought it out in England. Sent on her first national tour to promote the book, she discovered the writer's life isn't always glamorous. Her very first book signing was in the Men's Socks and Underwear Division of the Hudson's Bay store in Edmonton. The memory was comical: "I sat behind my little table watching the potential undershort buyers slink past with only the most furtive of looks in my direction."[25]

She'd had trepidations about publishing the novel (parts of it, she said, were such a farce), but the reviews were numerous and affirmative. George Woodcock, one of Canada's best critics, wrote in *The Toronto Daily Star* that it was a social novel of high perceptiveness and was extremely good. Robert Weaver commented on its wit, intelligence, intensity, and its precise concern with language. William French, of *The Globe and Mail*, remarked that seventeen novels (thirteen of them first novels) had been published that fall, a number well above the average. He particularly recommended Graeme Gibson's impressive first novel, *Five Legs*, and poet Margaret Atwood's *The Edible Woman*: "1969 may well be remembered as the turning point in our literary history," he commented.[26] Describing Margaret as "an Edmonton wife and Harvard PhD student," the reviewer of *The Peterborough Examiner* said the novel was witty, pungent, and masterful, and an extraordinarily good read. *The Vancouver Sun* called her an "all-Canadian girl poet" and a pro who knew exactly what she was doing with every phrase. One reviewer remarked on the fact that Miss Atwood's Toronto was really Toronto, not an old National Film Board movie, adding that it didn't feel like a "duty" to read this Canadian novel.

There were a few negative reviews. The most confounding came from C.F.P. of the Saskatoon *Star-Phoenix*, who wrote:

> Both Marian and her inventor fail to realize that her so-called psychoses and all her other troubles are due to a combination of laziness and promiscuity. Those who are steeped in all the modern jargon of psychology, convinced that fornication is normal, love is old-fashioned, and marriage is "out" will love this book. For the old-fashioned, more stable person, this book has nothing to commend it.[27]

But the real surprise for Margaret was that, in October, just weeks after the book appeared, Minotaur Film Productions of Montreal contacted her and bought the film rights to *The Edible Woman* for $15,000. The film was to be produced by John Kemeny and directed by George Kaczender in collaboration with Oscar Lewenstein Productions of London.

When news of the purchase became public, the headlines in *The Montreal Star* read: "A Tough Broad's First Novel Becomes A Film." The reviewer, John Richmond, explained that when he'd last reviewed Margaret Atwood, he'd called her "lady-like," and she'd written back indignantly: "I'm not at all lady-like. I am a tough broad."[28]

In 1969, there was virtually no film industry in Canada. The National Film Board was making only documentaries and animated films. In 1967, an astonishing breakthrough had momentarily seemed possible when Allan King produced a remarkably dramatic documentary called *Warrendale*, about a home for disturbed adolescents. It made people feel that there might after all be room for a national industry. But the CBC, which had commissioned the film, refused to air it. The language spoken by the wards of Warrendale was deemed too shocking for Canadian audiences, and suddenly King seemed doomed to waste his talent fighting Canadian censors. In optioning a Canadian novel, Minotaur Film Productions of Montreal was trying something very new.

Margaret spent the winter working on the film script of *The Edible*

Woman. Often it took her away from Edmonton for consultations with her producer. Suddenly, access to a larger life seemed possible.

The success of *The Edible Woman*, both a film contract and international publication, was almost unprecedented for a Canadian novel, and a first novel at that. Friends were warm in their praise. Gwen wrote:

> I didn't get a chance (other than saying that when I read Edible Woman I was appropriately unable to eat myself) that it's quite a delicious, tasty dish. I *did* devour it in a day, which I rarely do with a book. . . . Duncan is marvelous; he just slips into the book and sneaks around quite at will; he's very much *there*, I mean there's no suggestion of him having been *put* there, if you see what I mean, which I'm sure you do. Which makes me quite envious (note the green type-writer ribbon) of your facility to *move* characters around and have them do and say natural things. . . . It's all very Deep and Mysterious to me. Thank God, I muttered to myself as I read on, someone is writing something accurate about Woman for once.[29]

The response in Edmonton to Margaret's success was mixed. According to Diane Bessai, everyone in the English Department at the University of Alberta rushed out to buy the book. But Margaret's independent stance had made her some enemies. There were those who wanted to see her as one-dimensional, cool and controlling. They wanted to see Jim as the object of her satire, portrayed by the eccentric character Duncan, with little fictional transformation.

Jim discovered that, at a time when the disproportionate number of American academics on Canadian faculties was beginning to be noticed, he was being identified as one of the ugly Americans who'd come to take people's jobs. "There were only a few people, of course, but these same people," he remembers, "were not friendly to Margaret. This troubled me. I thought: why not celebrate this original and interesting talent, but of course they were threatened and they also insulted Northrop Frye and Jay Macpherson, the people Peggy revered. This made Peggy feel intensely uncomfortable, and me even more out of place."

Some took particular umbrage at a line in one of her poems, "84th Street, Edmonton," in which she'd said that in Edmonton there was "only more / nothing than I've ever seen."[30] Clearly, Jim felt, people were looking to be offended. But, as he saw it, Margaret was trying very, very hard to fit in. "She went on 'The Tommy Banks Show' and she read for an Avon Lady's poetry group, doing what she felt was expected. I felt both she and I were out of place. But we were trying. It wasn't that we were being intentionally eccentric and strange."

Diane Bessai remembered an incident:

> At one of the get-togethers in the faculty club (we did an awful lot of beer drinking in those days and usually ended up there after classes and on Fridays), one faculty member, who shall be nameless, got nasty with Jim. He often got nasty when he drank. He referred to Jim in a scathing way as "Mr. Peggy Atwood." Peggy was absent, but when she heard about it, she was enraged, and phoned to tell me so. Certain men in those days didn't like to see a woman, who was supposed to be the adjunct, get centre stage. It made them feel insecure. This belittling of Jim was outrageous to her.

To be put in the position of having to defend Jim was condescending to Jim; for Margaret, it was a deep source of frustration.

Margaret's success certainly occasioned some envy. Charlie wrote that he'd run into a former school chum of hers from Leaside High School at an "upper armpit cocktail party" in Toronto. The woman had said she resented seeing Margaret's name in print because she knew her when she was just "plain old Peggy at Leaside High." "I mean, who knew she'd actually be published?" He'd responded: "Well, I hate to spoil your illusions, dear, but she's still plain old Peggy on 107th St. in Edmonton." He ended his letter to Margaret: "Why do they do it? Why does the sea roar?"[31]

That fall, Diane's husband, Frank, was desperately ill. He was only forty-one, and was diagnosed with a brain tumour that would prove fatal. During the next ten months the world turned into a ghastly nightmare. Frank and Diane had four small sons. Their home became a meeting place for the friends and relatives who came to help.

Margaret and Jim visited together, and Margaret often came on her own to help with the children. She would gather them together upstairs and tell them stories. Diane remembers her visits, and the anticipation with which her children awaited those stories.

> She had a cape around her — I think it was just a blanket — and she had it up over her head. She held a flashlight up to her face, and the kids really knew they were in for something. There was nothing condescending in the manner in which Peggy did this. You know: now you're going to have a story. This was a dramatic, magic set-up.

Margaret was telling them her own version of the Grimms' fairy tales. Diane's oldest son, John, then six and a half, retained vivid memories of those evenings. He loved them. Obviously moved by the children's tragic situation, Margaret wrote the poem "Stories in Kinsman's Park." Diane had told her about a nightmare her younger son had had of a caterpillar eating the side of his head, an obvious worry about his father's illness. In the poem Margaret refers to the fairy tales we tell children, where "death can occur only / to witches and in / sanctioned ways," where wounds are imaginary or "cured by secret leaves," while in the real world we cannot keep our children safe from suffering.[32]

Margaret was fond of Frank Bessai. She wrote to Eli that he still carried on witty, though rambling, conversations, and was in less pain, and she said she hoped Eli would be coming to visit him soon. She wondered how she herself could live through such a thing. It was so very terrible. Somehow Diane was holding up.

Times were difficult, and the pressure was taking its toll on Margaret and Jim's relationship. She was writing poems about dreams. "Dreams," she said, "are a relief. As long as one keeps having them, one is assured (however falsely) of one's sanity."[33] Jim had had a dream in which he was eating his lunch in a bullfight arena, surrounded by colossal carved statues of bulls; he had something in his hand that he didn't want anyone to see. It turned out to be Margaret's head. Her own subconscious responded with a series of dreams in which she was getting married to someone else. This became the basis of the poem "Midwinter Presolstice":

The cold rises around
our house, the wind
drives through the walls in
splinters; on the inside
of the window, behind
the blanket we have hung
a white mould thickens.

We spend the days quietly
trying to be warm; we can't
look through the glass;
in the refrigerator old food
sickens, gives out.

I dream of departures, meetings,
repeated weddings with a stranger, wounded
with knives and bandaged, his
face hidden

       All night my gentle husband
sits alone in a corner
of a grey arena, guarding
a paper bag
       which holds
turnips and apples and my
head, the eyes closed[34]

Looking back, Jim remarks: "I don't really know to this day what that dream was about, though I remember Gwen had a benevolent interpretation of it. We did much dream work then. We were all dreaming a lot. I was reading Jung to try to figure them out. All those interpretations about one's inner life and the mystical life. We were a very occult crowd. Maybe being out there in the west, sane, logical west that it is, opened other doors."

Marriage, and the matching of two sensibilities, was not easy. Margaret never sentimentalized.

Habitation

Marriage is not
a house or even a tent

it is before that, and colder:

the edge of the forest, the edge
of the desert
                    the unpainted stairs
at the back where we squat
outside, eating popcorn

the edge of the receding glacier

where painfully and with wonder
at having survived even
this far

we are learning to make fire[35]

She was recording a common experience. All around her, marriages were disintegrating. Friends, like Dennis Lee and his wife, Donna, were divorcing. But she still wanted to share her life with someone. Weren't her parents in their Eden? She would work at this. With will, she and Jim would find their way through. She wrote poems about stamina, like "Carrying Food Home in Winter":

I walk uphill through the snow
hard going
brown paper bag of groceries
balanced low on my stomach,
heavy, my arms stretching
to hold it turn all tendon.

Do we need this paper bag
my love, do we need this bulk

of peels and cores, do we need
these bottles, these roots
and bits of cardboard
to keep us floating
as on a raft
above the snow I sink through?

The skin creates
islands of warmth
in winter, in summer
islands of coolness.

The mouth performs
a similar deception.

I say I will transform
this egg into a muscle
this bottle into an act of love

This onion will become a motion
this grapefruit
will become a thought.[36]

Much to Margaret's delight, Charlie had gotten a job teaching art at the University of Calgary the previous fall, and had been up to visit several times. In February 1970, he had an exhibition of his new graphics at the Canadian Art Galleries on 17th Avenue, and Margaret and Jim drove to Calgary for the opening. Charlie had discovered the West. Feeling almost "born again," as he put it, "overwhelmed by the prairie light, the mountains, the magnitude of everyday vistas," he had begun "appropriating" images. Mounties, cowgirls, grain elevators, Chinook arches, and the dome car of the CPR filled his new paintings.[37] He intended this as a delicious put-on, not satirical at all, but rather an affectionate parody of Western pop mythology.

For his grand opening, instead of having the requisite wine and cheese, he hired A & W from across the street to cater the affair. Girls with milk-shakes and change purses at their waists moved through the crowd, and someone wearing a Lois Lane name-tag walked around, interviewing people. The music of the Sons of the Pioneers (a kind of Western barber-shop quartet famous for songs like "Tumbling Tumbleweeds") blared from the loudspeakers. Later there was a lesson on how to hunt moose, complete with calls and moose-walking-in-water sound effects.

Friends had raided the bins of the Sally Ann shops, and were wearing costumes meant to parody the 1950s. Charlie received his guests in a black suit with sequined lapels, and spectator shoes. Margaret showed up in her high-buttoned boots, a maxi-skirt, and a black feather hat with a half-veil.

Charlie was a tireless pun artist. In paintings like *Noblesse Oblige*, of a Royal Canadian Mounted Policeman holding his horse against a yellow sky and wearing a mask borrowed from the Lone Ranger, he was both celebrating and sending up the bizarre hybrid myth of the West. It was camp, it was fun. The reviewers the next day seemed suspicious that this Toronto interloper was making fun of the locals. But Charlie loved Calgary: "It was in Alberta that I really discovered Canada," he says.[38] In fact, Alberta was producing its own parodists. Robert Kroetsch's hilarious novel *The Studhorse Man*, which parodied not only Western myths but the *Odyssey* and classical mythology as well, had just been published. The Prairie artists, as they would be called, would spearhead much of the change that would occur in Canadian art in the next decade.

That spring, Margaret travelled a lot. In April she went up to Prince George to give a reading and stayed in the home of the poet Barry McKinnon. As a travelling writer in those days, one took what one could get, and she slept on a mattress on the living-room floor, waking to find nine pups had been born in the next room overnight. The mother had sat on five of them and didn't know how to feed the other four. Margaret and Barry spent the day feeding the pups with an eyedropper. She wrote to Eli: "Nature isn't automatic. One sometimes wonders how it manages to keep going at all."[39] She thought perhaps she should have been a vet.

She was back in Toronto in May and attended the People's Poet Award party for the Maritime poet Milton Acorn, Gwen's ex-husband. He had been passed over for the Governor General's Award that year, and Irving Layton and Eli Mandel had put together an alternative award. Margaret was among those who had contributed money. She had never quite forgotten Layton's comment that women should not invade men's territory by writing, and told Eli that "Irving ethically should send my cheque back, since he doesn't approve of how I made my money (selling poems & other encroachments on male territory) . . . [but] I'll suppress my Scorpio tendencies for the moment."[40] She could distinguish between the man and his macho public persona. (She and Gwen would discuss how nice he was in private.) She admired the poet, and when she came to edit *The New Oxford Book of Canadian Verse in English* years later she featured his work prominently. But she wouldn't let him get away with his public dismissal of women writers.

The directors of *The Edible Woman* had been asking Margaret to come to London, and with the financial security that the film option provided she and Jim decided they could live there for a while. This meant Jim would be giving up a secure job, but he elected to forgo the safety of the academic box. Margaret wrote to Gwen that they were faced with packing and pulling up stakes, but they would be "very glad to shake Edmonton off our feet. It wasn't catastrophic but would have been if we'd stayed."[41] Looking back, Jim remarks: "After two years it had become clear that we weren't happy there and it was affecting our relationship. There was a movie to be made in London, there was international interest in her work, and it seemed certain that a major career — well, in fact, it still wasn't all that certain — but the thing she wouldn't be doing was the small campus thing she had imagined."

12

MYTHOGRAPHERS

Jim and Margaret moved to England. For three weeks, they stayed near Kew Gardens in an eighteenth-century house full of old harps, ornate furniture, and *objets d'art*; it belonged to a friend of Oscar Lewenstein, the producer of *The Edible Woman*. Soon they found a flat at 29 St. Dionis Road in Southwest London. The flat was adequate, with good working space, but it was filled with cat fleas. Living in furnished apartments had begun to get tiresome. Margaret had been doing that for ten years. She began to long for her own home.

London was plagued by endless strikes that winter. The first was the garbage strike. Pyramids of garbage filled the city's squares and greens, and rats crept into houses. The electricity strike and then the postal strike followed. As the weather turned cold and damp, Margaret and Jim were forced to huddle under blankets. They turned to each other and said: "We're back in Edmonton."[1] But it was wonderful to be in England, to be able to go to plays, operas, and museums, and to enter, however tentatively, the London film world.

Margaret had completed the first draft of the screenplay for *The Edible Woman* in April, so, when she and Jim arrived in London, George Kaczender was ready to think about casting. As the search for a lead actress got under way, they were hustled off to view film clips and to see plays and movies. It was an exciting time.

Yet, however glamorous it was, Margaret was not seduced by the film world. She was a writer and that meant writing. She decided to resurrect her "camp novel," "The Nature Hut," and thought she might have a first draft ready by mid-November. Its structure was immensely complex, narrated from the point of view of eight characters, and, after 250 pages, she abandoned it once and for all. But she would always consider it one of those salutary exercises in failure. Salutary because, to one who has failed and survived, the idea of failing again isn't so terrifying.

Little, Brown, Margaret's American publisher, had decided to bring out both *The Edible Woman* and *Procedures for Underground* that fall. She was still a young, unknown author, and the prospect was exhilarating. But something was happening in her country that overshadowed the American publication of her books.

On 6 October, the British newspapers reported that British Trade Commissioner James Cross had been abducted from his Montreal home by a revolutionary cell of the FLQ. On 10 October, Pierre Laporte, Quebec Minister of Labour and Immigration, was also kidnapped from his front yard by two masked men. Six days later, Prime Minister Pierre Trudeau and his federal Cabinet invoked the War Measures Act, suspending civil liberties in Canada.

When Margaret and Jim opened *The Times* on 17 October, the front page headline read: "Wartime Emergency Regulations Imposed on Whole of Canada." Declaring a "state of apprehended insurrection," the Canadian government had authorized a massive police operation in the early hours of the morning. According to *The Times*, one thousand parachute troops had been brought in from Edmonton, and another five hundred were coming up from New Brunswick. "Authorities believe there are 22 active FLQ cells with a total membership of 130. So far," Margaret read, "there have been more than 250 arrests."[2]

On the night of 17 October, the body of Minister Laporte was found in the trunk of an abandoned car parked near the St.-Hubert airport, one mile from an army encampment being used by troops taking part in the emergency measures. Laporte had been "executed." Arrest warrants were issued for three suspects whose names were already known to police.

Montreal, *The Times* reported, was "a city under siege."[3] Armed soldiers stood guard on the rooftops of almost every building within five blocks of Notre Dame Cathedral when Laporte's funeral took place three days later. The press and radio were in a state of hysteria: news was given out, then denied, then officially corrected. Speculations followed rumours. A young girl claimed that she'd been abducted by the FLQ, and showed the group's letters branded on her stomach. It took days before her story was exploded as a ruse.

The reports were so confusing that, in hopes of making sense of it all, Margaret and Jim took to going to Canada House to read the Canadian coverage. There they found fellow Canadian exiles in a state of mourning. Such things were supposed to happen elsewhere, not in Canada.

The army had virtually unlimited powers of search and detention. By the end of November, there had been 3,068 raids. Four hundred and fifty-three people had been arrested, many of them simply artists and students who had ideologically supported Quebec independence. There were allegations of brutality in Quebec jails. "Repression," reported *The Times*, "is not a way of curing anything."

Gwen MacEwen wrote to Margaret that it was a devastating time. "The last weeks since the Laporte murder have been bleak. One shouldn't be surprised, of course, but something went THUD in my stomach on October 17th, and there's an awful taste in my mouth which I can't get rid of."[4]

Fifty-nine days after his abduction, Cross was discovered in an apartment in the north end of Montreal. He was alive.

For Jim, whose own country had recently been through the Kennedy and the King assassinations, the event was not outside the realm of possibility, but to Margaret, as to most Canadians, the whole affair was inconceivable.

Many Canadians would never forgive the federal government for the arrests of so many innocent people. Margaret believed it demonstrated that Canada, like any country, was a "scary place." In the future she would be willing to go on record with her opposition to the War Measures Act. Addressing students at Dalhousie University in 1980, she would say: "If you think Canada is really a county dedicated to democracy and the principle of free speech, remember the War Measures Act. . . . Remember how few people spoke out. We are a timorous country, and we do tend to believe that what those in authority do must, somehow, be justified."[5]

Margaret told Gwen she doubted that the real story behind the scenes those few months in the fall of 1970 would ever be known. But the October Crisis confirmed what, in her darkest moments, she deeply believed: that the ground underfoot was unstable. Because of what had happened in Quebec, she went to the offices of Amnesty International in London, and became a member.

The American reviews of *The Edible Woman* began to come out that winter, and were almost invariably positive. In *The Milwaukee Journal*, Marjorie Bitker wrote: "Move over Muriel Spark, Honor Tracy, and all the other fiendishly clever female writers. Here is a young woman of 30, Canadian born, with four published books of poetry behind her, who has produced one of the funniest novels of many a year."[6] In a long review in *The New York Times*, Millicent Bell elaborated:

> We are all prone these days to gloomy laughter or comic despair as we consider our lives in consumerdom, the country where in the end we find ourselves consumed — that is, converted into waste by the things we acquire, the goods and packaged ideas dispensed along the supermarket aisles of our culture. In this first novel, however, a female hand gives an extra twist to the switchblade. The Canadian poet Margaret Atwood has written a work of *feminist* [my emphasis] black humour, in which she seems to say that a woman is herself likely to become another "edible" product, marketed for the male appetite that has been created (or, at least, organized) by the media. . . .
>
> But Miss Atwood's imagination is too wacky and sinister for situation comedy — and, to our considerable diversion, her comic distortion veers at times into surreal meaningfulness.[7]

Margaret was being inducted into the pantheon of the new "women writers." She found herself, for the first time, labelled a "feminist."

With the attention the novel received, Margaret suddenly had access to magazines interested in publishing her fiction. "Under Glass," "The Grave of the Famous Poet," "Encounters with the Element Man," and "Polarities" were written that year. Turning back to a novel she'd started in 1964–65, she began to work in earnest. Eventually she would call the novel *Surfacing*.

She wrote to Gwen that she was also working on a children's book for which she was doing the drawings and hand-setting the type in Letraset. "I seem to have lost interest come to think of it in the last couple of weeks — it may go the way of many of my Great Ideas. My latest is that someone should rent a small theatre and play re-runs of old radio shows completely in the dark; wouldn't you like to be able to drop in and listen to The Jack Benny Show, The Green Hornet, Inner Sanctum, Our Miss Brooks and many many more for $1.00 or so?"[8]

As she always did when feeling desperate at the turns the world took, Gwen resorted to humour, inviting Margaret to become a member of the Flat Earth Society, of which she was Canadian vice-president: "One of our immediate aims is to approach the United Nations with the request that a large fence be built around the Edge of the earth to save people from falling off into the Abyssmal Chasm, and also to discourage possible suicides. If you feel, then, that you are more or less on the Brink, you must join the club."[9] Margaret duly joined up.

That fall, *The Guardian* did a profile on Margaret as a young Canadian writer living in England. Deutsch had brought out *The Edible Woman* the previous winter. The interviewer, Raymond Gardner, was slightly officious. He remarked it was unusual that she should be writing a novel about a young woman trying to drop into society when the norm for first novels was the portrait of the artist dropping out. He asked her how much of *The Edible Woman* was autobiographical. She responded: "The book is about someone who does not know what to do with her life and that has never been my predicament."[10]

When George Woodcock asked if she'd met the author Julian Symons, who had written a glowing review of *The Edible Woman* in *The Listener*, she replied that they "hadn't made efforts to meet much of anyone to tell you the truth, because 1) busy and 2) don't want to come through like another pushy North American."[11] But her editor at Andre Deutsch, Diana Athill, made sure her young author felt comfortable and there were parties. Margaret and Jim were invited to dinner with Jean Rhys, then in her eighties, who took a shine to Jim. As they tried to talk literature, Rhys simply sat there glowing. Diana Athill explained: "You know, she likes chaps." They also met Brian Moore at Athill's, with whom Margaret talked passionately about the War Measures Act in Canada.

One important friendship was cemented in England. The Canadian novelist Margaret Laurence was living with her two children at Elm Cottage at Penn, a small village near High Wycombe in Buckinghamshire.

The two writers had seen little of each other since the Governor General's Award ceremony in 1966. When Laurence first tried phoning Margaret in London, she was informed that the number belonged to a telephone booth in Earl's Court Exhibition. When they finally spoke, Margaret said she'd long suspected that they lived in a phone booth. The flat was about the same size and temperature, and the phone seemed always to cut out mid-conversation. Agreeing to meet in January, Margaret asked whether there was anything she could bring Laurence from London — perhaps "some smog or a little of the mellowed garbage they hadn't collected yet?"[12]

The reunion was enthusiastic. Laurence delighted in Jim. She found they could talk about the small Midwestern towns they had come from, and about the eccentrics in them. Laurence liked to say she thought everyone was mad as bats, and "normality" was a "reassurance word" that really meant nothing. Jim had no trouble agreeing with this.

In their correspondence, Margaret and Laurence began to talk about feminism. Margaret had sent Laurence a copy of *Sisterhood Is Powerful: An Anthology of Writings from the Women's Liberation Movement*, which had come out in September 1970. The book contained two of the most influential articles from the Women's Liberation movement: "The Politics of Orgasm" and "The Politics of Housework."

Women's Liberation was a completely new thing. Margaret had, of course, read Betty Friedan's *The Feminine Mystique* (1963) and Simone de Beauvoir's *The Second Sex*, but the first time she had heard of the new feminism was in 1969 in Edmonton, when her old room-mate and friend, Sue Milmoe, had sent her a copy of the article "The Politics of Housework."

The new feminism was an American phenomenon. NOW (National Organization for Women) had been established in 1966. More radical groups like WITCH and the Coat Hangers had begun the same year with "rap sessions," "bitch sessions," and "consciousness raising" groups. By 1969, the demand for women's rights had snowballed and an astonishing number of women's groups were formed in cities throughout the United States (New York City alone had more than two hundred of them). In 1970 Gloria Steinem and Brenda Feigen formed the umbrella group WAA (Women's Action Alliance), and Kate Millett made the cover of *Time* magazine for her book *Sexual Politics*. Ms. magazine was founded by Steinem and Feigen in 1971.

But Margaret Atwood and Margaret Laurence had had their consciousnesses raised long before official feminism. Shortly after receiving the anthology *Sisterhood Is Powerful*, Laurence wrote back:

Elm Cottage. Friday.

Dear Peggy,

Very much thanks for sending me the Women's Lib publication and the poems of bill bissett. Haven't read the poems yet, but read some of the Women's Lib this morning. I guess I really do have an ambiguous attitude to Women's Lib — basically, I am in great agreement. I can't go along with some of the attitudes, but quite a few women in the movement can't, either. I'm not a joiner in the sense that I shall never find a cause with which I agree over detailed beliefs 100%, but of course that isn't so important. I thought "The Politics of Housework" was great! I recognized all the arguments from way back, of course. Except that in my case, I was too naïve and uncertain (yeh, even at 34) to do much more than argue sporadically or resent silently. I suppose I do find it emotionally trying to read the Women's Lib stuff, not because I disagree with most of it, but because in many ways I wish so profoundly that such a general movement had existed let's say 15 years ago. I feel as though I have in fact fought every single one of those issues, but alone and therefore not effectually from the point of view of relationships. The only solution for me, therefore, was to take off and learn to accept the fact that at 44 now, and considering the men of my generation, and also considering that my work is of enormous overwhelming importance to me, there's no way of having a partnership on the only terms I could bear now . . . a relationship of equals.[13]

In "The Politics of Housework," the art historian Pat Mainardi, inspired by the two hundred years (by her calculation) of housework her mother and aunts had contributed to civilization—"May our daughters be spared"—had written an amusing dialogue with men about who does the "shitwork."[14] Laurence was delighted.

But she also had some concerns. There was an ideological vehemence to feminism that disturbed her. She felt, rightly, that women like herself, who had made their own professional lives, were often resented. A second book that appeared in 1970, *Women's Liberation: Blueprint for the Future*, warned in its preface: "There has always been a small percentage of 'exceptional' women. We are not impressed. . . . In our efforts to organize a movement, we have become suspicious of creating an elite."[15]

And there was something else that Laurence found even more disturbing. Women, like herself, who had had children began to feel uncomfortable, as if they were somehow being accused of colluding with the patriarchy. Laurence complained to Margaret:

> I would say that if a woman doesn't want to have kids, that is her business and hers only. But if she deeply does, that does not mean she is not interested in anything else. I don't really feel I have to analyse my own motives in wanting children. For my own reassurance? For fun? For ego-satisfaction? No matter. It's like (to me) asking why you want to write. Who cares? You have to, and that's that.

Finally, in a postscript, Laurence added a note about the article "The Politics of Orgasm": "All that nonsense about vaginal organisms seems trivial to me. If you come, you come. . . . who needs charts? Let it be. Maybe it should just be accepted as your portion of grace, or part of it."[16]

Margaret, at thirty-two, was twelve years younger than Laurence, and had had a completely different experience. She had gone her own way from the beginning. She wrote back:

Dear Margaret: 18 Jan 71

> There's a lot in yr letter I'd like to talk about — the vaginal orgasm thing *is* important, not because of the charts or lying there wondering which part of yr bod is reacting, etc., leave

that to the scientists, but because it knocks the props out from under the whole Freudian superstructure. I think Freud is right most of the time about men, but he sure was way off base on women. He was making a construct — based on vaginal orgasm — which made men, or the Magic Penis, *necessary* for women. You see where that leaves lesbians (freaks, abnormal, unsatisfied, having to rely on carrots, etc; or fixated at a "childish" level of psychological development). It also made life very tough for women who were so constructed — or had men so constructed — that more than the Magic Penis was required   they were told they had Penis Envy & wanted to be men, & if they could get over that they would automatically have a Rich Full Sexual Life. It's not the orgasms *per se* that matter — it's the use (as weapons against women) it's been put to. Wipe out your identity & have Vaginal Orgasms, etc. I've had a bit of contact with the Freudian school of psychology as applied to women and wow. . . .

As for my so-called generation — most of them were raging male chauvinists of the most blood-curdling description, though I guess they had enough flexibility to be able to change a little. But the world is still full of them, and some of the worst are some of the youngest who haven't fought it through yet. I just decided at age 17 that I wasn't going to get married because it would kill me or my writing (same thing to me then) and had about 5 years of various kinds of hell. Jim is really a kind of exception, and it's hard for him a lot of the time — having a writer wife & getting asked condescendingly at parties "And what do *you* do?" etc.

The male writer thing is still around too — both the "male" writers of my generation had trouble with me at first, didn't know whether to shake my hand or grab my ass, but they're ok now. . . . The most comfortable thing for them seems to be to turn one into a sort of White Witch or Wise Woman, quasi-maternal, one who will Understand About Writing and also about Problems. Leading to some fairly grotesque situations.

> Yes, I think the Movement women do tend to resent those who've done it alone. . . . You've made it within the system and in a way you're a refutation of their feeling We All Have To Pull Together. . . . I hate groups so much that it would be a real sacrifice for me to join, but I might just try it. Yes I can see why you wouldn't want to get too deep into the women's lib theory part of it; but I feel that just writing the truth is in a way a better contribution anyway; as encountering real-life men & their attitudes is more convincing than reading theories about it.

Margaret felt that what Women's Lib did for her was simply give a sense of moral support. "It's really hard to go the way you know is write [right! what a pun!] for you and have everyone else (everyone else, not just men) think you're immoral or some kind of a freak. What a relief to discover there are those who think you may be right."[17]

But there was one area where the new Women's Liberation movement wasn't helpful. If you had devoted yourself to your work, and yet wanted children, how was this to be done? Margaret looked back with dismay at those stories she had written as a teenager, in which she had described the greatest horror as getting pregnant and ending up doing diapers and dishes. She now understood how condescending and naïve her young bohemianism had been.

Though Margaret found the feminists had gotten a lot right, she didn't need feminism to tell her she didn't have to have children. What she secretly wanted was someone to tell her that she could. That it cost her grief was clear. There is an eerie poem in her sequence *Power Politics*:

> This year I intended children
> a space where I could raise
> foxes and strawberries, finally
> be reconciled to fur seeds & burrows
>
> but the entrails of dead cards
> are against me, foretell
> it will be water, the

element that shaped
me, that I shape by
being in

    It is the blue
cup, I fill it

It is the pond again
where the children, looking from
the side of the boat, see their mother

upside down, lifesize, hair streaming
over the slashed throat
and words fertilize each other
in the cold and with bulging eyes [18]

Almost like a soothsayer or sibyl, she reads the Tarot pack and has drawn the card of the cup. In her world it is only words that fertilize, and she is their barren captive. The unclaimed children look to the drowning mother in the water. Margaret had written a kind of elegy for her generation of women who felt they had to forgo children for the sake of their professional work.

Margaret would always describe herself as a feminist, but not an ideological one. As her books *Power Politics* and *The Edible Woman* became increasingly well known, feminists thought they had found a champion, but she sometimes felt as if the movement were appropriating her. Jim puts it succinctly: "Peggy grew up on such a fringe of society, and tried to live up to all that entailed, and then she became classified — by the feminist literature movement and many another thing besides — which quite frustrated her at times. She sees herself as a feminist on some level, but that is not her major contribution."[19]

Two months after her letter to Laurence, in March 1971, Margaret's collection of poems *Power Politics* was published by the House of Anansi under the editorship of Shirley Gibson. (Harper & Row would publish it in the United States in 1973.) The first poems had been composed on the back of English Department memos at the University of Alberta. Amusingly, there appears on the back of a memo dated February 1970 what is probably the first draft of the famous opening quatrain of *Power Politics*: "You fit into me / like a hook into an eye / a fish hook / an open eye." On the other side is a list of English Department committee assignments. Margaret had sent out parts of the sequence to British magazines in 1970; the poems were all rejected.

Margaret described *Power Politics* as a book that deals with female–male power relationships at three levels: individual, political, and mythological. She added: "I don't believe poetry is or should be 'self-expression' in any naïve, personal sense. Rather I see it as a lens through which the human universe can see itself, an aural focusing through which human languages can hear themselves."[20]

When the poems came out, she was asked to make a selection, with commentary, for a broadcast by the CBC program "Ideas." She explained that she was looking at power as "our environment":

> We would all like to have a private life that is sealed off from the public life and different from it, where there are no rulers and ruled, no hierarchies, no politicians, only equals, free people. But because any culture is a closed system and our culture is one based and fed on power this is impossible, or at least very difficult. Unfortunately; since the exercise of power is the opposite of the practice of love. Love gives, but power takes, and justifies itself for taking. So many of the things we do in what we sadly think of as our personal lives are simply duplications of the external world of power games, power struggles. The amount of effort we expend concealing this state of affairs from ourselves and from each other is even sadder.
>
> The title of my collection of poems, *Power Politics*, was taken from a letter written to me by a close friend; she was describing a bad situation she herself was in. I saw the same phrase two days later in a newspaper. For me that's where the poems exist — halfway between letter and newspaper, the so-called public world and the so-called personal world.
>
> Poetry isn't a sermon or a solution or even an analysis. But

Oliver Cogswell

Margaret in Northern Quebec, 1971

House of Anansi Press, 1971.
Clockwise from left: Dennis Lee, Arden Ford, George Orr, Ann Wall, Byron Wall,
Shirley Gibson, Paul Meyer, Art Mayer, Christine McClymont

bp Nichol and bill bissett, early 1970s

Susan Sandler and Beth Appeldoorn, Longhouse Book Shop, Toronto

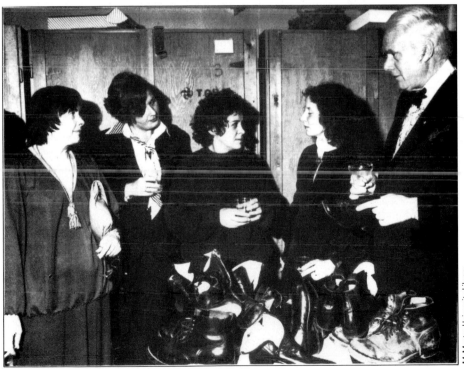

Writers' Union: Eclectic Typewriter Revue, 1977.
From left to right: Marian Engel, Ruth Clarke, Alma Lee, Margaret, Pierre Berton

*Margaret and Graeme
with Wook Kyung Choi, Alliston, Ontario*

Charles Pachter

*Graeme and Margaret on
Sullivan Street in Toronto, 1980*

Charles Pachter

Margaret and daughter, Jess

Margaret and Graeme

Pen Benefit at Harbourfront, 1985. From left to right: Mordecai Richler, Alice Munro, Brenda Davies, Robertson Davies, Timothy Findley. Greg Gatenby in forefront.

Harbourfront Literary Reading Series

Margaret and Michael Ondaatje

Margaret at Gracie's, Charlie Pachter's Queen Street restaurant, 1981

sometimes it's a reflection. We use reflections of ourselves in mirrors so we can see what we look like. If the sight is too horrible we sometimes make efforts to change. But with no recognition there can be no change.[21]

Margaret was insisting that the schizophrenic divide we make between the public and the private is nothing like as secure as we presume. We live as if we believed that the intimate and private world is a space we can retreat to, but there, too, we bring the games of power that inform our public world. Why should we expect it to be otherwise?

What we call love is as culturally conditioned as anything else we do. To loving, we import the mythologies that have accumulated from our culture. Love begins in a kind of mythomania; it carries its own histrionics and extremism. In modern culture, this includes the imagery from romantic cinema. We want love to be an epic story, which carries its own paraphernalia: the waltz, the dinner scene in the movie, the hotel with the potted palms, the love song and its string of aphorisms. Margaret was already looking at the idea of love as an addiction, and the self as constructed. Each gender has its iconic images: the woman as patient Penelope, as Daphne, as primitive cave goddess, and the man as questing adventurer, as conquering knight, as Bluebeard, as Dracula. Only from the outside does it look as if the man has all the power. Each side exercises power, and the capacity to hurt in love is astonishing.

In these poems, the woman is also a mythographer, demanding that the man be larger than life. When we get down to the deep mystery of love, we discover we invent each other; we dance with strangers. The poems are driven by a fierce, direct, unsettling (because often humorous) voice asking for truths about our most confusing human mystery: how a man and woman can be together and forgo the power struggle.

They are hostile nations

1

In view of the fading animals
the proliferation of sewers and fears

the sea clogging, the air
nearing extinction

we should be kind, we should
take warning, we should forgive each other

Instead we are opposite, we
touch as though attacking,

the gifts we bring
even in good faith maybe
warp in our hands to
implements, to manoeuvres

2

Put down the target of me
you guard inside your binoculars,
in turn I will surrender

this aerial photograph
(your vulnerable
sections marked in red)
I have found so useful

See, we are alone in
the dormant field, the snow
that cannot be eaten or captured

3

Here there are no armies
here there is no money

It is cold and getting colder
We need each others'

breathing, warmth, surviving
is the only war
we can afford, stay

walking with me, there is almost
time / if we can only
make it as far as

the (possibly) last summer

They were all inaccurate:

the hinged bronze man, the fragile man
built of glass pebbles,
the fanged man with his opulent capes and boots

peeling away from you in scales.

It was my fault but you helped,
you enjoyed it.

Neither of us will enjoy
the rest: you following me
down streets, hallways, melting
when I touch you,
avoiding the sleeves of the bargains
I hold out for you,
your face corroded by truth,

crippled, persistent. You ask
like the wind, again and again and
wordlessly, for the one forbidden thing:

love without mirrors and not for
my reasons but your own.

The poems were not personal exorcisms. They were not costly confessions. The cost of the poems came from standing up and breaking taboos: the unsayable was being said. They shattered romantic myths and altered the spectrum of assumptions and perceived possibilities in relationships between men and women. They suggested love took time and courage, and had to be nurtured.

For Margaret, of course, who always delighted in shaking things up, in claiming new territory and opening doors, it was exciting, heady stuff. Still, even she wasn't prepared for the persona of Medusa and ice maiden that would begin to attach to her public image.

The response to *Power Politics* was electric. Margaret Laurence wrote to her:

> The poems, as a matter of fact, hit me like the spirit of god between the eyes. The very very short beginning one . . . "You fit into me like a hook into an eye . . ." was, I felt, absolutely stunning because it expressed in hardly any words the whole man–woman thing in its painful essence or perhaps I mean in the essence of the pain which can be involved in it. I think the same is true of a great many of the poems in the book. They aren't bitter, which is good. They are sometimes vicious, as those who know about traps sometimes are. They also imply an enormous need of one another, a belief that men and women do not necessarily have to vitiate one another even tho they so often do.[22]

Laurence also wrote the same words to her friend Al Purdy, adding: "Wow, that is some book, eh? . . . I admire her poetry more than I can say. I also love her as a human, and somehow, once we really talked, did not find her frightening, as I thought I might. Instead, I felt I could level with her. And probably did."[23]

The reviews that came out in Canada were intriguing. Many had little to do with the poetry. Bruce Blackadar wrote in *The Windsor Star*: "Her face on the back cover is like [an] instant of utter honesty and horrifying self-revelation. . . . How long can we bear such intimacy?"[24] Peter Stevens wrote in *The Globe and Mail* that "the whole book seethes with cool outrage. Yet this chronicle of two people violating each other in the name of human love sets up its own limitations. . . . The language gives a sense of unconcern."[25] Sid Stephen reported in his review that, when he gave the book to a self-proclaimed male chauvinist, the man replied with delight that the poems reinforced his basic distrust of the opposite sex. "But don't they upset you?" Stephen asked. "Not a bit; she thinks like a man," he answered, "hard and clean and mean."[26] Another reviewer wrote:

> It must be rather easy, intellectually, to live in a world where solutions to wars, malnutrition, hunger, environmental dangers, the disastrous effects of technology, etc. have all one cause, and therefore one solution: find the man, kill him, create a sisterhood of love. This kind of "power politics," Margaret Atwood's words, seems so self-defeating, world-defeating, so infantile . . . that it might be entirely ignored were it not for the success of its special pleading among women poets who associate freedom with fanciful killing or with a liberated sexual vocabulary.[27]

Asked in 1976 whether she had been surprised by the animus of certain reviewers, Margaret replied: "Well, it's a question of what people find acceptable. Poems by men about the wicked behavior of women are part of a venerable tradition going back at least as far as the Elizabethans' Cruel Mistress, and few people bother to analyze conventional modes. We don't bat an eyelid when we read about bitch goddesses or when we see portraits of women with big tits and no heads. But women aren't supposed to say nasty things about men. It's not nice and it's not conventional."[28]

As she began to give public readings from *Power Politics*, Margaret found that, when she read her hook-and-eye epigram, the usual response was horror. But she had expected people would see the humour. "There are people who won't laugh unless you flash an orange neon sign that says

LAUGH NOW. You have to accept that," she remarked ruefully to an interviewer. "Here again it's a question of what is and is not acceptable. Irving Layton can read his extremely nasty poems about women and his audience finds them hilarious. My poems about men are not received that way, although I've never written a poem about a male academic who has pimples on his bum. I don't go in for explicit personal attacks like that. I don't know why. Maybe I have a lingering feeling that ladies should be polite."[29]

Two years later, the American reviews of *Power Politics* seemed less personal; mostly they looked directly at the poetry. Dick Allen, in *Poetry*, described *Power Politics* as a "top-flight sequence of poems about a love affair, written with intensity of feeling, careful craft, and harrowing imagery. . . . [It] is an honest, searching book which touches deeply; it goes about as close to the core of the love struggle as Sylvia Plath did at her very best; we emerge from the experience shaken and at once tough and tender."[30]

Helen Vendler, one of America's best poetry critics, reviewing three books in *The New York Times Book Review*, clearly found Margaret's the most impressive:

> Margaret Atwood's "Power Politics" is a true sequence, a death struggle between man and woman. . . . To those who take it straight [the book] moves almost unwillingly, but relentlessly, through a brilliant schema of unflagging suspense and pitches of drama. . . . Atwood is so accomplished that one can only hope that she will enlarge her poetic scope and scale, tune her vision to longer wavelengths.[31]

It would take time to assimilate what Margaret had done in these poems. She had exploded the myth of romantic love that held women in a kind of emotional vise. Women had been trained to believe that love is a life solution, that they must search for the other, the soul mate, who is the necessary completion to their own identity. It is the myth that, for centuries, has pervaded our literature, from high culture to the dime-store bodice-rippers. But, curiously, the love story never had a happy ending. The lovers died in their transcendent passion — the Tristan and Isolde story — or the women were abandoned and left to mourn the purity of their love — as in Elizabeth Smart's *By Grand Central Station I Sat Down and Wept*. Such love had little to do with living in the real world. Behind the façade of its high rhetoric, the myth of romantic love invited pose, accusation, counter-accusation, the victor/victim complex that so fascinated Margaret. When she called her sequence about love "Power Politics," she was signalling that, in a culture whose engine is power, and which is structured on the principle of domination through race, class, gender, to pretend that power does not function in personal relationships seems a deliberate and wilful blindness. Women should take a harder look. Margaret understood that the addiction to the emotional turmoil of love was a dangerous illusion for women, and women and men would better be served if that myth were exploded. But she wasn't simply interested in tearing down old myths. She imagined something more would be possible. "Being human? Have we achieved it?" she often asked. It might be possible to have a relationship with another that involved a compassionate recognition of that person's separateness, or, as she put it, that "broke the mirrors." Women spent so much time obsessed with love, that, paradoxically, it became self-obsession. Margaret was saying that women would be better off thinking of themselves in a context beyond the universe of two, creatively engaging with the world. In the end we must all take responsibility for ourselves since the only destiny we hold in our hands is our own. And only we hold our own destiny.

By April, it was clear that Minotaur Film Productions of Montreal was floundering and wasn't going to do the film of *The Edible Woman*, but suddenly the British director, Tony Richardson, who had directed two of the blockbuster films of the 1960s, *Tom Jones* and *A Taste of Honey*, picked up the option. Margaret reported to friends that prospects for the movie were looking up again, as the Tarot cards had said they would.

In May, she and Jim drove to the south of France. Richardson had invited them to stay at his villa so that he and Margaret could work on the script. Jim still remembers stepping out of the car in a small mountain town in Provence, only to discover Richardson had bought the whole town. It had about eleven buildings. Waiting to greet them was Sir John Gielgud. The house was filled with exotic parrots, and evenings were spent with Sir John recounting stories, like the one about the time he fell into the lobster salad at the Glyndebourne Opera House. Over the month that Margaret and Jim were there, other theatre and film people visited.

It was all rather dazzling, though Jim made the mistake one night of telling someone he was thinking of specializing in Canadian literature. This elicited the response: "Canadian literature! Why would you do such a thing, James. No. No. No. It's so boring." The scene was fun to watch, but it had little to do with him.

Margaret and Jim went on to Italy. They'd found a house in Anticoli Corrado, a small town in the mountains overlooking a gorge, just east of Rome. It was a spectacular summer. They spent two and a half months there while Margaret worked on *Surfacing*. Everyone they met was writing a novel, and so Jim sat down one day and did the same. He found an agent who liked it, and though publishers rejected it they were sufficiently interested to ask whether he could write short stories. It turned out he could; the first one he would write was published in *The Atlantic Monthly*. He also wrote some articles on animal-story writers in Canada that became the basis for a book published by Clarke, Irwin.

Jim and Margaret moved back to Canada at the end of August. Tony Richardson was in Toronto trying to raise Canadian money for *The Edible Woman*, but this was turning out to be difficult. His last few films hadn't been blockbusters like *Tom Jones* and *A Taste of Honey*, and financial backers were proving more elusive. "Part of the problem," Jim remembers, "was their British attitude. Their approach was: 'Of course you'll lend us money,' and the Canadian response was: 'Of course, we must look into this more carefully.'" Richardson hoped that finding a big enough star would attract backers, and briefly considered Barbra Streisand. He did get money from Telefilm Canada, and the film percolated on for a bit, but it was never made. Jim remarks: "It was a pity since the script was charming. It was to be in the tradition of the small films of the early seventies, like *John and Mary* or *Love Story*. But soon it was too late to resurrect it. Its time was past."

Margaret had been offered a job at York University. They bought a house, 27 Hilton Avenue, behind Casa Loma, and set up their studios, supplementing their income by renting rooms on the top floor to students, including Margaret's sister, Ruth.[32] It was too late in the year for Jim to find another teaching job, and, besides, the academic job market was frozen. Though he continued to send out résumés, he knew no one was hiring.

Outside the country Margaret and Jim had lived the odd symbiosis that comes from being foreign tourists together, but now, back in Toronto, the strain began to show. It was clear both of them were unhappy. At first,

Toronto was not Jim's town and he felt like the foreigner he was. There were friends, like Charlie, but he didn't know where to go in the city to find the life that was there.

Looking back, he remarks:

> It was becoming clear that whatever version of marriage we had had in our mind's eye, we were not following the script, and I didn't know what script we were going to follow. Peggy was very good at dissecting and analysing the expectations of the female role in those days. But neither this nor the male role had anything to do with what we were. I wasn't the model of that male but I didn't know what I was. Peggy certainly wasn't the conventional female. She knew what her calling was. This was never in question. I had some trouble with mine.
>
> Having never thought about marriage, I didn't expect her to cook and clean. None of that ever crossed my mind. One wonders what did cross my mind, or anybody's. What we were living had a certain experiment to it. Making it up as we went along.[33]

This was an extremely difficult time for both of them. In a letter to Margaret Laurence, Margaret described that autumn as awful. She was under enormous pressure, teaching at York, giving readings, doing Anansi work (she was now editing for Dennis Lee's publishing house). To Laurence, her only explanation for what she described as feeling abysmal and panic-stricken was that she had taken on far too much. To say more would have been disloyal to Jim.[34]

In the summer of 1972, after two very bad months, Jim moved out. He and Margaret would divorce in 1977.

It is strange how, in retrospect, what you thought of as your own personal experience often turns out to be part of a much larger general pattern. Jim says reflectively: "There were a lot of agonizingly unhappy relationships in those days because there were so many changes in expectations. Far more so then than there seem to be now, though perhaps it's just that I'm older."

Jim shared with the other young American males of his generation the anxiety of being draftable and the confusion of finding himself exiled in a foreign country. He really didn't know where he was. Years later, when he was interviewed by an academic writing a book on young Americans who came to Canada during the Vietnam War, he discovered his was a common plight. He told the interviewer his first marriage had broken up, and the man replied: "They all did. Every single one of them."

Years later Margaret and Margaret Drabble would look back and realize their lives had followed patterns that they hadn't been aware of at the time. The paradigms life offers are limited. The women of their generation were breaking down old paradigms at a time when new ones hadn't yet been invented and there were costs.

Margaret was interviewing Drabble for *Chatelaine* magazine and remarked that their generation was the first among women writers to be able to write whatever they wanted. When they'd first started out, their "female material" wasn't considered respectable. "You were one of the first people I can remember reading — the others were Marian Engel and Alice Munro — who would actually deal with what women said in the kitchen when men weren't there, what women thought in the bathtub and things like that, which I had never read before." Drabble replied: "I suppose that really had to do with my own — you could call it arrogant — certainty that what I find interesting, a million other people must find interesting too. I'm not abnormal, I know I'm normal."

In this retrospective interview they looked back at their lives and at what had been possible. Drabble recounts:

> It was difficult. I was brought up, as possibly you were, with this faith that one could do both [successfully combine writing and marriage], one could have a very full life. Of course, what we hadn't realized was that it was absolutely exhausting. A lot of the 60s was spent figuring out that, although in principle one could have children and work, in practice this was very hard.
>
> I was 21 when I had my first [child]. . . . I wasn't going to be silenced and sit at home with the babies. I wrote at home. I think it was hard but I don't think there was any prejudice against my doing it. Certainly, from my mother there was a great deal of encouragement, and even my first husband,

who hated my success, didn't directly oppose my work, if I
can make that distinction.

Margaret remarked that the marriages of a number of Canadian writers followed that pattern: early marriage, children, and a husband who, as
she put it, "then felt that something had been sprung on him that he
hadn't bargained for — namely the success of the woman."[35] Margaret
herself had chosen an alternative route. She had delayed domestic life and
children until later. But her marriage had disintegrated anyway, in part
because Jim had been subjected to and recoiled from the common prejudice: if a woman was powerful, the man she was with had to be an adjunct,
not a completely independent personality. It would take a while for society to allow successful women to be freed from the assumption that they
turned men into eunuchs.

During those two black months in the summer of 1972, Jim began writing short stories. The first one, titled "The Phrenology of Love," was a
hilarious, though poignant, send-up of his Montana roots. Set in a
fictional town called Hebb, its central figure is a middle-aged high-school
biology teacher, Evalt Jerome Gustavson, who falls in love with a bald lady,
Mrs. Grace Split, who plays bull fiddle in a Western band at the Liberty
Head on Highway 9. Jim has a great ear for comic dialogue and he caught
the repressed puritanical extremes of the Midwest. The story, accepted by
The Atlantic and published the next year, won the award for the best
fiction of the year.[36] At the time, he was writing to prove he could. Looking back, he realizes that the loneliness of that summer had been constructive. He remarks: "Now that it is all receding — it was twenty-five years
ago — it seems like a very creative and productive time for both of us."

In 1975, Margaret published her story "Hair Jewelry." It reads like a
kind of envoi, a gesture of affection after the relationship was over. She
and Jim are not the characters in the story, but in building the initial
romantic relationship between the two figures, she recovered a few details
of their time together at Harvard. For instance, the main characters build
a snow lady of Queen Victoria, as she and Jim had done. This was like
those Alfred Hitchcock cameos again, a private moment buried in a story
about something else. What it said was that it had truly been a love affair.
Jim responds: "Oh, yes, we were in love. This was a real thing for a while."

13

TRANSFIXED

While she and Jim were living in Italy, Margaret had received a letter from Dennis Lee asking if she would join the editorial board of the House of Anansi. His letter was really a cry of panic. When Anansi was established in 1967, Jack McClelland of McClelland and Stewart had predicted that the press would survive eighteen months. So far, it had lasted four years. But, in 1971, it was in trouble.

Anansi was really a phenomenon of the sixties. Legend has it that the founding of the press took place over beer at the Pilot Tavern in Toronto. It was said that Dave Godfrey and Dennis Lee could not get their own work published because it failed to interest American branch-plant publishers in Canada. They founded their own publishing house to create a space for themselves and for other new Canadian talent. But it was much more casual than that. Dennis Lee recalls that Anansi started as an improvisation: "Why don't we publish *The Kingdom of Absence*? Shall we make up a name so it sounds like a real publishing house?"[1]

Dennis and Dave set up the press in the subarctic basement of Dave's rented Edwardian house at 671 Spadina Avenue, next door to the Wing On Funeral Home. They converted one end of the cellar into an office, and shelved the press's inventory in the furnace room. Their first full-time employee was Doug Fetherling, a recently arrived poet and Vietnam War resister, whom Dennis described as a young eighteen-year-old of enormous manic energy. And a gifted poet. They paid him thirty-five dollars a week, fifteen of which he returned in rent for cot space in the same basement.[2]

The House of Anansi started with poetry books. They reprinted

Margaret's *Circle Game*, and published new books by young poets like Fetherling and Joe Rosenblatt, and soon they did Michael Ondaatje's *The Collected Works of Billy the Kid*. They also published fiction, including Godfrey's collection of stories, *Death Goes Better with Coca-Cola*. But they had another focus too. In January 1968, they brought out *Manual for Draft-Age Immigrants to Canada*, a detailed guide on how to survive as a draft dodger in Canada.

Dave was a young man with many causes. Dennis describes him as super-bright, with a tactical mind. "I think he woke up every morning and reinvented the universe. There was a splenetic, contained fury that nobody understood. He was constantly drawing targets around whatever an arrow would light on — foreign capital, big publishing houses, universities — and he invented the superstructure of the enemy in retrospect."[3]

One of Dave's causes was his own invention of a product called Makka, a powdered substance which, when mixed with water, was supposed to contain all the essential nutrients; it was to be a cheap means of feeding the hungry of Africa. Another was the Student Union for Peace Action. As the Vietnam War got hotter, deserters and draft dodgers crossed the Canadian border. Dennis and his wife, Donna, counselled deserters one night a week in their home. In fact, a couple of them took up residence for a brief period.

The manual became a runaway success, and Anansi became the "apotheosis of the underground." Draft dodgers and would-be authors showed up at the front door of 671 Spadina, only to be redirected down the laneway to Anansi's inauspicious back-door entrance. Soon after the publication of the manual, the RCMP arrived with wire-tapping equipment.

It was the sixties and everyone was out to reinvent everything. While Dave was interested in "entrepreneurial activism," Dennis wanted to change education. He was teaching at his old alma mater, Victoria College, but had come to the conclusion that the modern bureaucratized university could no longer work. So he invented his own college. In 1968, he and Howard Adelman (then teaching philosophy at York University) founded Rochdale College.

The evolution of the college was rather baroque. As a young student, Adelman had become president of the Campus Co-operative Residences Incorporated, an organization whose purpose was to provide low-cost housing for students. By the mid-sixties, his pet project was to build a cost-effective high-rise student residence. With the University of Toronto's co-operation, he gained legal college status for what came to be called the "Rochdale project." But soon the Co-op's Education Committee, fired up by Dennis, changed this housing experiment into a radical experiment in co-operative education. Rochdale was to be an in-your-face rebuke to the WASP establishment of the university.[4]

In 1968, six run-down Co-op houses were designated as Rochdale College, while Dennis and Adelman waited for the completion of the eighteen-storey high-rise at the corner of Bloor and Huron sreets. Their intention was to create a college where students could live and work independently in a context of unstructured education: "no faculty, no grades, none of the oppressive infrastructure of the old way." Rochdale was unwilling "to prescribe or proscribe any activity whatever as educational for the person carrying it on," as Dennis later put it.[5] The idea was that it would be run democratically, and the students would decide what they needed to learn. Only the sixties could have come up with such an experiment. Rochdale did spawn important new ideas in co-operative art (the artists General Idea, and Theatre Passe Muraille, were hatched there), but it was also destined to spin off into disasters. In a way, like the sixties themselves. It took less than a year for Rochdale to degenerate, as Doug Fetherling later put it, into a Haight-Ashbury of the north — "the biggest drug supermarket that Canada and maybe the eastern half of North America had ever seen. More importantly, it was a closed dystopian society of the most rigid kind, an authoritarian nightmare of a place where biker gangs, hired as security forces, set up checkpoints in the lobby and patrolled the corridors with vicious dogs; precisely the opposite of what poor Dennis had envisioned." Dennis resigned and the other young "idealists were soon given the sack."[6] Because Dennis was associated with both Rochdale and Anansi, the two were linked in people's minds, which wasn't entirely to Anansi's advantage.

The House of Anansi was always more than a publishing house because the energies of those involved were funnelled off in so many directions. It soon became obvious that Dave and Dennis had different commitments. Yet, both had moral claims on the press. Certainly, Dave wanted a more entrepreneurial, business-like focus. Rumours flew that he and Dennis were headed for a rupture but, in fact, there was no showdown. As Dennis remembers things, "it was a matter of two young alpha males, both on fire, recognizing that they did things in different ways and weren't going to be able to work together indefinitely."[7] Dave left for a year in France to work on his novel, and when he returned, with his friends Roy MacSkimming and Jim Bacque, he decided to found New Press on Sussex Avenue, a short distance from Anansi. But clearly, there *had* been a conflict of tempera-ments between him and Dennis. Years later Dave's wife, Ellen, published a mystery novel titled *The Case of the Cold Murderer*. The setting was a small press. One of the owners, a furrowed-browed WASP literary editor, turned out to be a twisted, psychopathic murderer. Dennis thought briefly of suing.

Fiction had been Dave's turf, but now, as managing editor, Dennis took it over. It was clear he had a shrewd editorial eye for both fiction and poetry. The first novel Anansi published after Dave's departure in 1969 was Graeme Gibson's *Five Legs*. Dennis was sure it would bankrupt the house, but he felt it had to be done because it was brilliant. It turned out to be a publishing triumph. The first week or so it was outselling American pulp writer Jacqueline Susann. Its run of 1,700 sold out within the month and it was reprinted three times that first year. In 1970 Anansi broke new ground with Marian Engel's feminist novel *The Honeyman Festival*. They also published Quebec novelist Roch Carrier's *La Guerre, Yes Sir!* translated from the French by Sheila Fischman, the first in an irregular series of Quebec fiction. Civic activism was not abandoned. Dennis initiated *The Bad Trip* (1970) to protest the proposed construction of the Spadina Expressway, which would have cut the heart out of the city. Anansi was too cash-strapped to bring it out and so it was done as a co-op venture with New Press.

Soon, Anansi decided to test American legislation by printing five thou-sand copies of Allen Ginsberg's *Airplane Dreams* and sending more than half the print-run to the United States in bulk. There was something called the "Manufacturing Clause" in the States, which put a limit on how many copies of a book manufactured outside the country could be imported. But Canada had no equivalent legislation. While American publishers could dump their over-runs across the Canadian border at will (which they did), Canadian publishers had to knuckle under and print their books in the U.S. Anansi was disgusted that Canada, as usual, didn't protect its own. The gesture, however, proved quixotic. The Americans applied their legislation and *Airplane Dreams* was pulped. Anansi lost several thousand dollars.

By 1971, Dennis was feeling burnt out. It was already apparent that, as a rebel publisher, Anansi was helping to create a radical cultural shift in Canadian literature, but being a small Canadian publisher was no longer a novelty. There were now many small presses. Even the bigger branch plants were becoming interested in Canadian authors. And the government was offering grant money to support Canadian titles.

By the summer of 1972, Dennis was ready to give up. Interpersonal relationships at the press had become so involved that, according to Jim Polk, who had joined Anansi's editorial board the previous year, some took to calling it "the House of Atreus."[8] There were internecine politics, divorces, love affairs, and one writer had committed suicide. A warehouse fire the previous year had destroyed half the stock, the accounts were in arrears, and the printer was foreclosing. Perpetually cash-strapped, Anansi explored the possibility of some kind of formal association with Macmillan of Canada, but that publisher wasn't interested. Professing good will, they offered to buy Anansi for a symbolic dollar. It was a brutal slap in the face.

The press staggered on. Jim Polk claimed that the sales of Margaret's *Survival: A Thematic Guide to Canadian Literature* got the press out of this dark period. To everyone's surprise, it turned out to be a best-seller.

When Margaret came on the board in the fall of 1971, Anansi had already left Spadina for a house near the CBC on Jarvis Street. It was not a glamorous place to work. Anansi had not yet become a legend. The only question was how to keep things going.

Margaret was reading manuscripts in time taken from her writing and teaching. Dennis was always astonished by how she could take off with a manuscript, sit down for four hours on a Sunday morning, "and there would be — bang, bang — detailed notes on something that needed catalytic work. Impeccable, local editing, and then she'd pull back and on to the next thing."

Margaret was susceptible to the argument that it was her civic duty to help the "Canadian" cultural project. Anansi had been publishing manuals. They had brought out *Law! Law! Law!* by Paul Copeland and Clayton Ruby, which was a pocket guide to the law, offering, among other things, advice on what to do "when you and the law get acquainted." It wasn't hard to get arrested in the late sixties. They also brought out *VD: The People-to-People Diseases* for the hippies in Yorkville.

Margaret proposed to write a manual too, something along the lines of a reader's guide to Canadian Literature. (Jim would say she was conned into it.) But the idea interested her. She was teaching Canadian Literature at York University, and had discovered that nobody else on the faculty knew the books. At Harvard, the academic centre of the universe, she had always been amazed that professors like Perry Miller and Alan Heimart had been able to pore over the turgid sermons of seventeenth-century Americans as if they were literature, while in Canada even the most interesting Canadian writers didn't merit a footnote. A manual that outlined what was out there would be valuable.

Reverting to some of the theories she had worked out in the early sixties about the cultural peculiarities of Canadians, she set to work on her thesis. She had read Perry Miller's *Errand into the Wilderness*, which located American identity in the obsessive drama of the conquest of nature. Americans had made the frontier their symbol; it expressed their optimism and their Puritan belief that they were the elect, the chosen. Canadians, however, looked at nature differently. They didn't want to conquer it; they just wanted to survive it. Nationally and culturally, they were always worried about surviving. The risk of such a preoccupation, though, was being saddled with a victim complex. *Survival*, in fact, was a kind of political manifesto telling Canadians to get over their waffling and value their own. Margaret was tired of the Great Canadian Victim Complex. This she encapsulated at the time as: "Look at poor innocent us, we are morally better than the Americans. We do not burn people in Vietnam, and those bastards are coming in and taking away our country."[9] Well, the real truth of the matter, according to Margaret, was that Canadians were selling it.

In order to meet the fall 1972 deadline, the final assemblage of *Survival* took many comic-opera twists. Jim remembered coming home one unbearably hot August day to find the cast of Anansi assembled in their Gothic house behind Casa Loma. The rooms were full of people with typewriters and notecards scrawled in Margaret's cuneiform handwriting. She herself was in a corner, busily writing, while Dennis paced back and forth, throwing out suggestions. Shirley Gibson, who would become Dennis's successor at Anansi, brought the gin.

Survival was a huge success. By 1975, it had sold more than fifty thousand copies. Ten years earlier, Northrop Frye had claimed that Canadians were less perplexed by the questions of personal identity — "Who am I?" — than by questions of cultural identity — "Where is Here?" *Survival* sold because it seemed to be offering answers to the national obsession.

By the early seventies, among writers at least, there was an enormous sense that something entirely new was happening.

While he was working on *Eleven Canadian Novelists*, his collection of interviews with Canadian writers, Graeme Gibson made the discovery that there were other writers with whom he shared a set of common axioms, an imaginative climate. This was both regional — it came to be called "Southern Ontario Gothic" — and national:

> There was a kind of imaginative climate that Marian Engel, Alice Munro, Tiff Findley, James Reaney, Peggy, all of us, were part of. One felt one was living in a kind of village, an imaginative village. Or even perhaps better, one could talk of a kind of repertory theatre. You know those films about Humphrey Bogart or Ingmar Bergman or whomever — who shared a common project. We had that. We believed we could do whatever we were up to. We would not be stopped by stuff outside ourselves. In fact, we would be fed by it. And there was a consensus that the culture — if not the public culture which was failing in many ways — at least the imaginative culture was on a roll that carried us. The group was better than the sum of the individuals. We discovered that that romantic nonsense that the individual artist has to be isolated was absolute crap.[10]

Nineteen seventy had been a watershed year. Ryerson Press (the oldest Canadian publishing house, established in 1829, with Canadian classics on its list like Archibald Lampman and Robert Service) was sold to the American firm McGraw-Hill on 1 December 1970. When the government didn't intervene to protect it, the response was outrage. This was a time to build, not eviscerate, Canadian institutions. A committee called "The Friends of Egerton Ryerson" was formed. Graeme Gibson remembers climbing the twenty-foot statue of Ryerson in front of Ryerson Polytechnical Institute and draping it in an American flag, while the demonstrators sang "I'm a Yankee Doodle Dandy." "To our astonishment," Graeme remarks, with a certain amusement at his younger self, "all the press turned out. We were all interviewed and as soon as it was over, we ran home and watched ourselves on television. We discovered we had power. Before that it would never have occurred to us that we could have gotten on television with our concerns or that a newspaper would look twice at us. We were, as they say, empowered by what we believed in."

Soon the Ontario government established the Royal Commission on Book Publishing with three high-profile commissioners: Richard Rohmer, a Toronto lawyer, businessman, and popular novelist (several of his political thrillers dealt with attempts by the United States to annex Canada); Dalton Camp, former president of the Progressive Conservative Party; and Marsh Jeanneret, director of the University of Toronto Press. Rohmer noted with alarm that every professional organization except the writers had formal representation at the hearings. He approached his friend Max Braithwaite, a writer for radio and television, and said: "Get the goddam writers here." Braithwaite called David Lewis Stein, Margaret Atwood, Gwen MacEwen, Marian Engel, and Graeme Gibson and, with other writers, they were invited to outline the problems that writers in Canada confronted. Out of these hearings came the call to establish a writers' union, a body devoted to the legal and financial rights of writers.

When *Survival* finally came out in the fall of 1972, it proved to be exactly what was needed. For the first time, it seemed the public was keenly interested in Canadian writing. New literary magazines were cropping up everywhere: *Descant*, *Waves*, *The Antigonish Review*, *Ariel*, *event*, *Capilano Review*, *Canadian Fiction Magazine*, *Exile*, *Open Letter*, and *Books in Canada*, to name only those that would last. Even educational institutions began to think of including Canadian literature on their curricula.

Longhouse, the first bookstore devoted to Canadian literature, opened its doors in March 1972. Beth Appeldoorn had been running the York University bookstore. "Coming from the Netherlands," she remarks, "I found Canadians really backwards when it came to their own writers. Nobody recognized anybody. Nobody cared."[11] Appeldoorn and her partner, Susan Sandler, asked to meet with Margaret, Dennis Lee, and Bill

Toye from Oxford, and over coffee at Dennis's house they floated the idea of a store devoted exclusively to Canadian books. "They told us to go for it and offered us some money, though we didn't need it; we had our own. Jack McClelland said we should get in touch with him if we ever needed money, but he was sure we would go down the tubes."

Appeldoorn and Sandler called their motives political. They were inspired by the nationalist economist Mel Watkins, who, in 1968, had chaired the influential government task force on the state of foreign ownership in Canadian business and industry. The task force had called for the repatriation of the economy. Longhouse was intended to change Canadians' indifference towards their own culture. Soon after the March opening, Margaret began to spend time at Longhouse, doing research for *Survival*. She would sit downstairs to write and come upstairs to consult the books. "I think she got as much strength from us as we did from her," Appeldoorn remarks.

Longhouse became a showcase for Canadian books, and Appeldoorn and Sandler became unpaid ambassadors for Canadian literature. The store had seven thousand titles in its inventory. While most of the books were textbooks, the stock included French- and English-Canadian fiction and poetry, as well as an international collection of children's books. Soon universities in England, Holland, Germany, and Scandinavia were writing to Longhouse to inquire about bibliographies because, under a project supported by External Affairs, they had begun to set up Canadian Studies programs. Appeldoorn and Sandler found themselves compiling Canadian Studies lists, using *Survival* as a guide since it was the obvious place to start. There was no book like it. "It was such a clever book," says Appeldoorn. "I think many writers were jealous because they hadn't written it." Writers, publishers, and movie producers looking for film scripts started showing up at Longhouse. Appeldoorn and Sandler stayed after hours and helped pay for impromptu dinners. It was a wonderful time. Canadian literature was indeed on a roll.

Every story had a subtext. During that fall of 1972, two writers began to meet privately in the downstairs office of Longhouse. Margaret and Graeme Gibson had recently become lovers, though they were not yet ready to declare this publicly.

They had first met briefly two years earlier at that party for Milton

Acorn at Grossman's Tavern when he was awarded the People's Poet Medal in lieu of the Governor General's Award for Poetry. It had been a great party, raucous and celebratory, with Milton ending the evening in tears. Both Graeme and Margaret had also been shortlisted for a Governor General's Award that year, he for *Five Legs* and she for *The Edible Woman*. (The fiction award had gone to the prairie novelist Robert Kroetsch, for *The Studhorse Man*.) At Grossman's, Margaret approached Graeme and said: "I thought your book should have won the Governor General's Award." And then she drifted away. [12]

It had fallen to Graeme to take authors' photographs for House of Anansi book covers. When Margaret returned briefly to Toronto in the spring of 1971, he was assigned the task of taking her photograph for the back of *Power Politics*. The occasion still carries a particular resonance for him. It was one of those seemingly innocuous moments that, like stones in a stream, haphazardly change the course of one's life. Graeme remembers that Margaret's hair was up and she had on a hat. After three rolls of film, he asked her to take off her hat and brush her hair. And she obliged. The resulting photograph was haunting. "Looking through the camera, I found myself, well, transfixed. I was really fascinated. When you use a lens that comes right in on the face, there's an intimacy. Her eyes, her hair. I was looking through that camera for a long time. I was completely fascinated by her."

They did not meet again until Margaret's return from England in the fall of 1971. Their paths crossed professionally, since her *Power Politics* and his second novel, *Communion*, were released in the same season. In an interview they did for the CBC, in which the producer had asked them to interview each other, Graeme remarked that he almost felt he could have written some of her lines in *Power Politics* and that she could have written some of his sentences in *Communion*. There was an uncanny resemblance in sensibility. She concurred. Before long they were working together at the House of Anansi and also on the politics of the incipient Writers' Union.

Graeme does not remember when or how they first started "seeing each other," but he does recall the first time they went out together, to a Japanese restaurant upstairs at the corner of Bloor and Spadina. "Remember, I was very impressed by this woman already. On Peggy's plate there was some of that green wasabi mustard. Now she, coming out of Leaside, mistook this for some kind of cream cheese. So with her chopsticks, I watched her pick up the whole blob of mustard, put it in her mouth, and eat it. She didn't flinch." He was amused and touched by the brave front she put up.

Graeme was in his late thirties when their relationship began. He was an extremely handsome man with an intense energy that was compelling. Where she had grown up in a strange isolation, his childhood had been one of continual displacement.

Graeme was born in London, Ontario, in 1934. His father was a professional soldier with the Royal Canadian Regiment. Beth Appeldoorn remembers "the Brigadier." They used to go out drinking together and he'd talk of the involvement of his Canadian unit in the liberation of Holland. The Brigadier was proud of his son. Appeldoorn made sure there was a special display of *Five Legs* at the York University Book Store when the novel came out.

Graeme's mother had been born in Australia, the daughter of a Canadian father and an Australian amateur opera singer. As a young woman she returned to London, Ontario, where she met the "dashing" young subaltern in the Royal Canadian Regiment with the handsome blond moustache. They fell in love. Because the marriage was delayed by military regulations, she went out and got a job with CFBL Radio. Soon she had her own program, singing songs and playing the ukulele, and acquired a reputation as "the Australian songbird." That, at least, was how her son affectionately recounted the parental saga.

The family moved around a lot, living for various stretches in London (Ontario), London (England), Halifax, Fredericton, Toronto, Ottawa, and Sydney, Australia. Graeme was educated at a long string of schools. At the last one, Collège Militaire Royale de St-Jean, in St-Jean, Quebec, he discovered not only that he was an excellent marksman, but that he had "leadership" potential. At Waterloo College, he imagined himself a journalist "in a trench coat standing in the rain somewhere in Vienna." He transferred to the University of Western Ontario to take English and Philosophy. Soon he began to think of a writing career and moved on to the University of Edinburgh, where he had a "gloriously romantic year" writing and fantasizing about going off to Hungary to drive an ambulance in the Hungarian uprising of 1956. He contacted various groups that were heading for Hungary, but, as he puts it, "I was so obviously demented and wild-eyed, they said 'thank you very much' and sort of patted me on the head." He returned to the University of Western Ontario to finish his degree, and though he had been an indifferent student did brilliantly on his general exams. He was offered a teaching fellowship.

Just like the young Margaret, he believed that, if he was going to be a writer, he should be in Europe somewhere, working at a menial job, living in an attic, and writing a novel. Instead he stayed in London, Ontario, to take his Master's degree. It was at this time that he met his first wife, Shirley. The two married in 1959 and did set off for London, England, with $79 between them. Graeme was determined to be a writer and, while working as a supply teacher in the tough Notting Hill Gate public schools, he started writing *Five Legs*. Soon their first son was born. They then found an apartment through a friend in a villa on Cap d'Antibes, and in those eight months Graeme devoted himself to writing.

The family returned to Canada, where Graeme secured a job at Ryerson Polytechnical Institute. After three years of teaching, he was awarded a Canada Council grant and suddenly had a free year. By now the couple had a second son. At Shirley's insistence, the family house was sold, the kids were bundled up, and they moved to Oaxaca, Mexico. As Graeme recalls, "battling with that book felt like psychological terror." But he completed *Five Legs*, and back in Canada he set about looking for a publisher. When the novel was turned down by four companies, friends suggested he take it to Dennis Lee. Lee recognized its experimental brilliance, and it was published in 1969. Soon both Shirley and Graeme were working at Anansi. She would become president when Dennis Lee left in 1972 to pursue his own writing.

By the early seventies, Graeme and Shirley's marriage had ceased to be conventional. In a way that was not unusual in the sixties, they were no longer a consistent couple. The marriage was virtually over when Graeme met Margaret.

In 1972, Graeme and Shirley Gibson formally separated and he rented a house near the town of Beeton, north of Toronto. His sons, Matthew and Graeme, with whom he was very close, often came to visit. As did Margaret.

By the fall of 1973, it was clear to both Margaret and Graeme that something substantial was happening. When Graeme's rented house in Beeton was put up for sale, he and Margaret bought a hundred-acre farm together near Alliston, about fifty miles north of Toronto. He was the man with whom she would share her life.

14

MULMUR TOWNSHIP

Mulmur Township, just north of Highway 89, sits between Alliston and Shelbourne, north of Adjala. The area was first settled in the 1820s and '30s by Irish, mostly Protestant, immigrants. In 1973, when Margaret and Graeme moved there, families like the Greens, the Irelands, and the Murphys had been farming the land for 150 years. The township was just far enough out of the way to have escaped the hobby farmers and weekend people who went to the Bruce Peninsula, and the land was just good enough to establish a rich farming tradition. In some ways it was a remarkably closed, cut-off world (electricity didn't come to the area until 1952), and allegiances went back to nineteenth-century Ireland. While the Orange lodges had mostly disbanded (at the euchre parties you could now find both Protestants and Catholics), the stories persisted. The old stone house that had been in the Walker family for 120 years was remembered as the place where the women and children were hidden during the Catholic Fenian raids of the 1840s. The area still adhered to Protestant fundamentalism. Some families wouldn't touch alcohol, and the young men who wanted to drink sat outside in their trucks in the laneways.[1]

The house Margaret and Graeme lived in was a classic Ontario farmhouse built in the 1840s. Margaret described it as the "'dream' home that would have followed the log shanty of the first settlement period." It was a "half-chimney" house, with the chimney on the second floor and an iron stove to heat the first. It had a front parlour with deep window mouldings, as well as a back parlour. These mouldings and the piles of rocks in back of the house were, to Margaret, an impressive demonstration of the back-breaking labour that obviously had gone into the house's construction. It was still known as the "Noble house," named after the family who had originally settled it, though no one by that name had lived there for decades.[2]

It was Graeme who was committed to farming the land. "To her credit," he says, "Peggy went along with it." Graeme didn't realize it, but when he had first moved to the area he was subconsciously setting the scene for his next novel, *Perpetual Motion*. As he says: "I had imposed all this on my family because I was going to write a book about a nineteenth-century farmer. When I got up there, I even started shaving with a straight razor. My rationale to myself was that I wouldn't be wasting razor blades, but the first sense I had of my character, Robert Fraser, was in shaving before a mirror with a straight razor."[3]

After they moved in, a fourteen-year-old boy from down the road came over each day to visit. Graeme asked him: "If one was to farm this land, where would one get the equipment?" The boy told him about farm auctions, and together they went off to buy the second-hand plough, tractor, bailer, and so forth, that the farm needed. About half of the local auctions were the result of failure or tragedy. Someone had gotten too old to work, or someone had died. There was a fatalism about those auctions that Graeme found deeply moving, and by buying locally he was supporting the community.

Soon Graeme had thirty-five acres under cultivation and was bringing in winter wheat. He, Margaret, and his sons were able to take 1,800 to 2,300 bales of hay off the fields in the summers. They kept a large kitchen garden and many animals: at various times they had chickens, ducks, geese, horses, cows, a black Persian cat called Patience, a tabby called Ruby, and two Irish wolfhounds. They were not dairy farmers, but the cows kept them busy, breaking loose at night. Margaret was surprised to learn cows could dive. They would swim out to the middle of the pond and under the barbed-wire fence strung across it to keep them in.[4] She liked to tell friends the story of the chicken that committed suicide by getting into the garbage can where the feed was stored and smothering when the lid fell closed. She gave her stepsons, Matthew and Graeme, the chicken to bury, but after the dogs dug it up several times they decided on a tree burial, hanging it in a bag in one of the trees on the lot line.

Each year after that the boys secretly went to check and see if the chicken had mummified.[5]

The farm lost money, of course, and Margaret and Graeme became familiar with the hazards of farming. There were the hailstorms that destroyed the crops, the equipment that broke down, and the animals that got sick ("If you're going to have livestock," as their neighbour had warned them, "you're going to have deadstock").[6]

While her public life accelerated, the private life Margaret had established for herself was essentially domestic, and, as friends recalled, unselfconsciously casual. In the old white farmhouse, the front door was rarely used. You entered from the side. The guest room was crammed with a freezer, sewing machine, and bottles of fermenting home-made beer. Pipes were exposed in the half-finished bathroom. Soon, Margaret and Graeme built a two-storey guest cabin to house the visitors. An evening might be spent in the rural dining room, with the iron stove pumping heat, reading *Pears' Cyclopaedia* out loud and laughing at the almanac's advice on obesity, neurosis, masturbation, and happiness. The lamb stew might have been cooked by Graeme, and the dishes could be left to the morning. Or perhaps Graeme might talk into the early morning about his latest project. As she listened, Margaret might be crocheting an afghan, a way to keep her hands occupied. She didn't like to waste time.[7]

As any writer would, Margaret was absorbing this landscape for future use. She was impressed by how "the landscape . . . was an organic whole — the landmarks, the families, the feuds, the stories, the ghosts, the history — 'Over there's the barn where we hid the women and children, the time the Fenians came,' someone told us, and it was that *we* that was instructive. All of this was held together in the minds of the living." Ontario was old enough to have accumulated quite a few long-standing feuds, local traditions, and ghosts. "It was a thick, rich, suggestive mix."

There were two aspects of the community that appealed to Margaret as a writer. The people still had a "highly ornamented way of speaking, heavily laced with figures of speech." They still spoke in an Irish/English idiom that had survived from the nineteenth century. She was delighted when one of the farmers said he wished to retire before they put the wooden overcoat on him. When they referred to slightly demented people they used the expression "two bricks short of a load."

Even more important was her encounter with local folk beliefs. Many of these had to do with weather predictions, or practical devices: when one wanted to put in a well, one called on the dowser or witcher, who used the traditional peeled willow fork to divine water. It always worked better than commercial well-drilling. There was also a tradition of healing. "Some people," she recalls, "were thought to be blood stoppers — that is, they could stop any flow of blood, such as a nose bleed or cut hand, if you just told them about it. Some could even do it over the phone."[8] A necessary art, when there were so many farm accidents.

"Other beliefs," she added, "were about fortune telling, and others were about clairvoyance, especially premonitions of disaster." If you inadvertently invited thirteen people to dinner, you had to set a fourteenth place or one of the guests would be dead within two weeks. Margaret's neighbour could tell her numerous instances when this actually happened. Graeme remembered the lady on the next farm over who claimed that she smelled blood on the stairs when a death was about to happen, and she had smelled blood. Within three days, one of the neighbours had turned his tractor over on himself.

The locals also had practical advice on what to do about ghosts. "We were told quite early on that, if we were bothered by a ghost, the best thing to do was to leave some food out for it at night. That way it would know that its presence was acknowledged and that you had admitted its right to share space with you, and it would feel welcomed and go away."[9] Margaret connected this piece of folk wisdom with the Welsh tradition of the sin eater, the subject of her story by that name.

Margaret and Graeme did indeed have a ghost. Graeme was amused that it chose to visit him, since he was the one who was most sceptical about such things. The farmhouse had a central staircase that went straight up to the back of the house and connected to a balcony that ran around to the front. He remembered being alone in bed one winter night when Margaret was away in California. He heard someone in the vestibule below.

> I had spoken to Peggy on the phone that day and knew she couldn't have come back in that short time. The way the drive was set up, the lights of any car coming towards the house shone straight into the bedroom window. And Mac,

our bluetick hound, barked insanely at anything that happened. I heard footsteps on the wooden stairs. And I decided it was a woman's footsteps. If it had been a man's I'd have been out of bed — I would have had a defence mechanism. But I was puzzled at the prospect of a woman's steps and the house locked. She walked towards the hall door and I shouted a couple of times: "Who is it?" She stopped outside the bedroom door and entered what must have once been the nursery. I realized I would have to pass her to turn on the light. And I lay there thinking: It is houses, not people, who are haunted. We haven't been here long enough for this thing to have anything against me. So I wished it well and eventually I went to sleep. The next morning I woke up and asked myself how much I'd had to drink. Was it a dream? And so I let it go. I told Peggy about it and then we forgot it.

There were many independent confirmations. Years later, when the subject came up, a guest who had minded the house said the apparition had appeared before him three times. A young *au pair* who worked for Margaret and Graeme encountered a woman in a long blue dress, looking very sad. After they left the farm, they rented it out to some people from Northern Ireland. When Graeme went to collect the rent, the young Irish woman had said: "So tell me about the ghost." Her husband had seen a woman in her nightdress approaching the nursery.

"I don't know what one does with an experience like that," Graeme remarks, "since it has no structure. There's no explanation, and all I can say is that it happened." No history for the ghost was ever uncovered, but Margaret and Graeme assumed it must have had something to do with a dead child. They tried doing some local research to find out whose ghost it might be, but there were no legends of violent deaths in their house. Someone, though, did tell them that there had once been a marble gravestone in their cellar. It had been stolen from a nearby cemetery and used for cooling candy. There was indeed a Gothic flair to life in Mulmur Township.

During that first year at the farmhouse, Margaret was working on the poems that would eventually become her book *You Are Happy*, published in 1974. How quickly she absorbed the imagery of the rural landscape to locate the complex emotions that were the legacy of the past few years:

Spring Poem

It is spring, my decision, the earth
ferments like rising bread
or refuse, we are burning
last year's weeds, the smoke
flares from the road, the clumped stalks
glow like sluggish phoenixes / it wasn't
only my fault / birdsongs burst from
the feathered pods of their bodies, dandelions
whirl their blades upwards, from beneath
this decaying board a snake
sidewinds, chained hide
smelling of reptile sex / the hens
roll in the dust, squinting with bliss, frogbodies
bloat like bladders, contract, string
the pond with live jelly
eyes, can I be this
ruthless? I plunge
my hands and arms into the dirt,
swim among stones and cutworms,
come up rank as a fox,

restless. Nights, while seedlings
dig near my head
I dream of reconciliations
with those I have hurt
unbearably, we move still
touching over the greening fields, the future
wounds folded like seeds
in our tender fingers, days
I go for vicious walks past the charred
roadbed over the bashed stubble

admiring the view, avoiding
those I have not hurt

yet, apocalypse coiled in my tongue,
it is spring, I am searching
for the word:
>   finished
>   finished

so I can begin over
again, some year
I will take this word too far.[10]

Even digging in the manure pile becomes a meditation:

Digging

In this yard, barnyard
I dig with a shovel

beside the temple to the goddess
of open mouths: decayed
hay, steaming
in the humid sunlight, odour
of mildewed cardboard,

filling a box with rotted dung
to feed the melons.

I dig because I hold grudges
I dig with anger
I dig because I am hungry,
the dungpile scintillates with flies.

I try to ignore my sour clothes,
the murky bread devoured

at those breakfasts, drinking orange
and black acid, butter
tasting of silt, refrigerators,
old remorse . . . [11]

It was as if she was pulling together all the imagery she had accumulated so far. In a sequence of poems called "Songs of the Transformed," she
returns to an old obsession with metamorphosis, that obsession she shared
with her father about animal transformations and which she found
confirmed in classical mythology. But now she was writing about animals
from the farm and field. She wrote "Rat Song," "Crow Song," "Pig Song,"
"Owl Song," "Song of the Worms," "Song of the Fox," "Song of the Hen's
Head," all from the perspective of the animals. They were elaborate games
she was playing, deadly serious games. Worms sing of love which "disgusts
the soles of boots, / their leather strict religion," and dream of revenge
against humans. Rats are parasites who live off human leavings, but
humans live off leavings too. The crow feels defrauded; he sings of "Hope,"
but his baffled people hear only the word "Win." But it is the "Song of the
Hen's Head" that is the most Gothic. Other poets might write of the
decapitation of a chicken in the barnyard, but few would think to speak
from the point of view of the severed head. Margaret was, of course, a
witness to this farmyard event, so precise is her description:

After the abrupt collision
with the blade, the Word,
I rest on the wood
block, my eyes
drawn back into their blue transparent
shells like molluscs;
I contemplate the Word

while the rest of me
which was never much under
my control, which was always
inarticulate, still runs
at random through the grass, a plea

for mercy, a single
flopping breast,

muttering about life
in its thickening red voice.

Feet and hands chase it, scavengers
intent on rape:
they want its treasures,
its warm rhizomes, enticing sausages,
its yellow grapes, its flesh
caves, five pounds of sweet money,
its juices and jellied tendons.
It tries to escape,
gasping through the neck, frantic.

They are welcome to it,
I contemplate the Word,
I am dispensable and peaceful.

The Word is an O,
outcry of the useless head,
pure space, empty and drastic,
the last word I said.
The word is No.[12]

Margaret had a thing about necks. She had hoped she'd inherited the neck of her witch ancestor, Mary Webster. She would speak of the neck as being like an isthmus that separates mind and body, that keeps the rational mind from feeling the body's pain and love. We live in our heads, cut off from the world. In this macabre poem, the discarded head of the chicken cries "No" as its body, muttering about life in its bloodied voice, becomes sweet money. Margaret's humour is black and precise.

But there is another tone entirely in *You Are Happy*. Margaret did not easily offer her intimate life to outsiders, but it was clear to her friends that she and Graeme were very much in love. Timothy Findley remembers his first meeting with Margaret and Graeme. That first autumn, Graeme, who was already a close friend, brought her with him to Stone Orchard, the farmhouse where Findley and his companion, Bill Whitehead, lived.

Findley remembers Margaret sitting in his living room, crocheting; she was working on a colourful afghan, or perhaps it was a scarf. He had not met her before, other than to shake hands, and knew nothing of her background. They were discussing cluster flies, since Stone Orchard was suffering an invasion of them. Margaret asked if they overwintered in the house or laid eggs and hatched in the spring. He was amused. He realized she wanted to know him but didn't want to ask a direct question about who he was. She was inviting him into her arcane world of biological facts. They went for a walk with the dogs through the field, and Findley remembers his first image of the two of them as a couple. "Peggy and Graeme went to their car and came away enveloped in capes which they had put on shyly, and in a funny sort of way I fell in love with them. They were so wonderful together, Graeme matching her intelligence and both clearly finding each other such fun." Findley was delighted. Margaret already had the reputation of a distant figure, with the mystique that had begun to attach to her with the publication of *Surfacing* and *Survival*. He discovered "the icon could giggle."[13]

In fact, in her disconnected jottings for the poems she was working on in drafts in 1972 and 1973, Margaret was writing poems out of emotions that were being fed by her new relationship. She jotted lines for a poem that would become "Four Evasions": "Unable to say how much I want you / unable even to say / I am unable."[14] She looked for ways to resurrect the word love. How do you speak of love when the word has become stale and emptied by cliché? Later she would write "Variations on the Word Love":

> This is a word we use to plug
> holes with. It's the right size for those warm
> blanks in speech, for those red heart-
> shaped vacancies on the page that look nothing
> like real hearts. Add lace
> and you can sell
> it. We insert it also in the one empty
> space on the printed form

that comes with no instructions. There are whole
magazines with not much in them
but the word *love*, you can
rub it all over your body and you
can cook with it too. How do we know
it isn't what goes on at the cool
debaucheries of slugs under damp
pieces of cardboard? As for the weed-
seedlings nosing their tough snouts up
among lettuces, they shout it.
Love! Love! sing the soldiers, raising
their glittering knives in salute.

Then there's the two
of us. This word
is far too short for us, it has only
four letters, too sparse
to fill those deep bare
vacuums between the stars
that press on us with their deafness.
It's not love we don't wish
to fall into, but that fear.
This word is not enough but it will
have to do. It's a single
vowel in this metallic
silence, a mouth that says
O again and again in wonder
and pain, a breath, a finger-
grip on a cliffside. You can
hold on or let go.[15]

Trying to find a new way to speak, she wrote the love poem called
"There Is Only One of Everything." It was published in *The Nation* in
January 1973.

Not a tree but the tree
we saw, it will never exist, split by the wind
                    and bending down
like that again. What will push out of the earth

later, making it summer, will not be
grass, leaves, repetition, there will
have to be other words. When my

eyes close language vanishes. The cat
with the divided face, half black half orange
nests in my scruffy fur coat, I drink tea,

fingers curved around the cup, impossible
to duplicate these flavours. The table
and freak plates glow softly, consuming themselves,

I look out at you and you occur
in this winter kitchen, random as trees or sentences,
entering me, fading like them, in time you will disappear

but the way you dance by yourself
on the tile floor to a worn song, flat and mournful,
so delighted, spoon waved in one hand, wisps of
                    roughened hair

sticking up from your head, it's your surprised
body, pleasure I like. I can even say it,
though only once and it won't

last: I want this. I want
this.[16]

What we call love usually involves possessing the other for the sake of
our own security — a demand for a fixed permanence that smothers and
destroys. When asked about this poem, Graeme replied that, by insisting

that love be for ever, "you submit it to the vagaries and dangers of fate. And as soon as you start doing that, then it's the old hostages-and-fortune thing. It's enough. It's almost too much to want it now, and insist upon it now."[17]

Margaret always selected the last poem in her books carefully, and it usually serves as a coda to what precedes. She ended *You Are Happy* with a poem titled "Book of Ancestors," in which love is seen as a kind of sacrifice of the self to risk, without guarantees. To love is "to take / that risk, to offer life and remain / alive, open yourself like this and become whole."[18]

Living with Graeme in Mulmur Township, Margaret was astonished to find that she had ended up with a life "pretty close to the leaves-in-the-back-yard model" that her parents had set her. It wasn't what she'd expected for herself. She had thought that, if she wasn't dead by thirty, she would at least have followed the "red-shoes model" of the woman artist. By now she should have been somehow damaged, warped, suicidal, or at least have rotted her brains with absinthe. When she first started out, it was supposed to be impossible to be a woman and a writer and still fall within the range of the normal. In 1975, she told an interviewer:

> It would be impossible for me to live with anyone who
> didn't allow me to be a writer. But it cost me a lot of blood,
> let me tell you. I missed out on a lot of things other women
> had — children, a husband for a long time. Now I know
> that I may not have missed anything at all. But the point is,
> I thought I did.[19]

Looking back at it, the idea that the artist had to be doomed seemed like some kind of collective romantic neurosis. The only thing writers had in common was that they wrote. Now she could laugh: "If Shakespeare could have kids and avoid suicide, so could I, dammit."

She explained that she owed at least some of her new-found equanimity to two things: she had "the aid of some business assistants, and a large man who likes kids and cats, and has an ego so solid it isn't threatened by mine. This state of affairs was not achieved without struggle, some of it internal — but it was reached."[20]

In the mid-seventies, however, the question of how a woman could connect her art and her gender still lurked in the background, and Margaret often found herself asked how she managed her private life. In a long interview published in *Communiqué* in 1975, as a special for International Women's Year, Susan Swan, then a young journalist, was particularly persistent in questioning Margaret about her evident self-confidence as a writer. She asked Margaret when she had started to believe in herself as an artist. Margaret replied: "I'm not sure what that means and because I'm not sure, probably there never was a point at which I didn't."[21]

Margaret explained to Swan that her sense of confidence had to do with "family background." Her parents had allowed her to evolve her own imperatives and had not put any pressure on her to be the same as everyone else. Childhood is "enormously important," she remarked, and unfortunately "you can't change your family." You can spend years overcoming internalized feelings of self-contempt inherited from childhood. She admitted that her self-confidence and independence as a young woman were probably an exception for women of her generation.

Thinking about a composer friend of hers, Swan remarked that one of the most difficult things for a woman writer was not "to put a man's business before her own." Women "had difficulty putting [their] work first or giving it equal time with a man's need."

Margaret's response was straightforward:

> I don't know. I don't think so. I like men who are able to take care of themselves — who can cook dinner if they feel like it. And I don't mend anybody's socks. If Graeme has to go somewhere in a hurry, I take care of the farm. But then when I go somewhere, he takes care of it. So we spell it off that way. There's nothing here that both of us can't handle except during the summer, when there's certain machinery things that I don't do. But I think it would be as peculiar for me to say that I can't go out and feed the cows as it would be for him to say he can't get his own meals. I think being an adult involves being able to do these things whether you like them or not. Men aren't helpless and I have more respect for them than to assume that they're incapable of running their own housework, if need be.

Swan wondered about the mistakes women make in relationships with men. Perhaps women wanted to see men as Prince Charming. Or perhaps they were trying to show men how indispensable they were.

Margaret replied with a joke: "I had a thought about Cinderella the other day. The real reason that Prince Charming chooses Cinderella over the other two sisters is that she is the only one who can do housework. She thinks she is being carried off to a life of ease but, in fact, she's being carried off because she can do the housework and they can't."

But she added thoughtfully: "I don't think women are indispensable to men. And I don't think men are indispensable to women and that's very nice because it means that you don't feel trapped, that you don't absolutely need this person. You can be with them if you enjoy it. That's what it should be, I think. Otherwise all kinds of resentments can grow."

But, Swan wanted to know, how had she resisted female guilt? Women seemed to be trapped by guilt: "If they do what they want, they feel guilty; if they don't, they feel guilty. Has this been a problem for you?"

Margaret responded: "In a situation like that I would feel frustration rather than guilt. I think women are brought up to assume other people's happiness depends on them and therefore if those people are not happy, it's their fault. I've certainly been in situations like that. But if you have good will and you try and it still doesn't work, you figure out that these people's happiness does not depend on you. You cannot make anybody happy. You can make them unhappy, but that's a different thing."

Two things were of utmost importance: to find the inner strength to be who you are, and to have a sense of humour. "I think one thing that's very difficult for women is coping with the idea that they may be considered too self-directing — too threatening or aggressive or dominating."

Margaret, however, had always been willing to take the rap. If there were people who would always be threatened by her, no matter what she did, she decided she might as well just be the way she was. It was really their problem.

Still, Margaret concluded the interview by adding that she hated to sound as if she were an advice-to-the-lovelorn columnist. "I don't know what's good for other people. I can't say, 'Ok, the word is coming out from Margaret Atwood that now you can have a good relationship. It's Ok, girls, you don't have to be angry all the time.'"

She was neither a propagandist nor a lifestyle critic nor an exotic; she was a writer, someone who sat in a messy office, typing. These questions were extraneous to writing. But they were a product of the time, and she understood why.

In the fall of 1972, when reviews began to appear of Margaret's new novel, it had been more than a year since she'd finally completed the manuscript in London. She'd spent months mulling over a title, rejecting at least twenty, including *What's Dead*, *Camouflages*, and *A Place Made of Water*, before settling on *Surfacing*. Like all writers, she felt as if she had dropped her book into a void. And then she waited. The book proved to be a triumph.

She was being trumpeted as a feminist and a nationalist (both of which she could admit to), but in her own mind she had written a ghost story.

She remarked to one interviewer: "*Surfacing* is a ghost story which follows a certain formula. The heroine . . . is obsessed with finding the ghosts, and once she's found them she is released from that obsession. The point is my character can see the ghosts but they can't see her."[22]

Margaret was serious about the ghosts. She'd always been fascinated by them. She explained:

> There are various kinds of ghosts you can see. You could have just a simple straightforward ghost story in which somebody sees a ghost which has no relation to them whatsoever. You could have a sort of primitive myth in which dead people are as alive as living people and they're just accepted. Nobody is too surprised by it because it happens all the time. Or you can have the Henry James kind, in which the ghost that one sees is in fact a fragment of one's own self which has split off, and that to me is the most interesting kind and that is obviously the tradition I'm working in. But I wanted to write a ghost story for the same reason that I'd like to make a good horror film. It's an interesting area which is too often done just as pulp.[23]

There are three ghosts in *Surfacing*: the protagonist's mother and father and the strange ghost at the end of the story:

I'm not frightened; it's too dangerous for me to be frightened
of it; it gazes at me for a time with its yellow eyes, wolf's eyes,
depthless but lambent as the eyes of animals seen at night in
the car headlights. Reflectors . . .

Then its head swings away with an awkward, almost crippled motion: I do not interest it, I am part of the landscape,
I could be anything, a tree, a deer skeleton, a rock.[24]

Margaret had been a child in the bush all those years back. She knew
what terrors the bush held. She also knew its potent magic. The northern
woods, to anyone who has spent time in them, seem almost like an
animistic presence. Someone, something, sits at your back, watching.

The ghost Margaret conjured is a nature god, a lost fragment of the
human self. As she explained: "Everybody has gods or a god," but the gods
must "come out of the place where you are, [out of] the reality of your life.
. . . The assumption of the book, if there is one, is that there are gods that
do exist here, but nobody knows them. . . . How that fits in with the book
I don't know, but I'm sure it has something to do with it."[25]

Margaret had thought of using an epigram for *Surfacing*, but later
dropped the idea. It was to be a quotation from a 1651 text by John
Holland, *Smoke of the Bottomless Pit or A More True and Fuller Discovery
of the Doctrine of Those Men Which Call Themselves Ranters or the Mad
Crew* (such was her reading): "They maintain that God is essentially in
every creature, and that there is as much of God in one creature as in
another. . . . I saw this expression in the Book of Thieves, that the essence
of God was as much in the Ivie leaf as in the most glorious Angel."[26]

Her point, if she had one, was to rearrange the hierarchies that put man
above nature. Nature is not there simply for our exploitation. It is not raw
material for our technologies or our romantic projections. We must respect
its autonomy. We destroy it at our peril.

"Ideas in fiction," she would say, "are closer to algebra than you might
think. Given X, then Y. It's a human activity and valuable to tell a story."[27]
Once the plot is set, a story has its own logic. Hers followed the logic of a
woman possessed by ghosts (of an aborted child, lost parents, lost gods)
whom she will have to confront and reclaim.

Still, asked what *Surfacing* had to do with her life as a writer, she replied: "A great deal. . . . For me it came out of pressures that are oppressively Canadian. The constant pull of two embattled languages, the threat of extinction, the amorphousness of identity; and, physically, the water-and-rock of the northern Shield country, where lakes are mazes and you cannot travel without your reflection and your echo."[28]

Margaret's publisher, Jack McClelland, had warned her that *Surfacing* wasn't going to be as easy a sell as *The Edible Woman*, but it turned out that, continent-wide, the reviews were amazingly good.[29] George Woodcock wrote in *The Nation*: "What Atwood has accomplished is to bring us up to date on how we are related to some of our deepest hopes, for ourselves and for our continent."[30] *Maclean's* called *Surfacing* "simply superb." *The New York Times* described it as "first-rate" and "thoroughly brilliant." *The New York Times Book Review* concluded: "Denying Emerson's maxim that the true art of life is to skate well on surfaces, Atwood shows the depths that must be explored if one attempts to live an examined life today."[31] It doesn't get much better for a young writer at the age of thirty-three.

But Margaret felt that to believe in success, to make that your measure, is dangerous. Success can always be taken away from you. There were only two things that were important: the writing for its own sake, and a centred private life. When asked by a reporter in the fall of 1972 what she wanted, it wasn't fame. Rather, turning and smiling at Graeme, she said: "Just more of the same. I have it now. There are only a few little wrinkles to be ironed out."[32]

According to Graeme, this never changed. He says:

> Peggy's a writer and she has to write. She has to work at it, of course, but she can turn her hand to anything: she can write poetry, essays, children's stuff, she can write nonsense. In that sense, she's an instinctive writer. We've been together a long time and I'm astonished how little fame has changed her. Talking about morality, personal morality, for her own sake, artistic morality, whatever it is, she has managed to sustain this completely. I don't know how she does it, remain largely unchanged.[33]

15

SURVIVALWOMAN

I have an image in my mind of Margaret: living in Mulmur Township in a farmhouse something like her grandmother's, telling her own kitchen stories, reclaiming her female heritage. But even such an innocuous fantasy would make her uncomfortable. It is dangerous, she would say, to hold life hostage to myth, or to turn individuals into models. A model was never something she aspired to be.

By 1973, after the publication of *Survival* and *Surfacing*, myths seemed to attach to her as readily as Velcro strips. She was becoming, as she described herself, "one of those idea chips that people move around." Some reviewers had called her Medusa; others, the ice maiden. She could laugh at this: "I've been accused of hating women. I've been accused of hating men. I've been accused of not hating either of them enough." She told one interviewer: "People find me pretty terrifying [because] they confuse me with my work."[1]

The need to create this Atwood iconography seemed to start with the publication of *Power Politics* in 1971. Graeme felt that the Medusa myth began with the gaze she offered to the public in the photograph he'd taken of her for the back cover: her eyes are seductive and yet so direct that they seem to nail the viewer to the spot. To some she personified female revenge. He felt a certain amused chagrin that he had helped to create that image. A number of reviewers fell into the trap of reading the poems as straightforward autobiography. In the seventies, male reviewers seemed to be expecting female revenge of some sort.

Of course, it went deeper than that. Margaret did seem to frighten people. Timothy Findley reflects:

> How does one read the mystique that began to attach to Peggy? There was something about her in those days. The minute you heard her name some kind of bell rang. One didn't think of Marian Engel or Margaret Laurence or Adele Wiseman in that way. She was totally herself, a figure enclosed in some kind of — not mystical light, by any means, but there was a sort of — I don't want to use the word "mystique" because it's wrong — but there was something around Margaret Atwood that set her apart from everybody else in the writing world, at that moment. I remember once, after the Writers' Union had been established, she wrote a note in the newsletter: "for chrissakes stop treating me like the Queen Mother." She had garnered this superabundance of respect, which was for her very troubling and quite wrong. But, on the other hand, there was something understandable about this. She emanated a kind of confidence none of the rest of us had. She knew who she was, what life was about, how you persist as a writer.
>
> I think my first wave of love for her came when we were sitting in a restaurant on Yonge Street after a Union meeting. We didn't really know each other, all of us sitting at this great table, having wine and spaghetti. I watched her and I kept thinking: "This is one of the funniest women alive." And yet others were treating her as though "we mustn't laugh." She knew what people thought of her, and how ridiculous most of it was, and not only ridiculous but wrong. They saw only the icon. She was called cold and removed and arrogant. That was all just bullshit. She was phenomenally generous. She gave and gave and gave.[2]

Graeme would add:

> You had this startlingly attractive young woman, who was fiercely right, and imaginatively very interesting. There are

all kinds of people that are going to jump through hoops, both men and women, trying to figure out how to handle her. And Peggy does not suffer fools gladly. That, even when they're not fools. She's very direct. It was certainly intensified by the fact that she's a woman. But even a man gets called up for being outspoken. Although women are supposed to be nurturers and all that, and she is, she carried an aura of authority. There was an assurance about her writing and about her public persona from early on. And some people saw this as arrogant or manipulating. But anyone who has that kind of clear-sighted intelligence and clear ability is going to run into a kind of mythic thing.[3]

Perhaps one of explanations for this was that the Canadian cultural community had never quite seen her like before. She did not shy away from ambition. All those years ago, she had told Patrick Lane and John Newlove they were chumps for not aspiring to the Nobel Prize. She assumed that a Canadian writer had as much chance as anybody of being a great writer. You had to give it a shot. She did not confess to self-doubt.

Canada was not used to taking its writers for granted, and there had been no Melville or Henry James, no Shakespeare or Milton, to give its writers a sense of tradition. Even though the writers were there — Margaret herself would point to P.K. Page, Margaret Avison, Jay Macpherson, Robertson Davies, Margaret Laurence — their presence had only just begun to enter the public imagination.

In a colonial culture, Margaret's confidence brought its own cost. Alice Munro described the cultural syndrome of cutting people down to size most accurately in the title of one of her collection of stories, *Who Do You Think You Are?* It was "the tall poppy syndrome." One was expected not to get too far above oneself or take oneself too seriously.

Margaret was unprepared for the backlash that set in after the initial success of *Survival*. By December 1972, she had begun to feel its sting. An aggressively nasty poem by Robert Read called "Atwood as Acupuncture" appeared in the December 1972 issue of *The Canadian Forum*.[4] In the poem, Read imagines himself under Margaret's power and, as she inserts her needles into his flesh, he is overwhelmed. "Atwood as Acupuncture" ends with her swallowing his still bumping and bleeding heart down her icy throat.

Presumably this was meant to be read as a satirical riposte to *Power Politics*, but it was an unpleasant attack. Margaret had once made fun of the male poets and their ejaculatory theory of poetry, but it was never *ad hominem*, and to find herself with this bumping heart shoved down her throat was a bit much. When she wrote a letter of protest to the *Forum*'s editorial board, they explained that the poem had somehow slipped through in the Christmas rush without being approved by the collective. She let the matter drop.

Soon reviews of *Survival* started coming in to Anansi. As they came across Jim Polk's desk, he was shocked. "There were reviews that said Peggy's thesis about Canada's obsession with survival was simply an expression of her own neurosis; they said she was trying to turn it into a religion. I began to wonder whether in Canada it was impossible to read a book except as a biblical script you must believe in."[5] Anansi had billed *Survival* as, simultaneously, a book of criticism, a manifesto, and a collection of personal and subversive remarks. People seemed to be missing the humour and the deliberate provocation.

There were many, certainly the majority, who were delighted by *Survival*. Margaret must have spoken of her anxieties about the book to Margaret Laurence because Laurence sent a personal note. *Survival*, she felt, was:

> the first attempt, EVER, to state why Can writing is not the same as Amer or Eng. I could see, finishing the book, your worry that a) teachers might think — Aha! This is Everything We Need to Know About Can Writing; and b) writers might think — Have I A Suitable Victim, Human Or Animal, And If Not, What In Hell Is The Matter With Me? But worry not. These are the chances we have to take. . . . The book is good, provocative, and (I think) true.[6]

The novelist Adele Wiseman also wrote a letter:

> By the way, I hope you don't mind my mentioning that I have been appalled at the way the pack has been snarling

after you this past while. For a long time I've had this theory
that many people, having been partially smothered themselves at some time, cannot bear having an exceptional
vitality in their midst. . . . [7]

Friends were perhaps being overly protective. After all, *Survival* was on
the best-seller list for months, and between 1972 and 1975 it sold fifty
thousand copies. However, the invective of a number of review articles
was unexpected.

One of the most prominent nationalists, Robin Matthews, took on
Survival in the pages of *This Magazine*. He began by saying the book "has
to be looked at clearly, without the delicacies writers usually accord one
another in order to stay friends, to live together in the small literary world
Canada has. . . . We cannot afford to lie to each other." He claimed
Margaret had selected the negative side of Canadian literature, the literature of surrender, but had neglected the indigenous "struggle literature."
He felt that the books she selected to discuss used "the language of struggle" of the United States, thereby "accepting U.S. terms of behaviour."
She had left out works that celebrated Canada with a "perfect sense of
being . . . home."

Margaret had dedicated her book to Northrop Frye, Eli Mandel, and
Doug Jones, whom Matthews called "some of the leading intellectual 'negro
kings.'" Anansi, whose books he accused her of referring to disproportion-
ately, was "home for the suffering, rather chic, rather experimental, nicely
nationalistic writers of a hand-wringing we'll-probably-lose-so-don't-let's-
be-anti-American-or-too-militantly-political-type." In sum, Margaret
Atwood had engaged "in a put-down of the Canadian imagination."[8]

This Magazine invited Margaret to respond even before she had the
chance to read the article. Her eventual riposte was twenty-one pages
long. Robin Matthews, she complained, "thinks the battle [to overcome
the Canadian inferiority complex] is well on its way to being won, so it's
time to cheer. I think it's just beginning, and to waste your mouth foam
on cheering is a luxury we cannot yet afford."

But for the most part she was polite. She was a serious nationalist. She
felt that as long as Canadians saw themselves as victims, declaring themselves helpless before America's superior economic and cultural power,

they would never take responsibility to shape their own culture. Matthews, she felt, had done truly admirable work on the nationalist campaign to hire Canadians at Canadian universities. But he was "in danger of becoming a one-man garrison society walled up in his own paranoia, scanning the critical and literary scene like a periscope and going Bang at anything that moves."[9]

That fall of 1972, Margaret had been appointed writer-in-residence at the University of Toronto. Sam Solecki, then a young professor at St. Michael's College, remembers her giving the mandatory spring lecture that went with the position. She was hot. Everyone was talking about *Survival*, *Surfacing*, and *The Journals of Susanna Moodie*. He recalls that her lecture was a summary of *Survival*. "She was genial, open, witty, informative." The first questions from the audience came from the "old troglodytes" at St. Mike's, as Solecki called them. It wasn't clear to him whether they were more upset because she was a woman and "divorced" or because she hadn't included certain writers in her study of Canadian Literature. He had the sense of watching the old guard looking at the new, and they weren't happy.

Marshall McLuhan stood up. He was exploring the idea of masks, of putting on oneself as a mask. "It had some meaning for him in the McLuhanesque sense, though what he was on about wasn't clear to anybody. 'Miss Atwood,' he inquired, 'would you say that you put us on, not only that you have a mask, but that you have a variety of selves?' The question went on for about four minutes, with Margaret leaning on the lectern. She eventually gave an answer about writers and masks. And McLuhan replied: 'No, no, you have missed my whole point.' She countered: 'I have nothing to add, but perhaps we can talk about it later.' She was taking on the great Marshall. It was impressive. The self-confidence was there in front of the Establishment."[10]

Attacks against *Survival* continued. The most aggressive was launched by the poet Frank Davey in the summer 1973 issue of *Open Letter*. Davey took on *Survival* in a critical article that began with the sentence "In Margaret Atwood's poetry the overwhelmingly dominant subject has been what it is like to be Margaret Atwood." He went on to attack her fiction as rigidly controlled and contrived. He claimed Margaret had succumbed to the temptation of "the writer as power politician." *Survival*, he wrote, "could with equal justice have been subtitled a guide to House of Anansi Literature. A full 42% of Anansi's currently in print poetry and fiction are recommended in the book's various reading lists." Furthermore, Anansi's Graeme Gibson appeared to be Atwood's favourite novelist. The review was not subtle. Davey accused Margaret Atwood of naïvety; of "sketchiness and superficiality" in her research; of being ingratiating to the academic community; and of taking the "'power politics' expedient of suppressing" writers who didn't fit her thesis. Davey claimed that the book's success would be disastrous for those writers who hadn't expressed the "'right ideas' to make the Atwood canon."[11]

The review was barbed and nasty, and Margaret was deeply insulted. She responded by letter with her own statistical evidence. Having documented the references per chapter, she indicated that the majority of authors were not Anansi authors, and that there were authors who got more references than Graeme Gibson.

The sideways attack on Graeme was unusual. Until now he had escaped the opprobrium and reverse sexism that Jim Polk had had to suffer at the hands of those who had called him Mr. Atwood. In the literary community, respect for Graeme was high, both for his writing and for his work in cultural politics. He could only remember one occasion (on his promotion tour for his novel *Perpetual Motion*) that he was asked by an Alberta TV interviewer: "What it's like to live with Margaret Atwood?" He had replied, "None of your goddam business." He remarks: "In fact, Peggy's success never bothered me because we had both established the kinds of writers we were before we got involved and both of us had had the necessary success you need at the beginning, which sustains you."

There were other reviews of *Survival* that accused Margaret of being "trendy" and the book of being "shoddy." Some claimed she was a "Canadaphile"; others that she was contemptuous of Canada. She told George Woodcock she was thinking of getting some cards printed up: "Margaret Atwood is dying of a foul disease . . . and is unable to communicate with you in any way whatsoever."[12]

From her reading of Perry Miller's *The Raven and the Whale*, Margaret already knew that a period of cultural nationalism always creates ideological invective among writers. She had often remarked how damaging the nationalistic literary wars had been to Herman Melville in the nineteenth century. Melville was vilified by the "Young Americans" (as the nationalist school of writers called themselves) as not being American enough, and by the Anglophile critics as being too parochial, and thus lost the two communities that might have supported his writing. Perry Miller had concluded that Melville had been destroyed by the cultural politics of his time. After the fierce debate over *Moby Dick*, his reputation sank like a stone and he fell into silence for thirty years.

But Margaret was not about to be silenced. She took up the banner and fought back. There were some, like Dennis Lee, who thought she was altered by this in some ways. "There began to be a ferocity about her. She seemed to divide the world into We/They. I was part of the 'We,' so I can say this. She wanted to be sure 'We' weren't taken advantage of. It was complex. An unquestionable goodness of heart, very generous, went along with another 'kick 'em in the balls' kind of self."[13]

But soon Margaret was able to make fun of the whole kerfuffle. By 1975, she was writing a comic strip for *This Magazine* called "Kanadian Kultchur Komics," under the pseudonym Bart Gerrard. Her lead character was called Survivalwoman, "otherwise known as the flying Kotex® (Canada Limited)," who lived in her survival lair under the Bloor Street viaduct. As the comically inept Survivalwoman, Margaret got to make fun of everything from the Writers' Onion (the Writers' Union, which she had helped to establish); to Ceebeecee politics; to herself as saviour of Can Lit, with her rush to the rescue: "Blithering Beavers . . . it's a cry for Help!"[14] In one of her comic strips, the plot line is the CIA's (Cultural Infiltration Agency) efforts to penetrate the Writers' Onion. Their mole needs to have written a book. He proposes *The Joy of Sex*. "Not Kanadian enough," he's told. "Here's one, *The Joy of Socks*, by Alex Contort . . . it's a book on the survival of the foot." Margaret would always say: "It's a question of having a sense of humour. That's the only thing that's going to get you by."[15]

Looking back from this perspective in time, the seventies in Canada was the decade of fierce nationalist debate. In his famous "Conclusion" to the first edition of the *Literary History of Canada*, Northrop Frye had said that "cultural history has its own rhythms. . . . there must be a period, of a certain magnitude, in which a social imagination can take root and establish a tradition."[16] Canada, he lamented, had never had such a period. Written in 1965, that essay had served as a wake-up call.

Suddenly everyone, from Robertson Davies to Margaret Laurence, was talking about Canadian cultural identity. Davies proclaimed that his novel *Fifth Business* was about "the bizarre and passionate life of the Canadian people." Margaret Laurence spoke of her Manawaka series as novels of "homecoming." The Prairie novelist Rudy Wiebe talked about the need to acknowledge foundation cultural myths.

The same thing was happening in the other arts. In 1973, Charlie Pachter was busily working on a series of paintings called *Homage to the Colonial Mentality*. They were witty portraits of Queen Elizabeth: sitting astride a moose; or superimposed on a Lawren Harris landscape with a moose swimming towards her; or greeting Canadians in the forest like an angelic apparition with her tell-tale purse and gloves. His point seemed to be that the iconography at the core of the Canadian imagination was false, a foreign import.

In the visual arts, a kind of nationalism had taken root in 1967 when a group of painters, through the impetus of Jack Chambers, had started Canadian Artists' Representation (CAR) to protect artists' rights. By 1971, locals had been established in virtually every artistic community across the country. The energy was everywhere, but what was happening in Toronto was indicative. Artist-run galleries were opening, such as the Electric Gallery (1970), A Space (1971), and the Nightingale Arts Council (1970), and magazines were founded, including *Proof Only* (1973) and *Parachute* (1975). Native art was beginning to be recognized. Norval Morrisseau, an Ojibwa, and Carl Ray, an Anishnabe, in 1973, were instrumental in establishing the Native-run Ojibwa Cultural Foundation on Manitoulin Island.[17]

The theatres were busy too. In the mid-sixties it appeared that nothing much was happening in theatre in Canada. To the young radicals, the Stratford Theatre, in Stratford, Ontario, which concentrated on classical drama, seemed hidebound and conventional. But then seasoned actors, with five or six years of theatre under their belts and greedy for something new, flocked to the new Toronto companies, such as Theatre Passe Muraille, Tarragon, and Factory Lab, which had begun to open up after 1968. And suddenly the talent was there. In 1973, Passe Muraille launched *1837*, an experimental play written by Rick Salutin. It became a kind of touchstone for nationalists. Its subject was Canada's only armed rebellion, which occurred in 1837 when William Lyon Mackenzie, a newspaper editor and, briefly, mayor of Toronto, led some 750 rural supporters in a violent uprising against the British colonial government. The rebellion failed; many of the rebels were exiled, and a number were hanged. For Paul Thompson, the director of Passe Muraille, theatre was on a roll. He approached Margaret with the idea of producing a musical of *Survival*, though the project eventually died on the drafting table.

Journalists, too, carried on the nationalist debate. Margaret was a contributing editor to *This Magazine*. (It had originally been called *This Magazine Is About Schools*, but abbreviated its moniker to *This Magazine*, which always invited the joke: Which magazine?) She could always be counted on for her Bart Gerrard strip and for poems and the occasional article. Some of the country's best journalists and writers, including Rick Salutin, Carole Corbeil, Susan Crean, Myrna Kostash, Joyce Nelson, Ian Adams, and Stan Persky, cut their teeth at *This Magazine*.

Even those who did not identify themselves as nationalists, like the authors at Coach House Press, were caught up in the sense of new possibilities. Michael Ondaatje, looking back, would say "there was a real sense of a community that was doing things that came up from underneath — it was as if we were underneath the official culture of the time. There was an atmosphere of storming the gates."[18]

The writers discovered they had a common cultural project, to create art in Canada (only a brief ten years back, ambitious artists had felt compelled to leave the country). And there was public support for Canadian art. The Canada Council (established by Parliament in 1957 to support the arts, humanities, and social sciences) was now deeply involved in funding individual writers, magazines, and publishing houses. An article in the Montreal *Gazette* of December 1972 remarked that the number of Canadian books had increased by 25 per cent: "It would be over-simple to explain this phenomenal growth of Canadian writing in terms of Government assistance alone. Still, the confidence stimulated by this support has allowed Canadian-owned publishers to successfully expand an industry whose very existence seemed threatened a year ago."[19]

Finally, another important cultural institution opened. It was the product of a desperate election ploy in 1972 by the Liberal government of Pierre Trudeau. Trudeau had called an election but, as the campaign unwound and the prospect of a minority government seemed something to hope for, the

Liberals were looking for a way to shore up votes in Toronto. The Minister of Urban Affairs arrived in Toronto with a blank cheque and expropriated two kilometres of lakefront property. The old derelict harbour was to be transformed into a cultural park. After a two-year clean-up and many cultural probes (artists like Maureen Forrester and intellectuals like Marshall McLuhan were hired to lead groups of eighty to a hundred people on walk-abouts to discuss use of the site), Harbourfront opened in June 1974, with fireworks and parties that seemed to last all summer. In March of the next year, a young writer named Greg Gatenby left McClelland and Stewart to take over the literary reading series, and soon transformed it into a national forum. Most Canadian writers, both the well known and the esoteric, ended up reading at Harbourfront. "It was an intensely national-ist period," Gatenby remarks. "We wanted to hear our own voices. It was wonderfully exciting to hear them."[20]

Ideological skirmishes and internecine warfare were to be expected. Nationalists were accused of being chauvinists, and anti-nationalists were sell-outs. Margaret detested this debate. Like many, she wanted national-ism to have a positive thrust. She wrote to George Woodcock on the subject of Canadian publishers: "My only messages are: paranoia of all kinds — region afraid of region, old publishers afraid of new ones, new ones afraid of old ones, ones of different political views afraid of each other — should be avoided. Publishers should not hate & compete with each other; they should work together to improve the entire climate. How's that for a nice Sunday speech?"[21]

It was a wonderful time to be writing. Looking back today, most writ-ers of Margaret's generation regard the seventies with great nostalgia. Timothy Findley remarks: "We were a very lucky generation. I'm ten years older than Peggy, but I enjoyed the same thing. We had a kind of confi-dence, a sense that we could go for it. There was a lot of mutual support. We were inventing ourselves and the culture."[22]

Of course a backward glance always minimizes the difficulties. Making art in Canada was still fraught with problems, but perhaps it was the excitement of the fight for attention and the sense of solidarity in the battle that were the source of all that energy. Findley went through an eight-year drought, a "dark, dark period," before he published his break-through novel, *The Wars*, in 1978. It was the first book he went on tour to promote. There had been a devastating review in *The Globe and Mail*. The reviewer, Donald Jack, had found the book "absolutely trivial. Men don't cry, and so on." His friend and partner, Bill Whitehead, recalls that they were staying in an Edmonton hotel. "Tiff was still devastated from the *Globe* review. In the strange lobby of this hotel, there was only a small source of sky from the vaulted ceiling. *The Financial Post* had been couriered to us by Tiff's publisher, and we couldn't find any decent light to read it. So Tiff went into this little patch of sunlight to find out why they had sent the newspaper to him. It was Peggy's review of *The Wars*. She said that in Canada there were many KOOBS (Jack McClelland's word for commercial pop books) but this was a real book. Which just reopened Tiff's life."[23]

Findley adds: "That review saved my life. It was the most thoughtful commentary on the book. I doubt I would have been able to do the rest of the tour had there only been the *Globe* review."

In *The Raven and the Whale*, Perry Miller had pointed out that many of the great foundation books of American literature had been written within a fifteen-year period between 1845 and 1860, including Melville's *Moby Dick*, Hawthorne's *Scarlet Letter*, Whitman's *Song of Myself*, Thoreau's *Walden, or Life in the Woods*, Poe's stories, and Emily Dickinson's poems. Those years had been a period of self-conscious nationalism, of national articulation, when the writers threw off their colonial deference to Britain and created their own literature. All New World cultures went through this phase, though for most, including the cultures of Latin America, Australia, New Zealand, and Canada, the process had been much slower. In retrospect, Canadians would discover that, largely because of the nationalist movement from 1965 to the end of the 1970s, which changed perceptions, and also because of the financial assistance of the Canada Council, Canada had become a place where writing was possible. They also discovered there had been pioneer writers before this time who had gone largely unrecognized or had been dismissed. In sum, there was a Canadian tradition.

For both Margaret and Graeme, who were caught up in the process, nationalism was a pragmatic commitment. If the country's national literature was to survive, writers had to be protected and enabled to make a living. There were no standard contracts for writers, no avenues for grievances with publishers, no literary agents. Canadian copyright was murky, and tax laws applying to writers needed reform. The novelist Hugh MacLennan told Margaret an old horror story about his friend the writer Gwethalyn Graham that served as a kind of worst-case scenario. Gwethalyn Graham had published a novel, *Earth and High Heaven*, in 1944. It had become an international best-seller and had earned her $450,000. MacLennan elaborated: "Because an author's income was then regarded as 'unearned,' and 1945 was the highest taxation year ever, she was left with $10,500 by the government. The government made a settlement in Equity, as they put it, for about $30,000. She died in poverty."[24]

What was needed was a writers' union. And it was obvious to most people that the person to organize it was Graeme. He had the political skill. In 1972, he started writing to individuals across the country and meeting with such people as Mavis Gallant, Farley Mowat, Pierre Berton, John Metcalf, Clark Blaise, and Robertson Davies to discuss a union. Money for a conference was supplied by an enlightened arts director at the Ontario Arts Council named Ron Evans, and at the end of the year thirty writers were flown into Toronto for a first meeting. Frank Scott, with a committee that included Harold Horwood, Marian Engel, and Austin Clarke, drew up a constitution. Clark Blaise, who was there as the designated link between Toronto and Montreal, recalls those planning sessions: "We shook each others' hands with the exaggerated respect of self-conscious, self-important young people launching a movement. . . . We were a literary generation."[25] The initial debates were tough. Many people were sceptical of the idea of organizing writers, and wondered who was to be let in. But the constitution was ratified, and all published writers were invited to join.

The Writers' Union of Canada dated its inception as 3 November 1973. By the time Graeme was elected chair in 1974, the union had well over two hundred members.

Both Margaret and Graeme could always be counted on to support those causes they believed in, with time and money. Giving blood. In 1984, they would be instrumental in founding the English-Canadian Centre of PEN, the international organization devoted to fighting on behalf of writers whose human rights had been violated. The early meetings were held in their dining room, and the first problem was chairs. There weren't enough, until Timothy Findley brought along his bridge chairs. Margaret and Graeme came up with the idea for the initial fund-raising project, a Can Lit cookbook, which made enough money to hire an executive director.

As she fought along with others for cultural issues on the home front, Margaret found her international reputation was growing. In 1973, plans were under way for an American edition of *Survival*, to be published in 1975. Margaret was a bit surprised that there was American interest in a book on the subject of Can Lit, as it was affectionately called. She told George Woodcock: "Maybe the U.S. is Canadianizing at the same rate Canada is being Americanized? Well, not the same rate maybe."[26] Frances McCullough, her American editor at Harper & Row, said she was excited by the prospect that the book would lead American readers into Canada. In discussing revisions for the American edition, McCullough apologized for her "appalling . . . ignorance about the simple physical facts of Canada" and asked Margaret to provide footnotes for some of the more obscure phrases: "Tom Thompson [sic] jack pine, Toronto Annex, Orange Day parade, a house in Rosedale, defense of the Long Sault, and Canadian Shield." "Do you think its hopelessly inane to include something about geography and early settlement and who speaks what language and the Indians and the fact that you can freeze to death very fast and all that! . . . What about Joual or whatever it's called?"[27] She told Margaret that rats had infested her country house, but had only eaten Norman Mailer's book on Marilyn Monroe (the left cheek) and had bypassed the bedside copy of *Survival*. She liked the idea that even the American country rats were beginning to respect Canadian books. As it turned out, because of contract issues, an American edition of *Survival* was never published.

16

NO TRAINS IN SIGHT

In 1974 Margaret published her tenth book, *You Are Happy*. Already, many were anxious to correct the iconography that attached to her. One of the most intelligent efforts was by a young twenty-three-year-old poet, Susan Musgrave. Musgrave began her review of *You Are Happy* by describing the publication of a new Atwood book as an "event," like "a new Brando film or a new Dylan record used to be." Margaret Atwood had always been identified with her poems, she complained, and "to judge the poems is to judge the poet." The mythical "para-Atwood" was "laconic, embattled, shrewish. . . . It's monstrously unfair of us and only a culture that lives on the fag ends of romanticism would try it," wrote Musgrave.[1]

The image of the mythical para-Atwood got its best expression in Alan Pearson's review of *You Are Happy* in *The Globe and Mail*:

> In the iconography of the bookshop poster, she is seen as a snaky-haired Medusa; a glance at those steely eyes confirms that the country behind them is steeped in everlasting November. No edible woman this. The male psyche knows to beware as this sinewy female unleashes all the thermotropic weaponry of her rhetoric. . . . If not a Boadicea born into prominence on the whinnying mares of nationalism and women's liberation, then certainly a tocsin belle of Canadian letters.
>
> One begins to get a spectral image of the Atwood persona: a long-gowned figure, haunting the mildewed sedges of icy

banks, a fey creature feeding the shy deer and stepping delicately between patches of snow, wild hair blowing, a mind full of bitter thoughts, defiant and demon-haunted by turns, a Brontean figure in a landscape of bare branches, iron grey sky and an acrid smell of woodsmoke on the air.

There are mica glints of . . . meaning but what? Siren Song tells us how boring it is for a woman to be obliged to attract men by appealing to them for help. . . . After an evening with this book I reach gratefully for a Bloody Mary.[2]

When she taught Canadian Literature at York University in 1971, Margaret participated in a project examining sexual bias in the media. Her students were assigned the task of investigating bias in reviewing. They sent letters to writers asking whether they believed sexual bias existed, and also examined a large number of reviews. Seventy-five per cent of the male writers who replied to the question said there was no evidence of sexual bias, while 25 per cent said perhaps there was some. But, among the women, 50 per cent said, yes, there was bias; 25 per cent said maybe; and 25 per cent said no.

When the reviews themselves were examined, however, Margaret could say that, "in all honesty, we didn't find as much sexual bias as we'd expected." She and her students concluded that things were reasonably good for women. Sexual bias was not explicit, but there was a double standard.

Twenty-five years ago, it was fashionable to draw a distinction between a masculine style and a feminine style of writing. This Margaret called the "Quiller-Couch Syndrome," after the turn-of-the-century Trinity College, Oxford, critic who defined masculine as vigorous and feminine as vague. In a humorous article describing her students' survey, she listed the stereotypes attached to women. There was the "sexual compliment put-down": "she writes like a man." The domestic put-down: "when a man writes about things like doing the dishes, it's realism; when a woman does, it's an unfortunate feminine genetic limitation." The "panic reaction": "the book threatened the male reviewer." And the "Ophelia syndrome": "the writer as crazy freak, or Doomed Brontë."

In a way, it was just that women were catching up to men. As she put it, "male-author stereotypes" included the "Potted Poe, Bleeding Byron,

Doomed Dylan, Lustful Layton, Crucified Cohen, etc." For women there was the "Elusive Emily," "Reclusive Rossetti," and "Suicidal Sylvia." Stereotypes like these, even when the author complied with them and became a cult figure, did no one any good.[3]

Margaret did not want writing to be viewed as magic, madness, or trickery, or as an evasive disguise for a message. Rather, it was a legitimate profession: "The woman writer exists in a society that, though it may turn certain individuals into revered cult objects, has little respect for writing as a profession, and not much respect for women either." Reviewers and the media, she explained, deeply affect the tangibles of a career: how a woman is received or reviewed, and how much money she makes. But they are "a false arena. The real one is in her head, her real struggle the daily battle with words, the language itself. . . . Writers are makers of books."[4]

As late as 1978, Joyce Carol Oates asked Margaret in an interview: "You must be disturbed by the journalists' efforts to categorize you — to package you as 'The Reigning Queen of Canadian Literature,' or a national prophetess, or even a Medusa. What have your reactions been?"

Margaret replied:

> I dislike the kinds of titles you mention; I find "Reigning Queen" a particularly offensive one, implying as it does that literature, as practiced by women anyway, is either a monarchy or a beehive. In any case, there's only room for one "reigning queen," who will presumably be stung to death later on when she can't lay more eggs. Such titles are insulting to the many fine women writers in this country (Marian Engel, Alice Munro, Margaret Laurence, to name three) and threatening to me. I suppose Canada is hungry for a few visible "stars," having been without any for so long. The danger to the writer is early stellification — one may become a vaporous ball of gas. But only if captivated by one's image. Luckily, my image here, as reflected in the press, has not been very captivating, at least to me. I can do without Medusa."[5]

The Pearsons of this world were taking their potshots at Medusa, but the feminist movement's attachment to her was problematic in a different way.

The novelist and journalist Lesley Krueger remembers meeting Margaret in December 1973 at a week-long conference of Canadian University Press (CUP), an organization of student newspapers across the country. Krueger was nineteen at the time and news editor of *The Ubyssey* at the University of British Columbia. The Women's Caucus of CUP had invited Margaret to speak on a panel and asked her to attend a preliminary meeting to discuss the upcoming agenda. As Krueger recalls:

> We were very excited because Margaret Atwood was just then beginning to emerge in everyone's consciousness. I remember very clearly, however, that as I listened to the discussion I had a growing impression that people weren't asking her anything. They were trying to tell her what they wanted her to say. To be fair there was so much denigration of feminists then, even within an organization with radical leftist principles like Canadian University Press. These were feisty, assertive young radicals, yet they still found them-selves assigned to making the coffee. Here was this identi-fied feminist icon coming to speak and everybody wanted her to say exactly what they believed. They revered her but they weren't interested in listening to her; they were inter-ested in injecting her with their beliefs.[6]

Lesley Krueger was elected chair of the panel and felt that Margaret had somehow identified her as an ally, and seemed to be grateful for her presence. Of course, she herself was "impressed half to death" with Margaret, and wonders now if she might have been reading into Margaret's motives. But her assumption coming out of that first meeting was that Margaret felt she would need a defender. She seemed nervous, which struck the young Krueger enormously. Margaret was old enough to be one of her professors.

In the interim before the panel, Krueger had been planning to meet a friend who lived in Toronto. She hadn't seen her in several years, and hadn't been able to reach her by phone. Finally someone answered her call, only to tell her that her friend had died very suddenly that morning. Her friend had not been sick. She had died from an aneurysm. Krueger was devastated. She hadn't known anyone her own age to die as suddenly as that. The afternoon turned surreal. Krueger remembers:

> I went into the washroom at Ryerson. It was one of those washrooms with white cubicles and white sinks, and the floor tiles had a yellowish tint. I have a clear memory of sitting on the floor, and Margaret Atwood came in. She asked if I was all right? I told her that my friend had just died and that I couldn't do the panel. I would lose it. She looked shocked and dismayed. I was looking up at her from my position on the floor. And I suddenly noticed her hands begin to shake. I have this very clear image of these hands shaking. She comforted me and said nothing about the panel, but I suddenly felt that she also realized she would be left on her own with the lions — with all those eager young women who wanted her, they wanted to possess her and to have her speak their ideas. And the one person who had emerged as her ally was out of it. I had a clear understanding—the way one does at periodic times — of the individuality of someone else. I thought: How much this costs her! Here was a person who was for us so famous, so admirable, and yet she was surprisingly human. She was sad and nervous and alone and young. I think I remember feeling that she wasn't so old after all.

Margaret called herself a feminist, and she certainly wanted to help young women. But she didn't want to be cornered into being a mouthpiece. She believed that "the proper path for a woman writer is not an all-out manning (or womaning) of the barricades. . . . The proper path is to become better as a writer."[7]

Margaret had only one ambition: to be a good writer, and for her this meant being a self-supporting professional writer. Which is why, from early on, she turned her hand to all kinds of writing, from her high-school jingles and puppet plays to her mature magazine journalism and television scripts. By the mid-seventies she had begun to make a comfortable living as a writer and she incorporated herself in 1976 under the name "O.W. Toad" (an acrostic for "Atwood"). In addition to an agent, she could afford an assistant who could handle all the requests and inquiries regarding her work. Indeed, students and researchers were beginning to engage in what would become the Atwood-criticism industry.

She took herself seriously as an artist, which demanded much more courage and originality than would, at first, seem obvious. There were two problems. A lot of women still had difficulty believing they could be writers at all, given the Romantic cult of genius that still attached to the writer. It took guts to believe in oneself enough to demand a room of one's own, but then to assume the authority to subordinate others to one's work, to assume that the assistant, researcher, agent, and publicist were all appropriate adjuncts to one's professional life — that was a departure.

There was also the lingering cliché that treating one's art as a professional activity somehow soured the source of inspiration. Art was pure. It had little to do with the practicality of living in the world. Others were meant to take care of the artist. In fact, this Romantic notion often did work, especially for the male artist. Had people been willing to look behind the scenes in those days, they would have seen that many male writers indeed had assistants — unpaid assistants in the form of wives or lovers, who not only took care of their correspondence, but often held down outside jobs in order to make enough money to free the writers to write. Behind so many male artists, particularly poets, were the women who kept the performance going.

Margaret was dismissive of the Romantic fantasy of the bohemian artist. She once said: "In a bourgeois, industrial society, so the theory goes, the creative artist is supposed to act out suppressed desires and prohibited activities for the audience."[8] She had a different model: the Victorian man or woman of letters (like Dickens or George Eliot) who was an active participant in society and lived by his or her work. And she had no intention of using her mate as a breadwinner. Graeme was not to be commandeered into being her assistant or her financial back-up. As a writer, she had a responsibility to make her own living and, anyway, he had his own career.

However, even this professionalism provoked suspicion. There were many who felt Margaret kept her finger on the cultural pulse and that her themes were dictated by a shrewd eye for what would sell. One reviewer remarked that she was "blessed with the gift of ceaseless relevance." And she would find herself on the defensive. She told one interviewer: "Nothing I do has anything to do with market demands, except in the TV script department. . . . I've always felt my writing was somewhat eccentric."[9]

One interviewer, Linda Sandler, remarked: "You seem to pick up the right signals, because The Edible Woman pre-dates feminism, Surfacing is about the wilderness, Lady Oracle is about a cult figure, and these are all stories people want to hear."

Margaret replied: "I don't have any special clairvoyant gifts. As 'prophecies,' reading my books is rather like going to the fortune teller. She peers into her crystal and she says: 'Babble, babble, babble.' You forget most of it, but then you meet a dark stranger and you say, 'Gee, what clairvoyance!' Plugging into the popular sensibility is not peculiar to me."[10]

Margaret had always been fascinated by the popular sensibility and by what she called its "social iconography," the myths that lie buried beneath our assumptions. This could be charted all the way back to her childhood, to that young girl who surfaced from her forest world as an outsider to social conventions. She was someone introduced to social conventions too late ever to mistake them for natural states of being.

Jim Polk comes closest to expressing this when he explains, "She was really from the bush, and with her background she could look at things as if from afar, as it were, and seemed to see everything through her special lens. She could make a comedy of it when it was her mood, or see ordinary things in an odd, surreal, hushed, Gothic way."[11]

She once said that she felt "like a curious, often bemused, sometimes disheartened observer of society."[12] In her interview with Graeme in 1971 for Eleven Canadian Novelists, she had asked: "Does anyone ever achieve it [being human]?" Being human seemed, inevitably, "just out of reach."[13]

One of her richest meditations on this theme is the centrepiece to You Are Happy, the Circe/Mud Poems. Much of the human story is a story of war, of sexual conquest, and of killing. When looked at from a woman's perspective, it is a ruthless history. In Homer's Odyssey, four thousand years back, the story was already fixed. Two icons meet: the male as warrior and the female as temptress. For Margaret these two "counterfeit" images defined a route to much of the sickness that plagues the human psyche. While it is assumed that her vision is ironic or cynical, in fact her vision is often dark. In those poems she took on the voice of Circe speaking from despair and loneliness and anger:

> Men with the heads of eagles
> no longer interest me . . .
>
> I search instead for the others,
> the ones left over,
> the ones who have escaped from these
> mythologies with barely their lives;
> they have real faces and hands, they think
> of themselves as
> wrong, somehow, they would rather be trees.[14]

What allows two people to live together and to sustain a relationship, despite the many pressures towards separation? Perhaps they must share a common gaze on the world. As writers, Margaret and Graeme shared a dark vision of society careering off the rails, as is evident from their respective works. *Surfacing* and *Communion* can almost be seen as companion pieces, written before they came to know each other, both meditations on the warping of the human psyche, on what Margaret once called "trapped and wounded life energies."[15] Graeme was looking at the male in ways that wouldn't be recognized as such until Robert Bly popularized the subject twenty years later. Together they worked as environmentalists, and volunteered for the Civil Liberties Association of Canada, and both would serve as presidents of PEN Canada. While they lived in the seeming isolation of Alliston, they continued to be as active as ever in their public lives.

The amount of work Margaret managed to do between 1973 and 1976 was extraordinary. She often said that she thought of herself as a lazy sort of person. She would later revise that and add, "at least in comparison to my family."[16] Increasingly, she was being asked to do free-lance work. Magazines like *The Atlantic* and *Ms.* were courting her, and the CBC was also interested. These commissions brought in a substantial portion of her income. She had passed that invisible ceiling where, instead of having to peddle her work, people came to her. It is what a writer hopes for.

George Jonas was a CBC television producer and director for a series called *The Play's the Thing*. He asked Margaret to send him something, and, in the fall of 1973, she wrote a two-act play called *The Servant Girl*, based on a sensational murder trial in Richmond Hill, north of Toronto. In 1843, a sixteen-year-old servant, Grace Marks, had been convicted of the double murder of her employer and his mistress. Margaret had first come across the story eight years earlier when she read Susanna Moodie's account of it in *Life in the Clearings*. When she began her research by going back to the newspapers of the time and the actual prison records, she found Moodie had got a lot of the story wrong. Her first idea was that the play could begin with Moodie's tour of Kingston Penitentiary in 1850 to visit the murderess Grace Marks. Margaret had good instincts. She mapped the floor plans of the kitchen, parlour, and bedrooms. Parts of the play could be set in an insane asylum and a jail.

The play was first aired on 7 January 1974. Twenty years later, Margaret resurrected the story for her much more complex novel, *Alias Grace*, explaining: "Years passed and Grace Marks continued to wander around in my head. . . . she kept insisting on being given a fuller hearing."[17] Suddenly the linearity of the drama could be expanded. She could play with phrenology and theosophy, with the foundations of psychology, with magic and with class. Margaret always told young writers that writing is organic. One work grows out of another. And the first law of writing is never throw anything away.

The film rights for *Surfacing* were bought by the Québécois director Claude Jutra. She wrote to George Woodcock in March 1974 that she was working on the screenplay and scaring herself silly over the ghost scenes.[18] She also joked that she was working on another "preposterous fiction. (If you thought the others were frank in their departures from realism, wait till you see this one)." It would be called *Lady Oracle*. By now she had a researcher to whom she could send her list "of strange requests":

1) a map of Italy.
2) an English–Italian, Italian–English dictionary.
3) a work on Italian architecture or history that contains the following information: which Pope had built (and when) the water-fountain papal residence at Tivoli? . . .

4) an Italian Photoramanze . . . they are cheesy magazines,
sort of like *True Romance* except that the story is told in
still black and white photos with captions and cartoon
balloons. . . .
5) a copy of *Jane Eyre*.[19]

Margot Kidder bought the film rights to *Lady Oracle* after the book
came out, though the film was never made.

Still, there was always time for fun. Charlie Pachter had been looking for
a venue to house his vision of a Picasso-like atelier for artists in Toronto
and, in 1974, he found a building at 24 Ryerson Avenue, off Queen Street.
No one yet saw any value in those downtown districts of second-hand
shops, cheap ethnic eateries, and spacious warehouses, and the building
was going cheap. When he told Margaret, she was enthusiastic and helped
him put together the down payment. Calling his place "Artists Alliance,"
he invited painters, print-makers, architects, designers, film-makers, writers — anyone who needed a place — to join. Soon, as he explains it,
"artists were living in nooks and crannies like mice with ladders, and with
the kitchens below and the beds above. It was a blast."[20] People started
calling him "the King of Queen Street."

It was there that Charlie put on the "Ugly Show" in 1975. The famous
and the unknown were invited to submit the worst work they had either
made or found. Margaret's contribution was an egg cup she had made in a
ceramics class and which had blown up in the kiln. It was a squat, bulbous
female figure, with the rotund body typical of prehistoric fertility images.
It might have stepped out of the landscape of her Circe/Mud poems. In
1976, Charlie did the "Stunning Show," a parody of exclusive fund-raiser,
black-tie auctions. Everyone came in Sally Ann tuxes and dresses, and the
starting bid for paintings was $100,000. Charlie bought ten *hor d'oeuvres*
and glued them to a silver tray, which was duly passed around.

In 1976, Charlie bought a farm in Oro, north of the town of Barrie and
not far from Alliston, which he called the Oro Fixation, and his Canada
Day parties on 1 July became a "real thing." When Graeme and Peggy
visited, they used to go to the local bakeries for butter tarts. Soon they were

going to farms for the local bake sales. He became the butter-tart maven, discovering subcategories of the confection. Presbyterian butter tarts were crustier; Catholic ones were deeper. His theory was that as the croissant is to France, and the doughnut is to America, so the butter tart is to Canada.

But work continued. Margaret was writing *Days of the Rebels: 1815–1840*, a history book for high-school students, published in 1977. She also published a number of the short stories that would appear in the collection *Dancing Girls* (1977). The CBC was particularly interested in the story "Rape Fantasies," and commissioned her to write a radio adaptation. In 1976, she wrote a TV script, *Memoirs of a Great Detective*, for the CBC, though they never used it. Her first *Selected Poems* came out that year with Oxford University Press, and *The Edible Woman* was published in Italy, the first of many European translations.

She was up to her neck in deadlines. She and Graeme had taken on the job of writing a screenplay for Margaret Laurence's *The Diviners*. She was also writing a piece for Ms. magazine on Henry Morgentaler, the doctor who led the Canadian campaign to legalize abortion. When Ms. editor Nina Finkelstein asked her to do a second piece, on Margaret Trudeau, she finally said no, but added: "I can recommend unreservedly a very excellent journalist up here, June Callwood. . . . The Writers' Union by the way includes a whole bunch of good female writers."[21] She also sent Finkelstein a book of poems by the Canadian poet, Pat Lowther, who had recently been murdered by her husband. "I knew Pat," she wrote. "Her death made me very angry. She deserves a wider audience."[22]

There was always fund-raising to be done for the Writers' Union. An earlier idea of the union editing an anthology of pornography had fizzled out when it became clear that good writers made bad pornographers, though Marian Engel's *Bear* was seeded by the project. In 1977 Margaret and Graeme floated the idea of staging a theatrical revue. Writers across the country were pulled in to write skits, and Paul Thompson of Theatre Passe Muraille was brought on side as director. Held on 9 May, the show was called "The Eclectic Typewriter Revue."

Thompson recalls: "There was a lovely spirit of subversion in it all that I remember quite clearly. Peggy was in there scribbling away, writing stuff. My favourite skit was the one in which she and two other women writers did a snowshoe dance in honour of Farley Mowat. And Rudy Wiebe, with

George Riga's daughter, sang some song about the poor wee boys of Ontario. Writers were making fun of themselves and that indicated a new confidence. The glee and the fullness of energy that Peggy discovered when she went into it all was wonderful to see. She came up with most of the interesting ideas."[23]

Thompson gradually realized that Margaret would make a wonderful collaborator. He remarks: "When I playfully proposed the idea of a musical of *Survival*, I didn't realize how desirous or seductive Peggy found this. Until we did 'The Eclectic Typewriter Revue.'" She seemed deeply attracted by the collective anarchy that this kind of theatre represented. In fact, Thompson sensed that she was totally hooked, and might have turned more fully towards theatre, except "she would have had too much fun with it and it would have affected her work. She would have had difficulty controlling it and giving it the same kind of arc, the same kind of complexity, that she required in her other writing." He felt that Margaret had "looked at temptation" and then had turned back, almost reluctantly, to the solitary, sedentary world of her art.

Margaret had a writer's will and self-discipline. When she was repeatedly asked why she wrote, the question always struck her as bizarre. Why does a dancer dance or an athlete run? To one questioner she replied: "For the joy of it." "The thing about writers that people don't realize is that a lot of what they do is play. You know, playing around. That doesn't mean that it isn't serious or that it doesn't have a serious meaning or intention."[24] To another she said: "It's exhausting, but not a bad kind of exhausting."

When Graeme had asked her in his 1971 interview: "What do you like most about your own writing?" she had responded: "Doing it. . . . I think the book you always like best is the one you're about to write. And what you think about the ones you have written is what you did wrong, or how you would do it if you were going to do it over again, or whether you would ever do it again."

He'd asked: "Who do you write for?" And she had joked: "Once upon a time I thought there was an old man with a gray beard somewhere who knew the truth, and if I was good enough, naturally he would tell me that this was it. That person doesn't exist, but that's who I write for. The great critic in the sky . . . I would say that's a personification of some ideal which is unattainable."[25]

Like a long-distance runner, she kept writing to exceed her own limits.

For several years, Margaret had been thinking of having a child. In the fall of 1975, she found she was pregnant. She would soon be thirty-six. Of course she worried about her age and about whether she had waited too long. There was a great deal of propaganda at the time about older mothers and their risk of having babies with birth defects. Soon she found it difficult to read for sustained periods — "a trial but not a catastrophe." Her doctors advised her to delay getting her vision corrected until after the birth.

She didn't stop working. That November, a young Canadian professor at Harvard, David Staines, invited her down to Cambridge to give a lecture on Canadian Literature. He, too, had done his thesis under Jerome Buckley, and had first met Margaret at one of Buckley's Thanksgiving dinners. Professor Buckley organized a dinner for her and introduced her lecture, which she'd called: "Canadian Monsters: Some Aspects of the Supernatural in Canadian Fiction." Graeme accompanied Margaret, and Staines, discovering they both loved lobster, took them for a lobster orgy. It was the beginning of a long friendship. From time to time, Staines and Margaret talked of the fact that she'd never completed her thesis, though she'd written two-thirds of it. She would say that she'd been writing so much that she'd had no time for the thesis, but he understood that it rankled in a mild sort of way. She did not like to leave things unfinished. When his own thesis was published as a book, he gave her a copy, joking: "Some of us do finish our theses."[26]

In her seventh month of pregnancy, Margaret put the finishing touches to Lady Oracle. (It had taken her two years to write it.) Her daughter, Jessica, was born on 17 May 1976. She reported to friends that Graeme was overjoyed. He had so wanted a girl.

"Everything went well, baby is magnificent," she told Nina Finkelstein.[27] Despite sleep deprivation, she reported that she was functional again, and could proceed. At the end of May she wrote to George Woodcock that she was "a little more tired than usual, but not much and about to begin work again (tho slowly)."[28]

A practical matter she had delayed for a long time had to be confronted. She had never learned to drive: "In my youth I made the mistake of trying to learn through relatives and friends." Now that she had a baby, she would have to learn and she wasn't feeling all that confident. While taking the lessons, she discovered she was blocked about writing letters. "I suppose I was feeling generally incompetent," she explained. But she did get her driver's licence.

Beth Appeldoorn might have been right in her assessment of Margaret: "She's totally down to earth. There is no crap around her. What you see is what you get."[29]

Soon Margaret was being asked to explain the significance of wanting a child. One particularly young, or particularly obtuse, interviewer asked: "What does pregnancy mean in your writing?" Margaret replied patiently: "You can't say pregnancy is one thing. It's many things, like making love. I mean it's not just one thing that ought to have one meaning. It's one of those profoundly meaningful human activities which can be very multi-faceted and resonant. It can have a very positive meaning for some and a very negative meaning for others."[30] It was certainly annoying to find herself saying the obvious. More annoying that the obvious needed to be said.

Wanting to have children was like wanting to write, absurd to look for reasons why. After her daughter was born, Margaret wrote "Giving Birth." The story moves so organically through its meditations that to extract any moment is to diminish that moment. It is both graphically physical in its details and mysteriously elusive, like the experience itself.

Margaret was able to find a wonderfully direct and yet intimate narrative voice for her story. "But who gives birth and to whom is it given?" the narrator asks. The verb itself seems inept, and she thinks: "Language, muttering in its archaic tongues of something, yet one more thing that needs to be re-named. It won't be by me though."

Who *is* it that gives birth? she wonders. The narrator splits into several selves: the woman speaking; the woman who "gave" birth (who is distant from the narrator now, almost a past self); the woman who accompanied her like a phantom to the hospital who doesn't want to give birth to a child; the writer (Margaret Atwood); the reader (whoever she or he is): all are wraiths, echoes, reverberations in the brain. Life itself is ephemeral; identity is fluid. "But," says the narrator, "real enough."

Surely giving birth must bring some unexpected vision:

> She is, secretly, hoping for a mystery. Something more than this, something else, a vision. After all she is risking her life,

though it's not too likely she will die. Still, some women do. Internal bleeding, shock, heart failure, a mistake on the part of someone, a nurse, a doctor. She deserves a vision, she deserves to be allowed to bring something back with her from this dark place into which she is now rapidly descending. . . . [She] tries to reach down to the baby, as she has many times before, sending waves of love, colour, music, down through her arteries to it.

But the story proceeds without epiphanies. "As for the vision, there wasn't one. [She] is conscious of no special knowledge."

The epiphany is the simple meeting of mother and child in gestures of love. "The baby isn't crying; she squints in the new light. Birth isn't something that has been given to her, nor has she taken it. It was just something that has happened so they could greet each other like this."

But Margaret does end the story with a vision, of a kind. Weak from just having "given birth," the woman leans through the window of her hospital room looking out over the city:

> All she can see from the window is a building. It's an old stone building, heavy and Victorian, with a copper roof oxidized to green. It's solid, hard, darkened by soot, dour, leaden. But as she looks at this building, so old and seemingly immutable, she sees that it's made of water. Water, and some tenuous jellylike substance. Light flows through it from behind (the sun is coming up), the building is so thin, so fragile, that it quivers in the slight dawn wind. Jeannie sees that if the building is this way (a touch could destroy it, a ripple of earth, why has no one noticed, guarded against this accident?) then the rest of the world must be like this too, the entire earth, the rocks, people, trees, everything needs to be protected, cared for, tended. The enormity of the task defeats her; she will never be up to it, and what will happen then?

Like any woman who has given birth, she discovers that life is fragile.

And precious. It must be protected. And soon life begins again, with its ordinary demands. Her child is carried in to the hospital room, "solid, substantial, packed together like an apple."[31]

And public life began again for Margaret. She was distressed to discover that, after she became a MOTHER, people wanted to see her differently:

> People's attitudes towards me changed remarkably. . . . You wouldn't believe it. It's not that I'm a different person. I'm exactly the same person as I always was, pretty well, give or take a little evolutionary change. But it's not as though becoming a mother suddenly renders you this warm, cozy, cookie-handing-out individual, if you weren't before. I always have handed out cookies, as a matter of fact.[32]

Having a child was a personal choice. She was old enough to remember the time when women were told they had to get pregnant and have babies to fulfil their femininity. She also remembered the time when women were told that they oughtn't to have babies, that it was anti-feminist to do so. She liked neither line. She remembered when women who had children casually excluded her from their frame of reference, as if from some secret knowledge or some private cabal. It was tiresome and cruel. She had sworn then that she would never do this to any woman who did not have children.

In her mind she was simply a woman who wrote books and had a child. And that was miraculous enough. She hadn't expected it. All those years back, when she had started out, there was the moral of *The Red Shoes*. She had been told, and half believed, she couldn't be a woman and an artist. If she tried, she would end up jumping in front of a train.

There was no train in sight.

AFTERWORD

Looking back at the sixties and seventies, it's now possible to say that those were the years when English-Canadian culture finally got over its colonial cringe. In future, young writers would no longer have to waste good energy wondering whether they could practise their craft in Canada. They could look back at the numerous artists who had stayed and made careers in their own country.

Clark Blaise remembers: "In those fifteen Canadian years [1966–81], more of the dream came true than I might have dared to wish. I was a young writer present at the birth of contemporary Canadian writing. (It was like a coffeehouse experience in Paris; everyone together in a single time and place, an agenda to discuss, anthologies to collect, publishing houses to launch, the young getting started, the literary midwives returning from Europe, the friendly journalists crouching on the edges.)" It was the time when it was "possible to know everyone."[1]

These same young mavericks have become the Establishment. And many of the institutions they started — theatres like Passe Muraille, publishing houses like Anansi, and organizations like the Writers' Union — have lasted, becoming venerable; some even tired. Longhouse, the bookstore devoted solely to the sale of Canadian books, disappeared. It was no longer necessary. The nationalist movement achieved what it set out to do: to give Canadian culture a mirror in which to view itself.

The problems of colonialism that had haunted the culture, what Northrop Frye had called the "frostbite at the roots of imagination," turned out to be a matter of perception, as any post-colonial or feminist theorist could tell you. When you are caught shadow-boxing with a sense of cultural, or indeed personal, inferiority, continually on the defensive, flinching at the ambivalences and vagaries caused by self-doubt, then energies are suppressed, or deflected into anger. It's curious how hard the process is, but eventually "coming of age" means moving in from the margins and finding your own place. Or as Margaret Atwood would put it: you reach phase four in the dynamic of survival. You accept your own experience for what it is. And begin to look outward.

From the mid-eighties on, Canadian writers became players on the international scene: Robertson Davies, Margaret Laurence, Mordecai Richler, Alice Munro, Mavis Gallant, Margaret Atwood, Michael Ondaatje, Rohinton Mistry, Carol Shields, Timothy Findley and Jane Urquhart. And in the mid-nineties, even young writers like Anne Michaels, Dionne Brand, and Ann-Marie MacDonald shot into international prominence. On the home front, what had been a predominantly WASP culture opened. Native writers moved to the fore, as did writers from elsewhere who had made Canada home.

Unfortunately, coming of age does not make life any easier. It simply means inheriting new problems, the ones that plague everybody. Canadian writers may now have a sense that Canada is a good place to start from, but what then? Starting out now has a different set of hazards. Publishing houses come and go, often at the whim of multinationals driven by profit margins. It's only a slight consolation to know that one is in good company worldwide. How the creative arts are to survive in a consumer society may be the dilemma for the new generation. There may be stars, but will there be a culture behind them? Two decades ago, in his book *The Gift: Imagination and the Erotic Life of Property*, Lewis Hyde insisted that, until we give a place to creativity in our market-driven economies, and see the work of art as a gift and not a commodity, we won't get things right. Art is a human activity. The human mind seems to need it for psychological equilibrium. As Margaret once said, the real question about writing, and all other artistic activities, is not why do some people create art? but rather why doesn't everyone?

And what about Margaret herself in the last twenty years? Margaret's life has unfolded as the cards said it would.

She and Graeme left Alliston and moved back to Toronto in 1980, first living on Sullivan Street, off Spadina in Toronto's original Chinatown. There were periods of residence outside Canada: in Scotland, Germany, Alabama, and France.

Margaret structured her writing day. She hired a babysitter four hours a day, five days a week, and wrote in the afternoons. If she was engrossed in a new novel, she might also write at night. She usually worked in an office elsewhere, not at home. In the early eighties, she kept an office on Manning Avenue, a few blocks from Sullivan Street. Writing was a matter of discipline: of emptying the mind of everything and letting it fill with whatever fiction, poetry, or prose she was working on.

There would be adjustments for travel with a child. In Scotland in 1978, she wheeled her daughter off twice a week to the Mothers' and Toddlers' Playgroup in the Anglican church hall where room was made for the internationals. When she mentioned the fact that she wrote novels, she was asked if she had a publisher, and she would find that, under the polite shifting of eyes, she became defensive. It would have been easier to explain her presence with "My husband has a job at the university" (Graeme was on a Scottish–Canadian writers' exchange), but she didn't. She never had explained what she did in terms of someone else. Still, it amazed her how, once out of her environment, she had to insist on the fact that she was a writer in order to keep believing it herself. She was surprised how quickly the trappings of success fell away.[2]

She came to describe her three priorities as family, writing, and the environment. She once thought that she would have to forgo the dream of family because domestic life would destroy the writer. As a young woman, she had warned herself: "Sartre, Samuel Beckett, Kafka, and Ionesco . . . did not have major appliances." Now she could revise that: "I bake (dare I admit it) chocolate-chip cookies and I find that doing the laundry with the aid of my washer–dryer is one of the more relaxing parts of my week." Though home, husband, two stepsons, and a daughter sometimes stood between her and the typewriter, the rewards were much greater than the frustrations. However, she would add: "A family and writing is OK, even a job and writing is OK. But a job, a family, and writing is not on. Only two out of the three is manageable."[3]

On their way to an Australian writers' conference in 1978, Margaret and Graeme decided to go the long way round, stopping in Iran,

Afghanistan, and India. With them on their nine-week tour went their twenty-month-old daughter. They packed powdered milk and orange crystals, stuffed animals, and books. One major problem they'd overlooked was what to do with themselves once their daughter was asleep in the hotel room, and they took to squeezing a chair into the adjacent bathroom, where they could read and write while keeping an eye on her. It was that or sitting in the dark.

In an article titled "Travels of a Family Man,"[4] Graeme wrote about their trip. In Afghanistan, he was most struck by the women, or, more precisely, by their absence. On the streets of Kabul were mostly men and boys. The few women who ventured out were dressed in Moslem chadors, shrouded in anonymity. (Margaret actually bought herself a purple chador. She wanted to know what it felt like to wear one.) A young man they met by chance invited them to tea and showed wedding photos in which the bride was absent. In this world Margaret was treated as though she were invisible. In Australia, it was the opposite. Graeme was consoled by writers, male and female, when they saw him looking after the child while Margaret worked. In the article he mused on the nature of sex roles and sex stereotypes, and ended the piece by claiming that the best of this fascinating trip was that he and his wife were able to share it with their child. In "Travels of a Family Man," he comes across as a man who has worked his way thoughtfully to a kind of equanimity. Normal life has its beauties. When questioned about relationships, Graeme Gibson makes it clear he does not trust romantic metaphors. Hunting for a working analogy, the most he will say is that "a relationship between two people can be like lichen," which is a thallophytic plant in a symbiotic union with an algae. In other words, two organisms intertwined but completely independent.[5]

Margaret's writing remains central to her sense of self. In the last two decades, she has written four new books of poetry, four short-story collections, six more novels, four children's books, and numerous magazine articles. Her success has surprised her. In 1978, she remarked: "It constantly amazes me — and this isn't false modesty — that my work sells as well as it does. I consider it rather quirky and eccentric." She regards herself as "one of the few literary writers who has gotten lucky."[6]

What is the nature of her appeal as a writer? It has something to do with her empathy for her reader. Her books always seem to connect with something real in people's lives.

Lady Oracle, which came out in 1978, was a book about the conflict between a woman's romantic fantasies and the reality of actual life. The central character, Joan Foster, secretly writes escapist Gothic romances, and lives her life as if it were one, too. Margaret said: "She's someone who is attempting to act out a romantic myth we're all handed as women in a non-romantic world."[7] She understood the hook of these books: "Escape fiction . . . is a kind of wide-awake dreaming."[8] It's the dream that we all secretly have — that everything will work out in the end. But, instead of dismissing female fantasy, she affirmed it, saying that it had its place. We need the optimism of a little fantasy to keep going in a reductively literal-minded world. The real problems in writing *Lady Oracle* were the artistic ones. She wrote the novel in the second person, and then switched back to the first, and had to struggle with a complex cast of characters.

Lady Oracle stayed on best-seller lists for months. It was also slammed by the British critic Brigid Brophy, who wrote: "I feel like a tourist set reverently down in front of a national monument and obliged by conscience to blurt, 'Sorry, it looks to me like a fake.'"[9]

Margaret once remarked that, coming after her two earlier novels, *Lady Oracle* ended a unit of three. *Life Before Man* came out in 1980. She described it in 1979 as the first of another unit of three. She knew where she was going. She had to. Time was still at a premium, though now for different reasons.

Calling on old memories of the Royal Ontario Museum, Margaret made her main character in *Life Before Man* a paleontologist who studied dinosaurs. Beneath the novel was an acknowledgement that human life, too, might become extinct. She considered this her most domestic novel. Since it was about a triangular relationship between two women and a man, she had to create an equilateral triangle — three points of view, with each version of reality having veracity. Reality, as she always said, is a malleable substance, and differs, depending on who is experiencing it. Again she was placed on the defensive, this time for creating a weak male character. She responded that Nate was the only optimist in the book. What fascinated her, in fact, was sixties morality. "The 60s confused people. They tried to enjoy themselves and not worry about restricting their lives in artificial, puritanical ways. . . . When they stomped on morality, ethics got thrown out too."[10] The question was how can people determine ways to act when they must shape their own moral codes.

For Margaret, the most satisfying review of *Life Before Man* was one in a paleontology journal, which claimed hers was a very accurate description of a paleontologist's work. "I was flattered. I like to get things right," she remarked.[11]

Through the eighties, Margaret's range of vision, the area of society she wrote about, was expanding. *Bodily Harm*, published in 1981, explored her fascination with the body in our culture, how we fetishize it differently, depending on cultural training. It was her first novel set outside North America. She and Graeme had made their first trip to the Caribbean in 1973, when a friend had invited them to the island of Bequia. They continued to visit, but it took seven years of collecting scenes and images before the landscape became familiar enough to begin to enter her poems and fiction. The novel surprised her: "If you had told me in 1960 that I would sometime be writing a novel about human rights violations in the West Indies I would have told you you were crazy," she remarked.[12] Her focus, however, was less on the politics of the island than on the distorted perception of the situation by her main character, Rennie. Margaret made Rennie a lifestyles journalist, a manufacturer of chic: "We can afford to worry about personal health, personal fitness, personal romance," she explained. Most of the world can't. "I wanted to take somebody from our society and put her into *that*, and cause a resonance."[13] Margaret wanted to say that our belief in freedom — "thinking that freedom means a choice of everything" — is naïve, narcissistic, and exploitative. In sum, it is imperialistic. Most of the world does not live that way, and neither, realistically, do we. "You have a choice between A, B, or C," she remarked, "and that is it for your own life."[14] In the Caribbean, Rennie suddenly discovers she is not exempt from suffering.

The response to this novel was mixed. Some felt it was partly commercial, partly serious. What intrigued women reviewers, however, was that the novel took its character into the world of political action, a place not many female characters had been before.

In the early 1980s Margaret published two new volumes of poetry, *True*

Stories and *Interlunar*. In such poems as "Notes Towards a Poem that Can Never Be Written," it is clear that her work for Amnesty International had brought her into abrupt contact with the tragedies of the Latin American revolutionary wars of the seventies. The poem is dedicated to a young poet named Carolyn Forché, who had become a friend. She wrote a blurb for Forché's remarkable book *The Country Between Us*, describing her work as "a poetry of courage and compassion."[15] Forché had spent time in El Salvador in 1978 at the invitation of the poet Claribel Alegría, and had been witness to the brutality of the death squads and the official violence there. She left the country in 1980 at the urging of Archbishop Oscar Romero, just six days before he was assassinated while saying Mass in the chapel of Divine Providence Hospital. She was probably one of the last foreigners to spend time with him. No poet captured the brutality of that world better than Forché. Margaret, too, felt the need to speak out, not to look away.

Once Margaret had wondered whether to identify Toronto as the setting of her first (unpublished) novel. Would anyone recognize the city? Twenty years later, she could set her novels anywhere. Since 1981, she had been thinking of a novel tentatively titled *Offred*. As a teenager she had read Second World War histories in the basement of her family home and had been fascinated by totalitarian systems. She and Graeme had been to Afghanistan. What about a novel set in the near future about a totalitarian takeover? It was the challenge that seduced her. She always wanted to do something she'd never done before. Could she pull it off?

Where to set such a novel? She thought of Toronto and of Montreal. But it wouldn't fly in Canada; Canada, with its genius for compromise, didn't veer towards extremes. She thought of Cambridge, Massachussetts, where she'd spent four years. The mind-set of her fictional Gilead would be close to that of the seventeenth-century Puritans whom she'd studied. They were, after all, her ancestors. She began collecting clippings: on cults; on environmental pollution such as lead poisoning, toxic dumps, Agent Orange, and PCBs; on infertility. The clippings had headlines like "IUD Tied to Infertility," "The Breeding Crisis in the West," "Sexual Engineering and the Super-Race of Children Left After Hitler's Death," "16,500 Fetuses to Get Burial in L.A." She noted a book by Ben J. Waltenberg titled *The Birth Dearth*. As she wrote, she discussed bits of the novel with Graeme. "He thought I was going bonkers," she said, "but he egged me on."[16]

Most people were thinking of dictatorships in their conventional form: a new Stalin or Hitler or Pinochet. But what if people were looking in the wrong place? What would happen if pollution led to infertility? Margaret imagined a totalitarian society run by Bible-thumping fundamentalists in which women were turned into fertility slaves. Reading *Genesis*, she came upon her final title, and she found the model for the handmaid's clothes on the Dutch Cleanser cans of her childhood — the logo of a woman with her face concealed beneath her hat had always frightened her.

As she wrote *The Handmaid's Tale*, Margaret worried that people would think her merely paranoid. The responses were multiple. Canadians asked: Could it happen here? The British said it was realistic. Americans wondered how long before it actually occurred.[17]

The Handmaid's Tale, published in 1985, brought Margaret international fame, and was the first of her novels to make the Booker Prize list. It was on *The New York Times* Best-Seller List, and got a rave from John Updike and a slam from Mary McCarthy. It was made into a film starring Faye Dunaway, Robert Duvall, and Natasha Richardson, and scripted by Harold Pinter.

It doesn't always happen that the writer can be an effective spokesperson. Margaret is. There have been political issues in Canada that have demanded writers' attention: the North American Free Trade Agreement, censorship, copyright law, obscenity laws, the status of women, the environment. There were always causes to support: the African National Congress, the Canada–India Village Aid Association, PEN. She was chairman of the Writers' Union in 1981–82, and president of PEN from 1984 to 1986. In the nineties, she waded into the debates about federalism and the recognition of Quebec as a distinct society.

By the time *Cat's Eye* came out in 1988, critics were noting a new ease in Margaret's work. In retrospect, she explained that, in writing the book, she had "wanted a literary home for all those vanished *things* from my own chldhood — the marbles, the Eaton's catalogues, the Watchbird Watching you, the smells, sounds, colors. The textures."[18]

She once remarked that she was sometimes drawn to stories because she noted an absence — why had no one written about little girls? They had mostly been excluded from fiction. Their dramas, secrecies, betrayals, and cruelties were not considered serious literary material. Writing that novel felt like a risk — there would inevitably be those who said the subject was trivial or that she had painted it too blackly. Yet, she managed to conjure up the world of childhood, with all its intensities and its irresolutions.

By the time *The Robber Bride* appeared, in 1993, Margaret's work was being described as "among the most intricate, consciously constructed and metaphorically dense being written in English."[19] A British poll placed her with Angela Carter and Toni Morrison as the three most studied writers on U.K. campuses. Her story was of three women who support one another through the emotional havoc wrought by a predatory fourth. Again there'd been a gap she'd wanted to fill. She once joked that evil women had disappeared from fiction after the war and it was intriguing to bring them back. Critics reported *The Robber Bride* was the "author's warmest, most emotionally accessible book yet."

In 1995, she published *Morning in the Burned House*. People had been asking why she had abandoned poetry, and she always responded that poetry had abandoned her. But poetry came back, and she had lost none of her power. Poetry, she had said, often came from the melancholy side of the brain. After a protracted illness, Carl Atwood had died in 1993, and the book is pervaded by an elegiac sense of loss, of love for the father who was gone. She dedicated the book to her family.

When she was in Europe on a book-promotion tour for *The Robber Bride*, Margaret had an inexplicable visitation. Looking out the window of her hotel, she thought about Grace Marks, the woman about whom she'd written a play almost two decades earlier. She had a sudden image of Marks in the cellar of the Canadian farmhouse that was the scene of the murders she'd been accused of committing in 1843. Margaret sat down and began writing on the hotel stationery. It was not unusual for her to write this way. She often said that being on a plane or in a hotel room where no one can reach you was conducive to writing. Or perhaps it was the jet lag. *Alias Grace* was to be her first work of historical fiction. She held to the facts, where they were available, and then invented. It was from the things that couldn't be verified that the novel emerged. The kind of research she undertook involved going back to the actual location of the murders, finding the graves of the dead, tracing genealogies, reading tracts on Victorian prison reform and Spiritualism, and also mid-nineteenth-century newspaper accounts of the trial, with their political editorializing. Grace Marks was infamous in her day, a female murderess who attracted both scurrilous and sentimental attention. A kind of Lucia di Lammermoor. At least that's how Margaret thought of her: "[She] is both the innocent person with the white nightgown and the person who has just killed her bridegroom."[20] One way of looking at the novel is that Grace Marks is always trying to resist people's inventions of her, to escape their definitions, yet she is fated to play to those inventions. And one thinks, yes, "Alias Margaret."

A *Times* reviewer wrote:

> A petite and courteous woman, Margaret Atwood seems an unlikely authority on malevolence. She lives in a leafy suburb near the university in Toronto where the streets have well-clipped lawns and the greatest excitement is the tittle-tattle of a donnish dinner party. Yet, sitting in the back garden of her home beneath a brooding sky, one feels a hint of wildness, a sense of something dark, melodramatic. Gothic.[21]

Those who know the city can only guffaw at the reviewer's sentimentalized portrait of downtown Toronto, where Margaret, in fact, lives.

People were still inventing her. When she was awarded the National Arts Club's medal of honour for Literature, the headline read: "New York Fetes Atwood." "Americans may complain about getting Canada's bad weather, but they were only too happy to welcome a blast of acerbic Canadian air last night as Margaret Atwood was honoured with one of New York's toniest literary awards." Margaret began her acceptance speech in French, and went on to describe Robertson Davies, the only other Canadian winner of the award, floating in the air above her, intoning: "Do not get a swelled head. You must not forget the dark folkways of your people."[22]

In some ways, Margaret has become the model she dreaded: she proved that a writer could make it in Canada. She has become an adjective, and even an answer on *Jeopardy*. ("I'll take Authors for $600, Alex.")[23] The prizes have come, the honorary degrees, and all have mattered. She cherishes her international readership. Still she refuses definitions. Why limit yourself to one voice? Reverting to her high school puppet-show days, she remarks: "You can be Little Red Ridinghood and you can also be the wolf."[24] She is still daunting, refusing to let generalizations slide. She demands accuracy and does not demur.

I hold two anecdotes of Margaret Atwood in my mind. Because few people can see *her* through the cloak of their perception of the famous novelist, such anecdotes are, of course, only partial truths. Still, that is not so odd. We are all filtered through the perceptions of strangers.

In 1987, Margaret participated in a "Save the Temagami Wilderness" campaign. Temagami is northwest of North Bay, the largest wilderness area in Ontario south of the fiftieth parallel. The novelist M.T. Kelly had come up with the idea of witnessing the impact of the clear-cut lumber industry first-hand by canoeing through the wilderness. The trip was to last five days, and it included Margaret, her eleven-year-old daughter, M.T. Kelly, and his friend, David Carpenter. Graeme had injured his knee and had to back out at the last minute. An MP from Rainy River was among the others. They flew in groups into Florence Lake in a four-seater Cessna with canoes strapped to the pontoons. The plan was to canoe down the Lady Evelyn system of rivers.

The rough-and-ready camping was challenging. There were difficult portages, twenty-foot climbs up vertical cliffs, and shallow streambeds where they had to wade the canoes through waist-high water, feeling their way among slimy rocks. There were waterfalls to see on the Lady Evelyn, and the network of *nastawgan* — traditional aboriginal trails and portages still largely intact, complete with pictographs. Everyone on the trip was shocked by the impact of the clear-cutting on the forest.

David Carpenter describes the trip: "Peggy was fine, but some of the others on the trip were soon falling apart. The guide, Bruce Hodgins, was driving us too hard."

In particular, Carpenter remembers their rest-stops, when they all jumped into the river to cool off.

> It was as if we'd ceased to exist. Peggy would swim with her daughter and it was as if they were both five years old. Playtime in the water. A wonderful relationship. It was lovely to watch. She and her daughter would sing old TV

commercials: Pepsodent and Drano. She never wanted to talk books.

By the last day, tensions were running high. Two canoeists were down, done in. Finally Peggy wanted to challenge Bruce's competitiveness, the way he had been pushing us, and suggested we phone ahead for a launch to pick us up at the beginning of the last portage and tow us into camp. It would, of course, have meant Bruce had failed. But we talked it out and Peggy's insurrection was defeated. She was good-natured about it. She gave me and M.T. neck massages that night. We paddled through the last bay in an electric storm. She was wonderful. She carried her load, and more so.[25]

At the end of the trip, they visited Chief Gary Potts, head of the Temagami Band, who was fighting further bush-road development on tribal lands. Margaret did what she could; she wrote an article for the *Toronto Star* titled "The True North Weak and Threatened: The Temagami Wilderness under Pressure."

I think of a second anecdote involving a young PhD student. He was writing a thesis about Margaret Atwood, and attended a Toronto conference devoted to her work. One of the participants suggested they go on an excursion to explore what he called "Atwood territory." Feeling slightly odd, he joined the group of eight or ten as they headed for the subway. On the connecting St. Clair bus, the group scattered among the seats. At the front of the bus, a woman was sitting quietly, her wool cap pulled down low against the cold. She blended in, and it was a while before they recognized her. Margaret Atwood: it was as if she had suddenly materialized, like her character Susanna Moodie. At the end of *The Journals of Susanna Moodie*, Moodie rides the St. Clair bus, revealing that the city is an unexplored, threatening wilderness. With trepidation, one of the students approached her and explained that they intended to visit her ravine. She immediately offered: "I'll take you down."

The small group walked down to the bridge and she said: "This is a new concrete bridge." The old one from her childhood had been rickety and precarious. It was December, the midst of winter, a sunny but quite cold day, yet Margaret seemed to be enjoying her role as tour guide. She pointed to the water, and looked at them with an amused, mischievous grin: "That water is coming from under Mount Pleasant Cemetery. This is where the dead bodies are washing under the bridge." At least that is how the young man remembered it. They walked up the other side of the ravine, and she pointed out the houses in the neighbourhood that had been there in her childhood. They parted ways. The group went on to Mount Pleasant Cemetery, and she turned in the direction of her mother's house. It felt like a Gothic moment. When the young man thought about the conversation on the bridge, he couldn't figure out what was behind her enigmatic grin. Was she teasing them? Was she serious? She remained mysterious to him, which is as it should be.[26]

The books are out there. Margaret Atwood's work speaks for her. She has turned her hand to such a variety of subjects that the direction she will take is impossible to predict. The only certainty is that there will be other books to add to the more than thirty-five she has published. She has carried her load.

NOTES

INTRODUCTION: THE RED SHOES

1. Joyce Carol Oates, "Interview with Margaret Atwood," *New York Times Book Review*, 21 May 1978; reprinted in *Margaret Atwood: Conversations*, ed. Earl G. Ingersoll (Willowdale ON: Firefly Books [hereinafter cited as *Conversations*]), 1990, p. 72.
2. "Articles and Essays," Atwood Papers, Box 56, file 29. Thomas Fisher Rare Book Library, The University of Toronto.
3. Barbara Wade, "Margaret Atwood: Interview," *Maclean's* In-Class Program, 1981. Atwood Papers, Box 56, file 58, p. 2.
4. "Articles and Essays," Box 56, file 29.
5. Wade, "Margaret Atwood: Interview," p. 1.
6. "Figure It Out: Margaret Atwood," in *Lives & Work: Interviews*, ed. Bruce Meyer and Brian O'Riordan (Windsor, ON: Black Moss Press, 1992), pp. 2–3.
7. Author's interview with Margaret Atwood, 12 February 1997.

1: KITCHEN STORIES

1. Valerie Miner, "The Many Facets of Margaret Atwood," *Chatelaine*, June 1975, p. 69.
2. Joyce Carol Oates, "Interview with Margaret Atwood," *New York Times Book Review*, 21 May 1978; reprinted in *Conversations*, p. 70.
3. David D. Hall, ed., *Witch-Hunting in Seventeenth Century New England: A Documentary History, 1638–92* (Boston: Northeastern University Press, 1991), p. 4.
4. "Ancestral File (TM)-ver 416F," *Pedigree Chart*, The Church of Jesus Christ of the Latter-Day Saints, 1993.
5. Richard Weisman, *Witchcraft, Magic, and Religion in 17th-Century Massachusetts* (Boston: University of Massachusetts Press, 1984), p. 76. See also Carol F. Karlsen, *The Devil in the Shape of a Woman: Witchcraft in Colonial New England* (New York: W.W. Norton, 1987).
6. Cotton Mather, "Memorable Providences," in *Narratives of the Witchcraft Cases 1684–1706*, ed. George Lincoln Burr (New York: Charles Scribner's Sons, 1914), p. 132.
7. Samuel G. Drake, ed., *Annals of Witchcraft in New England* (New York: Benjamin Bloom, 1869; 1967), pp. 169–81.

8. *Records of the Court of Assistants of the Colony of the Massachusetts Bay, 1630–1692*, Vol. I. Printed under the assistance of John Noble (Boston: County of Suffolk, 1901), p. 229.
9. Drake, ed., *Annals of Witchcraft*, p. 176.
10. Sally Smith Booth, *The Witches of Early America* (Mamaroneck, NY: Hastings House, 1975), p. 84.
11. Ibid., p. 155.
12. Margaret Atwood, "Half-hanged Mary," in *Morning in the Burned House: New Poems* (Toronto: McClelland & Stewart, 1995), pp. 58–59; 66–67.
13. "Graduate Society Medal Winners: Witches: the strong neck of a favorite ancestor," *Radcliffe Quarterly*, September 1980, p. 5; reprinted as "Witches" in Margaret Atwood, *Second Words: Selected Critical Prose* (Toronto: Anansi, 1982 [hereinafter cited as *Second Words*]), p. 331. Since family genealogy has been traced back only as far as John Killam (born 16 August 1740), the connection to Mary Webster remains a "kitchen story."
14. Rev. J.R. Campbell, *A History of the County of Yarmouth, Nova Scotia* (Saint John, NB: J. & A. McMillan, 1876), pp. 21–22.
15. Col. Leonard H. Smith Jr. and Norma H. Smith, comps., *Nova Scotia Immigrants to 1867: From Manuscripts* (Baltimore, MD: Genealogical Publishing Co., 1992), p. 128.
16. Miner, "The Many Facets of Margaret Atwood," p. 33.
17. Beverly J. Freeman, *Reverend Jean-Baptiste Moreau* (Auburn, MA: Freeman, 1984), p. 18.
18. Margaret Atwood, "Great Aunts," *Family Portraits: Remembrances by Twenty Distinguished Writers*, ed. Carolyn Anthony (New York: Doubleday, 1989), pp. 4–5.
19. Ibid., p. 5.
20. Ibid., p. 4.
21. Margaret Atwood, "Landfall: Nova Scotia," *New York Times Magazine*, 18 March 1984, p. 100.
22. Ibid., p. 101.
23. Ibid.

2: READING FAMILIES

1. Margaret Atwood, *The Labrador Fiasco*, (London: Bloomsbury, 1996), pp. 13, 19.
2. C.E. Atwood, "Studies on the Apoidea of Western Nova Scotia with Special Reference to Visitors to Apple Bloom," *Canadian Journal of Research* 9 (1933): 442.
3. "Great Aunts," p. 7.
4. Margaret Atwood, "True North," *Saturday Night*, January 1987, p. 143.
5. Ibid.
6. Ibid., p. 144.
7. Miner, "The Many Facets of Margaret Atwood," p. 68.
8. Sue Fox, "Margaret Atwood: A Childhood," *New York Times Magazine*, 7 May 1994, p. 50.
9. Margaret Atwood, *Reader's Companion to* Alias Grace (Toronto: Doubleday, 1996), p. 2.
10. Author's interview with Margaret Atwood, 12 February 1997.
11. Margaret Atwood, "Approximate Homes," in *Writing Home: A PEN Canada Anthology*, ed. Constance Rooke (Toronto: McClelland & Stewart, 1997), p. 7.
12. Ibid., p. 6.
13. Geoff Hancock, "Interview with Margaret Atwood," in *Canadian Writers at Work: Interviews* (Toronto: Oxford University Press, 1987); reprinted in *Conversations*, p. 212.
14. Margaret Atwood, "Hurricane Hazel," in *Bluebeard's Egg* (Toronto: McClelland and Stewart, Seal Books, 1983), p. 21.
15. Author's interview with Harold Atwood, 26 March 1998.
16. Margaret Atwood, "My Mother, My Friend," *Chatelaine*, May 1985, p. 93.

17. Karla Hammond, "Interview," *Concerning Poetry*, 8 July 1978; reprinted in *Conversations*, p. 100.
18. Ibid.
19. Miner, "The Many Facets of Margaret Atwood," p. 68.
20. Fox, "Margaret Atwood: A Childhood," p. 50.
21. Catherine Sheldrick Ross and Cory Bieman Davies, "Interview," *Canadian Children's Literature* 42 (1986); reprinted in *Conversations*, p. 155.
22. Miner, "The Many Facets of Margaret Atwood," p. 66.
23. Atwood, "Hurricane Hazel," in *Bluebeard's Egg*, p. 29.
24. Carol Saline, "Margaret Atwood and Her Daughter, Margaret Atwood," in *Mothers and Daughters* (Toronto: Doubleday, 1997), p. 63. See also Miner, "The Many Facets of Margaret Atwood," p. 33.
25. Michael Rubbo, *Atwood and Family*, National Film Board, 1985.
26. Margaret Atwood, "Significant Moments in the Life of My Mother," in *Bluebeard's Egg*, p. 15.
27. Margaret Atwood, "Most Influential Book," *New York Times Magazine*, 12 June 1983, p. 43.
28. Ibid., p. 43.
29. Hermione Lee, *Margaret Atwood. Writers in Conversation* (London, England: Institute of Contemporary Arts; Rolland Collection, Northbrook, IL 1983).
30. Author's interview with Margaret Atwood, 23 April 1993.
31. Le Anne Schreiber, "Interview," *Vogue*, January 1986, p. 208.
32. Ibid.
33. Saline, "Margaret Atwood and Her Daughter, Margaret Atwood," p. 65.
34. Atwood, "Significant Moments in the Life of My Mother," in *Bluebeard's Egg*, p. 17. In a film interview with Hermione Lee (*Margaret Atwood: Writers in Conversation*), Margaret Atwood remarked with regard to *Bluebeard's Egg*: "I tried to write fairly autobiographical stories: the first and last and two others. I write out of settings I know but usually not out of personal experience or my real life. I put in my real parents because people confused them with the parents in *Surfacing*, who are darker because it's a ghost story."
35. Atwood, "Significant Moments in the Life of My Mother," p. 11.

3: PRELUDE: THE BUSH

1. "Balloons," Atwood Papers, Box 90, file 22.
2. Margaret Atwood, "Toronto, the City Rediscovered," *New York Times*, 8 August 1982, p. 14.
3. Doris Anderson, *Rebel Daughter* (Toronto: Key Porter Books, 1996), p. 81.
4. Ibid., p. 95.
5. Author's interview with John McCombe Reynolds, 23 February 1998.
6. Earl G. Ingersoll, "Interview," *The Ontario Review* 32 (Spring–Summer 1990); reprinted in *Conversations*, p. 236.
7. Robert Fulford, *Accidental City* (Toronto: Macfarlane Walter & Ross, 1995), p. 37.
8. "Ravines," Atwood Papers, Box 90, file 22.
9. Charles Trick Currelly, *I Brought the Ages Home* (Toronto: Ryerson Press, 1956).
10. Margaret Atwood, "A Night in the Royal Ontario Museum," in *The Animals in That Country* (Toronto: Oxford University Press, 1968), pp. 20–21.
11. Margaret Atwood, "My First Museum Love," *The Globe and Mail*, 9 May 1987.
12. "The Royal Ontario Museum," Atwood Papers, Box 90, file 21.
13. "Ox Eyes," Atwood Papers, Box 90, file 22.
14. Atwood Papers, Box 91, file 20.
15. "War," Atwood Papers, Box 92, file 6.

16. Margaret Atwood, "Nationalism, Limbo, and the Canadian Club" (1971), reprinted in *Second Words*, p. 84.
17. Elizabeth Meese, "Interview," *Black Warrior Review* 12 (1985); reprinted in *Conversations*, p. 182.
18. Margaret Atwood, "Theology," *Now*, 26 September–2 October 1985, p. 29.
19. Margaret Atwood, "Interview," *Publishers Weekly*, 23 August 1976, p. 6.
20. Atwood Papers, Box 3, file 2.
21. Ellsworth Jaeger, *Wildwood Wisdom* (Toronto: Macmillan, 1945).
22. "Correspondent Piece," 20 October 1989, Atwood Papers, Box 147, file 6.
23. Lee, *Margaret Atwood: Writers in Conversation*.
24. William Toye, ed., *Oxford Companion to Canadian Literature* (Toronto: Oxford University Press, 1997), p. 1054.
25. Ernest Thompson Seton, *Wild Animals I Have Known* (1898; Toronto: McClelland & Stewart, 1991), p. iv.
26. Atwood, "The Animals in That Country," in *The Animals in That Country*, p. 2.
27. Meese, "Interview," p. 182.
28. Schreiber, "Interview," p. 209.
29. Rubbo, *Atwood and Family*.
30. Judith Timson, "The Magnificent Margaret Atwood," *Chatelaine*, January 1981, p. 64.
31. Judith Timson, "Atwood's Triumph," *Maclean's*, 3 October 1988, p. 60.

4: THE THENNESS OF THEN

1. David Brownstone and Irene Franck, *Timelines of War* (Boston: Little, Brown, 1994).
2. Doug Owram, *Born at the Right Time: A History of the Baby-Boom Generation* (Toronto: University of Toronto Press, 1996), p. 18.
3. Ibid., pp. 77–78.
4. Ibid., p. 79.
5. Margaret Atwood, "English Teachers Speech," *Indirections* 11 (1 March 1986): 9.
6. Author's interview with David Carpenter, Leaside High School, 29 January 1998.
7. Atwood Papers, Box 91, file 20.
8. "English Teachers Speech," p. 9.
9. *The Clan Call*, Vol. 1, no. 4, (1952–53), p. 87.
10. "Embarrassment Story for Marta Kurc," Atwood Papers, Box 16, file 16.
11. *The Clan Call*, Vol. 1, no. 6 (1954–55), pp. 24–25.
12. Author's interview with M.T. Kelly, 3 November 1997.
13. *The Clan Call*, Vol. 1, no. 7 (1955–56), p. 28.
14. "Hazardous Experiences," Atwood Papers, Box 90, file 22.
15. "Some Words of Advice to the Graduating Class of 8T3 from Margaret Atwood," *University of Toronto Bulletin*, 20 June 1983, p. 9.
16. Wade, "Margaret Atwood: Interview," p. 2.
17. Atwood, "Approximate Homes," pp. 5–6.
18. Leaside High School video, 40th Anniversary, 1985, interview with Margaret Atwood.
19. Margaret Atwood, "Under the Thumb: How I Became a Poet," *Utne Reader*, September–October 1996, p. 79.
20. Margaret Atwood, "Nine Beginnings," in *The Writer and Her Work*, ed. Janet Sternberg (London: Virago), pp. 79–80.
21. Miner, "The Many Facets of Margaret Atwood," p. 68.
22. Ibid.
23. Leaside High School video, 40th Anniversary.
24. "Synthesia: Operetta in One Act (1956)," Atwood Papers, Box 3, file 3.

25. "Poetry and Audience," Atwood Papers, Box 56, file 2.

26. Owram, *Born at the Right Time*, p. 21.

27. Ibid., p. 13.

28. Ibid.

29. Ibid., p. 14.

30. Anderson, *Rebel Daughter*, p. 119.

31. Ibid., p. 129.

32. Ibid., p. 54.

33. Jim Davidson, "Interview," *Meanjin* 37 (1978); reprinted in *Conversations*, p. 96.

34. Margaret Atwood, "My Mother, My Friend," p. 94.

35. Fulford, *Accidental City*, p. 35.

36. Atwood, "Hurricane Hazel," pp. 45–46.

37. Leaside High School video, 40th Anniversary.

38. *The Clan Call*, Vol. 2, no. 1 (1956–57), p. 20.

5: Peggy Nature

1. Margaret Atwood, "Fifties Vic," *CEA Critic* 42/1 (November 1979)· 19.

2. Ibid.

3. Ibid.

4. Ibid., p. 21.

5. Atwood, "Significant Moments in the Life of My Mother," p. 17.

6. Ibid., p. 18.

7. Author's interview with Sam Solecki, 3 January 1997.

8. Atwood, "Fifties Vic," p. 20.

9. Author's interview with Professor A. Johnston, 27 March 1997.

10. Ibid.

11. Margaret Atwood, "Dennis Lee," *Canadian Magazine*, Atwood Papers, Box 74, file 2. See Dennis Lee, *Nicholas Knock and Other People* (Toronto: Macmillan, 1974), p. 20.

12. Author's interview with Dennis Lee, 7 March 1997.

13. "Draft," Atwood Papers, Box 90, file 22.

14. Author's conversation with John Sewell, 27 February 1998.

15. Author's interview with Charles Pachter, 13 November 1997.

16. Ross and Davies, "Interview," p. 160.

17. This is Charles Pachter's account. Rick Salutin, who was also a counsellor at Camp White Pine, records a slightly different version of the evening in *Marginal Notes* (Toronto: Lester & Orpen Dennys, 1984), p. 28.

18. Margaret Atwood, "Foreword," in *Charles Pachter*, text by Bogomila Welsh-Ovcharov (Toronto: McClelland & Stewart, 1992), p. 4.

19. Margaret Atwood, "Northrop Frye Observed," in *Second Words*, p. 400.

20. Atwood, "Fifties Vic," p. 21.

21. Author's interview with Margaret Atwood, 12 February 1997. See Atwood, "Northrop Frye Observed," p. 401.

22. Atwood, "Fifties Vic," p. 20.

23. Beatrice Mendez-Egle, "Interview," in *Margaret Atwood: Reflections and Reality* (Pan American University Press, 1987); reprinted in *Conversations*, p. 165.

24. "Poetry and Audience," Atwood Papers, Box 56, file 2.

25. Margaret Atwood, "That Certain Thing Called the Girlfriend," *New York Times Book Review*, 11 May 1986, p. 3.

26. "Atwood 90 (Part I: Interview 10/19 version)," Atwood Papers, Box 146, file 37.

27. Bonnie Lyons, "Interview," *Shenandoah* 37 (1987); reprinted in *Conversations*, p. 226.

28. Author's interview with Jay Macpherson, 20 May 1997.
29. Author's interview with James Reaney, 27 October 1997.
30. Ibid.
31. Margaret Atwood, "The Glass Slippers," *Acta Victoriana* 82/3 (March 1958): 16.
32. Ibid.
33. Margaret Atwood, "A Cliché for January," *Acta Victoriana* 83/4 (February 1959): 7–9.
34. Milton Wilson, letter to Margaret Atwood, Atwood Papers, Box 1, file 84. "Small Requiem" appeared in *The Canadian Forum*, December 1959, p. 202.
35. Atwood Papers, Box 4, file 30.
36. Shakesbeat Latweed, "The Expressive Act," *Acta Victoriana* 85/3 (April 1960): 16.
37. Atwood, "Northrop Frye Observed," p. 403.

6: THE SIBYLLINE TOUCH

1. Fulford, *Accidental City*, pp. 1–2.
2. William Weintraub, *City Unique: Montreal Days and Nights in the 1940s and '50s* (Toronto: McClelland & Stewart, 1996), p. 6.
3. Ibid., p. 284.
4. Harold Town, *Albert Franck: Keeper of the Lanes* (Toronto: McClelland and Stewart, 1974), p. 19.
5. Author's interview with Don Cullen, 2 March 1993.
6. Author's interview with Margaret Atwood, 8 August 1993. See also Margaret Atwood, "Isis in Darkness," in *Wilderness Tips* (Toronto: McClelland & Stewart, 1991).
7. Brenda Longfellow, *Shadow Maker: Gwendolyn MacEwen*, Gerda Productions, 1998. See also "Tyson Concert," Atwood Papers, Box 2, file 13.
8. Author's interview with Margaret Atwood, 8 August 1993.
9. Advertisement for the Bohemian Embassy in *The Sheet*, 1960.
10. Author's interview with Margaret Atwood, 8 August 1993.
11. Author's correspondence with Margaret Atwood, 1998.
12. Author's interview with Aviva Layton, 13 February 1997.
13. Author's interview with David Layton, 12 July 1995.
14. Anderson, *Rebel Daughter*, p. 122.
15. Author's interview with Margaret Atwood, 8 August 1993.
16. Ibid.
17. Robert Graves, *The White Goddess* (London: Faber & Faber, 1961), p. 24.
18. Author's interview with Margaret Atwood, 8 August 1993.
19. Ibid.
20. Margaret Atwood, "Great Unexpectations," *Ms.*, July/August 1987, p. 79.
21. M.E. Atwood, *Double Persephone* (Toronto: Hawkshead Press, 1961), p. 1.
22. Ibid., p. 4.
23. Ibid., p. 7.
24. Letter from Gwendolyn MacEwen to Margaret Atwood, 1961, Atwood Papers.
25. Margaret Atwood, "Insula Insularum," *Acta Victoriana* 85/3 (February 1961): 6–11.
26. "Atwood [Speech]," p. 3. Atwood Papers, Box 56, file 3.
27. Ibid., p. 2.
28. Atwood, "Fifties Vic," p. 22.
29. Author's interview with Professor A. Johnston, 27 March 1997.
30. "Draft: Atwood," Atwood Papers, Box 90, file 22.

7: THE CANADIAN CLUBBERS

1. Letter to Charles Pachter, 28 October 1961, private collection of Charles Pachter.

2. Marian Cannon Schlesinger, "Across the Common," in *My Harvard, My Yale*, ed. Diana Dubois (New York: Random House, 1982), p. 18.
3. Alison Lurie, "Their Harvard," in *My Harvard, My Yale*, p. 35.
4. Heather Dubrow, "On First Looking into Sandy's Ovid," in *College in a Yard II*, ed. David Aloian (Cambridge, MA: Harvard University Press, 1985), p. 188.
5. Linda Greenhouse, "Separate, Inseparable Worlds," in *College in a Yard II*, p. 191.
6. Faye Levine, "When the Bright Colors Faded," in *My Harvard, My Yale*, p. 99.
7. Ibid., pp. 99–100.
8. Faye Levine, "The Girls Who Go to Harvard," in *The Harvard Book: Selections from Three Centuries*, ed. William Bentinck-Smit (Cambridge, MA: Harvard University Press, 1982), p. 347.
9. Beth Gutcheon, "Folk Tales," in *My Harvard, My Yale*, p. 111.
10. Anne Fadiman, "Where Is the Grace of Yesteryear?" in *The Harvard Book*, p. 350.
11. Margaret Atwood, "The Curse of Eve—Or, What I Learned in School," (1978) in *Second Words*, p. 217. See also "Witches," in *Second Words*, p. 330. She was irritated enough by this to have repeated the anecdote in several articles and interviews.
12. Joyce Carol Oates, "Interview," *The Ontario Review* 9 (Fall–Winter 1978–79); reprinted in *Conversations*, p. 77.
13. "Growing Up Lucky under the Union Jack," speech at Wheaton College, November 1984, Atwood Papers, Box 90, file 20.
14. Letter to Margaret Atwood from Gwendolyn MacEwen [undated], Atwood Papers.
15. Ibid.
16. Atwood, "Witches," p. 330.
17. Letter to Charles Pachter from Margaret Atwood, 28 October 1961, private collection of Charles Pachter.
18. Ibid.
19. Atwood, "Witches," p. 329.
20. Author's interview with Jerome Buckley, Boston, 10 April 1997.
21. Author's interview with Margaret Atwood, 12 February 1997.
22. Roger Rosenblatt, *Coming Apart: A Memoir of the Harvard Wars of 1969* (Boston: Little, Brown, 1997), p. 164.
23. Atwood, "Growing Up Lucky under the Union Jack," p. 6.
24. Margaret Atwood, "Canadian–American Relations: Surviving the Eighties," *Second Words*, 1982. Address delivered to the Harvard Consortium in International Relations, Fall 1981.
25. "Beginning," Atwood Papers, Box 95, file 1.
26. "Canadian Clubbers and Canada Dry," Atwood Papers, Box 95, file 1. Margaret Atwood confirms that this piece was written largely in 1962.
27. Marie-Claire Blais, *American Notebooks: A Writer's Journey*, trans. Linda Gaboriau (Vancouver: Talonbooks, 1996), p. 12.
28. Ibid., p. 18.
29. Northrop Frye, *The Bush Garden* (Toronto: Anansi, 1971), p. 225.
30. Perry Miller, *The Raven and the Whale: The War of Words and Wits in the Era of Poe and Melville* (Westport, CT: Greenwood Press, 1955), p. 249.
31. Ibid., p. 187.
32. Meese, "Interview," p. 185.
33. Atwood Papers, Box 7, file 30. When Margaret Atwood donated her papers to the University of Toronto, it was difficult for her to be precise in dating the early work, which comprises easily a thousand pages of draft material.
34. Atwood Papers, Box 17, file 3.

35. Ibid.
36. Atwood Papers, Box 1, file 5.
37. Hancock, "Interview with Margaret Atwood," p. 217.
38. Author's interview with Jim Polk, 24 July 1997.
39. "The Cliff Dwellers in the Heart of the City," Atwood Papers, Box 6, file 5.
40. Levine, "My Harvard," p. 105.
41. Oates, "Interview," p. 77.

8: "A Descent through the Carpet"

1. Atwood, "Some Words of Advice to the Graduating Class of 8T3 from Margaret Atwood," p. 9.
2. "Margaret in Marketland," p. 4. Atwood Papers, Box 90, file 17.
3. Ibid., p. 10.
4. Ibid., p. 14.
5. Ibid., p. 13.
6. Author's interview with Jim Polk, 24 July 1997.
7. Letter to Margaret Atwood from Kay Grant, associate editor, Abelard-Schuman, 26 August 1964, Atwood Papers.
8. Letter to Margaret Atwood from Clarke, Irwin & Co., 25 January 1965, Atwood Papers.
9. *The Trumpets of Summer*, with John Beckwith, Atwood Papers, Box 41, file 3.
10. Margaret Atwood, "The Grunge Look," in *Writing Away: The PEN Travel Anthology*, ed. Constance Rooke (Toronto: McClelland & Stewart, 1994), p. 1.
11. Author's interview with Jim Polk, 24 July 1997.
12. Atwood, "The Grunge Look," p. 1.
13. Ibid.
14. Al Purdy, *Reaching for the Beaufort Sea: An Autobiography* (Madeira Park, BC: Harbour Publishing, 1993), p. 230.
15. Author's interview with Sam Solecki, 3 January 1997.
16. Author's interview with Jim Polk, 24 July 1997.
17. Letter to Charles Pachter from Margaret Atwood, 23 September 1964, Atwood Papers.
18. Letter from Charles Pachter to Margaret Atwood [undated], Atwood Papers.
19. Letter from Margaret Atwood to Charles Pachter, 17 October 1964, Atwood Papers.
20. Atwood, "Under the Thumb: How I Became a Poet," p. 107.
21. Letter from Margaret Atwood to Al Purdy, 18 December 1964, University of Saskatchewan Archives.
22. bill bissett, ed., "Introduction," *The Last blewointment Anthology*, Vol. I (Toronto: Nightwood Editions, 1985), p. 7.
23. bp Nichol, "Introduction," in *The Last blewointment Anthology*, Vol. II, ed. bill bissett (Toronto: Nightwood Editions, 1986), p. 9.
24. Margaret Atwood, "Some Old, Some New, Some Boring, Some Blew, and Some Picture Books," *Alphabet*, No. 17 (December 1966), in *Second Words*, p. 65.
25. Letter from Margaret Atwood to Charles Pachter, 17 October 1964, Atwood Papers.
26. Margaret Atwood, "A Descent through the Carpet," in *The Circle Game* (Toronto: Anansi, 1966), p. 21.
27. Margaret Atwood, "The City Planners," in *The Circle Game*, p. 27.
28. Margaret Atwood, "Evening Transition Before Departure," in *The Circle Game*, p. 15.
29. Margaret Atwood, "A Meal," in *The Circle Game*, p. 33–34.
30. Margaret Atwood, "A Sibyl," in *The Circle Game*, p. 51.
31. Margaret Atwood, "Pre-Amphibian," in *The Circle Game*, p. 63.
32. Margaret Atwood, "Against Still Life," in *The Circle Game*, p. 65.

33. Margaret Atwood, "Letters, Towards and Away," in *The Circle Game*, p. 69.
34. Karla Hammond, "Interview," *American Poetry Review* 8 (1979); reprinted in *Conversations*, p. 117.
35. Atwood, "Under the Thumb: How I Became a Poet," p. 107.
36. "Growing Up Lucky under the Union Jack," Atwood Papers, Box 90, file 20.
37. Letter from Margaret Atwood to Charles Pachter, 17 October [1964], Atwood Papers.
38. Letter from Margaret Atwood to Charles Pachter, 23 September [1964], Atwood Papers.
39. Margaret Atwood, "The Circle Game," in *The Circle Game*, p. 41.
40. Letter from Margaret Atwood to Charles Pachter, 17 October [1964], Atwood Papers.
41. Letter from Margaret Atwood to Charles Pachter, 15 March 1965, Atwood Papers.
42. Margaret Atwood, "Introduction" to *Women Writers at Work: Paris Review Interviews*, ed. George Plimpton (New York: Penguin, 1989).
43. Patrick Lane, "John Newlove & Margaret Atwood c. 1966," *Geist* 17 (1995): 31.
44. Letter from Margaret Atwood to Charles Pachter, 18 July 1965, private collection of Charles Pachter.
45. Letter from Margaret Atwood to Al Purdy, 5 March [1964], University of Saskatchewan Archives.
46. Margaret Atwood, "An Introduction to *The Edible Woman*," in *Second Words*, p. 369.
47. Letter from Margaret Atwood to M. McIntyre [undated], Atwood Papers, Box 95, file 29.
48. "Jacket Copy," *The Edible Woman*, Atwood Papers, Box 95, file 19.
49. Letter from Margaret Atwood to Marge Piercy, 2 August 1973, Atwood Papers.
50. "Logic," Atwood Papers, Box 10, file 1.
51. Atwood, "Under the Thumb: How I Became a Poet," p. 107.
52. Author's interview with Jim Polk, 24 July 1997.

9: THE WALL

1. Letter from Margaret Atwood to Charles Pachter, 9 March 1966, private collection of Charles Pachter.
2. Margaret Atwood, "Dancing Girls," in *Dancing Girls* (Toronto: McClelland and Stewart, 1977), pp. 221–36.
3. Rosenblatt, *Coming Apart: A Memoir of the Harvard Wars of 1969*, p. 50.
4. Ibid.
5. Margaret Atwood, "A Night in the Royal Ontario Museum," in *The Animals in That Country* (Toronto: Oxford University Press, 1968), p. 20.
6. Margaret Atwood, "It is dangerous to read newspapers," in *The Animals in That Country*, pp. 30–31.
7. "Speeches for Dr. Frankenstein," in *The Animals in That Country*, p. 44.
8. Margaret Atwood, "Backdrop Addresses Cowboy," in *The Animals in That Country*, p. 50.
9. Margaret Atwood, "The Shadow Voice," in *The Animals in That Country*, p. 7.
10. Letter from Margaret Atwood to Peter Miller, 20 October 1966, Atwood Papers.
11. Author's interview with Jerome Buckley, Boston, 12 April 1997.
12. Letter from Margaret Atwood to George Woodcock, Victoria Day, 1974, Atwood Papers.
13. "The Uses of the Supernatural in the Novel" (student essay, third year, for Jay Macpherson), Atwood Papers, Box 3, file 3.
14. Author's interview with Margaret Atwood, 12 February 1994.
15. "The Metaphysical Romance from the 1880's to the 1940's," PhD thesis—draft introduction, Atwood Papers, Box 50, file 19.
16. Margaret Atwood, "Superwoman Drawn and Quartered: The Early Forms of *She*," *Alphabet*, No. 10 (July 1965), in *Second Words*, p. 54.
17. Author's interview with Jim Polk, 24 July 1997.

18. Letter from Margaret Atwood to Charles Pachter, 19 October 1965, private collection of Charles Pachter.
19. Letter from Peter Miller to Margaret Atwood, 29 September 1965, Atwood Papers. See also Peter Miller, "Contact Press: The Later Years," *Canadian Notes & Queries*, No. 51 (1977):1, pp. 4–14.
20. Letter from Margaret Atwood to Charles Pachter, 24 January 1966, private collection of Charles Pachter.
21. Letters from Margaret Atwood to Charles Pachter, 27 July 1967 and 9 March 1966, private collection of Charles Pachter.
22. Letter from Margaret Atwood to Al Purdy, 23 July 1967, Queen's University Archives.
23. Letter from Margaret Atwood to Al Purdy, 13 November 1967, Queen's University Archives.
24. Letter from Margaret Atwood to Charles Pachter, 9 March 1966, private collection of Charles Pachter.
25. Letter from Margaret Atwood to Charles Pachter, 24 October [1966], private collection of Charles Pachter.
26. Letter from Margaret Atwood to Al Purdy, 28 June 1966, Queen's University Archives.
27. "A Failure," unpublished manuscript, 1998.
28. Ibid.
29. Author's interview with Sue Milmoe, Harvard, 12 April 1997.
30. Letter from Margaret Atwood to Peter Miller, 22 June 1966, Atwood Papers.
31. "Great Aunts," pp. 15–16.
32. Ibid., p. 16.
33. Letter from D.G. Jones to Margaret Atwood, 14 November 1966, Atwood Papers.
34. Letter from Margaret Atwood to Daryl Hine, 13 January 1967, Atwood Papers.
35. "A Jest of God," Atwood Papers, Box 146, file 28. The third female recipient of a Governor General's Award was Marie-Claire Blais, who won the prize for French fiction. It was the first time in twenty-two years that three of the six major prizes went to women.
36. James King, *The Life of Margaret Laurence* (Toronto: Knopf Canada, 1997), p. 245.
37. Letter from Margaret Atwood to Al Purdy, 7 January 1967, Queen's University Archives.
38. Letters from Margaret Atwood to Al Purdy, 17 January 1967 and 10 April 1967, Queen's University Archives.
39. Author's interview with Daryl Hine, 8 April 1997.
40. Author's interview with Margaret Atwood, 12 February 1997.

10: THE SUMMER OF LOVE

1. Nicholas Jennings, "Rolling on the River," *Toronto Life*, November 1996, p. 151.
2. Matt Cohen, "The Tunnel of Endless Pleasure," *Toronto Life*, November 1996, p. 102.
3. John Allemang, "Something Happened Here," Culture Section, *The Globe and Mail*, 21 June 1997.
4. Owram, *Born at the Right Time*, p. 216.
5. Ibid., p. 211.
6. Ibid., p. 212.
7. Todd Gitlin, *The Sixties: Years of Hope, Days of Rage* (New York: Bantam Books, 1987), p. 244.
8. Norman (Otis) Richmond, "Slugfest," *Toronto Life*, November 1996, p. 147.
9. Pat McDonagh, Culture Section, *The Globe and Mail*, 21 June 1997.
10. Susan Swan, "Only a Go-Go Girl in Love," *Toronto Life*, November 1996, p. 136.
11. Ronnie Hawkins, Culture Section, *The Globe and Mail*, 21 June 1997.
12. Swan, "Only a Go-Go Girl in Love," p. 136.
13. Shari Ulrich, Culture Section, *The Globe and Mail*, 21 June 1997.

14. Gitlin, *The Sixties: Years of Hope, Days of Rage*, p. 363.
15. *blewointment*, Fascist Court Issue (1970), p. 33.
16. Chris Rodley, ed., *Cronenberg on Cronenberg* (Toronto: Knopf Canada, 1992), p. 15.
17. Author's interview with Dennis Lee, 7 March 1997.
18. Dennis Lee, "Cadence, Country, Silence: Writing in Colonial Space," *Open Letter*, Ser. 2, No. 6 (Fall 1973).
19. Author's interview with Margaret Atwood, 12 February 1997.
20. Sarah Sheard, "The Heady Fumes of Ink and Ideas," *Toronto Life*, April 1997, pp. 52–54.
21. Author's interview with Paul Thompson, 12 November 1997. The story is contained in Marcel Aymé, *Le passe-muraille* (Paris: Gallimard, 1943). For a good review of alternative theatre in Canada see Denis W. Johnston, *Up the Mainstream: The Rise of Toronto's Alternative Theatres, 1968–1975* (Toronto: University of Toronto Press, 1991).
22. William Thorsell, "Expo 67's Happy-faced Idealism Was Misleading," *The Globe and Mail*, 26 April 1997, p. C13.
23. Margaret Atwood, "Bowering Pie . . . Some Recollections," *Essays on Canadian Writing* 5/3 (Summer 1989), p. 4.
24. Author's interview with Jim Polk, 14 October 1997.
25. "Sir George Piece," Atwood Papers, Box 56, file 28.
26. Ibid.
27. "Bowering Pie . . . Some Recollections," p. 4.
28. Douglas Fetherling, *Travels by Night: A Memoir of the Sixties* (Toronto: Lester Publishing, 1994), p. 240.
29. Clark Blaise, *I Had a Father: A Post-Modern Autobiography* (Toronto: HarperCollins, 1993), p. 122.
30. Author's interview with Jim Polk, Toronto, 4 March 1993.
31. Letter from Margaret Atwood to Charles Pachter, 18 November 1967, private collection of Charles Pachter.
32. Draft letter to Hope Leresche (agent), Atwood Papers, Box 95, file 8.
33. Letter from Hope Leresche (agent) to Margaret Atwood, 16 March 1966, Atwood Papers, Box 92, file 1.
34. Author's interview with William Toye, 4 October 1997.
35. "Susanna Moodie," Atwood Papers, Box 91, file 4.
36. Margaret Atwood, "Further Arrivals," in *The Journals of Susanna Moodie* (Toronto: Oxford University Press, 1970), p. 13.
37. Atwood, "Afterword," in *The Journals of Susanna Moodie*, p. 64.
38. Ibid., p. 62.
39. Letter from Margaret Atwood to Bill Toye, 13 March 1968, Atwood Papers, Box 95, file 5.
40. Letter from Margaret Atwood to Charles Pachter, 13 August 1968, private collection of Charles Pachter.
41. Author's interview with Jim Polk, Toronto, 4 March 1993.

11: LEARNING TO MAKE FIRE

1. Margaret Atwood, "Four Poets from Canada: Jones, Jonas, Mandel and Purdy," *Poetry*, 114, No. 3 (June 1969); reprinted in *Second Words*, p. 55.
2. Author's interview with Diane Bessai, 14 August 1997.
3. Letter from Margaret Atwood to Eli Mandel, 30 October 1968, Atwood Papers.
4. Letter from Margaret Atwood to Al Purdy, 28 January 1969, Queen's University Archives.
5. Letter from Margaret Atwood to Charles Pachter, 14 December 1968, private collection of Charles Pachter.
6. Letter from Margaret Atwood to Al Purdy, July 1969, Queen's University Archives.

7. Letter from Margaret Atwood to Charles Pachter, 28 December [1968], private collection of Charles Pachter.
8. Margaret Atwood, "Spell for the Director of Protocol," in *Procedures for Underground* (Toronto: Oxford University Press, 1970), p. 45.
9. Letter from Margaret Atwood to George Bowering, 16 July 1969, Atwood Papers. See also letter to Charles Pachter, 17 July 1969, private collection of Charles Pachter.
10. Letter from Margaret Atwood to Charles Pachter, 13 August, 1968, private collection of Charles Pachter.
11. Letter from Margaret Atwood to Eli Mandel, undated [1969], Atwood Papers.
12. Letter from Margaret Atwood to Al Purdy, 18 October [1964], University of Saskatchewan Archives.
13. Margaret Atwood, "Eden Is a Zoo," in *Procedures for Underground*, p. 6.
14. Margaret Atwood, "A Dialogue," in *Procedures for Underground*, p. 12.
15. Letter to Margaret Atwood from Eli Mandel, undated [1969], Atwood Papers.
16. Letter from Margaret Atwood to Eli Mandel, undated [1969], Atwood Papers.
17. Margaret Atwood, "Dream: Bluejay Or Archeopteryx," in *Procedures for Underground*, p. 9.
18. Letter from Margaret Atwood to Gwendolyn MacEwen, 24 September 1969, Atwood Papers.
19. Letter to Margaret Atwood from Gwendolyn MacEwen, 2 December 1968, Atwood Papers.
20. Letter from Margaret Atwood to Gwendolyn MacEwen, 26 July 1969, Atwood Papers.
21. Letter to Margaret Atwood from Gwendolyn MacEwen, 16 August 1969, Atwood Papers.
22. Margaret Atwood, "MacEwen's Muse," *Canadian Literature*, No. 45 (Summer 1970); reprinted in *Second Words*, p. 69.
23. Author's interview with Jim Polk, 14 October 1997.
24. Letter from Margaret Atwood to Gwendolyn MacEwen, 24 September 1969, Atwood Papers.
25. "Margaret in Marketland," p. 11. Atwood Papers, Box 90, file 17.
26. William French, "Books & Bookmen," *The Globe and Mail*, 4 October 1969.
27. C.F.P., "Food Taboos," Saskatoon *Star-Phoenix*, 7 November 1969.
28. John Richmond, "A Tough Broad's First Novel Becomes a Film," *Montreal Star*, 9 April 1970.
29. Letter to Margaret Atwood from Gwendolyn MacEwen, 22 September 1969, Atwood Papers.
30. Margaret Atwood, "84th Street, Edmonton," in *Procedures for Underground*, p. 52.
31. Letter to Margaret Atwood from Charles Pachter, 18 January 1969, private collection of Charles Pachter.
32. Margaret Atwood, "Stories in Kinsman's Park," in *Procedures for Underground*, p. 38.
33. Letter from Margaret Atwood to Eli Mandel, New Year's Day [1970], Atwood Papers.
34. Margaret Atwood, "Midwinter Presolstice," in *Procedures for Underground*, p. 20.
35. Margaret Atwood, "Habitation," in *Procedures for Underground*, p. 60.
36. Margaret Atwood, "Carrying Food Home in Winter," in *Procedures for Underground*, p. 73.
37. Welsh-Ovcharov, *Charles Pachter*, p. 130.
38. Author's interview with Charles Pachter, 17 March 1998.
39. Letter from Margaret Atwood to Eli Mandel, 20 April 1970, Atwood Papers.
40. Ibid.
41. Letter from Margaret Atwood to Gwendolyn MacEwen, 22 March 1970, Atwood Papers.

12: MYTHOGRAPHERS

1. Author's interview with Jim Polk, 14 October 1997.
2. "Wartime Emergency Regulations Imposed on Whole of Canada," *The Times* (London), 17 October 1970.

3. "Montreal a Siege City for Funeral," *The Times* (London), 21 October 1970.

4. Letter to Margaret Atwood from Gwendolyn MacEwen, October 1970, Atwood Papers.

5. Margaret Atwood, "An End to an Audience?" address delivered in the Dorothy J. Killiam Lecture series, Dalhousie University, October 1980, in *Second Words*, p. 354. See also "What to Write," in *For Openers: Conversations with 24 Canadian Writers*, ed. Alan Twigg (Madeira Park, BC: Harbour Publishing, 1981), p. 222.

6. Marjorie M. Bitker, "Books of the Week," *The Milwaukee Journal*, 17 January 1971.

7. Millicent Bell, "The Edible Woman," *New York Times Book Review*, 18 October 1970.

8. Letter from Margaret Atwood to Gwendolyn MacEwen, 31 December 1970, Atwood Papers.

9. Letter to Margaret Atwood from Gwendolyn MacEwen, 13 January 1971, Atwood Papers.

10. "In a Strange Land," Women's Section, *The Guardian*, Atwood Papers, Box 126, file 6.

11. Letter from Margaret Atwood to George Woodcock, 18 January [1971], Atwood Papers.

12. Letter from Margaret Atwood to Margaret Laurence, 10 December 1970, Atwood Papers.

13. Letter to Margaret Atwood from Margaret Laurence, Friday, [undated], Atwood Papers.

14. Pat Mainardi, "The Politics of Housework," in *Sisterhood Is Powerful: An Anthology of Writings from the Women's Liberation Movement*, ed. Robin Morgan (New York: Vintage Books, 1970), pp. 447–54.

15. Sookie Stambler, ed., *Women's Liberation: Blueprint for the Future* (New York: ACE Books, 1970), p. 9.

16. Letter to Margaret Atwood from Margaret Laurence, Friday, [undated], Atwood Papers.

17. Letter from Margaret Atwood to Margaret Laurence, 18 January 1971, Atwood Papers.

18. *Power Politics* (Toronto: House of Anansi, 1971), p. 41.

19. Author's interview with Jim Polk, 14 October 1997.

20. "I find it very difficult," Atwood Papers, Box 90, file 2.

21. "Notes on *Power Politics*," *Acta Victoriana* 97/2 (April 1973): 7.

22. Letter to Margaret Atwood from Margaret Laurence, 15 November 1971, Atwood Papers.

23. John Lennox, ed., *Margaret Laurence–Al Purdy: A Friendship in Letters* (Toronto: McClelland & Stewart, 1993), p. 242.

24. Bruce Blackadar, "The Lady's Eyes See Terrible Beauty," *Windsor Star*, 27 March 1971.

25. Peter Stevens, "Deep Freezing a Love's Continual Small Atrocities," *The Globe Magazine*, 24 April 1971.

26. Sid Stephen, "Margaret Atwood winds up Poetry Reading Series," Atwood Papers, Box 126, file 5.

27. "Seven Women Poets," Review Section, *Carleton Miscellany* 14/2, (Spring/Summer 1974): 123.

28. Linda Sandler, "Interview," *The Malahat Review* 41 (January 1977); reprinted in *Conversations*, p. 51.

29. Ibid.

30. Dick Allen, "*Power Politics*," *Poetry*, July 1973, pp. 239–40.

31. Helen Vendler, "Do Women Have Distinctive Subjects, Roles, and Styles?" *New York Times Book Review*, 12 August 1973, pp. 7–8.

32. For addresses of Margaret Atwood's residences in Toronto, see Greg Gatenby, *Literary Guide to Toronto* (forthcoming).

33. Author's interview with Jim Polk, 14 October 1997.

34. Letter from Margaret Atwood to Margaret Laurence, 30 January 1972, Atwood Papers.

35. "Margaret Atwood Talks to Margaret Drabble," *Chatelaine*, April 1987, p. 73.

36. Jim Polk, "The Phrenology of Love," *The Atlantic* 232/4 (October 1973).

13: TRANSFIXED

1. Author's interview with Dennis Lee, 7 March 1997.
2. Fetherling, *Travels by Night*, pp. 106–7. Among the best personal memoirs on Toronto in the late sixties, it covers the founding of Anansi and Rochdale.
3. Author's interview with Dennis Lee, 7 March 1997.
4. Johnston, *Up the Mainstream: The Rise of Toronto's Alternative Theatres, 1968–1975*, pp. 30–34.
5. Fetherling, *Travels by Night*, p. 132.
6. Ibid., pp. 130–31.
7. Author's correspondence with Dennis Lee, 23 April 1998.
8. James Polk, "A Spider's Life: Anansi at Fifteen," *Canadian Forum*, June/July 1982, pp. 19–21.
9. Graeme Gibson, "Margaret Atwood," *Eleven Canadian Novelists* (Toronto: Anansi, 1973), pp. 22–23.
10. Author's interview with Graeme Gibson, 4 November 1997.
11. Author's interview with Beth Appeldoorn and Susan Sandler, 26 August 1997.
12. Author's interview with Graeme Gibson, 4 November 1997.

14: MULMUR TOWNSHIP

1. Author's interview with Ted Chamberlin, 12 November 1997.
2. "Southern Ontario Gothic," Atwood Papers, Box 91, file 27.
3. Author's interview with Graeme Gibson, 4 November 1997.
4. "Southern Ontario Gothic," Atwood Papers, Box 91, file 27.
5. "The Suicidal Chicken," Atwood Papers, Box 2, file 6.
6. Author's interview with Graeme Gibson, 4 November 1997.
7. Miner, "The Many Facets of Margaret Atwood," p. 68.
8. "Southern Ontario Gothic," Atwood Papers, Box 91, file 27.
9. Ibid.
10. Margaret Atwood, "Spring Poem," in *You Are Happy* (Toronto: Oxford University Press, 1974), p. 22.
11. Margaret Atwood, "Digging," in *You Are Happy*, p. 19.
12. Margaret Atwood, "Song of the Hen's Head," in *You Are Happy*, p. 41.
13. Author's interview with Timothy Findley and William Whitehead, 26 October 1997.
14. Margaret Atwood, "Four Evasions," in *You Are Happy*, p. 77.
15. Margaret Atwood, "Variations on the Word Love," in *True Stories* (Toronto: Oxford University Press, 1981), p. 82.
16. Margaret Atwood, "There Is Only One of Everything," in *You Are Happy*, p. 92.
17. Author's interview with Graeme Gibson, 4 November 1997.
18. Margaret Atwood, "Book of Ancestors," in *You Are Happy*, p. 96.
19. Miner, "The Many Facets of Margaret Atwood," p. 68.
20. Margaret Atwood, "Great Unexpectations," *Ms.*, July/August 1987, p. 196.
21. Susan Swan, "Margaret Atwood: The Woman as Poet," *Communiqué*, May 1975, pp. 9–11.
22. Sandler, "Interview with Margaret Atwood," p. 43.
23. Gibson, "Interview with Margaret Atwood," p. 18.
24. Margaret Atwood, *Surfacing* (Toronto: McClelland and Stewart, 1972), p. 201.
25. Gibson, "Interview with Margaret Atwood," p. 19.
26. "Surfacing," Atwood Papers, Box 21, file 1.
27. Sandler, "Interview with Margaret Atwood," p. 43.
28. "Ich Uber Mich," Atwood Papers, Box 56, file 35.

29. Sam Solecki, ed., *Imagining Canadian Literature: The Selected Letters of Jack McClelland* (Toronto: Key Porter Books, 1998), p. 154.
30. George Woodcock, "Books and the Arts," *The Nation*, 19 March 1973.
31. Paul Delany, "Clearing a Canadian Space," *The New York Times Book Review*, 4 March 1973, p. 5.
32. Marci McDonald, "A New Literary Star Emerges in Canadian Letters," *Toronto Star*, 21 October 1972.
33. Author's interview with Graeme Gibson, 4 November 1997.

15: SURVIVALWOMAN

1. "Figure It Out: Margaret Atwood," p. 2. See also Margaret Atwood, "What to Write," in *For Openers: Conversations with 24 Canadian Writers*, p. 228.
2. Author's interview with Timothy Findley and William Whitehead, 26 October 1997.
3. Author's interview with Graeme Gibson, 4 November 1997.
4. Robert Read, "Atwood as Acupuncture," *Canadian Forum*, December 1972, p. 10.
5. Author's interview with Jim Polk, 14 October 1997.
6. Letter to Margaret Atwood from Margaret Laurence, 3 November 1973, Atwood Papers.
7. Letter to Margaret Atwood from Adele Wiseman, 29 October 1974, Atwood Papers.
8. Robin Matthews, "Survival and Struggle in Canadian Literature," *This Magazine* 6/4 (Winter 1972–73): 109–24.
9. Margaret Atwood, "Matthews and Misrepresentation," *This Magazine* 7/1 (May–June 1973); reprinted in *Second Words*, pp. 148–50.
10. Author's interview with Sam Solecki, 3 January 1997.
11. Frank Davey, "Atwood Walking Backwards," *Open Letter*, No. 5 (Summer 1973): 74–84.
12. Letter from Margaret Atwood to George Woodcock, 30 November 1972, Atwood Papers.
13. Author's interview with Dennis Lee, 7 March 1997.
14. Margaret Atwood wrote her comic strip in *This Magazine* from the January/February 1975 issue to the July/August 1978 issue.
15. Swan, "Margaret Atwood: The Woman as Poet," p. 10.
16. Northrop Frye, "Conclusion to a *Literary History of Canada*," in *The Bush Garden: Essays on the Canadian Imagination* (Toronto: Anansi, 1971), p. 219.
17. Dennis Reid, *A Concise History of Canadian Painting*, 2nd ed. (Toronto: Oxford University Press, 1988), p. 375.
18. Brenda Longfellow, *Shadow Maker*, documentary film on Gwendolyn MacEwen, 1998.
19. Sarah E. McCutcheon, "Government Aid Gives New Heart," *Gazette*, 2 December 1972.
20. Author's interview with Greg Gatenby, 19 March 1998.
21. Letter from Margaret Atwood to George Woodcock [undated], Atwood Papers.
22. Author's interview with Timothy Findley and William Whitehead, 26 October 1997.
23. See Atwood's review: "Timothy Findley: *The Wars*," *The Financial Post*, 12 November 1977; reprinted in *Second Words*, pp. 290–95.
24. Letter to Margaret Atwood from Hugh MacLennan, 2 July 1975, Atwood Papers.
25. Blaise, *I Had a Father*, p. 121.
26. Letter from Margaret Atwood to George Woodcock, 1 September 1973, Atwood Papers.
27. Letter to Margaret Atwood from Frances McCullough, 3 January 1974, Atwood Papers.

16: NO TRAINS IN SIGHT

1. Susan Musgrave, "Atwood: A Wary Lowering of Defenses," *Victoria Times*, 9 November 1974.
2. Alan Pearson, review of *You Are Happy*, *The Globe and Mail*, 28 September 1974, p. 33.

3. Margaret Atwood, "On Being a Woman Writer: Paradoxes and Dilemmas," *Women in the Canadian Mosaic*, ed. Gwen Matheson (Toronto: Peter Martin Associates Limited, 1976); reprinted in *Second Words*, pp. 197–204.
4. Ibid.
5. Joyce Carol Oates, "Interview with Margaret Atwood," *The Ontario Review* 9 (Fall–Winter 1978–79); reprinted in *Conversations*, p. 80.
6. Author's interview with Leslie Krueger, 11 December 1997.
7. Atwood, "On Being a Woman Writer," p. 204.
8. Ibid., p. 200.
9. Hancock, "Interview with Margaret Atwood," p. 205.
10. Sandler, "Interview with Margaret Atwood," p. 43.
11. Author's interview with Jim Polk, 14 October 1997.
12. Oates, "Interview with Margaret Atwood," p. 71.
13. Gibson, "Interview with Margaret Atwood," p. 26.
14. Margaret Atwood, "Men with the heads of eagles," *You Are Happy*, p. 47.
15. Atwood, *Survival*, p. 83. This comment is made by Margaret Atwood in reference to Gibson's novel *Communion*, which she called a "memorable work of art."
16. Author's interview with Margaret Atwood, 12 February 1997.
17. Atwood, *Reader's Companion to* Alias Grace, p. 2.
18. Letter from Margaret Atwood to George Woodcock, 23 March 1974, Atwood Papers.
19. Letter from Margaret Atwood to Donya, 6 January 1974, Atwood Papers.
20. Author's interview with Charles Pachter, 17 March 1998.
21. Letter from Margaret Atwood to Nina Finkelstein, 23 February 1977, Atwood Papers.
22. Letter from Margaret Atwood to Nina Finkelstein, 4 April 1977, Atwood Papers.
23. Author's interview with Paul Thompson, 11 November 1997.
24. J.R. Struthers, "Interview," in *Essays on Canadian Writing* 6 (1977); reprinted in *Conversations*, p. 65.
25. Gibson, "Interview with Margaret Atwood," p. 7.
26. Author's interview with David Staines, 15 February 1997.
27. Letter from Margaret Atwood to Nina Finkelstein, 8 August 1976, Atwood Papers.
28. Letter from Margaret Atwood to George Woodcock, 29 May 1976, Atwood Papers.
29. Author's interview with Beth Appeldoorn and Susan Sandler, 26 August 1997.
30. Jo Brans, "Interview with Margaret Atwood," in *Listen to the Voices: Conversations with Contemporary Writers* (Dallas: Southern Methodist University Press, 1988); reprinted in *Conversations*, p. 142.
31. Atwood, "Giving Birth," in *Dancing Girls*, pp. 239–54.
32. Struthers, "Interview," p. 65. See Atwood's review "Adrienne Rich: Of Woman Born," in *Second Words*, pp. 254–57, for her views on the mythology of mothering.

AFTERWORD

1. Blaise, *I Had a Father*, p. 121.
2. "Playground on the Fringe of Empire," Atwood Papers, Box 56, file 37.
3. Timson, "Atwood's Triumph," p. 61.
4. Graeme Gibson, "Travels of a Family Man," *Chatelaine*, March 1979, p. 36.
5. Author's interview with Graeme Gibson, 4 November 1997.
6. Oates, "Interview," p. 76.
7. Hammond, "Interview," *Concerning Poetry* (1978); reprinted in *Conversations*, p. 107.
8. Mendez-Egle, "Interview," p. 167.
9. Brigid Brophy, "A Contrary Critic Takes a Crack at *Lady Oracle*," *The Globe and Mail*, 9 October 1976, p. 35.

10. Alan Twigg, "Interview," *Strong Voices: Conversations with Fifty Canadian Authors* (Madeira Park, BC: Harbour Publishing, 1988); reprinted in *Conversations*, p. 123.
11. Lesley White, "Interview with Margaret Atwood," *The New York Times*, 16 April 1992.
12. Meese, "Interview," p. 179.
13. Lyons, "Interview," p. 227.
14. Meese, "Interview," p. 189.
15. Carolyn Forché, *The Country Between Us* (New York: Harper & Row, 1981).
16. Hancock, "Interview with Margaret Atwood," p. 200.
17. "The Handmaid's Tale—Before and After," Atwood Papers, Box 96, file 11.
18. Earl G. Ingersoll, "Interview," *The Ontario Review* 32 (Spring–Summer 1990); reprinted in *Conversations*, p. 236.
19. Val Ross, "Playing the Atwood Guessing Game," *The Globe and Mail*, 7 October 1993.
20. Graham Wood, "A Woman Possessed," *The Times*, 14 September 1986.
21. Ibid.
22. "New York Fetes Atwood," *The Globe and Mail*, 5 February 1997.
23. Letter to Margaret Atwood from Greg Gatenby, 12 December 1994, private collection of Greg Gatenby.
24. Mel Gussow, "Alternate Personalities in Life and Art," *New York Times*, 30 December 1996.
25. Author's interview with David Carpenter, 29 January 1998.
26. Author's interview with Helmut Reichenbächer, 20 March 1998.

ACKNOWLEDGEMENTS

I would like to thank all those people who have helped me in writing this book: Margaret Atwood, who responded to my questions, and who was always generous with permissions and with her trust, leaving me to make my own errors; and Sarah Cooper at O.W. Toad, who assisted me with factual inquiries and was unfailingly patient in the complex process of permissions. I would like to extend particular thanks to Graeme Gibson, Jim Polk, Charles Pachter, Timothy Findley, Jay Macpherson, Greg Gatenby, Dennis Lee, Diane Bessai, Beth Appledoorn, Susan Sandler, Sue Milmoe, Jerome Hamilton Buckley, David Staines, Sara Stambaugh, Paul Thompson, Daryl Hine, Peter Buitenhuis, Aviva Layton, M.T. Kelly, Sam Solecki, P.K. Page, James Reaney, Ted Chamberlain, William Toye, Leslie Krueger, and Alexandra Johnston,; in fact, to all those who helped, in interviews and in correspondence, with the research for this book.

I would like to thank those who read my manuscript, or parts of it, and offered constructive criticism: my perfect reader, Arlene Lampert, and also Richard Teleky, Sam Solecki, Dennis Lee, and my sister, Sharon Sullivan.

I would like especially to thank Mildred Pierce, who helped me in the complex research into family genealogy; Jennifer Gerstel who helped with tape transcriptions; and Helmut Reichenbächer. Others assisted me with their support: Gail Singer, John Evans, Carol Wilson, Lawrence Stone, Max Ryan, and Bill Hubacheck.

Without the assistance of the remarkable librarians who staff our libraries, my research would not have been as fascinating as it was: particularly Edna Hajnal at the Thomas Fisher Rare Book Library and the other excellent staff; Carl Spadoni, Research Collections Librarian at McMaster University; Randall Ware of the National Library of Canada; George F. Henderson, Archivist, Queen's University Archives; Shirley A. Martin, Head of Special Collections at the University of Saskatchewan Library; Ruth Wilson of the United Church/Victoria University Library; and Lynne Wood of Leaside High School.

I had the enormous good fortune to be awarded a Killam Research Fellowship to work on this book, and would like to thank the Canada Council for administering the grant and the Killam Fellowship board for their generous support. I would also like to thank the Department of English of the University of Toronto.

I would like to thank Nicole Langlois and Beverley Beetham Endersby for their patience. Most of all I would like to thank all the staff at HarperCollins, and, in particular, my editor, Iris Tupholme, Vice-President, Publisher, and Editor-in-Chief of HarperCollins Canada. Despite her gruelling schedule, she was always ready to respond to my least anxiety. I cannot imagine a finer editor.

I would like to thank my partner, Juan Opitz, who makes it all worthwhile.

To O.W. Toad for permission to quote from the Margaret Atwood Papers at the Thomas Fisher Rare Book Library, the University of Toronto, as well as letters, unpublished manuscripts, and literary journalism, copyright W.W. Toad.

To Oxford University Press for permission to quote from *You Are Happy*, *True Stories*, *Procedures for Underground*, *The Journals of Susanna Moodie*, *The Animals in That Country*.

To House of Anansi for permission to quote from *The Circle Game*, *Power Politics*, *Second Words*.

To McClelland & Stewart for permission to quote from *Surfacing*, *Bluebeard's Egg*, *Dancing Girls*, *Morning in the Burned House*.

To Andre Deutsch, London, for permission to quote from *Surfacing*.

To Jonathan Cape, London, for permission to quote from *True Stories*.

To Bloomsbury, London for permission to quote from *The Labrador Fiasco*.

To Virago, London, for permission to quote from *Morning in the Burned House*, *Bluebeard's Egg*, *Dancing Girls*.

To Houghton Mifflin, New York, for permission to quote from *Morning in the Burned House*, *Bluebeard's Egg*.

To Doubleday Bantam, New York, for permission to quote from *Reader's Companion to Alias Grace*.

To Simon & Schuster, New York, for permission to quote from *Surfacing*, *True Stories*, *Dancing Girls*.

INDEX